To Wyndham

Thomas Jefferson and Executive Power

JEREMY D. BAILEY

University of Houston

CAMBRIDGE
UNIVERSITY PRESS

CAMBRIDGE UNIVERSITY PRESS
Cambridge, New York, Melbourne, Madrid, Cape Town, Singapore, São Paulo, Delhi

Cambridge University Press
32 Avenue of the Americas, New York, NY 10013-2473, USA

www.cambridge.org
Information on this title: www.cambridge.org/9780521868310

First published 2007

Printed in the United States of America

A catalog record for this publication is available from the British Library.

Library of Congress Cataloging in Publication Data

Bailey, Jeremy D., 1974–
Thomas Jefferson and executive power / Jeremy D. Bailey.
    p. cm.
Includes bibliographical references and index.
ISBN 978-0-521-86831-0 (hardback)
    1. Executive power – United States – History.   2. Jefferson, Thomas, 1743–1826.
3. United States – Politics and government – 1783–1809.   I. Title.
JK511.B35   2007
352.23'50973 – dc22   2006036502

ISBN   978-0-521-86831-0 hardback

Contents

List of Figures and Table

Figures

Table

Preface

The scholarly understanding of presidential power rests on two distinctions. The first distinction concerns the extent of the president's formal powers and the place of the presidency in the constitutional order. The other distinction contrasts the Founders' presidency against the modern presidency by emphasizing the extraconstitutional powers of twentieth-century presidents. The first distinction is often characterized as arising from the differences in the political thought of Alexander Hamilton and Thomas Jefferson, that is, between a generous and a narrow reading of the Constitution's grant of authority to the president. The second distinction supposes that the modern presidency escaped from the constraints imposed by the Founders' careful plan to separate and check power by looking beyond the Founders' Constitution for its resources and became, in some cases, precisely what the Founders tried to prevent.[1] Because recent presidents eagerly exploit the constitutional hinges that allow the presidency to be strong, and because they bolster this strength with extraconstitutional devices, it is easy to conclude that the current presidency is both Hamiltonian and modern. As this scholarly understanding of the presidency puts it, Hamilton's case for implied powers, with its broad reading of the vesting clause in Article One, opened the space for later presidents to claim, as Theodore Roosevelt did, that they possess any power, not forbidden by the Constitution, to act on behalf of the people and for FDR to argue that the presidency needs the institutional resources to secure rights under modern conditions.

[1] Raymond Tatalovich and Thomas S. Engeman, *The Presidency and Political Science: Two Hundred Years of Constitutional Debate* (Baltimore: The Johns Hopkins University Press, 2003), 214–29.

But this formulation points to an obvious difficulty: how compatible is the seemingly democratic modern presidency with the Hamiltonian presidency? The modern presidency is both powerful and popular, but the one seems to undermine the other. Because elections have become more democratic, and because the science of polling allows, as Dick Morris taught us, "every day" to be "election day in modern America," a president can be both caretaker and creature of the popular will. Yet presidents increasingly rely on secrecy and administrative fiat to pursue their ambitions. Presidents use executive orders to avoid working with Congress, and, since Watergate, presidents have asserted executive privilege while calling it something else. Among scholars and presidents, the current understanding of the war power is that the president, not Congress, is responsible for determining when the nation is at peace or war. At the same time, presidents appeal to the people to justify their policies and their extraordinary acts of executive power.

Moreover, several scholars have found that the modern and premodern classifications rest on an uneasy theoretical foundation. Harvey Mansfield Jr. has argued that the distinction between the Founders and the moderns fails to appreciate the extent to which the modern presidency grows out of the modern doctrine of constitutionalism, which allows the formal and informal presidency to occupy the same office.[2] And, as Stephen Skowronek has written, the distinction between the Founders' presidency and the modern presidency fails to appreciate the more serious similarities among presidents who face similar political challenges, namely being associated with or opposed to a resilient or vulnerable regime.[3] Twentieth-century presidents have new tools, but does this make them new?

More important, even though modern presidents employ methods in the spirit of the Hamiltonian presidency, they have not wholeheartedly embraced it. FDR, for example, appealed to Hamilton's defense of national power only after discrediting Hamilton's suspicion of democracy.[4] Although Hamilton's reputation as an opponent of democracy is perhaps undeserved, his reasoning in *The Federalist* No. 70 illustrates the dilemma for modern presidents: where is the president who would argue that if republican government is antithetical to an energetic executive, then it must mean that the republican form, not energy in the executive, must be discarded? Where is the president who will

---

[2] Harvey C. Mansfield Jr., *Taming the Prince: The Ambivalence of Modern Executive Power* (Baltimore: The Johns Hopkins University Press, 1989); and David K. Nichols, *The Myth of the Modern Presidency* (University Park: Pennsylvania State University Press, 1994).

[3] Stephen Skowronek, *The Politics Presidents Make: Leadership from John Adams to George Bush* (Cambridge, MA: Harvard University Press, Belknap Press, 1993).

[4] Sidney M. Milkis, *The President and the Parties: The Transformation of the American Party System Since the New Deal* (New York: Oxford University Press, 1993), 21–51.

say in public, as TR did in private, that the people's love of Jefferson is a discredit to his country?

The Problem with Inventing the Presidency

More than relics of a lost world, such questions force us to examine the heart of the modern presidency. Today, presidents use their elections to claim a mandate from the people; they claim that the Constitution confers upon them the ultimate power of defending the Constitution and therefore tacitly grants them the power to use any means to do so; they appeal directly to the people to get Congress to pass their proposals and to encourage executive officials to do their bidding; and they carefully cultivate public opinion in order to make these appeals more useful. These aspects of the modern presidency are well known and well studied, but they can be better understood with reference to their institutional origins. The case for mandates presumes a particular kind of presidential selection and would have been incomprehensible under the original Electoral College; the argument for the constitutionality of executive prerogative requires a particular understanding of the relationship between necessity and fundamental law; and appeals to the public had to first be defended as a legitimate, and useful, practice in democratic government. Even a quick reading of the Constitution and its interpretation in *The Federalist* reveals that none of these developments can be taken for granted. Rather, somebody had to invent them.

But, as scholars affiliated with American Political Development argue, such inventions come about at particular intersections between political and institutional paths.[5] Or, as Karen Orren and Stephen Skowronek put it, instead of searching for "prime movers and master organizing mechanisms," scholars would do well to present "more circumspect specifications of order."[6] Put differently, the functional bias behind the question of who invented a particular institutional reform should be replaced by less normative and more historically subtle investigations of the interaction between established commitments, institutional rules, and new politics – what Orren and Skowronek call "intercurrence."[7] Consider, for example, the rival explanations of the apportionment scheme in the U.S. Senate. According to one interpretation, equal apportionment reflects the sovereign status

[5] Karen Orren and Stephen Skowronek, *The Search for American Political Development* (Cambridge: Cambridge University Press, 2004); Keith E. Whittington and Daniel P. Carpenter, "Executive Power in American Political Development," *Perspectives on Politics* 1 (2003): 495–513.

[6] Orren and Skowronek, *Search*, 16.

[7] Ibid., 112–18.

of the states.[8] According to another, the apportionment scheme grew out of the primary concern for the size of the Senate, which was paramount because the Senate was meant to be an elite body in the style of the House of Lords.[9] But if Frances E. Lee and Bruce I. Oppenheimer are to be believed, such functional accounts should be replaced by one more attentive to "path dependency."[10] For these scholars, equal apportionment arose because small-state delegates at the Constitutional Convention assembled a coalition that managed to protect equal apportionment by connecting it to past steps in the path: voting rules (which accorded each state one vote) and bicameralism (which presumed that one of the two houses of Congress be small) worked to the advantage of the small states and resulted in the Great Compromise. The same has been said of presidential leadership. Presidents can be agents of institutional change, yet the opportunities for change are confined by historical contingencies and previously traveled paths.

But, as the example of equal apportionment in the Senate suggests, the attractiveness of path dependency is also its danger. It can include rival, functional, interpretations even as it attempts to explain events as "historical contingencies." Could equal apportionment remain a viable option without the previous commitment, held by some would-be advocates of proportionality in apportionment, that the ideal Senate was a small Senate?[11] At the same time, there is a second functional explanation for equal apportionment: some of Madison's opponents insisted on equal representation because they shared a commitment to state authority, if only because the check on national authority would serve their respective interests.[12] In other words, equal apportionment in the Senate arose because the small states, with voting rules that were advantageous to their interests, exploited particular functional theories about what a senate should be.

All this is to say that the third president provides an important case study for those who study institutional development. More than any other president – with the possible exceptions of Madison and Wilson – Jefferson was a lifelong student of political change, and, with Madison, he was the founder of the nation's first opposition party. Consequently, Jefferson had

---

[8] *The Federalist* No. 62, p. 396.

[9] Elaine K. Swift, *The Making of an American Senate: Reconstitutive Change in Congress, 1787–1841* (Ann Arbor: University of Michigan Press, 1996).

[10] Frances E. Lee and Bruce I. Oppenheimer, *Sizing up the Senate: The Unequal Consequences of Equal Representation* (Chicago: University of Chicago Press, 1999).

[11] Daniel Wirls and Stephen Wirls, *The Invention of the United States Senate* (Baltimore: Johns Hopkins University Press, 2004), 71–103.

[12] David Brian Robertson, *The Constitution and America's Destiny* (New York: Cambridge University Press, 2005), 132–49; David Brian Robertson, "Madison's Opponents and Constitutional Design," *American Political Science Review* 99 (2005): 225–43.

to preside over a government that had undergone its first change of power, but the nature of that change was altered by how Jefferson wanted it to take place. Not a Framer of the Constitution of 1787, Jefferson had his own ideas about how to reconcile political change with constitutionalism. Consider, for example, his continued fascination with term limits: with the first transfer of power, Jefferson reconstructed the timing of the constitutional order itself by connecting presidential elections to constitutional transformation. Put differently, Jefferson reordered political time.

The Revolution of 1800 was thus a moment of opportunity, but, more than others, it had its limits because Jefferson's own project was confined by his attentiveness to his own place within it. With the exception of Washington, Jefferson was more aware than any other president of the importance of precedent, so his institutional transformations were almost always accompanied by an explanation. But, ever the revolutionary, he was famously enthusiastic about reform and suspicious of broad interpretations of the government's authority, so he attempted to combine electoral and institutional change with a strict construction of the law. A lifelong politician, however, he was forced to make compromises and seek alternative paths. Always subject to contingency, his political world required strategic choices, yet his writings and actions reveal a politician trying to find a theory of executive power that would be acceptable to republican theory and would not be undone by the events lawful republicans could not anticipate. Throughout his writing, then, runs the tension between a politician always conscious of the potential effect of his words and a theorist who wanted above all else to present coherence to future readers. Ideas and paths converged, partly because Jefferson had forged those paths.

Acknowledgments

My first acknowledgments must be to my teachers at Rhodes College who introduced me to politics; to my teachers at Boston College who taught me how to read; and to my teachers at both who taught me why these things mattered. They know who they are. With regard to this book, some deserve special mention. Robert Scigliano introduced me to Jefferson and to *The Federalist*. I know that I will always find his gentle footsteps among those pages. Marc Landy was a probing yet cheerful dissertation advisor and showed me that I could both love democracy and admire what lies under the covers. Robert Faulkner always insisted that I say what I mean, and, more important, he showed me how to do it. New Englanders and democrats, they taught me to suspect the worst in Jefferson *and* hope for the best.

This work has benefited from the advice and support of many others. Richard Bensel and Peter S. Onuf read the entire manuscript, offered timely words of encouragement, instructed me how to think about history, and were patient enough to save me from error again and again. Books by Henry Adams, Dumas Malone, Harvey Mansfield Jr., and Stephen Skowronek, have, as the following pages will show, influenced this work. Daniel Klinghard and Andrew Veprek were present in 1999 when this idea was formed in speech and thus shoulder some responsibility for it. Others who have read all or parts of this book and offered valuable suggestions include: Dennis Hale, Keith Quincy, Dan Sisson, Jim Headley, Joseph Wantuck, Robert Strong, and Don Brand. Deserving of special mention are the librarians and staff at the Library of Congress, the Alderman Library of the University of Virginia, the Robert H. Smith International Center for Jefferson Studies, and the Gumberg Library of Duquesne University. Research and preparation for this book were made possible by generous support from Boston College, the Institute for Human Sciences in Vienna, the International Center for Jefferson Studies at Monticello, Eastern Washington University, the National Endowment for the Humanities, and Duquesne University. Lew Bateman has been the model editor. Last, but perhaps most important, this work would have been impossible without the labors of the generations of editors who have made, and are making, Jefferson's papers available to the general public. Work on Jefferson can truly begin whey are finally finished.

Sections of Chapter 7 are published with the permission of the editors of the *Journal of Contemporary Thought*, Baroda, where they were originally published. Sections of Chapter 9 were published in *Presidential Studies Quarterly* 34 (2004), pp. 732–54, and are used with permission.

My mother and father, in their own ways, imparted to me the love of the written word. My wife, to whom this book is dedicated, sacrificed her mornings, demanded that I finish what I started, but always reintroduced me to the good life.

Abbreviations

Adams	Henry Adams, *History of the United States of America during the Administrations of Thomas Jefferson* (New York: Library of America, 1986)
Cappon	*The Adams-Jefferson Letters: The Complete Correspondence between Thomas Jefferson and Abigail and John Adams*, ed. Lester J. Cappon (Chapel Hill: The University of North Carolina Press, 1959)
The Federalist	Alexander Hamilton, James Madison, and John Jay, *The Federalist: A Commentary on the Constitution of the Unites States*, ed. Robert Scigliano (New York: Modern Library 2000)
Ford	*The Writings of Thomas Jefferson*, ed. Paul Leicester Ford, 10 vols. (New York: G. P. Putnam's Sons, 1892–99)
Jefferson	Thomas Jefferson
L&B	*The Writings of Thomas Jefferson*, ed. Andrew A. Lipscomb and Albert Ellery Bergh, 20 vols. (Washington, DC: 1903–04)
Malone	Dumas Malone, *Jefferson and His Time*, 6 vols. (Boston: Little, Brown, 1948–82)
PTJ	*The Papers of Thomas Jefferson*, ed. Julian Boyd et al., 32 vols. (Princeton, NJ: Princeton University Press, 1950–2005)
Smith	*The Republic of Letters: The Correspondence between Thomas Jefferson and James Madison, 1776–1826*, ed. James Morton Smith (New York: Norton, 1995)

Washington   *The Writings of Thomas Jefferson*, ed. Henry A.
                  Washington, 9 vols. (Washington, DC: 1853–54)
WTJ   *Thomas Jefferson: Writings*, ed. Merril D. Peterson
                  (New York: Library of America, 1984)

"The execution of laws is more important than the making of them"

Reconciling Executive Power with Democracy

Your Administration, will be quoted by Philosophers, as a model, of profound Wisdom; by Politicians, as weak, superficial, and short-sighted.

John Adams to Thomas Jefferson, 3 July 1813

Mr. Jefferson appears to me to be a man who will embody himself with the house of representatives. By weakoning the office of President he will increase his personal power.

John Marshall to Alexander Hamilton, 1 January 1801

But it is not true as is alleged that he [Jefferson] is an enemy to the power of the Executive, or that he is for confounding all the powers in the House of Rs. It is a fact which I have frequently mentioned that while we were in the administration together he was generally for a large construction of the Executive authority, & not backward to act upon it in cases which coincided with his views.

Alexander Hamilton to James Bayard, 16 January 1801

Historians and philosophers have written countless studies of Jefferson's life and ideas, but few have examined Jefferson's understanding of executive power.[1] So, too, with political scientists: in the issue of *Presidential Studies Quarterly* marking the bicentennial of the United States Constitution, scholars reexamined the presidency as understood by George Washington, James Madison, John Adams, Alexander Hamilton, James Wilson, and Gouverneur

---

[1] See, for example, Drew R. McCoy, *The Elusive Republic: Political Economy in Jeffersonian America* (Chapel Hill: University of North Carolina Press, 1980); Richard K. Matthews, The *Radical Politics of Thomas Jefferson: A Revisionist View* (Lawrence: University Press of Kansas, 1984); Garrett Ward Sheldon, *The Political Philosophy of Thomas* Jefferson (Baltimore: Johns Hopkins University Press, 1991); and Jean M. Yarbrough, *American Virtues: Thomas Jefferson on the Character of a Free People* (Lawrence: University Press of Kansas, 1998).

Morris – but not Jefferson.[2] There is a reason for this omission. Jefferson has been remembered by admirers and critics alike as preferring a weak executive, and partisans of feebleness do not make good subjects for studies of the presidency.

To the extent that scholars have examined Jefferson and the presidency, there is a consensus that he was in principle an enemy of executive power. According to this account, Jefferson had advocated a weak executive before he became president, and although he embraced executive power after he won the presidency, he did so unwillingly. Furthermore, his confession to Madison that he was not a "friend" to "energetic government," like his First Inaugural's description of good government as "frugal," was consistent with his summary of the difference between Federalists and Republicans as the "shade of more or less power to be given to the Executive or Legislative organ."[3] After all, he did not even include his two terms as president when prescribing the inscription for his own tombstone.[4]

The father of this scholarly consensus, of course, is Henry Adams. After documenting Jefferson's use of power – the Louisiana Purchase, the impeachments of Federalist judges, the arrest and trial of Aaron Burr, and the Embargo – Adams concluded if the difference between Jefferson and his opponents was the amount of power given to the executive it "was hard to see how any President could be more Federalist than Jefferson himself."[5] Since Adams's monumental work, scholars have followed Adams in charging Jefferson with constitutional inconsistencies as well as finding in Jefferson a lesson about the triumph of practice over principle. Under this formulation, Jefferson the president yielded to temptation, proving that the Jeffersonian presidency was impossible.[6]

To be sure, as the quotations by John Adams and John Marshall at the beginning of this chapter show, the consensus on Jefferson and the presidency can accommodate different approaches. Some have followed John

---

[2] Thomas E. Cronin, ed., "Origins and Inventions of the American Presidency," special issue, *Presidential Studies Quarterly* 17 (1987): 226.

[3] Jefferson, First Inaugural Address, *TJW*, 494; Jefferson to James Madison, 20 December 1787, *PTJ*, 12:442; Jefferson to Thomas McKean, 24 July 1801, Ford, 8:78.

[4] Thomas Jefferson, "Epitaph," *TJW*, 706–7.

[5] Adams, 354.

[6] Merrill D. Peterson, *Thomas Jefferson and the New Nation: A Biography* (New York: Oxford University Press, 1970), 775–6; Paul A. Rahe, "Jefferson's Machiavellian Moment," in *Reason and Republicanism: Thomas Jefferson's Legacy of Liberty*. ed. Gary L. McDowell and Sharon L. Noble, 53–84 (Lanham, MD: Rowman and Littlefield, 1997); Sidney M. Milkis and Michael Nelson, *The American Presidency: Origins and Development, 1776–2002*. 4th ed. (Washington, DC: Congressional Quarterly Press, 2003), 102; Garry Wills, *Negro President: Thomas Jefferson and the Slave Power* (Boston: Houghton Mifflin, 2003); and Raymond Tatalovich and Thomas S. Engeman, *The Presidency and Political Science: Two Hundred Years of Constitutional Debate* (Baltimore: Johns Hopkins University Press, 2003), 36.

Adams to argue that Jefferson's philosophy of opposition bound the exercise of power and made execution of the laws under his administration impossible.[7] Others, however, have marveled at Jefferson's party leadership by considering Jefferson's skill at the political art of persuasion, and as a result have confounded John Adams's prediction that future politicians would find Jefferson's methods shortsighted.[8] Others have emphasized Jefferson's reforms of the presidency to confirm John Marshall's prediction that Jefferson would bring about a shrinking of the office: Jefferson's abolition of presidential levees, conspicuously republican attire, delivery of presidential addresses to Congress in writing rather than in person, and advocacy of the two-term limit confirm Jefferson's suspicion of energy and foreshadow presidential decline under later Jeffersonian presidents.[9]

Only a few scholars have challenged the traditional account. Ralph Ketcham, for instance, wrote that the Jefferson as flexible or hypocritical thesis misunderstands Jefferson's activities as opposition leader: "In that position he had continued to accept *both* radical Whig scorn for imperial government and the idea of the patriot king, and he sought earnestly to find a mode of republican leadership retaining the values of each."[10] So, according to Ketcham, "the real essence of Jefferson's disagreement with the Federalist presidents" was not that Jefferson sought to "to make the office of the president less powerful" but, rather, that "Jefferson sought to make it *more popular*." Similarly, David N. Mayer warns that the dichotomy between a "strong" and a "weak" presidency fails to appreciate Jefferson's concern for constitutional propriety: "Where the Constitution assigned powers exclusively to the president, Jefferson vigorously exercised them; where powers were assigned to or shared with other branches, however, Jefferson preached and exercised restraint."[11] And, in an important article, Gary Schmitt found

[7] Forrest McDonald, *The Presidency of Thomas Jefferson* (Lawrence: University Press of Kansas, 1976), 162; Lance Banning, *The Jeffersonian Persuasion: Evolution of a Party Ideology* (Ithaca, NY: Cornell University Press, 1978), 273–302.

[8] James Sterling Young, *The Washington Community, 1800–1828* (New York: Columbia Univ. Press, 1966); Robert M. Johnstone Jr., *Jefferson and the Presidency: Leadership in the Young Republic* (Ithaca, NY: Cornell University Press, 1978).

[9] Clinton Rossiter, *The American Presidency* (New York: Mentor, 1960), 90; Stephen Skowronek, *The Politics Presidents Make: Leadership from John Adams to George Bush* (Cambridge, MA: Harvard University Press, Belknap Press, 1993), 92; Sidney M. Milkis and Michael Nelson, *The American Presidency: Origins and Development 1776–2002*, 4th ed. (Washington, DC: CQ Press, 2003), 107–8; and Joyce Appleby, *Thomas Jefferson* (New York: Times Books, 2003), 32 and 133.

[10] Ralph Ketcham, *Presidents Above Party: The First American Presidency, 1789–1829* (Chapel Hill: University of North Carolina Press, 1984), 106.

[11] David N. Mayer, "'The Holy Cause of Freedom': The Libertarian Legacy of Thomas Jefferson," in *The Noblest Minds: Fame, Honor, and the American Founding*, ed. Peter McNamara (Lanham, MD: Rowman and Littlefield, 1999), 110.

that Jefferson did not object to the use of "potentially expansive executive authority" even if he did have qualms about formalizing such power.[12]

If the scholarly minority is correct, then the consensus on Jefferson and the presidency is terribly wrong. If Jefferson was, as Hamilton reported, for a strong executive in the early 1790s, that is, if Jefferson eagerly embraced presidential power rather than being forced to it, then the traditional account has explained Jefferson's presidency in terms of a contradiction that need not exist. We are forced, then, to ask whether the events of Jefferson's administrations can be better understood by asking whether Jefferson brought to the office a particular understanding of presidential power. Stepping from the shadow of Henry Adams, we can examine Jefferson's view of presidential power as Jefferson presented it and with a proper understanding of political time. It is significant, after all, that Hamilton said he preferred Jefferson over Burr because Burr lacked a "theory."[13]

Two recent bicentennials illustrate the point. The Louisiana Purchase and the Twelfth Amendment, ratified in 1803 and 1804, reconfigured the geographical and political shape of the Union. The first, of course, doubled the size of the country and lessened the likelihood that the European powers would one day be meddlesome neighbors. The second corrected a flaw in presidential selection by requiring members of the Electoral College to "designate" whom they meant to elect as president and as vice president, thus lessening the possibility of an embarrassing stalemate in the House of Representatives. Each was a step in national development: the Purchase, as Abraham Lincoln said, settled the question of acquisition of territory, and the Twelfth Amendment, as John C. Calhoun noted, made it more likely that presidents would represent a national majority.[14] Each violated the Jeffersonian creed by lessening the authority of the individual states: the addition of new territory diluted the power of the existing states, just as the reform of the Electoral College made it less likely that state delegations in the House

---

[12] When the *Presidential Studies Quarterly* special issue was published as a book, Thomas E. Cronin included Schmitt's article on Jefferson. Although I encountered Schmitt's essay after I had developed the argument of this book, and believe it is wrong on several central points, it confirms some of my argument. Gary J. Schmitt, "Thomas Jefferson and the Presidency," in *Inventing the American Presidency*, ed., Thomas E. Cronin 326–46 (Lawrence: University Press of Kansas, 1989).

[13] "As to his theory, no mortal can tell what it is." Hamilton to James Ross, 29 December 1800, *PAH*, 25:280.

[14] Abraham Lincoln "Message to Congress," 3 December 1861, *Collected Works of Abraham Lincoln*, ed. Roy P. Basler (New Brunswick, NJ: Rutgers University Press, 1953), 5: 48. John C. Calhoun, Disquisition on Government and Discourse on the Constitution and Government of the United States in *Union and Liberty: The Political Philosophy of John C. Calhoun*, ed. Ross M. Lence, (Indianapolis, IN: Liberty Fund, 1992), 109–16, 208–13.

would choose the president. And each event can be interpreted according to the scholarly consensus. In the case of the Louisiana Purchase, Jefferson doubted its constitutionality and even drafted an amendment giving the government requisite authority yet remained silent with his doubts when the fate of the treaty, what he must have known would be his biggest accomplishment as president, was insecure. So, too, with the Twelfth Amendment: because the amendment guaranteed his own reelection, he could overlook the tension with states' rights. In each case, the opportunity was more important than the principle.

But questions remain. If expediency triumphs over constitutional scruple, why not simply proclaim that the Louisiana Purchase *was* constitutional? More perplexing, if the purchase of Louisiana made the United States safer – and Jefferson believed it did – why not assert its constitutionality on those grounds? And what was so pressing about the Twelfth Amendment? Was there *any* likelihood that Republicans would repeat their miscalculation of 1800, when they gave Jefferson and Burr the same number of electoral votes? Did it matter that Congress debated each at the same time? Was Jefferson paying attention to, even organizing, party strategy? Did Jefferson and his party choose one amendment over the other? Just as we do not yet understand the administration of the third president, we do not yet know all that there is to know about two important events in our political history.

1800 as Revolution in Executive Power

It is well known that Jefferson described his election as a revolution, and that this revolution resulted in the party system, but a recent book is the first to argue that the 1800 brought about a revolution in the presidency. According to Bruce Ackerman, the electoral deadlock between Jefferson and Aaron Burr helped transform the partisan question of who would be president into a larger question about the place of the presidency in the political system.[15] When Republicans argued that more people intended their votes to make Jefferson president, Federalists pointed out that the Constitution provided no such way to gauge such intent. That is, because of the "mistake" of the Framers, the Constitution was ill-equipped for the Republican claim that more people wanted Jefferson to be president than Burr, and it had to be modified to accommodate Jefferson's victory. The election of 1800 could have been resolved differently, with Jefferson presiding over the

---

[15] Bruce Ackerman, *The Failure of the Founding Fathers: Jefferson, Marshall, and the Rise of Presidential Democracy* (Cambridge, MA: Harvard University Press, Belknap Press, 2005), 36–92.

Constitutional Convention of 1802, but, because of a few fortunate events, the Constitution of 1787 was preserved, but only in name. In place of a congress of elites, the informal Constitution of 1800 placed popular presidents as leaders of the democratic system. For Ackerman, then, the election in the House was more than a crisis in terms of who would rule, for it was really a constitutional moment that decided whether the presidency should represent the people or whether a technical reading of the law could resolve the crisis without recourse to public opinion. Put differently, Federalists and Republicans pursued the paths that would lead to their own success, but Jefferson's accidental victory transformed the constitutional presidency into the democratic presidency.

Ackerman is right to notice that the debate over the resolution of 1800 changed the way that Americans thought of the presidency, but what he fails to consider is how prepared Jefferson was to exploit this twist of fortune.[16] Although Ackerman masterfully shows that the different strategies of Federalists and Republicans reflected different notions of authority, he does not really say whether Jefferson or others considered the mandate theory of the presidency before 1800. Put differently, he leaves it to the reader to assume that the mandate theory of the presidency was latent in the Republican opposition until the botched election of 1800 forced Republicans to make their partisan case for control of the presidency.

The truth is that by the time Jefferson sought the presidency, he had already devoted much of his efforts to thinking about executive power and constitutionalism. As constitutional reformer, wartime governor of Virginia, delegate to Congress under the Articles of Confederation, ambassador to France, Secretary of State, and opposition leader, Jefferson had devoted over two decades to reconciling the theoretical requirements of constitutional democracy with the practical realities of political life. Because Jefferson was convinced that democratic government required a strong chief executive, he focused his efforts not only on preventing what he believed to be Hamilton's monarchical designs but also on strengthening the presidential office. Consequently, his "Revolution of 1800" was a victory for the democratic principle *and* for a particular doctrine of presidential strength. By bringing his doctrine of presidential power to the presidency in 1800, he meant to connect the presidency to its democratic origins.[17] But this plan for the democratic

---

[16] Jack N. Rakove observes that the partisan fights over the meaning of the Constitution during the 1790s allowed the parties in 1800 to exploit the Constitution in the way that they did. "The Political Presidency: Discovery and Invention," in *The Revolution of 1800: Democracy, Race, and the New Republic*, ed. James Horn, Jan Ellen Lewis, and Peter S. Onuf (Charlottesville: University of Virginia Press, 2002), 54.

[17] I have chosen to emphasize the word *democratic* in spite of its historical inaccuracy. Jefferson used the word *republican*, and his enemies used *democratic* to criticize him. Nevertheless,

executive has not received the attention it deserves. Although we know the twists and turns of the election of 1800, and though we know that Jefferson called it a revolution, we do not fully understand why Jefferson believed it was a revolution.[18]

In this regard, Bruce Ackerman is right to argue that the Revolution of 1800 was part and parcel of the actual American Founding, but his account of 1800 is flawed because it, like the traditional scholarly account of Jefferson, misunderstands Jefferson's project. The Revolution of 1800 was more than a dangerous-yet-fortunate convergence of partisan politicians who had not yet embraced parties and a Constitution that had ignored parties, because the figurehead of that Revolution had a plan for the presidency. This is not to insist that Jefferson was "consistent," for the simultaneity of the Louisiana Purchase and the Twelfth Amendment forced Jefferson to choose opportunity over consistency. But it is to say that the fullness of this choice has been obscured by generations of scholars who presume that Jefferson wanted a weak presidency. By assuming that Jefferson wanted a presidency other than the one he created, scholars have failed to appreciate Jefferson what attempted to accomplish as politician and lawgiver. Because we do not yet know why Jefferson wanted to be president, it is time that we get around Henry Adams by revisiting Jefferson's understanding of executive power.[19]

Alexander Hamilton and Energy in the Executive

Before we turn to Jefferson's understanding of executive power, we should consider Alexander Hamilton's defense of executive energy in *The Federalist*. After a careful buildup, in which the presidency had been only delicately introduced, Hamilton addressed the "idea" that "a vigorous Executive is inconsistent with the genius of republican government." Hamilton

---

because of confusion arising from twentieth-century scholarship about the *republican* origins of the Constitution, *democratic* conveys the point more clearly today. Because I rely on Jefferson's words, however, I sometimes use *republican*. I do not mean to draw a distinction between the two or between those terms and another, *popular*.

[18] Possible scenarios are explored in James E. Lewis Jr., "'What is to Become of Our Government?': The Revolutionary Potential of 1800," and "'The Soil Will Be Soaked with Blood': Taking the Revolution of 1800 Seriously," in *Revolution of 1800* (see note 19), 3–29 and 59–86.

[19] Jack N. Rakove reminds us that it is significant that Jefferson allowed himself to be forward as candidate for president; Bruce Ackerman reveals Jefferson acting behind the scenes as presiding officer of the Senate to bend the Constitution to make his own election possible; and Stephen Skowronek's attention to political time brings into focus Jefferson's attention to the timing of his assumption to the presidency; in Jefferson's calculation, Washington was wise to retire "just as the bubble is bursting" and leave Adams to be blamed for Washington's difficulties. Jack N. Rakove, "The Political Presidency: Discovery and Invention," in *Revolution of 1800* (see note 4), 30–58; Ackerman, *Failure of the Founding Fathers*, 55–76; Skowronek, *Politics Presidents Make*, 65–66.

admonished the "enlightened well-wishers" of republican government that
they should hope that an energetic executive was consistent with republican
government, as "Energy in the Executive is a leading character in the definition of good government." According to Hamilton, an energetic executive
was essential to good government in times of emergency as well as during the
daily routine of governance. In the first case, energy was necessary to guard
"the community against foreign attacks" and to protect property against
"irregular and high- handed combinations which sometimes interrupt the
ordinary course of justice." Hamilton's illustration on this point did not
pull punches: the fact that the Roman republic was often "obliged to take
refuge in the absolute power of a single man, under the formidable title of
Dictator," to be saved from internal intrigue or external dangers, proved
that executive energy was essential to Rome's very survival. But however
necessary executive energy is during times of emergency it is also essential
for a "steady administration of the laws." Here, Hamilton's argument was
straightforward: even during the quiet routine of peace the effective execution of the laws was preferable to ineffective execution. The simplicity of
the argument was meant to convince republicans that their preferred form
of government would have to be conducive to energy if it was to be a good
government. "There can be no need, however, to multiply arguments or
examples on this head. A feeble Executive implies a feeble Execution of the
government. A feeble execution is but another phrase for a bad execution;
and a government ill executed, whatever it may be in theory, must be, in
practice, a bad government." Having forced republicans to choose between
their theories and their interest, Hamilton went on to list the ingredients
of energy: unity, duration, fixed salary, and competent powers. In the formulation of Madison's No. 51, in which "the interest of the man has to be
connected with the constitutional rights of the place," the first three might
be considered as giving the president the "will" to use the fourth, that is,
the powers he would need to execute the office. One of those three, a fixed
salary, is straightforward – in order to for the president to have its own will it
could not be dependent on another department of government for his pay –
but the other two deserve more attention.[20]

Hamilton's first two ingredients of energy are unity of office and duration. Unity, as opposed to plurality, offers the president the chance to act with
"decision, activity, secrecy, and dispatch," as there will not be co-presidents
or an executive council to leak information or aid the opposition when they
disagree with a policy.[21] Duration in office is linked to the principle that

[20] *The Federalist* No. 70, pp. 447–8.
[21] *The Federalist* No. 70, p. 449.

"a man will be interested in whatever he possesses, in proportion to the firmness or precariousness of the tenure by which he holds it."[22] Simply put, an adequate time in office with the possibility of reelection was necessary in order to attract and retain men of ability as well as provide presidents the space to carry out "extensive and arduous enterprises for the public benefit" and "dare" to act their "own opinion."[23] Separately, they embolden the executive to move beyond the "negative merit of not doing harm" and aspire to "the positive merit of doing good."[24] Together, they point to accountability and ensure that executive energy remain republican.

As the following chapters argue, Jefferson's understanding of executive power came to include the ingredients listed by Hamilton. With Hamilton, Jefferson came to believe that the executive branch could be unified, and therefore energized, by removing the executive council, and Jefferson was among the first to argue for providing the executive with a fixed salary. With regard to duration, Jefferson did not believe that a sitting president should be eligible for reelection, but his case for a term limit presumed that a term limit would strengthen, not enfeeble, the presidential office. And although Jefferson would later disagree with Hamilton concerning the powers of the president, he added the removal power to Hamilton's list of powers needed by the president: to connect the formal powers of the Constitution to his role as agent of the people, Jefferson placed the hitherto unsettled removal power under the president's command by attaching it to public opinion. This is not to say that Jefferson was "Hamiltonian," for Jefferson was suspicious of Hamilton's attempt to empower the executive branch, but it is to point out how striking it is that, once the Constitution was set in place, Jefferson attempted to make the president, not Congress, the leading agent of democratic change.

The central objective of this book, then, is to present Jefferson's understanding of executive power, which consisted of three principles. First, the president unifies the will of the nation and thereby embodies it. The source of the president's claim to embody the will of the nation is his mode of election; because the president is the single nationally elected officer, the president can claim, more than members of Congress, to represent the national will.[25]

---

[22] *The Federalist* No. 71, p. 457.
[23] *The Federalist* No. 71, pp. 464, 459.
[24] *The Federalist* No. 72, p. 463–4.
[25] The emphasis here is on the breadth of the electoral base, not its representativeness. To be sure, in almost two thirds of the states presidential Electors were chosen by state legislatures rather than by voters, and suffrage laws varied from state to state. The point, here, is that Jefferson emphasized the national basis for presidential selection. Stanley Elkins and Eric McKitrick, *The Age of Federalism* (New York: Oxford University Press, 1993), 741.

Because the president must be able to execute that will, it must be surprisingly strong, or energetic. Second, because a constitution can never be adequate for the opportunities and emergencies that will arise, and because the executive is caretaker of the public good, the executive must sometimes act outside the law, or even against it, on behalf of the public good. But the condition for such discretionary action is that the executive "throw himself" on the people for judgment, and, in order to make that judgment as accessible as possible, the executive must avoid broad constructions of the Constitution. Third, in order to provide a standard by which the people can judge executive action, the executive provides "declarations of principle." Such declarations allow for political change but also preserve constitutional limitations on power by enabling the people to judge executive discretion. Because this book presents this understanding as it unfolded over time, the remainder of this chapter will lay out these three components of Jefferson's theory of democratic energy.

Executive Unity and Public Opinion

Before he became president, and more than any of his contemporaries, Jefferson spent considerable effort thinking about the connection between public opinion and constitutional change.[26] On some occasions, Jefferson went so far as to suggest that constitutions and forms of government were less important than the majority will.[27] But, on others, he allowed that the public could be wrong. On the simplest level, he admitted that his "fellow citizens" could be "hood-winked" by "extraordinary combination of circumstances" or by partisan maneuvering, and he characterized the Federalist period as a "storm" of "delusion."[28] More important, he also believed that it was difficult for most people to rise above the horizon of their early education: "I have great confidence in the common sense of mankind in general: but it requires a great deal to get the better of notions which our tutors have instilled into our minds while incapable of questioning them; & to rise superior to antipathies strongly rooted."[29] Accordingly, after he retired from public life, Jefferson founded the University of Virginia, partly because he

---

[26] Declaration of Independence, *TJW*, 19; Jefferson to Patrick Henry, 27 March 1779, *PTJ*, 2:237–45; Jefferson to David Humphreys, 18 March 1789, *PTJ*: 14:676–9; and Jefferson, "Response to the Citizens of Albemarle," February, 1790, *TJW*, 491.

[27] Jefferson to Thomas Pinckney, 30 December 1792, *PTJ*, 24:802–4; Jefferson, *Anas*, in Paul Leicester Ford, ed., *The Works of Thomas Jefferson*, (New York: GP Putnam's Sons, 1904), 1:249; and Jefferson, "Opinion on the French Treaties," 28 April 1793, *TJW*, 422–34.

[28] Jefferson to John Dickinson, 6 March 1801 and Jefferson to Dr. Joseph Priestley, 21 March, 1801, *TJW*, 1084–6.

[29] Jefferson to Jeremiah Moor, 14 August 1800, *PTJ*, 32:102–3; and Jefferson, "Second Inaugural Address," 4 March 1805, *TJW*, 520.

disapproved of the curriculum at William and Mary. Although he believed that the will of the majority would suffer "honest, solitary and short lived" errors, he did acknowledge that it would "sometimes err."[30] It is therefore important to remember that Jefferson spent much of his life studying, drafting, commenting on, and proposing constitutions. In the *Notes on the State of Virginia*, Jefferson criticized the Virginia Constitution on the grounds that "the ordinary legislature may alter the constitution itself" and recommended that a new constitution be written to include a provision for an amendment process through constitutional convention.[31] Similarly, Jefferson's famous advocacy for a strict construction of the Constitution suggested he believed that constitutions were required to make public opinion discernible.

But there were requirements for constitutions, too, and the executive power occupied a central place in Jefferson's constitutionalism. In July 1789, for example, Jefferson described the U.S. Constitution as organizing the legislative, executive, and judicial departments of government around the standard of popular government. "We think in America that it is necessary to introduce the people into every department of government as far as they are capable of exercising it; and that this is the only way to ensure a long-continued & honest administration of it's powers." In the judicial branch, for example, the people may not be able to judge law, but they can judge fact and therefore serve on juries. Similarly, although the people are "not qualified to exercise themselves the EXECUTIVE department," they "are qualified to name the person who shall exercise it." After laying out the popular principle in the American system, Jefferson added a hypothetical: "Were I called upon to decide whether the people had best be omitted in the Legislative or Judiciary department, I would say it is better to leave them out of the Legislative." Jefferson's choosing to leave the people out of the legislative branch rather than the others reflected his fear that Congress would dominate the president and judges, but it also grew out of his discovery of the relationship between the executive branch and popular rule: "The execution of laws is more important than the making of them."[32]

As the following chapters will argue, Jefferson was an early advocate of unity in the executive because he found that a plural executive blurred accountability. For now, consider his extension of the principle to his observations of French politics and France's plural executive. Although he was a lover of France and a partisan of its Revolution, he criticized the Jacobins for domineering "over their executive so as [to] render it unequal to it's

---

[30] Jefferson, "Response to Citizens of Albemarle," *TJW*, 491.
[31] Jefferson, *Notes on the State of Virginia*, *TJW*, 246–7, 345.
[32] Jefferson to Abbe Arnoux, 19 July 1789, *PTJ*, 15:282–3.

proper objects."[33] In 1796, he wrote, "I fear the oligarchical executive of the French will not do, since a "small council" necessarily gets into "cabals and quarrels, the more bitter and relentless the fewer they are."[34] As Jefferson put it, the French should have learned from the American experience under the Articles of Confederation, and the remedy for the inconveniences of a small council was a single executive, not a larger council: "We saw this in our committee of the states; and that they were from their bad passions, incapable of doing the business of their country. I think that for the prompt, clear and consistent action so necessary in an Executive, unity of person is necessary as with us." Then, and later, Jefferson cast the American and French republics as "experiments" on the question of unity or plurality. In 1800, he predicted that Napoleon would see it in his interest to advocate a "single executive, limited in time and power" and therefore unite all the parties in France and conclude forever the republican experiment of a plural executive.[35] Furthermore, Napoleon could neither keep the plural executive directory, because "perpetual broils & factions" resulted in a "standing division" of three against two, nor could he "declar[e] for royalty," as he would be assassinated by "a Brutus." Napoleon's ambition, then, would lead the French to "think the experiment decided in favor of our form." After he retired from the presidency, Jefferson wrote to a pamphleteer that the "untimely fate" of the French Directory "cut short the experiment," but whether or not the internal dissensions of the Directory were the cause of its overthrow, he continued to suspect that the dissensions were "incident to a plurality."[36]

In 1811, Jefferson continued his campaign against the plural executive when wrote Destutt de Tracy to praise his critical commentary of Montesquieu's *Spirit of the Laws.* Jefferson argued that Tracy had at least one problem in his work, that is, that the doctrine of a plural executive would "probably not be assented to here," because American experience in 1784 and the simultaneous experiment in France proved to "the wise" that a plural executive was "impracticable with men constituted with the ordinary passions." Furthermore, the American experiment had demonstrated that a unitary executive corrected a defect inherent in republican government: "The tranquil and steady tenor of our single executive, during a course of twenty two years of the most tempestuous times the history of the world has ever presented, gives a rational hope that this important problem is at length

[33] Jefferson to Madison, 29 June 1792, *PTJ*, 24:134.
[34] Jefferson to Adams, 28 February 1796, *PTJ*, 28:618.
[35] Jefferson to Harry Innes, 23 January 1800, Ford, ed., 7: 412–13.
[36] Jefferson to Judge Woodward, 27 May 1809, Washington, 5:449.

solved." The problem was that republican government hitherto lacked the unity of action of a monarchy, but the invention of the president would make republican government at least as effective as a monarchy, since the president "produces unity of action in all the branches of the government." By unifying democratic wills under a single-minded administration, the presidential system could enjoy one benefit of monarchy.[37]

But unity was not enough. To ensure that representative government within the extended republic remained true to its democratic origins, Jefferson continued to advocate frequent elections. "Governments are more or less republican as they have more or less of the element of popular election and control in their composition."[38] And, "Governments are more are less republican in the proportion as this principle enters more or less into their composition": "action by the citizens in person, in affairs within their reach and competence, and in all others by representatives" is the "essence of a republic."[39] The will of the nation is the foundation for legitimate government. By submitting to the will of the majority, rather than to the one or the few, government is made "rational" in the sense that the errors of the majority will be more "honest, solitary and short-lived" than the errors of the one or the few.[40] Serving as a "rational and peaceable instrument of reform," elections replace the "sword" as the method by which a nation can "declare" its "will."[41]

But the relationship between public opinion and the president also moves in the other direction. The primary source of the president's unique relationship to the majority will is the national election, which, in Jefferson's hands, became an occasion for the president to summarize and direct the majority will in an inaugural address. Two days after his First Inaugural, Jefferson wrote John Dickinson that he hoped the American government would "be a standing monument" for other countries to imitate, that the Americans would prove "free government" to be the "most energetic" and would therefore "ameliorate the condition" of people everywhere.[42] But his First Inaugural would serve as another kind of monument: because the Election of 1800 marked the return of a previously "hood-winked" people to their "principles," the Inaugural would serve to remind other would-be leaders that the people can be taught "to see for themselves."[43] To one such

---

[37] Jefferson to A. L. C. Destutt de Tracy, 26 January 1811, *TJW*, 1243–4.
[38] Jefferson to Taylor, *TJW*, 1395.
[39] Jefferson to P.S. Dupont de Numours, 24 April 1816, TJW, 1387.
[40] Jefferson, "Response to Citizens of Albemarle," *TJW*, 491.
[41] Jefferson to Judge Spencer Roane, 6 September 1819, *TJW*, 1425.
[42] Jefferson to John Dickinson, 6 March 1801, *TJW*, 1084–5.
[43] Ibid.

reformer, Jefferson spoke of the relationship between the leadership and the majority will in nautical terms: "The storm we have passed through proves our vessel indestructible," and "A few hardy spirits stood firm to their posts, and the ship has breasted the storm."[44] Reflection suggests that the veracity of the first statement rests on the reliability of the second.

The electoral procedures of representative government alone, then, would not satisfy the larger condition that democratic government take its bearings from the will of the nation, because, the majority will has to be carried out. As he wrote in 1816, the "mother principle" of republican government was, for Jefferson, that "governments are republican only in proportion as they embody the will of their people, and execute it."[45] At the simplest level, the execution of laws is more important than the making of laws because execution puts to action what would otherwise remain purely theoretical. Like the extension of the republic beyond the direct democracy of a New England township, the execution of laws requires conforming the people's desires, as expressed in laws written by their representatives, to the requirements of political life. More than a craving for popular approval, the appeal to public opinion makes democratic politics executable: "The approving voice of our fellow citizens, for endeavors to be useful, is the greatest of all earthly rewards."[46] Like a constitution that takes into consideration the people it governs, the executive reconciles theory with practice: "What is practicable must often controul what is pure theory: and the habits of the governed determine in a great degree what is practicable."[47]

In the extended republic, that what is practicable comes from what is just depends on executive leadership. In the debate between Madison and Jefferson over the need for a bill of rights, Madison argued that the extended republic, and the multiplicity of interests it would include, would ensure that minority rights not be trampled by the majority. Later, to Madison's famous argument that a large republic would divide and conquer majority faction, Jefferson added that the president alone can see the "whole ground," that is, the president can uniquely claim to represent a national majority, and, perhaps, with the resources of the executive branch, that the president is uniquely able to distill the public good from the pool of interests. Madison's solution, under Jefferson's reformulation, provides the very foundation for

44 Jefferson to Lafayette,1 March, 1801, Washington, 4:363.
45 Jefferson to Kercheval, *TJW*, 1396.
46 Jefferson to the Society of the Methodist Episcopal Church at New London, Connecticut, 4 February 1809, in *The Complete Jefferson: Containing His Major Writings, Published and Unpublished, Except his Letters*, ed. Saul K. Padover (New York: Duell, Sloan & Pearce, 1944), 544.
47 Jefferson to Dupont de Numours, 18 January 1802, *TJW*, 1101.

presidential leadership: rather than leaving the national majority diluted and weak, the president allows, perhaps, members of the majority to "discover" again their "strength" and, like newly acquainted friends, to direct once separate sentiments to "act in unison."[48] When Jefferson defended the Louisiana Purchase in the Second Inaugural on the grounds that a larger republic would be less shaken by local interests, Jefferson was setting forth this larger argument for the democratic presidency. Jefferson found in the presidency another way for constitutional majorities to effect change without amending the Constitution.

Scholars have thus correctly perceived in Jefferson's letters a shift toward direct democracy, beginning around 1816, but this movement was more a logical extension than a rejection of his prior thoughts.[49] In several well-known definitions of a republic, he advocated a kind of direct democracy, writing that a government is "more or less republican" to the extent that its citizens engage in "direct action."[50] That Jefferson proposed ward republics only serves to confirm that he was wary of direct democracy on the basis that it was impracticable "beyond the extent of a New England township." Although Jefferson's views of federalism are too subtle to be worked out here, there is reason to believe that Jefferson preferred the election of representatives in the extended republic to the direct democracy of the New England township (and his association of direct democracy with political practice in New England was revealing), and he spent most of his political career attempting to extend the boundaries of the republic. This is certainly true for executive power. It is significant that, in 1816, when Jefferson explained that he and others in 1783 did not understand republicanism, he added that executive power was the source of their confusion.[51]

Prerogative and the Constitution

Democratic energy requires a new understanding of executive prerogative. Because the president acts in "constant agency" for the will of the nation, the president is responsible for accomplishing the objects expressed by the will of the nation and for guiding it during occasions of necessity. Acting as agent for a will to which he must defer, the president must, at times, be extraordinarily indirect with the people and the law: because instances of

---

[48] *The Federalist* No. 10, p. 60.

[49] Michael P. Zuckert, *The Natural Rights Republic: Studies in the Foundation of the American Political Tradition* (Notre Dame, IN: University of Notre Dame Press, 1996), 232; Sheldon, *Political Philosophy of Jefferson*, 83–102.

[50] Jefferson to John Taylor, 28 May 1816, *TJW*, 1392.

[51] Jefferson to Samuel Kercheval, 12 July 1816, *TJW*, 1396.

great achievement or emergency require extraordinary actions, the president must be willing to transgress, albeit temporarily, the will of the nation as expressed in the laws. Just as he tacitly conceded to Madison regarding the privileges of habeas corpus, Jefferson understood that it was the executive's duty to meet occasions dealt by necessity – even if it required acting in the absence of legal authority or, in some cases, departing from the law.

Jefferson alluded to the tension between executive energy and popular government in his First Inaugural. There, Jefferson disputed the assumption that a republican government lacked the "energy to preserve itself" by boasting that the American government was the "strongest on earth" because each citizen would voluntarily "fly to the standard of law, and would meet invasions of the public order as his own personal concern." But later in that speech, Jefferson asserted that the president, not the citizens, would be the best guide during times of conflict (even though others in government might say otherwise) because, as president, he was uniquely able to see the whole ground. Although Jefferson used the word "prerogative" most often to condemn it, his writings and actions reveal that he was not opposed to its use.[52]

To a large extent, Jefferson relied on the classic formulation of prerogative given by John Locke. In his *Second Treatise*, Locke defined prerogative as the power to act in the silence of law, and sometimes against the law, for the public good. Because the legislature is, by virtue of its organization, inadequate to practice the prerogative – in "some Governments," the "Lawmaking Power is not always in being, and is usually too numerous, and so too slow, for the dispatch requisite to Execution" – the prerogative power properly rested with the executive power. The executive, then, is the more appropriate power to hold the prerogative partly because the executive power would be unified under a single person and would be "always in being."[53]

Locke cast his definition of prerogative in terms of the law and thus raised a question about the relationship of prerogative and the law. Should the law include express provisions for prerogative, or should the law be silent with regard to prerogative? In Locke's account, prerogative arises because of

---

[52] Jefferson, First Inaugural, *TJW*, 492–6.

[53] For the executive to have the prerogative, the legislative and executive powers must be in "distinct hands." See John Locke, *Second Treatise*, Section 160, in *John Locke: Two Treatises of Government*, student edition, ed. Peter Laslett (Cambridge: Cambridge University Press, 1988), 375. There are disagreements about Locke's definition. Robert Scigliano argues that Locke's example of forgiving a person who pulls down a house to stop a fire suggests that the executive prerogative is in pardoning the offense, not in commissioning or executing it. "The President's 'Prerogative Power'," in *Inventing* (note 17), 240. See also Thomas S. Langston and Michael E. Lind, "John Locke & the Limits of Presidential Prerogative," *Polity* 24 (1991): 49–68; and Lee Ward, "Locke on Executive Power and Liberal Constitutionalism," *Canadian Journal of Political Science* 38 (2005): 719–44.

institutional convenience (the legislative branch cannot be assembled indefinitely) but also because of the fundamental imperfection of the law (things are always in flux). Rephrasing the question, then, how does the law best constrain what it cannot predict and contain? Does the U.S. Constitution include the prerogative power? If not, should it?

Among modern scholars, there are several understandings regarding the U.S. Constitution and the prerogative power. Each understanding agrees that laws are imperfect with regard to the future and must therefore be pushed aside if required to preserve the nation. Furthermore, each concedes that the president, by virtue of his unity of office and duration, is the most convenient as well as the safest repository for emergency powers. The understandings differ on whether the Constitution acknowledges and grants these powers. One understanding argues that Article II's vesting clause, the commander in chief provision, and the oath of office provide the president with the constitutional, that is, the legal, foundation for using the prerogative.[54] According to this constitutional understanding, the Framers constitutionalized necessity by placing prerogative *inside* the Constitution.[55] Another understanding asserts that the Constitution is silent concerning the prerogative. Under this extraconstitutional understanding, the prerogative power is *outside* the Constitution, so its occasional exercise, although illegal, must be controlled by politics rather than the Constitution.[56] Because the Constitution is silent concerning the prerogative, it must be pushed aside, albeit temporarily, during times of necessity. Whereas the first understanding finds the latitude for executive discretion within the constitutional framework, this understanding locates executive discretion outside the Constitution. There is yet another scholarly approach that combines the two. Rather than assessing prerogative purely in constitutional, or legal, terms, this understanding holds that prerogative is left to institutional conflict under constitutional design. Under this view, judging prerogative involves debate about premises: Was there an

---

[54] Larry Arnhart, "'The God-Like Prince': John Locke, Executive Prerogative, and the American Presidency," *Presidential Studies Quarterly* 9 (1979): 121–30; Leonard R. Sorenson, "The Federalist Papers on the Constitutionality of Executive Prerogative," *Presidential Studies Quarterly* 19 (1989): 267–83.

[55] Harvey Mansfield Jr., *Taming the Prince: The Ambivalence of Modern Executive Power* (Baltimore: Johns Hopkins University Press, 1989), 247–97.

[56] Lucius Wilmerding Jr., "The President and the Law," *Political Science Quarterly* 67 (1952): 321–38; Donald L. Robinson, "Presidential Prerogative and the Spirit of American Constitutionalism," in *The Constitution and the Conduct of American Foreign Policy*, ed. David Gray Adler and Larry N. George, 114–32 (Lawrence: Kansas University Press, 1996); Mark Tushnet, "Emergencies and the Idea of Constitutionalism," in *The Constitution in Wartime: Beyond Alarmism and Complacency*, ed. Mark Tushnet, 39–54 (Durham, NC: Duke University Press, 2005); Benjamin A. Kleinerman, "Lincoln's Example: Executive Power and the Survival of Constitutionalism," *Perspectives on Politics* 3: 4 (2005): 801–16.

emergency? Was there a grant of authority (or was such authority forbidden) by Congress?[57] Do the "attitudes and opinions of the American community" support the action?[58] Because presidential action becomes prerogative only when the other two branches say so, this understanding holds both a constitutional prerogative, in that the rival ambitions of officeholders in the three departments constrict prerogative, and an extraconstitutional prerogative, in that determining whether discretion is in the public good is a matter of politics simply.[59]

As scholars have noticed, the problem of the constitutionality of prerogative reveals an important difference between Jefferson's and Hamilton's attempts to reconcile executive power with republican rule. As Hamilton's contempt for republican well-wishers suggests, Hamilton believed that the Constitution – although perhaps not the ordinary law – had to be sufficient for any contingency or else the contingencies would prove that constitutions were irrelevant for actual politics.[60] Jefferson held a different understanding of executive prerogative. For Jefferson, Hamilton's defense of prerogative, like Hamilton's assertion of implied powers, undermined the key principle of constitutionalism, consent. Rather than finding the source of the prerogative power in a particular clause in the Constitution (such as the oath of office, the commander-in-chief provision, or the vesting clause), Jefferson believed that the Constitution is silent with respect to presidential prerogative.[61] Instead of muting these departures from the law with constitutional argument, Jefferson's understanding submits acts of presidential discretion to popular judgment. By placing the prerogative power outside the Constitution, Jefferson meant to reconcile the future trajectory of the will of the nation with its constitutional origins by way of the doctrine of strict construction. Because the condition for executive discretion was that the executive later "throw himself" on the people for their approval or censure, Jefferson's use

---

[57] *Youngstown Sheet & Tube Co. et. al. v. Sawyer*, 343 US 579, 634–654 (1952) (Jackson, J., con. op.).

[58] John P. Roche, "Executive Power and Domestic Emergency: The Quest for Prerogative," *The Western Political Quarterly* 5 (1952): 592–618.

[59] George Thomas, "As Far as Republican Principles Will Admit: Presidential Prerogative and Constitutional Government," *Presidential Studies Quarterly* 30 (2000): 534–52.

[60] Clinton Rossiter, *Constitutional Dictatorship: Crisis Government in the Modern Democracies* (Princeton, NJ: Princeton University Press, 1948), 212–3; Larry Arnhart, "'The God-Like Prince'"; Leonard R. Sorenson, "The Federalist Papers on the Constitutionality of Executive Prerogative"; Clement Fatovic, "Constitutionalism and Presidential Prerogative: Jefferson and Hamiltonian Perspectives," *American Journal of Political Science* 48 (2004): 429–44.

[61] Schmitt observes that Jefferson considered the prerogative to be "extraconstitutional," but he concludes that Jefferson meant to "scale down" the formal powers of the president. "Jefferson and the Presidency," in *Inventing*, 340–3. See also Fatovic, "Constitutionalism and Presidential Prerogative," 433–5.

of the prerogative signals Jefferson's larger departure from the Hamilton's understanding of executive power.

But there is more to Jefferson's requirement that the executive throw himself on the people. Jefferson spelled out the democratic basis for a mild form of prerogative – presidential privilege – when he refused to answer John Marshall's subpoena to testify in the trial against Aaron Burr. To counter Marshall's argument from the equality presumed by the law (the president must appear in court since "all persons owe obedience to subpoenas"), Jefferson carved a presidential exception from constitutional design. As he explained in a letter to the chief prosecutor, "If the Constitution enjoins on a particular officer to be always engaged in a particular set of duties imposed on him, does not this supercede the general law, subjecting him to minor duties inconsistent with these?"[62] Part of Jefferson's objection rested on the distinction between the minor details of the law and the higher general purpose of the law: if the judiciary "could bandy him from pillar to post, keep him constantly trudging from north to south & east to west" to testify in courts, the president would not be able to meet his more important "constitutional duties." But, because Jefferson believed that the president was, by the Constitution, the most able officer to unite the will of the nation, his assertion of privilege also carried within it a popular element. Specifically, the president is immune to subpoena because he is constitutionally required to be activist, that is, he is required to execute the will of the people: "The Constitution enjoins his constant agency in the concerns of 6. millions of people."[63]

Jefferson's public statement regarding the subpoena thus resembled and transformed Locke's argument. Because necessity required the executive to be "always in function," especially to respond to crises in foreign relations, the president would be unable to appear in court. But Jefferson's defense of presidential privilege also marked a departure from Locke's account of the prerogative power. More than the lone officer "always in being," the American president, as Jefferson understood it, was the lone officer who could rightfully claim to see the whole ground, which means that a president can

---

[62] Jefferson to George Hay, 20 June 1807, *TJW*, 1179–80. Jefferson had previously written a milder public statement several days earlier. See Jefferson to Hay, quoted in Malone, 5: 322. Jefferson did accommodate the judiciary by making available some of the subpoenaed papers. Mayer, *Constitutional Thought*, 275–6.

[63] To be sure, Jefferson added that the president's answering the judiciary's call would, in practice, upset the "leading principle" of the Constitution, that is, the "independence" of the branches from one another. Nevertheless, Jefferson's belief that the president is required by the Constitution to be in "constant agency" of the people is central to his argument for presidential privilege.

say with justice that it is his duty, by virtue of his mode of election, to execute the will of the people. Rather than giving the executive the prerogative power on the grounds that the executive was uniquely attached to the people, Locke emphasized the difference between the legislative and executive powers by noting the representative function of the legislature: the legislative power could not always be "in being" because it would come to hold a "distinct interest" from the rest of the community.[64] Jefferson, however, emphasized the public and popular basis for executive prerogative: because the president can unify and direct public opinion toward national objects, the president's role as caretaker of the national will requires that he sometimes act against the law for the public good. Jefferson's "constant agency" democratized Locke's "always in being."

Within this advocacy lies the expansion of presidential prerogative. More than the president's last resort of self-preservation, the democratized prerogative can be used to effect a positive public good in addition to preventing a negative harm. In his First Inaugural, Jefferson spoke of "great occasions," and throughout his presidency he stated that citizens would sometimes have to protect the law by acting outside of it. Jefferson himself had acted against the letter of the Virginia Constitution during his tenure as governor, as did countless officers who impressed horses, confiscated boats, conscripted citizens, and destroyed private property in order to resist the British. As president, Jefferson exercised powers previously nonexistent in the Constitution when he purchased and incorporated the Louisiana territory, just as Robert Livingston and James Monroe went outside their official instructions when they brokered the deal for the entirety of Louisiana. Although Jefferson never explained this doctrine with regard to the Louisiana Purchase, he said his refusal to assert the constitutionality of the Purchase was designed to "set an example" against a broad construction of the Constitution. Moreover, he asserted his doctrine throughout the rest of his administration, used his "Special Messages" to Congress to defend acts of executive discretion by others, and explained his understanding of the prerogative power in private and public letters.

Consider the Election of 1800. Ackerman notes that Republican solutions to the deadlock were mostly extraconstitutional while Federalist solutions

---

[64] Locke, *Second Treatise*, Section 138, in *Two Treatises*, 361. To be sure, others have noted the popular aspect of Locke's executive. See Larry Arnhart, "'The God-Like Prince': John Locke, Executive Prerogative, and the American Presidency," *Presidential Studies Quarterly* 9 (1979): 121–30; Robert Faulkner, "The First Liberal Democrat: Locke's Popular Government," *Review of Politics* 63 (2001): 5–39.

included expansive readings of the Constitution.[65] Madison, for instance, proposed that Jefferson and Burr issue a joint proclamation convening Congress (as this "prerogative" "must reside in one or the other of them") and have the newly elected House choose between the two. As he put it, the "crisis" required the extraordinary solution: "The intentions of the people would undoubtedly be pursued. And if, in reference to the Const[itutio]n: the proceedings be not strictly regular, the irregularity will be less in form than any other adequate to the emergency; and it will lie in form only rather than substance; whereas the other remedies proposed are substantial violations of the will of the people, of the scope of the Constitution, and of the public order and interest."[66] Although Jefferson never issued such a proclamation, he, too, let himself be associated with extraconstitutional solutions. He told President Adams that "resistance by force" would be the likely Republican answer if the Senate attempted to name an interim president, he let others believe that he wanted a new convention to resolve the election, and he wrote Lafayette that the "details" of 1800 "cannot be put on paper."[67] Such solutions were surely the desperate acts of partisans creating multiple paths to office, and they call into question Jefferson's attachment to *the* Constitution.[68] But they also parallel Jefferson's belief that, during extraordinary occasions, it is better to go outside the law than to expand it by interpretation. The method was intertwined with the principle: with an appeal to the people, the Constitution could be saved by finding an extraconstitutional remedy for its deficiencies.

By examining Jefferson's understanding of prerogative, then, we can more seriously appreciate his project to transform executive power. Jefferson's assertion of executive prerogative was more than a defense of the principle that the executive must preserve the government against destruction, for it grew out of his belief that the executive was the representative of the popular will. Accordingly, Jefferson was the first to argue that the president, as the embodiment of what the people say every four years, lays out the whole ground as he sees it. Because Jefferson's solution to the problem of necessity does not include a doctrine of implied powers (indeed, it was formulated to

---

[65] Bruce Ackerman, *Failure of the Founding* Fathers, 36–54; Possible scenarios are explored in James E. Lewis Jr., "'What is to Become of Our Government?': The Revolutionary Potential of 1800," in *Revolution of 1800* (see note 4), 13–24.

[66] Madison to Jefferson, 10 January 1801, Smith, 1157–8.

[67] Jefferson to Monroe, 15 February 1801, L&B, 10: 201; and Jefferson to Lafayette,1 March, 1801, Washington, 4:363.

[68] James E. Lewis Jr., "What is to Become of Our Government?," in *Revolution of 1800*, 24; Wills, *Negro President*, 84–86.

counter it), and because it allows for prerogative to be used during times
other than self-preservation, Jefferson's conception of presidential prerogative is remarkably different from the alternative understanding of presidential
power. By expanding the prerogative power, Jefferson also meant to limit it.

Declarations of Principle

But the requirement that executives throw themselves on the people only
raises more questions. If the law is silent with respect to prerogative, and if
the executive is not to use the law to justify his actions, by what standard is
the executive to be judged? Will the people be overscrupulous in using the
law to discourage executives to act on their behalf, thus ushering in the feebleness mocked by Hamilton. Or will they, as Locke feared, not be watchful
enough, even being blinded by a "God like prince" who used prerogative for
the public good, and fail to notice when future executives use prerogative
against the public good? Because of such questions, Jefferson's solution to
the dilemma of prerogative and the law involved more than a strict construction of the Constitution. Specifically, Jefferson's institutional solution to the
problem of executive power, and his larger departure from Hamilton, was
political education.

Jefferson's understanding of executive power included faith in declarations of principle. To ensure that the president possesses enough energy to
secure liberty but does not use his prerogative to tread too far on that liberty,
the president enshrines rights in "declarations." By pointing executive energy
to the principles underlying the law, these declarations afford the president
leverage to carry out the purpose of the law when the limitations of the law
would otherwise prevent its execution. Furthermore, by defining the principles by which presidents administer their government, declarations provide
the standard by which the intent of presidential discretion can be judged.
Consequently, these declarations energize the presidency by gathering public opinion around the president. Serving as a text by which power can be
judged and as a platform around which a majority can be gathered, the
declaration of principle also brings public sentiment to a single point, edu-
cates it, and directs it toward administration. By connecting public opinion
to presidential declarations, declarations of principle place change outside
the Constitution while at the same time ensuring that government remain
constitutional.

More than a felicitous pen in a partisan cause, Jefferson used declarations
to frame for the public what he believed to be the purpose of democratic
government, that is, to create a kind of law where the laws were silent.
Accordingly, studies of Jefferson's role in founding an opposition party show

that he meant it to be a temporary and extraconstitutional solution to an emergency and that the democratizing role of parties helped alleviate the tensions inherent in democratic leadership.[69] At the same time, however, the First Inaugural's famous inclusive proclamation "We are all Republicans, we are all Federalists" was more than a shrewd offer of conciliation to the defeated foe of a close contest, for it fit within Jefferson's larger rhetorical aim of placing the president as the oracle of the national will.[70] As he himself put it, Jefferson used the First Inaugural to announce "promise" and his Second Inaugural to announce "performance" and thus transformed the inaugural address from a merely formal acknowledgment of taking the oath of office to a routine declaration of the principles of government.

As president, Jefferson employed declarations of principle to announce the foundations of authority and to unify and direct public opinion. Of his letter to the Danbury Baptist Association, in which Jefferson depicted religious liberty as a "wall of separation" between church and government, Jefferson explained to an advisor that a response to a citizen address could serve as an "occasion" for "sowing useful truths & principles among the people, which might germinate and become rooted among their political tenets."[71] On other occasions, he used his "special messages" to Congress, as well as some of his public letters, to praise instances of discretion employed by other executive officials. Jefferson came to rely on the use of public statements of principle not only to rally support for his party and administration but also to shape public opinion with the dual aim of energizing the presidency and more clearly marking its boundaries.

If the president could direct the public understanding of religious liberty, the presidency also could be the platform to which citizens would look for understanding the principles of their government. One goal of Jefferson's administration, then, was to instruct citizens how they might energetically pursue great democratic projects while at the same time protecting the principle of consent: the practical requirement of the appeal to the people would afford the people the facts with which they need to judge those they entrust with rule, and the regularized opportunity for a declaration of principles would allow that fundamental will to be preserved while being modified.

---

[69] Richard Hofstadter, *The Idea of a Party System: The Rise of Legitimate Opposition in the United States, 1780–1840* (Berkeley and Los Angeles: University of California Press, 1969); Johnstone, *Jefferson and the Presidency: Leadership in the Young Republic*; James W. Ceaser, *Presidential Selection: Origins and Development* (Princeton, NJ: Princeton University Press, 1979); Marc Landy and Sidney M. Milkis, *Presidential Greatness* (Lawrence: University Press of Kansas, 2000), 41–66.

[70] Jefferson, "First Inaugural Address," *TJW*, 492–6.

[71] Jefferson to Levi Lincoln, 1802 , Ford, 8:129.

Declarations thus made democratic consent possible by revealing the people to themselves. If is true that Jefferson's political philosophy hinged on his plan for education, it also true that his political science rested on his faith in declarations.[72]

The Understanding Developed

Rather than being an opponent of an energetic executive, Jefferson articulated his doctrine of executive strength throughout his public career. His numerous attempts to revise the Virginia Constitution as well as his use of executive power as governor of that state, reveal a consistent, if maturing, understanding of the relationship between prerogative and the law. As lawgiver, Jefferson avoided broad grants of authority to the executive even as he worked to make it unitary and less dependent on the legislative power. As governor, Jefferson confronted events in which the law made no provision for the executive action required by necessity, but he resisted broad interpretations of the law that would accommodate what the desperate times required. As a delegate to Congress and eventual critic of the Articles of Confederation, he was an early advocate of executive selection independent of the legislature and unencumbered by an executive council. Although this period reveals that Jefferson's understanding of the executive was not fully developed, it also shows that he advocated an executive that would have been remarkably strong and resorted to declarations of principle instead of broad interpretations of the law. Nevertheless, Jefferson had not arrived at his later argument that executive power made democracy possible.

The proposal and ratification of the U.S. Constitution provided the opportunity for Jefferson to complete his understanding of executive power. Although Jefferson had tinkered with rules governing elections and tenure of office, it was not until he and Madison had exchanged letters on amending the Constitution and until he had read *The Federalist* that Jefferson arrived at his idea that presidential selection could be combined with declarations of principle in order to make executive energy compatible with consent. Jefferson's advocacy for the bill of rights was thus one step in his long-standing project to make declarations practical, and his call for a two-term limit for presidents was meant to connect such declarations to routine democratic change. More than any of his contemporaries, he perceived the democratic potential of a popularly elected president.

---

[72] On education see, Zuckert, *Natural Rights Republic*, 220–32; Matthews, *Radical Politics of Jefferson*, 81–84; Sheldon, *Political Philosophy of Jefferson*, 53–82; and Yarbrough, *American Virtues*, 125–32.

Throughout his time in opposition, Jefferson left open the path for his democratic executive. By the time he had taken office as Secretary of State, Jefferson praised the merits of a single executive and recommended to reformers in other nations that their constitutions drop provisions for an executive council. At the same time, Jefferson undertook the project of democratizing the office of the president. This endeavor began with his "Response to the Citizens of Albemarle," and it is traceable throughout his participation with Madison throughout the Helvidius and Pacificus exchange, and in his continuing ambivalence with regard to the greatness of Washington. During his tenure as vice president, Jefferson undoubtedly used his influence to oppose the Federalist president, but he also observed that there were two views on the Constitution, those who considered it to be an "elective monarchy" and those who viewed "it as an energetic republic, turning in all it's points on the pivot of free and frequent elections."[73] No monarchist, Jefferson classed himself in the latter group and balanced his understanding of presidential power on the electoral pivot.

Jefferson's best opportunity for leaving his imprint on the meaning of executive energy came when he was president, and his two terms provide the most accessible example of his theory in practice. Jefferson attempted to empower executive administration by connecting it to public opinion, and he defended the president's removal power at a time when it might have disappeared. Moreover, he transformed the appointment power with public confidence in mind. In addition to serving as the "best criterion of what is best," public opinion "alone" could "give strength to the government."[74] Similarly, Jefferson's use of the prerogative as president fit within his lifelong attempt to place the prerogative outside the law while at the same time making the executive more energetic and more popular. Jefferson believed he had acted outside the Constitution by purchasing and incorporating the Louisiana Territory, but, because political necessity required that Jefferson then not throw himself on the people by recommending a constitutional amendment, he remained silent regarding the constitutionality of the Purchase. Rather than offering one of several constitutional arguments that were then available to him, Jefferson presented his extraconstitutional explanation elsewhere. Jefferson never recommended an amendment, because the Twelfth Amendment took precedence over a Louisiana amendment. The urgency was political and philosophic: Republicans needed to fix the Electoral College to ensure that the election of 1804 would not be manipulated by Federalists, and Jefferson used the Amendment to further connect the presidency to public opinion

---

[73] Jefferson to James Sullivan, 9 February 1797, *PTJ*, 29:289.
[74] Jefferson to Archibald Stuart, 25 April 1801, Ford, ed., 8:47.

by making presidential mandates possible. Finally, to institutionalize declarations of principle as the central platform of political change, Jefferson
invented the Inaugural Address as we know it and used Washington's example to get the term limit he had long advocated.

More than pointing the nation to its democratic birth, then, Jefferson's
victory in 1800 signified a turning point in the presidential office. In the
absence of Washington, and in the early divisions of a party system, the
presidency was in crisis. During the mounting crisis with France, Adams, who
had once proposed that presidents be addressed by the title "His Highness
the President of the U.S. and protector of their liberties,"[75] donned a military
uniform with sword to deliver inflammatory speeches against France. At the
same time, Adams created a standing army and, rather than commanding
it himself, designated Washington as Commander in Chief.[76] Worse still,
the Alien and Sedition Acts seemed to prove again that democracies would
vacillate forever between tyranny and disorder. Although Washington had
attempted in his Farewell Address to impart "confidence" in the presidency
to the "Yeomanry," his reputation had crippled his successor's ability to
inspire confidence in the electorate.

But the crisis in the presidency was more than theoretical, for it raised
the question whether the presidency could survive the parties.[77] Would presidents be so attached to their parties that they would be bound by their
cabinets, undermining the premise of accountability in the argument for
executive energy? When Adams attempted to regain control over his administration, by abruptly announcing that he would send an envoy to France
and by removing Hamilton's cronies from his cabinet, Hamilton responded
by publishing a pamphlet critical of Adams. There, Hamilton argued that
Adams lacked the "talents" necessary for presidency and possessed "great
and intrinsic defects" of "character."[78] More important, Hamilton criticized
Adams for ignoring the advice of his cabinet. When Burr acquired a copy of
Hamilton's pamphlet and, sensing a political opportunity, had it published
in the Republican papers, the advantage for the Republicans was twofold.
Jefferson was virtually guaranteed to win against a divided Federalist Party,

---

[75] Madison to Jefferson, 23 May 1789, *PTJ*, 15:147–8. Madison told Jefferson that such a title
would have "subjected" the first president "to a severe dilemma."

[76] Ackerman credits John Adams's later dismantling of the army as the key step for Revolution
of 1800. *Failure of the Founding Fathers*, 95–101.

[77] Skowronek formulates this question in terms of presidents who are loyal successors to
"reconstructive" presidents. *Politics Presidents Make*, 66–69.

[78] Alexnder Hamilton, "*Letter from Alexander Hamilton, Concerning the Public Conduct and
Character of John Adams, Esq. President of the United States*, 24 October 1800, *PAH*,
25:186–234.

and Hamilton's dividing his own party sowed enough discord that Hamilton lost his leverage as his party's leader.[79] On the morning of Jefferson's inauguration, Adams left the capital under the cover of darkness, leaving the first transfer of power to be attended only by the one on the receiving end of it.

Jefferson's victory in 1800 was more than a victory for the opposition against ruling Federalists, for it was also a unique opportunity for Jefferson to invigorate the presidency. By combining the opportunity of replacing an unloved president with the necessity to shape the presidency outside of Washington's reputation, 1800 could occasion a revolution in the executive office alongside a revolution in the electorate. When Jefferson said that his own election would demonstrate that "a free government is of all others the most energetic," he was reveling with fellow partisans and assuring opponents that the country would survive his administration, but he was also letting friends and foes know that he had a plan for the presidency.[80] We now turn to Jefferson's understanding of executive power.

[79] See especially Syrett's notes in *PAH*, 25:170–83.
[80] Jefferson to John Dickinson, 6 March 1801, *TJW*, 1084.

2

Executive Power and the Virginia Executive

Before he became president in 1800, and before the Constitution was written in 1787, Jefferson proposed two constitutions for Virginia. He proposed the first in 1776, about the same time when, as a delegate to the national congress, he offered his famous declaration for independence. He proposed the second in 1783, when he distributed his *Notes on the State of Virginia* to friends. In the interval, Jefferson had served as a wartime governor, and had determined that that the Virginia Constitution was flawed. In particular, one inadequacy of the Virginia Constitution – and of his own 1776 draft – was that it did not do enough to secure independence for the executive power. Indeed, Jefferson's actions as governor reveal his attempt to make executive power strong enough to meet the necessities of war but also remain compatible with constitutional government. By looking at the 1783 constitution informed by both the Virginia Constitution and Jefferson's 1776 plan, and by examining Jefferson's tenure as governor, it is possible to detect movement toward his mature doctrine of executive power.

The Virginia Constitution of 1776

A delegate to Congress in 1776, Jefferson made his famous argument for separation from Great Britain, but, at the same time, he was also thinking about forming a government in Virginia. When his request to return to participate in the Virginia legislature's attempt to write a constitution was turned down, he drafted a constitution of his own and sent it for Virginians to consider. As he explained, establishing a new form of government was then the "whole object" of the "present controversy" – "should a bad government be instituted for us in future it had been well to have accepted at first the bad one offered to us from beyond the water without the risk and expense of contest."¹ Although the Virginia legislature did not approve of most of Jefferson's plan, they did use some of Jefferson's draft for the preamble to the Virginia Constitution, and Jefferson later used it as a working draft for a portion of the Declaration of Independence.² But more than just a historical wind-up to Jefferson's felicitous enunciation of self-evident truths, Jefferson's proposed constitution for Virginia reveals Jefferson as a founder of political institutions as well as the scribe for revolutionary sentiment. Moreover, Jefferson's constitution included a stronger executive than the viable alternatives – which were submitted by John Adams and George Mason – and the constitution accepted by Virginian legislators.³ In articulating this argument against the king and in recommending a form of government, Jefferson went out of his way to show that he was no friend of the kingly office, but, at the same time, Jefferson left open the question of whether his animus was directed at an incompetent monarch rather than a powerful executive.

In order to form a new government, Jefferson had to show that the old one was insufficient. Like the list of grievances in the Declaration of Independence, the argument in the preamble offered the list of abuses committed by the king as evidence that the king who "heretofore entrusted with the exercise of the kingly office in this government hath endeavored to pervert the same into a detestable and insupportable tyranny."⁴ It is worth pausing here to note that the list of accusations levied against the king specified his outright aggressions against the colonies, but others indicated that the king's tyranny stemmed from his failure to execute his office. Two charges pointed to the king's failure to veto bad laws passed by parliament, and the ninth article accused the king of "combining with others to subject us to a foreign jurisdiction giving his assent to their pretended acts of legislation."⁵ The final charge made this claim broadly: the king's tyranny was revealed in his "abandoning the helm of government & declaring us out of his allegiance &

---

¹ Jefferson to Thomas Nelson, 16 May 1776, *PTJ*, 1:292.
² Jefferson, "Composition Draft of that Part of the Declaration of Independence Containing the Charges against the Crown," *PTJ*, 1:417–20.
³ The term "convention" is misleading. As Jefferson noted, Virginia did not send special delegates to form a special body to write a constitution, nor did the people at large ratify the finished document. Rather, the Virginia legislature simply wrote a constitution, leading Jefferson to argue that the Virginia constitution was no more fundamental than ordinary statute. *Notes*, TJW, 246–51. On other plans, see Julian Boyd's notes in *PTJ*, 1: 329–37. I use "viable" because there was another plan, attributed to Carter Braxton, which proposed a lifetime tenure for the governor and praised the British Constitution. Carter Braxton, "An address to the Convention of the Colony of Ancient Dominion of Virginia on the subject of government in general, and recommending a particular form to their consideration" (Printed by John Dunlap: 1776).
⁴ Jefferson, Third Draft of Constitution for Virginia, *PTJ*, 1:356.
⁵ Ibid., *PTJ*, 1:356–7.

protection."[6] To be sure, the rhetorical task at the time was to articulate a theory of the British Empire in which the colonies were connected to England by the king rather than by the real oppressor, parliament.[7] Nevertheless, it is significant that Jefferson did not make the case against the king simply by cataloging the ways in which the king was too energetic; rather, he showed that the king's tyranny derived from his being both too energetic and not energetic enough.

From these charges, the preamble concluded King George III should be "immediately deposed" and a new constitution formed because of George's "misrule."[8] But the one does not follow into the other. If George III had perverted his office such that it was insupportable, why not simply fill the kingly office with someone who would not exhibit George III's tyranny? This confusion was cleared near the end of the preamble: "And forasmuch as the public liberty may be more certainly secured by abolishing an office which all experience hath shewn to be inveterately inimical thereto and it will thereupon become further necessary to re-establish such antient principles as are friendly to the rights of the people and to declare certain others which may cooperate with and fortify the same in future."[9] After offering a list of grievances against one particular king, Jefferson appealed to "all experience" to support the conclusion that monarchy itself, rather than the weakness and strength of one king, was tyranny. The preamble's stated aim, to show that George III had made his kingly office a tyrannical one, was thus critically transformed by the preamble's conclusion, that the kingly office itself was necessarily tyrannical. In place of the kingly principle and prerogative, the constitution would lay out another principle to protect the more ancient one of popular liberty.

The body of Jefferson's constitution contained another contradiction regarding the king's authority. Although the office of the king would be abolished because the king had made the office tyrannical, the vesting clause in the executive article used kingship as the reference point for the powers of the governor, which he called the "administrator." Specifically, the administrator "shall possess the powers formerly held by the king: save only that, he shall be bound by acts of legislature tho' not expressly named."[10] But why

---

[6] Jefferson, First Draft of Constitution for Virginia, *PTJ*, 1:339. In his Summary View of the Rights of British America, Jefferson called on the "great office of his majesty, to resume the exercise of his negative power" in order to protect American rights. *PTJ*, 1:129.

[7] Carl Becker, *The Declaration of Independence: A Study in the History of Political Ideas* (New York: Random House, Vintage Books, 1958), 80–1, 102–16.

[8] Jefferson, Third Draft, *PTJ*, 1:357.

[9] Ibid., *PTJ*, 1:357.

[10] Ibid., *PTJ*, 1:360.

would Jefferson use the king as a model after having recommended that the kingly office be abolished? According to the vesting clause, the administrator would be like the king, except that he would be subordinate to the legislative branch. Furthermore, although the king's office would be the starting point for determining which powers would be granted to the administrator, many of the king's prerogatives were explicitly denied to the chief executive. In particular, the following powers were denied by Jefferson:

1. of dissolving, proroguing or adjourning either house of the Assembly;
2. of declaring war or concluding peace;
3. of issuing letters of marque or reprisal;
4. of raising or introducing armed forces, building armed vessels, forts, or strong holds;
5. of coining monies or regulating their value;
6. of regulating weights and measures;
7. of erecting courts, offices, boroughs, corporations, fairs, markets, ports, beacons, light houses, seamarks.
8. of laying embargoes, or prohibiting the exportation of any commodity for a longer space than [40] days.
9. of retaining or recalling a member of the state but by legal process pro delicto vel contractu.
10. of making denizens;
11. of creating dignities or granting rights of precedence.[11]

This list of prohibited powers is important because it reveals Jefferson's early reluctance to grant that some powers were executive by nature. But it is therefore significant in what it omits; the unnamed powers would have to belong to either the executive or legislative branch, except for those powers formerly exercised by the king, which would be granted to the executive. To summarize, why would the constitution first argue that George III had made his office tyrannical, then argue that history proved that the office itself was tyrannical, then use the kingly office as the starting point for a republican executive, and then forbid specific powers to the administrator?

Jefferson, it seems, was more eager than most Virginians to give power to the executive, but, at the same time, he was less eager than others to vest the executive with a grant of general power. Although the Virginians accepted Jefferson's argument in the preamble that King George had perverted his office, they rejected Jefferson's paragraph in the preamble abolishing the kingly office as well as his vesting clause that used the same office as the

[11] Ibid., *PTJ*, 1:360.

starting point for the new executive's powers.[12] When they attached Jefferson's preamble to their finished constitution, they dropped the section that pronounced the kingly office wholly "inimical" to the people's liberty and simply declared the former government "dissolved."[13] And, instead of Jefferson's convoluted attempt to give the administrator executive powers without giving the administrator *the* executive power, the Virginia Convention preferred George Mason's proposal that the administrator and Council "exercise the executive powers of government"[14] and went out of its way to ensure that the king would not be the model for executive power: "[A]nd he shall, with the advice of a Council of State, exercise the Executive Powers of Government according to the laws of this Commonwealth; and shall not, under any pretense, exercise any power or prerogative by virtue of any Law, statute, or Custom, of England."[15] Rather than using the king as a historical example for what executive powers might be, Mason's draft and the Virginia Constitution simply proceeded from the "executive powers of government." In this regard, Mason and the other Virginian legislators followed the Adams plan.[16]

More than others, Jefferson worried about the possibility that the people would reestablish the monarchy or call for one of their own. Jefferson summarized such fears to the president of the Virginia convention, Edmund Pendleton: "Should we not have in contemplation and prepare for an event (however deprecated) which may happen in the possibility of things; I mean a re-acknolegement of the British tyrant as our king, and previously strip him of every prejudicial possession? Remember how universally the people run into the idea of recalling Charles the 2. after living many years under a republican government."[17] The possessions discussed were "allodial" lands but they might as well have been governmental powers: the constitution would create an administrator who resembled a king but lacked his prerogatives. By replacing the king with an officer like a king but lacking the king's powers and prerogatives, the constitution could be used to quiet those who would inevitably argue for reinstalling the king or for following the British plan of government. Under Jefferson's constitution, the model of the kingly

[12] See especially Boyd's notes in *PTJ*, 1:336.

[13] "Text as Adopted," *PTJ* 1:379.

[14] "The Plan of Government as Originally Drawn by George Mason," *PTJ*, 1:367.

[15] "The Constitution as adopted by the Convention," *PTJ*, 1:380.

[16] John Adams to Richard Henry Lee, 15 November 1775, *Papers of John Adams*, Robert J. Taylor, ed. (Cambridge, MA: Harvard University Press, Belknap Press, 1977–2004), 3:307–8; John Adams, "Thoughts on Government," *Papers of Johns Adams*, 4: 86–92.

[17] Jefferson to Edmund Pendleton, 13 August 1776, *PTJ*, 1: 491–494. See Julian Boyd's discussion of the exchange on page 331.

office would be preserved in order to dim some of its royal glitter. Jefferson's plan for government, read alongside this statement to Pendleton, suggests that Jefferson's faith in democratic government carried with it some suspicion that the people desired monarchy. Even though Jefferson's 1776 attempt to write a constitution for Virginia does not represent Jefferson's final word on executive power, it indicates that Jefferson sensed in 1776 a connection he would later make, that is, the relationship between executive energy and popular affection.

Other features of the plan reveal that Jefferson favored a more powerful executive than did the others. Under Jefferson's plan, the executive power would be exercised by one administrator, with the assistance of a privy council. Both the administrator and his advisors would be selected annually by the House of Representatives.[18] Just as Jefferson would later work to limit the eligibility of sitting presidents to a second term, he then promoted a comparatively short tenure for Virginia's chief executive. Jefferson's limit of one year combined with three years' ineligibility was too strict for the Virginian legislators: following the Adams plan, the Mason plan required three years ineligibility and the Virginia Constitution four, but both allowed three successive terms of one year.[19]

For Jefferson, one reason why the executive would be selected by the House was to ensure that the executive not encroach on the legislative power, just as the provision that the House shall be "free" to follow its own "judgment and conscience" reinforced the idea that the Assembly, not an independent governor, would be the lawmaking body. But another reason for legislative appointment was to ensure that a person capable of executing the office be selected, as voters at large were not to be trusted with so important a task. From this observation to Pendleton regarding the selection of senators, it is evident that Jefferson had not yet found his faith in unfiltered popular

---

[18] The first draft would have prevented the possibility of corruption between the selecting body and the selected officer by disallowing the executive from taking office until the year-long term of the members of the House of Representatives who selected him was over. In the second and third drafts, Jefferson silently dropped the requirement that the appointing House's representatives' terms expire before the administrator assume office. *PTJ*, 1:337–65. John Adams, "Thoughts on Government," *Papers of John Adams*, 4:90.

[19] In practice, however, it seems that three-year limit served as a kind of guarantee that a governor would have three years in office. Before Jefferson, Patrick Henry served three terms as governor, and when Jefferson announced his plan to retire after two years, his friend John Page urged him to "Go on serve out the Time allowed by the Constitution[on]." Even Madison, who was not yet his friend but looked forward to Jefferson's coming leisure and its promise of increased correspondence, regretted Jefferson's decision to retire, assuming that his was his "final determination" rather than any possibility that the General Assembly would select another. Moreover, the Virginia Constitution arranged the tenure of privy council members to be at least three years. *PTJ*, 1:366–86.

elections: "I have ever observed that a choice by the people themselves is not generally distinguished for it's wisdom. This first secretion from them is usually crude and heterogeneous. But give to those so chosen by the people a second choice themselves, and they will generally chuse wise men."[20] Jefferson went on to emphasize his distrust of public opinion by writing that he "could submit, tho' not so willingly" to a lifetime tenure for senators if it were the only alternative to a "mere creation by and dependance on the people." Although Jefferson would have allowed "all male persons of full age and sane mind" having one-fourth of acre property in the city or twenty-five acres in the country the right to select members of the House, he did not yet believe they were up to the task of selecting Senators or members of the executive branch.[21] But Jefferson was ahead of his time. In 1776, most believed in legislative appointment of the executive: the Adams and Mason plans proposed that the governor be selected by joint ballot of the house and the senate, and this was the method accepted by the Virginia convention.[22] Because selection by joint ballot meant that the administrator would be twice removed from the people (senators would be selected by an electoral body rather than by voters), Jefferson's plan for selection by the House alone called for a more popular executive than did the alternatives.[23]

Just as important was whether the executive would be unitary or plural. As a rule, Americans in 1776 believed that the executive office should include a council to assist the governor – Jefferson was no exception – but the nature of the relation between the governor and his council was not yet settled.[24] Jefferson called for a privy council, which would be appointed by the lower house. However, Jefferson also provided for a Deputy Administrator to succeed the governor in office in case of death and, more important, "to assist his principal in the discharge of his office."[25] As Jefferson put it, the privy council "shall be able to give advice to the Administrator when called on by him."[26] But whether the administrator or his council was to be the final point of decision depends on what "advice" means. The language suggests

[20] Jefferson to Edmund Pendleton, 26 August 1776, *PTJ*, 1:503–507.

[21] Jefferson, Third Draft, *PTJ* 1:358.

[22] But Pennsylvania eliminated their executive, and the New York Constitution of 1777 called for election of the governor by voters with a freehold of 100 pounds. See Gordon S. Wood, *The Creation of the American Republic, 1776–1787* (Chapel Hill: University of North Carolina Press, 1969), 137. "Mason Plan" and "Constitution as Adopted by the Convention," *PTJ*, 1:367, 380.

[23] John Adams, "Thoughts on Government," *Papers of John Adams*, 4:86–92. "Mason Plan" and "Constitution as Adopted by the Convention," *PTJ*, 1:366, 380. Even the Braxton plan called for selection by the legislature, Carter Braxton, "An Address" (see note 3), 21–22.

[24] For the prevalence of the executive council, see Wood, *Creation*, 138–9.

[25] *PTJ*, 1: 349, 359.

[26] *PTJ*, 1: 350, 360.

that the council's job was to recommend rather than to direct. For instance, that "advice" was meant to be somewhat less than "advise and consent" is indicated by the fact that the constitution required the governor to obtain the council's "consent" in specific cases such as appropriating forfeited lands, whereas the governor's power to appoint general court judges and civil and military officers was subject to the council's "negative." Unless otherwise noted, then, "advise" seemed to mean giving advice in the simplest sense.

The Adams plan, the Mason plan, and the final Constitution went further in fastening the governor to a council. According to the Adams plan, the assembly would select "twenty or thirty" people to form another body, which would act like both an upper legislative house and an executive council. Whereas this council/senate would have "a negative voice in the legislature," it also would be a part of the executive power, as the governor's actions required "the consent of council."[27] Mason's plan called for the privy council's advice to "be entered of record in their proceedings."[28] Later, a special committee revised Mason's plan to require the council to have "their advice be entered of record, [and sign'd by the members giving such advice, to be laid before the general assembly when called for by them, but let not this be done, but on extraordinary occasions.]"[29] Similarly, the language of the constitution as adopted, which called for the council to enter their advice on record, including dissents, "to be laid before the General Assembly, when called for by them," suggests that the council's advice was meant to be a source of information by which the legislative branch could decide to refuse to reappoint an incompetent or corrupt administrator or even perhaps impeach and prosecute one after he had left office. But the Virginia Constitution offered more than the prospect of participating in impeachment proceedings, for council members' salaries would be divided proportionally according to attendance, and a council member could serve until he was removed by the legislative branch.[30]

Prerogative and the Dilemma of the Council

As Alexander Hamilton would later argue, a council allows the executive to hide from criticism when delicate questions of responsibility are raised,

[27] According to the Adams plan, if the legislative power were wholly in one assembly and the executive power wholly in a single person, there would be conflict and the "contest would end in war." To solve this dilemma, the Adams plan recommended a "distinct assembly be constituted as a mediator between the two extreme branches of the legislature, that which represents the people, and that which is vested with the executive power." John Adams, "Thoughts on Government," *Papers of John Adams*, 4:86–93.

[28] "Mason Plan," *PTJ*, 1:367.

[29] "Mason Plan as Revised by the Committee," *PTJ*, 1:370.

[30] "Constitution as adopted by the Convention," *PTJ*, 1:381.

and Jefferson's own governorship illustrated the difficulties of having such a council advise the executive. As governor, Jefferson would present himself as the clerk for the council when explaining his actions to potentially hostile parties – British generals and personal friends in particular.[31] Consider the controversial imprisonment of the British officer, Henry Hamilton.[32] The council's decision to put Hamilton in prison rather than granting him parole depicts Jefferson as the dutiful errand boy of his council: "This Board has resolved to advise the Governour that the said Henry Hamilton . . . be put into irons, confined in the dungeon of the publick jail, debarred the use of pen, ink and paper, and excluded all converse except with their keeper. And the Governour orders accordingly."[33] From Jefferson's letters to George Washington, however, it is clear that Jefferson then believed that he was the single official who had the power, if not yet the will, to decide whether Hamilton would be granted parole. Finding nothing in "those Books usually recurred to as testimonials of the Laws and usages of nature and nations" to assist him, he turned to Washington for advice because the latter's opinion could both settle the "public mind" as well as discern the "national faith."[34] Washington replied that most officers believed that Hamilton should be paroled but also trusted Jefferson to determine what was best "from motives of policy and to satisfy our people."[35] Later, when Washington's recommendation of parole became firmer, Jefferson paroled Hamilton, privately reporting that he had been persuaded by Washington.[36] For both Washington and Jefferson, then, it was presumed that Jefferson as governor, not Jefferson as the agent of an executive council, held the authority to grant Hamilton parole. Likewise, it may be debatable whether Hamilton "experienced the inhumanity of the executive power" as he later alleged, but it is probable that the executive Hamilton had in mind was more Governor Jefferson than the governor's council.[37]

Jefferson used this division of accountability on other difficult occasions. To William Davies's request for clothing, for example, Jefferson explained that he could not consult the council because its members had already adjourned for the day and because it was not in his power to issue

---

[31] Jefferson to William Phillips, 22 July 1779, *PTJ*, 3:44–9.
[32] "Order of Virginia Council Placing Henry Hamilton and Others in Irons," 16 June 1779, *PTJ*, 2:292–5.
[33] Ibid., 294.
[34] Jefferson to Washington, 17 July 1779, *PTJ*, 3:40–2.
[35] Washington to Jefferson, 6 August 1779, *PTJ*, 3:61–2.
[36] Washington to Jefferson, 23 November 1779, and Jefferson to Washington. 28 November 1779, *PTJ*, 3:198–9, 204–6.
[37] See Boyd's notes, *PTJ*, 3:96.

clothing: "The council have fixed by their rules the manner of issuing, and determined that it should be general, that all may fare alike."[38] Also, Jefferson would often speak in the formal terms of the council rather than the language of a single governor when declining the request of close friend. To John Page's request that he suspend an act for raising levies, Jefferson passed along the opinion of the Council that the request be denied and then explained the reasoning: "They think they cannot with any propriety suspend an Act after the Terms are all past which it should have been carried into execution. It would only answer the end of a remission of Penalties which would be an Abuse of the suspending Power given them by the latter Act. The Circumstances which produced that Law were that the militia of half the State had been called from their Counties on the invasion on very distant and long Services."[39] That responsibility within a plural executive is often hard to pinpoint was captured by the syntax of one Virginian who had requested supplies, "In the last two conversations I had with the Governor and the Council" ... "he was Pleas'd to Refer them [the supplies] to my management."[40] In fact, this tension between plurality and accountability was anticipated by Jefferson in his acceptance of the governorship: "My great pain is, lest my poor endeavors should fall short of the kind expectations of my country; so far as impartiality, assiduous attention, and sincere affection to the great American cause, shall enable me to fulfill the duties of any appointment, so far I may, with confidence undertake; for all beyond, I must rely on the wise counsels of the General Assembly, and of whom they have appointed for my aid in those duties."[41] As in his more famous First Inaugural Jefferson promised that insofar as patriotism, responsibility, and fairness were required, he would be more than capable of executing his office, but on occasions when executing the government would require more than personal virtues, he would look to the General Assembly and his council for assistance. But, as suggested by the distinction between normal duties and those "beyond," even if councils might provide aid in the form of wise counsel, Jefferson would still be the one determining when he would need to be counseled at all.

But emergencies raise more questions about plurality of office. What happens, for instance, if council members were not present to offer advice? When Jefferson was left without a council for the first time – when the British invasion forced him to remove the executive from Williamsburg to

---

[38] Jefferson to William Davies, 3 September 1780, *PTJ*, 3:587–8.
[39] Jefferson to John Page, 18 April 1781, *PTJ*, 5:491–2.
[40] John Syme to William Claiborne. 24 January 1781, *PTJ*, 4: 459.
[41] Jefferson, "Message Accepting Election as Governor," 2 June 1779, *PTJ*, 2: 277–8.

Richmond – he explained that until the council could meet he would do "such business as may be done by him, without the concurrence of the publick boards."[42] He executed at least three military actions without his council: he reported to General Muhlenberg the state of Virginia recruits for Continental service, offered "general Sentiments" regarding the location of a fortification along the mouth of the Ohio River, and ordered several lieutenants to "carry an expedition into the Indian country."[43] But until the council met, Jefferson was quite inactive – the "from" letters dominate this portion of Jefferson's correspondence and papers, and most of the surviving letters to others were unrelated to administration.

Jefferson took more initiative the next time he was left without council. When Arnold invaded in January 1781, Jefferson moved the council to Richmond to conduct executive business, and, in the transition, Jefferson found himself lacking a quorum but still having to direct the defenses of the state. By the time the council could achieve a quorum on 19 January, Jefferson had already ordered George Rogers Clark to proceed in his plans to capture Detroit, recommended Baron von Steuben to begin raising new levies sooner rather than later, ordered Steuben to discharge members of the militia who did not have firearms, informed the president of the Confederation Congress that forces would be necessary to replace Clarke's, written a complaint to the same official that Virginia had been required to play too great a role in supplying provisions for British prisoners, organized a system of express riders to convey intelligence, appointed an official to collect laborers to make repairs on buildings damaged by the British, commissioned the building of twenty "portable" boats, authorized an adventurer's plan to crash a flaming ship into the British fleet, impressed boats, transmitted to the Confederation Congress the General Assembly's resolution on ratification of the Articles of Confederation, and appointed someone to educate Steuben concerning the laws, customs, resources, and organization of Virginia's military.[44]

---

42 "Notice of Removal of Executive Office from Williamsburg to Richmond," 25 March 1780, *PTJ*, 3:333–4.

43 Jefferson to J. P. G. Muhlenberg, 12 April 1780, *PTJ*, 3:351–2; Jefferson to George Rogers Clark, 19 April 1780, *PTJ*, 3:354–5; Jefferson to George Rogers Clark [19 April] 1780, *PTJ*, 3:356–7. That Clark's expedition in the West and the hostilities with Native Americans had been a long time in planning, see Jefferson to George Washington, 15 February 1780, *PTJ*, 3:291–2. The point here is that Jefferson acted on the particular developments without a council, after he moved the location of the executive branch.

44 Jefferson to George Rogers Clark, 13 January 1781, *PTJ*, 4:348–9; Jefferson to Steuben, 13 January 1781, *PTJ*, 4:351–2; Jefferson to Steuben, 14 January 1781, *PTJ*, 4:356; Jefferson to Samuel Huntington, 15 January 1781, *PTJ*, 4:366, 369–71; Jefferson to Thomas Nelson, 15 January 1781, *PTJ*, 4:372; Jefferson to the Person Employed to Collect Workmen, 15 January 1781, *PTJ*, 4:373; Jefferson to James Maxwell, 16 January 1781, *PTJ*, 4:380; Jefferson to Thomas Nelson, 16 January 1781, *PTJ*, 4:382; Jefferson to George Weedon, 16 January

Another measure initiated by Jefferson without a council preserved Virginia's ability to muster forces to protect itself. In 1781, the British attempted to weaken Virginia's militia by guaranteeing "paroles" to Virginians who would pledge not to take arms against the British in the future. For the governor, who had already faced several outbreaks of insurrection among citizens who were displeased with conscription, these paroles must have been especially perplexing: without calling themselves Tories or Loyalists, Virginians could simply opt out of the military effort by claiming to have been forced to sign a pledge. Jefferson responded with his pen: with his council away, he drafted and redrafted a proclamation which explained the citizens were "incapable by law of contracting engagements which may cancel or supercede the duties they owe to their country while remaining in it."[45] The proclamation went on to say that all citizens who held conscientious obligation to "refuse obedience to the laws of their Country" were authorized and required to turn themselves over to the British forces. This proclamation, which explained that the laws would be enforced and that private citizens could not make a separate peace with an invading military, also provided Jefferson with the opportunity to teach Virginians the principles of the Revolution, that is, the logic of the Declaration of Independence. When Jefferson's council met on 19 January, it approved of the proclamation that had been drafted in its absence.[46]

In late April and throughout May, Jefferson's council rarely achieved a quorum throughout the complications of yet another British invasion. As Boyd notes, because of both the perils incident to the British invasion and general sporadic attendance, Jefferson was accompanied by only one other person from 25 April to 7 May.[47] On these days, some of Jefferson's letters spoke of the executive in terns of "we" and "our" even though no council was officially present.[48] From 7 May to 9 May, there were three members with whom Jefferson could "unofficially transact business." On 10 May, there were four members, constituting a quorum, and this council approved the previous actions taken by the executive: "The foregoing proceedings which have been done (through necessity) without the formality of a regular

1781, *PTJ*, 4:384; Jefferson to Richard Claiborne, 18 January 1781, *PTJ*, 4:393; Jefferson to Samuel Huntington, 17 January 1781, *PTJ*, 4:386–91; Jefferson to John Walker, 18 January 1781, *PTJ*, 4:400.

45 Jefferson, "Proclamation Concerning Paroles," *PTJ* 1:403–5.

46 H. R. McIlwaine, ed., *Journals of the Council of State of Virginia: Vol. II, October 6, 1777-November 30, 1781*, (Richmond: Virginia State Library, 1932), 273–6.

47 *PTJ*, 5:558, 614. The executive council journal records no business from 26 April to 6 May. McIlwaine, *Journals*, 341–2.

48 *PTJ*, 5:601–2. Boyd notes that some clerical errors can be attributed to the excitement of the period.

board, being now laid before the board and read, the same are approved."[49] Under Jefferson, a full council never gathered after 10 May.

That Governor Jefferson sometimes relied on his own lights more than those of his council was not missed by others. Again, the controversial question of paroles illustrates the tension then existing between civil and military powers. Responding to George Weedon's communication of a British general's request to exchange prisoners, Jefferson used the plural "we" to explain that the executive lacked the power to exchange Continental prisoners.[50] As Boyd notes, Weedon was not pleased with what he believed to be Jefferson's linguistic maneuvering and responded in kind, thanking Jefferson for the council's "resolution" and explained that he passed the "very words of the Council" to Phillips, even though Jefferson had sent Weedon his personal decision and not a formal council resolution. For Weedon, the difficulty in dealing with the governor and his council must have reinforced the his belief in military supremacy: he reported to the British general, "You are too well informed in of the Profession of Arms not to know the Military are by no means answerable for the Resolutions of the Civil."[51]

More than proceeding with business required by necessity, Jefferson couched difficult decisions in matters pertaining to the executive department in language of interpretation rather than command. For instance, to John Peyton's application that the draft law be suspended, Jefferson appealed to the principle of precedent: "I have at present no Council before whom I can lay it, but as the same Application had been made before by Colo. Page, and had been declined by the Council on the general principle that the suspending power given them was intended to be exercised only where such a proportion of Militia had been withdrawn from the County, as rendered the execution of the law impracticable, and as the two members present are of Opinion that the Draught should not be suspended in the present Instance, I apprehend that this may be considered still as the sense of the Executive, and that the Draught should proceed."[52] But the practical power of interpretation was learned by Jefferson even before he had to conduct business without a constitutionally sanctioned council. When communicating the council's decision, Jefferson would sometimes add his own thoughts to guide officials executing the law. To James Wood, for example, Jefferson sent the Council Order for

---

[49] McIlwaine, *Journals*, 344.
[50] Jefferson to George Weedon, 10 April 1781, *PTJ*, 5:401–2.
[51] George Weedon to Jefferson, 14 April 1781, *PTJ*, 4:456–8.
[52] Jefferson to Sir John Peyton, 5 May 1781, *PTJ*, 5:605–6. If Boyd is correct that only one other person accompanied Jefferson until 7 May, then Jefferson's use of "two members present" is particularly striking.

relocating British prisoners but also advised Wood on the best method of following it: "The advice of Council pretty fully explains itself, yet I will give you my ideas of the best mode of executing it, submitting them to your judgment."[53] In advising Wood, Jefferson enumerated what he saw to be the "most essential measure" and then directed Wood with details concerning place and time. Similarly, to George Rogers Clark, Jefferson explained that Clark's "distance from the scene of action" required Jefferson to trust Clark's "Discretion and Zeal for the good of [his] Country" as to whether Clark should quit one "Expedition" on behalf of another.[54] As he would recommend to other executives once he became president, Jefferson interpreted the law in such a way as to guide executive officers to execute what they believed to be the essential principle of law, even if executing the principle entailed transgressing some of the law's details.

Jefferson's language was indicative of his own moving in and out of the formal requirements of an executive connected to a council. Bound by a constitution that had required the executive to be directed by an advisory council, a stricture he himself had balked at in his own constitution, Jefferson found a way to acknowledge the laws and preserve the government in the face of necessity. That Jefferson took measures to defend his state even though he lacked his council is important because it modifies the common understanding that Jefferson was reluctant to take action as governor. Rather than representing a pre-presidential period in which a suspicion of executive energy crippled his ability to carry out the laws, Jefferson's actions as governor foreshadow his actions as president. More often than not, Jefferson found ways to energize the executive's direction of the military effort, ways that he also believed were compatible with the Virginia Constitution and securing rights. As later chapters show, Jefferson's working without his council reflects his larger efforts to keep executive discretion outside the law rather than placing it inside by way of interpretation. More important than the specific measures taken were the methods used, methods that Jefferson would later employ as president. Not simply acting because necessity demanded it, Jefferson kept records to ensure that the council and the assembly would be able to approve of his actions after the fact. The point for now, however, is that Jefferson's tenure as governor subjected him to the dilemma of necessity and the law, but it also offered the opportunity to look for a solution.[55]

---

[53] Jefferson to James Wood, 9 June 1780, *PTJ*, 3:428–9.
[54] Jefferson to George Rogers Clark, 19 April 1780, *PTJ*, 3:356–7.
[55] See, for instance, "The Board of War to Jefferson," 16 November, 1779, *PTJ*, 3:190–1.

Prerogative and Punishment

In his first two drafts of the 1776 constitution, Jefferson reserved the pardon power for the legislative branch but in the final draft, Jefferson deleted the pardon power from the list of prerogatives reserved to the legislature, choosing instead to deny the power completely: "nor shall there be power any where to pardon crimes or to remit fines or punishments."[56] Mason, however, allowed the governor the power of "granting reprieves or pardons, except in cases where the prosecution shall have been carried on by the Lower House of Assembly."[57] The Virginia Convention sided with Mason, allowing the administrator the pardon privilege, albeit under the advice of council.[58]

That Jefferson, who spent much of his legislative career trying to make punishment more humane, denied even the legislative body this authority reflects Jefferson's early anxieties about the former king's prerogatives. Put simply, he did not believe that the power to mitigate the law's severity should be entrusted to human judgment. As he explained to Pendleton, predictable and proportionate punishments would make the law milder even as it acted as a deterrent: "Punishments I know are necessary, and I would provide them, strict and inflexible, but proportioned to the crime. . . . Laws thus proportionate and mild should never be dispensed with. Let mercy be the character as the law-giver, but let the judge be a mere machine. The mercies of the law will be dispensed equally and impartially to every description of men; those of the judge, or of the executive power, will be the eccentric impulses of whimsical, capricious designing men."[59] Thus, the law would be freed from the uncertainty of executive discretion. Later, Jefferson prefaced his "Bill for Proportioning Crimes and Punishments" with the argument that "cruel and sanguinary laws defeat their own purpose, by engaging the benevolence of mankind to withhold prosecutions."[60] As governor, Jefferson would often tell petitioners that he lacked the authority to pardon certain crimes, such as desertion: "I have no power to remit the sentence of the law, nor do [I] know any power which can, except the General assembly."[61] Still concerned with royal prerogatives endangering rights, Jefferson was unwilling to allow discretion to executives who were to administer punishment.

Statements against executive discretion in punishment notwithstanding, Governor Jefferson did exercise his constitutionally authorized pardon

---

[56] Jefferson, Third Draft, *PTJ*, 1:359.
[57] "The Plan of Government as Originally Drawn by George Mason," *PTJ*, 1:367.
[58] "The Constitution as adopted by the Convention," *PTJ*, 1:380.
[59] Jefferson to Edmund Pendleton, 26 August 1776, *PTJ*, 1:505.
[60] Jefferson, "A Bill Proportioning Crimes and Punishments," *TJW*, 349.
[61] "Petition of Certain Deserters, with Jefferson's Observations," *PTJ*, 4:19–21.

power. Sometimes, he used the pardon even more vigorously than allowed by the Virginia Constitution. For instance, in a case in which Jefferson believed a slave had been falsely convicted of treason, he granted a reprieve from execution until the Assembly would be back in session to consider the indictment. This particular move was especially bold, for Jefferson at the time lacked a council and, as his term had nearly expired, he would be a private citizen within weeks.[62]

On other occasions, the state's interest in prosecution, not mercy, guided his use of the power. For example, when Jefferson learned that some Virginian soldiers had claimed horses abandoned by the British before the rightful owners could, Jefferson passed along a stern warning to the general of Virginia's militia, Thomas Nelson: "These Men being under your Command I beg you to take the most coercive measures for compelling a restitution and letting them know that the most vigorous and exemplary punishment will be inflicted on every Man who shall be known to have one of them and not to deliver him up. Such as are recovered be so good as to have brought up. The mischief done us by our Citizens, plundering one another has far exceeded what the Enemy did."[63] Even if Jefferson's promise that punishment would be "most vigorous" does not necessarily mean that punishment would exceed that allowed by law, it does suggest that the punishment would not be lightened. Indeed, there were times when executive duty spirited Jefferson's otherwise humanitarian demeanor: after Benedict Arnold's raid on Virginia's capital, Jefferson commissioned the capture of Arnold and, although he decided against it, seriously considered authorizing Arnold's execution – with or without a trial.[64] In another case of treason, Jefferson recommended that some of the accused "had better not be put under prosecution" so that they could be used as witnesses for the prosecution: "The reason is that if that they be prosecuted and convicted of treason the Executive have no power to pardon; by keeping them out of a course of law the executive will have in their power to recommend them to the Legislature ... if their conduct in the mean time shall be such as shews they merit to be so recommended."[65] The executive may not have the power to pardon in all cases, but he does have

---

[62] "From Mann Page, enclosing Court Proceedings against a Slave, together with Jefferson's Reprieve," 13 May, 1781, and Madison to Jefferson, 3 April 1781. *PTJ*, 5:640–3, 325–38.

[63] Jefferson to Thomas Nelson, 12 January 1781, *PTJ*, 4:344.

[64] Jefferson to J. P. G. Mulhenberg, 31 January 1781, *PTJ*, 4:487–8. Before Julian Boyd's verdict that the portion of the letter commissioned the mission but not the execution, Dumas Malone concluded that the letter "is better regarded as a revelation of Jefferson's state of mind than as an illustration of punitive action." Malone, 1: 341, n23a.

[65] Jefferson to James Calloway, *PTJ*, 3:519–20.

the ability to influence prosecution "out of a course of law," before a pardon becomes necessary.[66]

Like other executives, Jefferson observed firsthand the imperfection in the law, and he had to decide which criminals to prosecute and which laws to enforce. But what is striking about Jefferson's actions is that, long before he became president, he ordered executive and military officers to prosecute or release prisoners by terms not strictly found within the "course of law." The lawgiver had found that the silence of the law could be used on behalf of the public good.

Prerogative Power and Legislative Supremacy: Impressments

One power conspicuously absent from the executive article in Jefferson's 1776 constitution was the power of directing the military. Unlike the Mason plan and the Virginia Constitution, which authorized the executive to call out the militia with the advice of council and "when embodied shall alone have the direction of the Militia under the laws of the country," Jefferson's draft did not directly lodge the power in either branch.[67] Although the powers of declaring war and peace and raising armies would be lodged in the legislature alone, the administrator would have the power to appoint military officers with the consent of his council. However, Jefferson's constitution did not say whether the power of command would rest with the branch that raises the army and declares war or with the one that appoints officers. Because the administrator would possess the powers formerly held by the king except for those explicitly denied, precedent – which is another word for initiative – would have to decide whether leading the militia was one of the powers exercised by kings and not forbidden to the administrator.

Commanding the militia proved to be especially difficult for Governor Jefferson, and some of his contemporaries even went so far as to accuse him of cowardice or treason.[68] There is some truth to the argument that Jefferson did not as vigorously lead the military efforts as others would have: Jefferson wrote in his autobiography that he resigned from the governorship in order to allow the military and civil powers to be joined, that is, for General Nelson

---

[66] Other Virginians like Edmund Randolph expanded the use of the pardon further, arguing that the executive could pardon one charged with treason before the trial and that the executive should pardon criminals to contain the effects of jury rebellion. Edmund Randolph to Jefferson, 23 February 1781, and Boyd's notes, *PTJ*, 5:642–643.

[67] "The Constitution as adopted by the Convention," *PTJ*, 1:377–386.

[68] Jefferson's conduct as a war governor was examined and vindicated by the Virginia House of Delegates and the Senate. That his conduct as governor was questioned at all allowed later partisans to charge Jefferson the politician with military cowardice. See Malone, 1:361–5.

to serve as governor.[69] But if such arguments are meant to mean more than Jefferson should have physically led the military efforts then they must presume not only that Virginia's constitutional design insufficiently provided for the governor to defend the state against invasion but also that Jefferson should have recognized such a defect and discarded the constitution in order to save the state. That Jefferson never resorted to this course of action, although he was so urged by many, certainly demonstrates Jefferson's early and lifelong suspicion of prerogative, but, more precisely, Jefferson's chosen method of executive restraint reflects his movement toward a working theory of a democratic executive. Rather than using necessity to justify the aggrandizement of the executive or military power, Jefferson conscientiously worked within the limits of constitutional design and resisted attempts by military officials to overstretch their authority. This is not to say that Jefferson allowed a narrow interpretation of the law to obstruct the defense of the state; rather, it is to say that Jefferson adhered to a strict interpretation of the Virginia Constitution, and when necessity demanded that he move outside his constitutional authority, Jefferson acted and then afterward sought legislative approval. By being both an advocate of executive action and a defender of the legislative process, the governor expanded his office without treading upon the legislature's duty to write the laws.

In the practical division of constitutional authority, Jefferson often refused to direct military matters which he believed properly rested with the legislative power. These occasions illustrate the narrowing tendency of Jefferson's strict construction. Jefferson once refused Charles Harrison's request for new recruits for an artillery regiment on the grounds that the legislature gave the power of "officering and regimenting of these men" to Washington and that it was "therefore not in the power of the executive to interfere" and that the matter "rests altogether with the Legislature."[70] Similarly, to a request for raising a Legion, Jefferson laid the matter "before the General Assembly" because the request, in his estimation, went beyond the "powers of the executive to stipulate."[71] And when Jefferson did believe he possessed the authority over a particular military matter, he would sometimes pass its exercise along to Virginia's military leader, Baron von Steuben. To one

---

[69] Jefferson, *Autobiography*, *TJW*, 45. Dumas Malone concluded that the Assembly "went a considerable distance toward military dictatorship" in their granting additional powers to Jefferson's successor, Nelson. Malone, 1:361.

[70] Jefferson to Charles Harrison, 13 September 1780, *PTJ*, 3:641–2.

[71] In this instance, Jefferson's words again reveal the tension regarding the executive and his council: he says that he will lay the request before the assembly once it meets, as the council together has already called the assembly into session. Jefferson to Alexander Spotswood, 31 January 1781, *PTJ*, 4:490.

request for arms, for instance, Jefferson explained, "The Militia embodied in this State having been put under his [Steuben's] command, it is probable that any orders which may go out on this subject may go from him."[72] Thus, strict construction served as handmaiden to self-interest: as a matter of ordering the personal virtues, Jefferson believed that the life of the soldier was less likely to provide happiness than the life of a philosopher.[73]

Jefferson's mildness and strict understanding of the constitution notwithstanding, Jefferson did sometimes create the legal authority for himself to direct the military efforts. In October 1779, the General Assembly passed a law to create a foundery to manufacture weapons and to clear the James River, and it was Jefferson's job as governor to write the contract. The problem, however, was that a private citizen claimed to have been previously granted the contract to build the foundry. Jefferson's task, then, was to investigate the claim and lay it before the General Assembly. But Jefferson went further: he went back to legislative records of 1764 to show legislators "circumstances which are to be found among your own journals and acts" that "were necessary to continue the thread of the relation so as to render it intelligible, and are desired to be considered only as references to your records for more authentic and precise information."[74] The evidence, according to Jefferson, supported Jefferson's argument that the individual's claim must give way to the general good. Furthermore, after emphasizing that legislative deliberation had already blurred what should have been clear, Jefferson's contract included a section, written in his own hand, which would "more effectually enable the Governour" to execute the terms of the bill and, more important, allow Jefferson himself the opportunity to supervise the construction.[75]

Another difficulty in commanding the military effort was the disposition of the people and their laws. Although Jefferson would later claim that republican government was the most energetic because citizens of a republic would freely and voluntarily protect the public good as if it were in their private interest, Jefferson in 1781 did not yet believe that republicans would make good or even willing soldiers.[76] Before he had befriended Lafayette, Jefferson wrote to warn the future military hero of the differences between republican America and France: "Mild Laws, a People not used to war and prompt obedience, a want of the provisions of War and means of procuring

---

[72] Jefferson to Paul Loyall, 9 February 1781, *PTJ*, 4:570–1.
[73] Jefferson to Johann Ludwig de Unger, 30 November 1780, *PTJ*, 4:171.
[74] Jefferson to Benjamin Harrison, 30 October 1779, *PTJ*, 3:130.
[75] "Bill for Establishing a Manufactory of Arms and Extending Navigation through the Fall of James River," *PTJ*, 3:131–47.
[76] Jefferson, First Inaugural, *TJW*, 493.

them often render our orders ineffectual, oblige us to temporize and when we cannot accomplish an object in one way to attempt it with another."[77] This is not to say that Jefferson believed that a republic should organize its military according to republican standards.[78] Rather, it is to say that Jefferson doubted whether republicans would consent to the harsh wartime measures taken by him as executive. Curiously, Lafayette's letter of 20 March, which may or may not have been written before the arrival of Jefferson's, warned that "Necessity will some times oblige me to take the Unpopular Method of impress" and asked Jefferson for his suggestions in making the demands of necessity less rigorous on Virginians.[79] Accomplishing the objects of drafting citizens, ensuring compliance of lower officers, and, ultimately, winning the war, often required that harsh execution be put in soft words.

Legislative supremacy complicated the already difficult task of fighting the war. In January 1781, Jefferson called the legislature into session early because the state was running short on money, and military leaders had told Jefferson that the state would need more than a militia to protect itself. Alongside his "Proclamation Convening the General Assembly," which he believed to be the only requirement "in point of formality," Jefferson issued a private letter to assembly members to explain himself.[80] Jefferson opened his letter by explaining that circumstances regarding his decision to call the Assembly into session included some "which could not with propriety be explained in the publick proclomation." In addition to "Men and money," Jefferson offered another reason for calling the Assembly into session. Because the British had destroyed several printing presses, several laws providing for the recruiting of men and procuring supplies had expired before Jefferson could order county magistrates to execute them. But rather than waiting for the Assembly to convene and write more legislation, Jefferson had already ordered county magistrates to enforce the expired legislation as quickly as possible. Since some of these officials might have had "legal scruples" that would get in the way of their executing a law that no longer existed, he had offered a larger justification for enforcing the expired law. First, he had assured the magistrates that the Assembly, "influenced by the necessity which induced them to pass the act," would approve of the actions after the fact. Second, Jefferson had pointed to the purpose of the act, arguing that both legal principles as well policy making agree that "substance" (procuring supplies) was more important than "circumstance" (the date of

[77] Jefferson to Lafayette, 10 March 1781, *PTJ*, 5:113–4.

[78] Jefferson, "Notes Concerning the Right of Removal from Office," *PTJ*, 4: 281–2.

[79] It also worth noting that Lafayette enclosed his letter of introduction from Washington in this letter. Lafayette to Jefferson, 20 March 1781, *PTJ*, 5:188–9.

[80] Jefferson to Members of the Assembly, 23 January 1781, *PTJ*, 4:433–4.

carrying out the law). Third, Jefferson had appealed to a kind of patriotism that would eagerly endorse the triumph of substance over circumstance: "While we have so many foes in our bowels and environing us on every side, he is but a bad citizen who can entertain a doubt whether the law will justify him in saving his country, or who will scruple to risk himself in support of the spirit of a law where unavoidable accidents have prevented a literal compliance with it." To these three arguments, he had added an important qualification, pointing out that departing from the letter of the law in this would not cause private harm – "no man can say this will be an injury to him," as later compliance would mean that a person would not have to sacrifice his person or property on an earlier date.[81]

Within Jefferson's deference to the legislature, then, was a defense of his discretion as governor. By going out of his way to explain why he called members of the General Assembly into session early, Jefferson also informed them that he had to make good on the promise he had already made to county executives. Since the "zealous citizen" would have followed Jefferson's order and executed the substance of the law (unlike the "unwilling" citizen, who would have found "much room for objection"), the legislature's approval would confirm Jefferson's argument that the substance of a law was more important than its circumstance.[82] More to the point, it would provide an official approval of executive discretion. At least one magistrate, Robert Ewing, agreed that the assembly's approval would remove "future scruple" by confirming that the actions had been done according to the "spirit of the Law" in service of the public good.[83] For executives like Ewing, the "authority of the legislature" would convince the unwilling or at least lessen the likelihood of conflicts between the unwilling and the zealous.

Another difficulty was the division between the civil and military powers. Sometimes, military officers would pass questions to Jefferson, on the grounds that the matters involved were "civil," and Jefferson would respond that the problem was not civil but "military."[84] Also, military subordinates

---

[81] Jefferson to the First Magistrate of Each Council, 20 January 1781, *PTJ*, 4: 414–5.

[82] Circular Letter to Members of the Assembly, 23 January 1781, *PTJ*, 4:433–4.

[83] "Wee directed such orders as to put the act to purchass the waggon &c. compleat in execution, and then with the same court thought it expedient, according to the spirit of the Law: tho Not Literally so: with the present pressing call and &c. to direct farther that the Beef and clothing act with out Loss of time should be put in execution allso. Wee hope to have your Excellencys Aprobation, and could Wish to Remove future scruple the ensuing assembly may confirm what in such cases May have been dun for the publick good &c." Robert Ewing to Jefferson. 12 February 1781, *PTJ*, 4:587–8.

[84] Steuben to Jefferson, 8 March 1781, and Jefferson to Steuben, 10 March 1781, *PTJ*, 5:98–99, 117–9. The issue in question was whether to receive a British ship under truce to give aid to British prisoners.

would sometimes fail to comply with Jefferson's orders, citing necessity or changing circumstances. George Corbin, for instance, refused to obey Jefferson's order to collect the dispersed "public arms," as his county's proximity to the "disaffected part of Maryland" meant that patriotic Virginians would be subject to the revenge of loyalist Marylanders.[85] As Corbin put it, he had neither the "Power or Inclination to effect" Jefferson's order, so he asked that Jefferson either change his mind or select someone else to execute Jefferson's will.

The tension between the military and civil power went deeper than county lieutenants appealing to local considerations to modify their governor's commands. Jefferson's constitutional authority to "alone have the direction of the Militia under the laws of the Country," once the militia was "embodied," was sometimes challenged by the commander of the Southern Continental Army, Nathanael Greene. The general, who was appointed by Congress, believed that Jefferson's constitutional scruples obstructed his efforts to repel the British invasion.[86] Greene and Jefferson's disagreement as to what constituted the best way for a republican government to conduct war culminated in an extraordinary exchange of letters in spring of 1781. Their argument about the relationship between the military and civil powers reveals Jefferson as a tough-minded advocate of executive prerogative while confirming Jefferson's attentiveness to the legislative branch.

The difference between the general and the governor can best be seen in their disagreement over the impress of horses. On 24 March, Jefferson sent Greene the General Assembly's resolutions to return impressed horses to their owners. As Jefferson explained, the Assembly had heard reports of abuses by the officers who executed the impress: "They are said to have transgressed extremely not only by exceeding the Tract of the Country to which the warrants were restrained, but in the Kind of Horses on which they seised."[87] On 27 March, without having received Jefferson's letter about impressments,[88] Greene wrote Jefferson to warn of another problem: many Virginians were claiming that they had served their required time in the military. "The struggle here is great, the situation of the Army precarious. The least misfortune will bring the war to your doors. You will feel the necessity, therefore of giving

---

[85] George Corbin to Jefferson, 28 February 1781, *PTJ*, 5:21–22.

[86] For instance, Greene denied Jefferson's request for information on the location of the Continental Army on the grounds of the "necessity of secrecy." Greene to Jefferson, 28 February 1781, *PTJ*, 5:22–24.

[87] Jefferson to Greene, 24 March 1781, *PTJ*, 5:229–231.

[88] Greene wrote Jefferson that he had received the letter on 5 April. See Greene to Jefferson, 6 April 1781, *PTJ*, 5:360.

me immediate support."[89] To this plea for help, Greene added a rebuke and a threat: arguing that the number of men he had received already was "greatly overrated," Greene scolded, "An army on paper will give you no security," and reminded Jefferson that as governor Jefferson had as much at stake in the army's success as did Greene, as "the interest of one is connected with the other." Several days later, before Greene had received Jefferson's reply, the general wrote again to the governor, this time to request shoes and transportation. Alongside this request, Greene reminded Jefferson that Virginia's participation was crucial for the larger efforts of the Continental Army and lectured the governor on the proper relationship between the military and civil power. According to Greene, unless laws were accommodated to the "demands of the service," the army would "fall a sacrifice." Under Greene's military arithmetic, the laws were a feature of the civil power and as such would have to serve as handmaiden to the military: "I have long endeavored to impress upon the different Legislatures the impossibility of accomodating the operations of the Army to the civil convenience; and the more serious they grow the less practicable the measure. Indeed civil polity must accommodate itself to the emergencys of war, or the people submit to the power of the enemy. There is no other alternative."[90] For Greene, then, if the civil power failed to subordinate its interests to necessity, as understood by the military power, the civil power would risk losing the object for which it called out the military power in the first place.

Before Jefferson received Greene's celebration of military prerogative, he had already sent Greene a letter indicating his own understanding of the proper wartime relationship between the civil and military powers.[91] Jefferson opened his letter by shifting responsibility to the legislative body on the grounds that as governor he was only "to be the pipe of communication to the sentiments of others." But the governor went on to explain that the subject of impressments caused him such "uneasiness" that he felt compelled to write Greene "as a private man" – so private that he departed from his customary use of a clerk and wrote the letter in his own hand.[92] Even if Jefferson wrote as a private citizen, both the subject and the consequences of the letter were unmistakably public: Jefferson solicited the general's assistance in persuading the General Assembly to repeal its resolution to return the more valuable of impressed horses to their owners. According to Jefferson, returning the horses would be imprudent because the costs to the state of

[89] Greene to Jefferson, 27 March 1781, *PTJ*, 5:258–9.
[90] Greene to Jefferson, 31 March 1781, *PTJ*, 5:301–2.
[91] Jefferson to Greene, 1 April 1781, *PTJ*, Vol. 5:313–4. Boyd's note on p. 301 indicates that Jefferson received Greene's 31 March letter on 25 April.
[92] *PTJ*, 5:314.

paying for horses, even those that "may have been valued high," would be worth enabling the cavalry to more speedily attack the enemy: "they will be cheaply bought if they enable you to strike your enemy and prevent being stricken by him." As Jefferson explained, the problem with the resolution was one of fact and one of law: the Assembly had overestimated the reports of abuses by several officers who had executed the impress, and the Assembly had erroneously assumed that "furnishing horses to our two regiments was the separate expense of the state." Abuse by officers was Greene's duty to rectify, whereas the Assembly's error regarding the law was Jefferson's to correct. Although it was "too late" for Jefferson to "set them right" because the assembly had already adjourned, Jefferson was confident that assembly members would "be glad to have an opportunity of correcting what they did when the error they were under shall be made known to them."[93] By using Greene to write the Assembly with an explanation of both the abuses and the necessity, Jefferson found the legal resource for impressing horses.

Greene's 28 April response to Jefferson's request for an "approbation" to send to the legislature did not mince words. After granting that it was "lamentable" that some officers did not "exercise more discretion and prudence" when executing an order that "seems to invade the rights of Citizens not perfectly conformable to the Laws and constitution of the Land," Greene argued that it was "equally to be lamented" that a legislative body would, on account of the abuses by particular officers, "bring upon an Army employed in their service inevitable ruin." According to Greene, in punishing the army for a few officers' abuses Virginian legislators had embraced a principle that some might have considered "virtuous" but others would recognize as "impolitic": "Particular situations and particular circumstances often make measures necessary that have the specious shew of oppression, because they carry with them consequences pointed and distressing to individuals. It is to be lamented that this is the case, but pressing emergencies make it political and sometimes unavoidable." As Greene saw it, the legislature valued "the rights of Individuals" over the "safety of a community." Put another way, the General Assembly was guided by the wrong kind of arithmetic: "In politic's as well as every thing else a received and established axiom is, that greater evils should in every instance give way to lesser misfortunes. In War it is often impossible to conform to all the ceremonies of Law and equal justice; and to attempt it would be productive of greater misfortunes to the public from the delay than all the inconveniences which individuals may suffer." Greene's logic is unmistakably that of the military leader. Individual rights

93 Jefferson to Nathanael Greene, 1 April 1781, *PTJ*, 5:313–4.

are luxuries during wartime and therefore stand opposed to the demands posed by necessity: to enforce the resolution ending the impressments would be to decide that "Horses are dearer to the Inhabitants than the lives of Subjects or the liberties of the People."[94]

In May, Jefferson wrote to the Speaker of the House of Delegates to report on the state of the military efforts and to urge the assembly to consider new ways to defend the state. Here, Jefferson went out of his to show deference to the legislative authority:

In Compliance with the Desire of Assembly expressed in their Resolutions of March 7th. I wrote to the honble. Major General Greene inclosing the said Resolution, and asking the Favour of him to have such Reports made to me as would enable me to proceed in the Execution of the Resolution. Copies of my Letter and of his on the same subject I now inclose, together with Copies of my Letters to the Continental and State Quarter Masters who were employed in impressing Horses for the Enterprize meditated on Portsmouth; on the Discontinuance of that Enterprize most of the Horses were returned to their Owners, so that I am in Hopes the inconveniences which that important Attempt had rendered necessary are now reduced within very narrow Limits; full Returns are not yet made so as to enable us to state what the Public stands engaged for on that account.[95]

In spite of all this deferential passing of letters, Jefferson was actually giving the legislature a lesson on the necessity of the impressment. Submitting Greene's 28 April letter for legislative consideration and reporting that he had written Greene regarding the resolution to return impressed horses, the governor omitted his own private letter of 1 April and Greene's 27 March, 31 March, and 6 April letters. Presented with Greene's letter, the Assembly resolved that horses not yet returned to their owners "ought to be paid for," that is, permanently employed in the military effort.[96] In 1822, Jefferson described Greene as "second to no one in enterprise, in resource, in sound judgment, promptitude of decision, and every military talent."[97] In his dealings with Greene, Jefferson revealed himself as no less an enterprising executive: more than just an errand boy for the legislative will, Jefferson used his position as governor to set the legislature right on occasions when the legislative body's sensitivity to individual rights numbed it toward the demands of necessity. In short, Jefferson corrected the legislative branch without directly confronting it. The pipe had become the piper.

[94] Greene to Jefferson, 28 April 1781, *PTJ*, 5:567–70.
[95] Jefferson to the Speaker of the House of Delegates, 10 May 1781, *PTJ*, 5:626–9.
[96] See Boyd's note, *PTJ*, 5:629.
[97] From the context, it clear that Jefferson meant that he was not even second to Washington. Jefferson to William Johnson, 27 October 1822. Ford, ed., 10:223.

Prerogative Power and Civil Liberties: Insurrections

One of the situations in which the executive must act swiftly is during insurrection. On this matter, Jefferson's reputation has been misunderstood, partly because of the colorful statements Jefferson offered to Abigail Adams and others regarding Shay's Rebellion.[98] The most obvious problem with this reputation is that distorts Jefferson's actions within the political world.[99] In spite of his comments that revolutions were natural and healthy phenomena within politics, Jefferson's treatment of insurrections while governor reveals a muscular, and sometimes discreet, use of executive prerogative to put down civil unrest.

During the spring of 1781, Jefferson had to deal with insurrection on several occasions.[100] In April, Garret van Meter requested that Jefferson send cavalry to quell the "rioters" who has assembled and sworn "fidelity to each other" to resist the government's collection of taxes and implementation of the draft.[101] Jefferson's reply was direct. Although it was clear that the executive had no legal authority to raise cavalry, Jefferson replied that the insurrection "must be subdued," as "Laws made by common consent must not be trampled on by Individuals." Consequently, Jefferson recommended that County Lieutenants "mount and equip themselves" to "serve as mounted Infantry." Although not actually a cavalry, such mounted men might be "used as effectually as a Calvary," which was crucial for stopping the insurrections because "men on horseback have been found the most certain Instrument of public punishment." For the new informal cavalry, Jefferson added a more direct suggestion concerning method: "Their best way too perhaps is not to go against the mutineers when embodied which would bring on perhaps

---

[98] Significantly, John Adams wrote in 1791 that he and Jefferson "never had a serious conversation" concerning "the nature of Government" and that the "very transient hints" passed between the two were "jocular and superficial," John Adams to Jefferson, 29 July 1791, Cappon, 247–9. Later, however, Adams did allude with seriousness to Jefferson's "philosophical Tranquility": "What think you of Terrorism, Mr. Jefferson?", John Adams to Jefferson, 30 June 1813, Cappon, 347. See also Jefferson to Abigail Adams, 21 December 1786, and 22 February 1787, Cappon, 159 and 173; Jefferson to Madison, 30 January 1787, *PTJ*, 11:93; Jefferson to William S. Smith, 13 November 1787, *PTJ*, 12:356. For the standard account, see David N. Mayer, *Constitutional Thought of Thomas Jefferson* (Charlottesville: University Press of Virginia, 1994), 91; and Richard L. Matthews, *The Radical Politics of Jefferson: A Revisionist View* (Lawrence: University Press of Kansas, 1984), 83–86.

[99] To others, Jefferson happily reported of the quieting of "commotions" and "mobs" in France. See Jefferson to Francis dal Verme, 15 August 1787, *PTJ*, 12:42–3; and Jefferson to William Carmichael, 3 June 1788, *PTJ*, 13:229–35.

[100] For draft resistance in the lower counties, see George Mason to Jefferson, 6 October 1780, *PTJ*, 4:18–19. See also Samuel McDowell to Jefferson, 9 May 1781, and Commissioners for Collecting Taxes in Accomac County to Jefferson, 15 May 1781, *PTJ*, 5:621–2, 651–4.

[101] Garret Van Meter to Jefferson, 20 April 1781, *PTJ*, 5:513–5.

an open Rebellion or Bloodshed most certainly, but when they shall have dispersed to go and take them out of their Beds, singly and without Noise, or if they be not found the first time to go again and again so that they may never be able to remain in quiet at home."[102]

Jefferson's action is revealing for two reasons. First, rather than encouraging rebellion or reflecting on its beneficial purgative effects, the governor wanted to crush the insurrection before it could spread into the streets. Second, rather than finding in necessity the legal authority to raise a cavalry ("men on horseback have been found the most certain Instrument of public punishment"), he created a mounted infantry to stop the insurrection and punish its organizers.[103] More than the a "pipe of communication" between the legislative body and the military, Jefferson used his position as governor to actively advise and even direct Virginia's military. Always trying to soften the severity of the law, Jefferson also found ways of vigorously enforcing the law by working outside it.

Events like the April disturbance presented Jefferson with the dilemma of balancing the evidentiary requirements with the exigencies of war. In order to apprehend insurrectionists one must first distinguish insurrectionists from spectators as well as determine the standard of evidence to justify arrest, but these procedural requirements work to the benefit of the insurrectionists who may or may not choose to abide by the law. This was the case in May 1781, when Jefferson believed that some citizens had committed treason but had been able to "so disguise and conceal their Transactions" such that sufficient evidence was lacking for prosecution under a "due course of law."[104] For Jefferson, protecting the country against individuals who would "whenever they shall have opportunity, aid or advise the Measures of the Publick Enemy" and who had been able to thrive under Virginia's protection of the accused required a new method. Even though punishment was "indispensably necessary," Jefferson ordered his officers to set up a special enquiry, establish probable cause, and then obtain a warrant. But in cases in which officers could not find sufficient evidence for probable cause or lacked the time to obtain a warrant, and there were still "pregnant Circumstances of suspicion," officers could apprehend the suspected and then report the events to Jefferson himself. By detaining both the "formost" and the "daring" of the traitors until the governor himself could examine the evidence, Jefferson would "disable from doing Mischief" those who would destroy the state

---

[102] Jefferson to Garret Van Meter, 27 April 1781, *PTJ*, 5:565–6.

[103] Compare to Jefferson's discussion of "mounted infantry" in his "Sixth Annual Message," in Saul K. Padover, ed., *The Complete Jefferson: Containing his Major Writings, Published and Unpublished, Except his Letters*, (New York: Duell, Sloan & Pearce, 1943), 421.

[104] Jefferson to James Innes, 2 May 1781, *PTJ*, 5:593–4.

while at the same time preserving the liberties of most of its citizens. This was not the only time Jefferson removed suspected traitors from the course of law.[105] Although insurrection is like prerogative in that it replaces the rule of law with the rule of men, and even though Jefferson praised revolutionaries who resorted to violence, he was willing to use extralegal powers to put down insurrection.

The 1783 Constitution

While he was governor, the occasion to propose another constitution came in the form of a jumbled set of questions from the French naturalist François Barbé-Marbois, who was writing an account of the natural and political history of the New World.[106] After he retired, Jefferson organized his answers into under the title *Notes on the State of Virginia*. In this work, he set out to disprove the theory, held by Georges Buffon and others, that America was naturally inferior to Europe by comparing the natural world of both continents. But by providing a scientific account of America's natural characteristics, Jefferson would also offer a defense of America's social and political institutions. But more than providing Europeans with a partisan account of the New World, the *Notes* carried within it some criticisms of American politics, the implications of which Jefferson believed dangerous enough that he circulated the finished product only among friends. Alongside these passages on religion and slavery, Jefferson argued that the existing Virginia Constitution insufficiently separated the three powers of government, and when Jefferson realized that the *Notes* would be published whether he consented or not, he included his 1783 draft for a new constitution for Virginia.

In the chapter on the Virginia Constitution, Jefferson described the executive branch first.[107] Then, after describing the other two branches, Jefferson

---

[105] For another occasion in which Jefferson ordered county executives to make arrests for "a misprision of treason" so that suspects of treason would not be "absolutely cleared if the evidence will not support the charge of treason," see Jefferson to William Preston, 21 March 1780, *PTJ*, 3:325.

[106] According to Boyd, Jefferson received the questions sometime before November 30, 1780, and by the following March, Jefferson had collected only enough "materials" as to promise Marbois that he would soon have enough time to devote more of his energies to the project. Jefferson to Marbois, 4 March 1781, *PTJ*, 5:58–9.

[107] The structure of the *Notes* is significant, and Jefferson rearranged Marbois' queries. "Marbois Queries concerning Virginia," *PTJ*, 4:166–7. Harvey Mansfield Jr., "Thomas Jefferson," in *American Political Thought: The Philosophic Dimension of American Statesmanship*, ed. Morton J. Frisch and Richard G. Stevens (Itasca, IL: F. E. Peacock, 1983), 33–38. For Jefferson's displeasure on the structure of the French edition of the *Notes*, see Dorothy Medlin, "Thomas Jefferson, Andre Morellet, and the French Version of Notes on the State of Virginia," *William and Mary Quarterly* 3rd Ser., 35: 1 (1978): 85–99.

offered the following famous description: "This constitution was formed when we were new and unexperienced in the science of government. It was the first too which was formed in the whole United States. No wonder then that time and trial have discovered very capital defects in it."[108] Many of the flaws he had in mind reflect his neverending concern with the political equality of Virginians: representation was not broad enough, and representation was disproportionate between tidewater and hinterland counties. But Jefferson's most important complaints concerned the growing power of the legislative body – it had assumed executive and judicial powers, it could change the constitution with an "ordinary" act of legislation, and it could fix its own quorum.[109] With regard to the first problem, Jefferson's analysis has been quoted by many, including Madison in the *Federalist*: "All the powers of government, legislative, executive, and judiciary, result to the legislative body. The concentrating these in the same hands is precisely the definition of despotic government. It will be no alleviation that these powers will be exercised by a plurality of hands, and not by a single one. 173 despots would surely be as oppressive as one."[110] This practical problem of the Virginia Constitution resulted from its design: "no barrier was provided between these several powers." The assembly had "decided rights which should have been left to judiciary controversy," and it had treaded on executive territory so often that "the direction of the executive" had become "habitual and familiar."[111] Jefferson's 1783 constitution, then, aspired to fix the mechanics of separating the three powers of government, partly by arming the executive with more powers.

One way Jefferson's 1783 draft attempted to ensure executive independence was by explicitly forbidding the legislature to reduce or supplement the governor's salary during or even after his time in office.[112] This was a significant departure from his 1776 draft, which explicitly withheld salaries from all the major members of government, allowing only that "reasonable expenses" may be "borne by the public, if the Legislature shall so direct."[113] It would also have changed the Virginia Constitution, which provided that the governor would have an "adequate, but moderate Salary." Importantly, the Virginia Constitution guaranteed judges and other officers "fixed and adequate salaries," indicating a possibility that the governor's salary could be

---

[108] Jefferson, *Notes*, *TJW*, 243.
[109] Ibid., 245–55.
[110] Ibid., 245.
[111] Ibid., 246.
[112] Jefferson, Proposed Revision of the Virginia Constitution, *PTJ*, 6:299.
[113] Jefferson, Third Draft, *PTJ*, 1:363.

changed.[114] The prohibition on salary changes was accompanied by another benefit: the 1783 constitution also guaranteed that even the "lands, houses and other things appropriated to the use of the Governour, shall remain to his use during his continuance in office." More than a reflection of Jefferson's growing awareness of the sacrifices incident to being a public servant, these prohibitions also indicate the movement of Jefferson's suspicions away from the executive to the legislative power.[115]

Another step toward executive independence was a longer time in office. Under his 1783 constitution, the governor would enjoy a five-year term. But Jefferson retained a feature of ineligibility: after five years of service, the governor would be ineligible for office for five more years.

Although Governor Jefferson encountered the practical difficulties of assembling a council, his 1783 constitution retained an executive council. Under this constitution, the council would have both more and less power. Like the governor, the council would be selected by joint ballot of both houses, but the council members would enjoy seven years in office. That there would be some overlap of councils and gubernatorial administrations suggests that council members would see themselves as more independent from the governor they advise. Furthermore, their power to advise would be expanded: as in the 1776 draft, the council would advise the governor when he determined that he needed their advice. But in cases in which the governor did not think he needed such advice, the council could choose to give their advice anyway, thereby ensuring that any possible conflict be a part of the public record.[116] When "laid before either house of the assembly" the latter would be able to determine exactly whether particular members concurred or dissented in the advice given, as proceedings would be signed by each member "as approved or disapproved." Emboldened by the fact that they may come in or leave office at a different time than the governor, council members would independently make some judgment about the best way to execute the laws.

At the same time, Jefferson enabled the council to meet without the governor. Under Jefferson's 1776 constitution, the deputy administrator was selected by the House of Representatives and would assist "his principal" in his executive business as well as succeed him in case of death. Under the 1783 constitution, the council would annually choose its own president,

---

[114] "The Constitution as Adopted by the Convention" and "The Plan of Government as originally Drawn by George Mason," *PTJ*, 1:380–82, 367.

[115] Jefferson, *Notes*, *TJW*, 246.

[116] Jefferson, Proposed Revision of the Virginia Constitution, *PTJ*, 6:299–300.

who would become interim governor in case of the governor's death. But more important than the fact that an interim executive would be chosen by the executive council and not the legislature, the council's president would preside over the council whenever the governor was absent. Jefferson, who had himself grown weary of meeting with his council when he was governor, arranged a system in which a governor need not attend his council's meetings. But this could lead to a more independent executive, because the independent selection of the deputy administrator suggested a movement away from legislative interference, and, with someone else presiding, and with the council members entering their advice at their own determination of the public good, the governor would gain the time to shape and enforce the administration of the laws. While the council would go about its daily routine of giving advice, the governor could act.

With a governor concerned primarily with acting and an advisory council made up of members from different administrations, there would almost certainly be conflict within the council and between the council and the governor. Jefferson's 1783 constitution then can be seen as Jefferson's trying to reconcile energy with democratic accountability. By freeing the governor from meeting with his council, Jefferson leaned toward administration by a single executive officer. But by giving the council the opportunity to lay its advice before the legislative body even if the governor did not ask for it, Jefferson drew back from allowing the governor complete political independence. Conflict was part and parcel of executive action.

The movement from legislative supremacy toward coordinate equality can also be seen in the new vesting clause. Whereas in 1776 Jefferson used the king as a model for the governor and then strictly defined the governor's powers, in 1783 he went out of his way to disassociate the new governor from the former king: "By Executive powers we mean no reference to those powers exercised under our former government by the crown as of it's prerogative; nor that these shall be a standard of what may or may not be deemed the rightful powers of the Governor."[117] Rather than following his 1776 draft, which modeled the chief administrator after the king, Jefferson adopted the Virginia Constitution's explicit rejection of the kingly office as an appropriate starting place for executive power. But Jefferson took the rejection a step further by saying that the kingly office would not provide a standard by which executive powers would be granted or forbidden. Just as a governor could not claim a power by virtue of the king's example or royal precedent, the legislature and judiciary could not deny the governor a power simply on the basis of the king's example. As Jefferson's 1783 draft reveals, the Virginia

[117] Ibid., 6:298–9.

Constitution's clause that forbade the governor from justifying his powers by means of the king was flawed in that it left the example of monarchy available as a means by which the powers available to the governor could be *limited*. Jefferson's 1783 draft, then, marked a compromise between the Virginia Constitution and his own 1776 draft by attempting to remove the king altogether.

Where, then, would the governor look to understand the source of his power? To answer this question, Jefferson's constitution included a hinge on which executive action might swing. Neither granting him nor denying him the king's powers, the 1783 constitution granted the governor powers required by his job description, so long as such powers were neither legislative nor judiciary: "We give him those powers only which are necessary to carry into execution the laws, and which are not in their nature either legislative or Judiciary. The application of this idea must be left to reason."[118] This might be read as a restraint. The executive is granted only enough power to carry out the law and even this power is limited in that the executive is denied powers that are naturally legislative or judicial. According to this constitution, it seems the executive's power is natural, or inherent, if only to the extent that the executive is the errand boy for another branch's more obviously natural power.

But if some powers are legislative or judicial in nature, are there executive powers in nature? Jefferson did not completely narrow the executive's domain to carrying out the will of the legislative body, nor did he leave the executive a grant of general power. By this time, Jefferson had began to consider the difference between "necessary" and "indispensably necessary" actions – a distinction that he would later employ in his opinion on the bank bill. And, if others used "indispensably necessary" to convey military arithmetic and promote a particular vision of the general welfare,[119] Jefferson himself used the phrase to justify executive discretion. In a letter written perhaps before he received Jones's, Jefferson eased the concerns of a militia leader who acted without receiving orders from Jefferson first: "It was certainly not only justifiable but laudable and even indispensably necessary that you should have proceeded as you did."[120] And, when trying to curb the spread of insurrectionist fervor in Virginia, Jefferson defended his endorsement of swift punishment by saying that was "indispensably necessary to punish" insurrectionists "for their Crimes by way of Example to

[118] Ibid., 299.
[119] Steuben to Jefferson, 9 March 1781, *PTJ*, 5:107; Joseph Jones to Jefferson. 16 April 1781, *PTJ*, 5:469–71.
[120] Jefferson to William Preston, 21 April 1781, *PTJ*, 5:524.

others, or to disable them from doing Mischief."[121] It was, of course, this distinction between indispensably necessary actions and actions of convenience that he later emphasized in his argument that Congress did not have the power to create a bank. Whether adding the modifier "absolutely" to "necessary" offered a clear standard for narrowing implied powers will have to be addressed elsewhere, but, for present purposes, it is important to note that this distinction affords the executive the power to act outside of the law.[122]

To make sure that reason not overstep its bounds in determining which powers are necessary to execute the law, the 1783 Constitution ruled out some powers out in advance. "We do however expressly deny him the praerogative powers of erecting courts, offices, boroughs, corporations, fairs, markets, ports, beacons, lighthouses, and seamarks; of laying embargoes, of establishing precedence, of retaining within the state or recalling to it any citizen thereof, and of making denizens, except so far as he may be authorized from time to time by the legislature to exercise any of these powers."[123] But the list of expressly denied powers was much shorter than the list of forbidden powers in his 1776 draft. More precisely, the new constitution granted most of the powers forbidden under the 1776 draft to the governor, on the condition that such powers would be subject to legislative regulation and not interfere with the national authority of the Confederation Congress. As might be expected, these newly authorized prerogatives included what Locke called the Federative powers: the governor would have the power to declare war and conclude peace, to contract allies, to issue letters of marque, to raise armed forces, and to build armed vessels and construct fortifications.[124] Curiously, one power the 1783 constitution did not grant to the executive was the pardon. Although his 1776 draft would have forbidden the pardon from being exercised by any of the branches, the 1783 version denied the General Assembly the power "to pardon or give a power of pardoning persons duly convicted of treason or felony."[125] Rather, the Assembly could "substitute one or two more trials and no more."

[121] Jefferson to James Innes, 2 May 1781, *PTJ* 5:593–4.

[122] The term was used in Washington's cabinet on 15 June 1793. Dorothy Twohig, ed., *The Journal of the Proceedings of the President, 1793–1797* (Charlottesville: University Press of Virginia, 1981), 179.

[123] "Jefferson's Proposed Revision of the Virginia Constitution," *PTJ*, 6:299.

[124] Ibid. Locke defined the Federative Power as that comprehending "the management of the security and interest of the public without." John Locke, *Second Treatise*, section 147, *John Locke: Two Treatises of Government*, student edition, ed. Peter Laslett (Cambridge: Cambridge University Press, 1988), 365.

[125] "Jefferson's Proposed Revision of the Virginia Constitution," *PTJ*, 6:298.

The Retired President and the Virginia Executive

After Jefferson served as president and returned to private life, he wrote a broad defense of the unified, single executive in a letter to the governor of Virginia, James Barbour. The governor had written Jefferson to ask whether the early governors of Virginia would cast the deciding vote in cases where their council was divided. After giving a history of the practice, which recommended that the governor act on his own opinion when the council was divided rather than breaking the tie with a vote, Jefferson offered examples of other Virginia governors who acted without the advice of council. First, Jefferson cited when he was left without a council during Benedict Arnold's invasion: "[B]ut in the numerous and extraordinary occurrences of an invasion, which could not be foreseen, I had to act on my own judgment and my own responsibility. The vote of general approbation, at the session of the succeeding winter, manifested the opinion of the Legislature, that my proceedings had been correct." Next, Jefferson cited General Nelson, who traveled with the army while governor, acting without a council. Nelson's prosecuting the war without council did raise the question whether a governor could act without a council during emergencies, and some brought petitions against Nelson in the Assembly. "[T]he questions necessarily involved were whether necessity, without express law, could justify the impressments, and if it could, whether he could order it without the advice of council." According to Jefferson, the Assembly settled the question by defending Nelson: "The approbation of the Legislature amounted to a decision of both questions." To encourage Barbour and to clarify his own position: "I remember this case the more especially, because I was then a member of the Legislature, and was one of those who supported the Governor's proceedings, and I think there was no division of the House on the question."[126]

After appealing to two cases in which governors who had not only acted in the case of a divided council but in the absence of a council, Jefferson went on to offer a broad defense of executive discretion. In the event that a governor lacked the advice of his council, the governor must act according to his own judgment, for the framers of the Virginia Constitution could not have meant for "their Governor, the person of their peculiar choice and confidence, should stand by, an inactive spectator, and let their government tumble to pieces for want of a will to direct it." But more than defending the action on the basis of protecting the government from falling to pieces, Jefferson went on to defend executive discretion on the basis that action was preferable to inaction. In this case, the governor draws power from the

---

[126] Jefferson to James Barbour, 22 January 1812, Ford, 10: 334–337.

fact that he holds the executive power: "In executive cases, where promptitude and decision are all important, an adherence to the letter of a law against its probable intentions (for every law must intend that itself shall be executed), would be fraught with incalculable danger." To properly fulfill constitutional expectations, then, the executive must approach laws with a prejudice toward action. Put somewhat differently, the executive must interpret laws with the standing assumption that lawmakers intend for the laws to be carried out. Put in the terms of *Federalist* #70, Jefferson praised past Virginia governors who had chosen dispatch over deliberation.[127]

Jefferson went on to fit this praise of executive action within the larger distribution of powers. The executive retains a prejudice toward action because the legislative body is designed for deliberation and the judicial for judgment – "The three great departments having distinct functions to perform, must have distinct rules adapted to them." To illustrate the difference between judges (who "may await further legislative explanations") and executives (whose inaction "might produce irretrievable ruin"), Jefferson again appealed to the historical example of invasion: "The Sate is invaded, militia to be called out, an army marched, arms and provisions to be issued from the public magazines, the Legislature to be convened, and the council is divided. Can it be believed to have been the intention of the framers of the constitution, that the constitution itself and their constituents with it should be destroyed for want of a will to direct the resources they had provided for its preservation?" After setting up this scenario of military necessity, Jefferson went out of his way to tell the governor that strict construction need not stand in the way of protecting the state: "Before such possible consequences all verbal scruples must vanish; construction must be made *secundum arbitrium boni viri*, and the constitution rendered a practical thing. That exposition of it must be vicious, which would leave the nation under the most dangerous emergencies without a directing will." In this defense of executive prerogative, Jefferson emphasized the difference between judges and executives. Unlike the judiciary department, which can take its time to discern legislative intent, the executive relies on his own judgment to put action to the law. More important, this predisposition toward action is beneficial in that it renders the constitutional "practical." If the executive thrives on the opportunity to "risk himself," the judge relies on caution: "The cautious maxims of the bench, to seek the will of the legislator, and his words only, are proper and safer for judicial government. They act ever on an individual case only, the evil of which is partial, and gives time for correction. But an instant of delay in executive proceedings may be fatal to the whole nation.

[127] Ibid., 336; *The Federalist*, No. 70, pp. 449–52.

They must not, therefore, be laced up in rules of the judiciary department. They must seek the intention of the legislator in all the circumstances which may indicate it in the history of the day, in public discussions, in the general opinion and understanding, in reason and in practice." The central difference between the discretion of judges and executives, then, may be summed up with the term "energy." Not "laced up" by the requirements of determining legislative intent, not made "inactive" by a doctrine of construction, Jefferson's executive carries out the law under the understanding that he must do so energetically.[128]

When he was president, Jefferson used similar arguments to defend other executives who parted with the law on extraordinary occasions, but it is useful to note the development of Jefferson's treatment of the Virginia executive. Compared to his own efforts to reform the Virginia Constitution, the defense of Nelson is clear in its defense of executive discretion. And, though there are resemblances to the actions he took as governor, the argument is far beyond any that Jefferson had given by 1783. Indeed, Jefferson's use of the prerogative power illustrates better than anything else his failed attempt as governor to balance deference to the legislative power, obedience to the constitution, and military defense of his state. Importantly, even after he spent time as governor, his proposed revision of the Virginia Constitution was incomplete in its provision for the executive power: leaving the application of executive duty "to reason" fails to ensure that accountability guides discretion. Put differently, Jefferson's early efforts to form the Virginia executive lacked the popular dimension he would later bring to the presidency, because Jefferson and his fellow Virginians presumed legislative selection and because Jefferson had not yet made the connection between the majority will and executive energy. As he later wrote to Kercheval, even the 1783 constitution was filled with "gross departures" from "genuine republican canons": "In truth, the abuses of monarchy had so filled the space of political contemplation, that we imagined everything republican which was not monarchy."[129] Specifically, he and other constitution writers had not yet discovered the "mother principle" of republican government: "governments are republican only in proportion as they embody the will of the people, and execute it."[130] The point is worth repeating: there are two requirements for republican government, representing the majority will and executing it.

Although lacking both components of the central principle of republican government, Jefferson's early use of the prerogative nevertheless reveals his

[128] Jefferson to Barbour, Ford, 10: 336–337.
[129] Jefferson to Kercheval, *TJW*, 1395–1403.
[130] Ibid., 1396.

attempt to combine a strict construction of the law with a vigorous exercise of executive discretion to point the execution of the law over the "details" to its higher "purpose." Lacking a popular foundation for his office, that is, lacking one aspect of his claim to see the "whole ground," Jefferson employed proclamations to report on his own measures "out of a course of law" and to instruct Virginians on the democratic foundations of the law. By the time he was the victor in the election of 1800, Jefferson would amend his understanding of executive power to include both conditions of the mother principle of republican government. The important paths in the maturation of Jefferson's understanding were the framing of the Constitution and his own partisan effort to interpret it. Each further revealed to Jefferson the connection between executive energy and public opinion.

3

Executive Power and the Constitution of 1787

Between his efforts to reform the Virginia executive and his inauguration as president, Jefferson served as delegate to Congress, minister to France, Secretary of State, and vice president. He also continued to offer reforms for Virginia's legal system, collaborated with republican sympathizers in France, and organized the nation's first opposition party. It is for this period in his life that Jefferson has been most characterized as an enemy of executive power. Indeed, Jefferson seemed to invite such characterizations when demanding a bill of rights, sympathizing with French revolutionaries, or rallying his party against Federalist "monocrats." When he positioned himself for the presidency, for instance, he contrasted himself from those who desired a more powerful executive, "I am not for transferring all the powers of the States to the general government, & all those of that government to the Executive branch."[1]

The truth, however, is more complicated. When Alexander Hamilton campaigned against Aaron Burr's election in 1800, he wrote that Jefferson was a "contemptible hypocrite" whose ideas were "tinctured with fanaticism," but pointed out that Jefferson's tenure as Secretary of State proved that the author of the Declaration was for a strong executive.[2] That is, according to this account, Jefferson's break with Hamilton was over the application of executive power, not the amount of power the executive would have. Accordingly, Ralph Ketcham argues that Jefferson "despised not the idea of an active, independent executive" but, rather, Hamilton's schemes to corrupt the legislative branch and make it the instrument of the Treasury

---

[1] Jefferson to Elbridge Gerry, 29 January 1799, *TJW*, 1056.
[2] Hamilton to James A. Bayard, 16 January 1801, *PAH*, 25:319–24.

Department.[3] Jack N. Rakove is also right to say that Jefferson's decision to seek the presidency is important, for it shows that the opposition had determined that controlling the presidency mattered if only because foreign policy had demonstrated that the presidency would dominate political life.[4] If Hamilton and these scholars are correct, then Jefferson's complaint with the Federalist executive stemmed from a difference concerning policy not the presidency.

But as important as partisan charges of corruption and debates over foreign policy were, they distract attention from the fact that Jefferson understood that Americans also were choosing the path that would define the relationship between executive power and constitutionalism. Jefferson never wanted to reduce all political questions to the executive will, but, as the previous chapter argued, he had already spent considerable efforts trying to create an executive that could survive the demands of political life without destroying the written law. As constitutional reformer and governor, he had resisted broad grants of authority to the executive, and instead preferred that executives go outside the law instead of expanding it. So, too, throughout the period from ratification of the Constitution to the creation of an opposition party, where the unifying thread was Jefferson's attempt to make executive power compatible with a written constitution by advocating the doctrine of strict construction.[5] But Jefferson was no fundamentalist, and strict construction was not an end but was instead a necessary means to preserve consent, since a broad construction would make the law too complex for popular judgment. More simply, for Jefferson, strict construction would make a majority will possible.

---

[3] Ralph Ketcham, *Presidents Above Party: The First American Presidency, 1789–1829* (Chapel Hill: University of North Carolina Press, 1984), 102.

[4] Jack N. Rakove, "The Political Presidency: Discovery and Invention," in *The Revolution of 1800: Democracy, Race and the New Republic*, ed. James Horn, Jan Ellen Lewis, and Peter S. Onuf, 30–58 (Charlottesville: University of Virginia Press, 2002).

[5] "Strict" should be interpreted as opposed to "broad" or "loose." There are problems with this term, but this book is not meant to be an examination of the possibilities of constitutional construction, and I have resisted inventing a new term. The implication of this book may be that Jefferson and his opponents favored competing "purposive" constructions. The latter term, of course, raises the question whether Jefferson's purposive construction results in strict construction or vice versa. These are questions for another study. See David N. Mayer, *Constitutional Thought of Thomas Jefferson* (Charlottesville: University Press of Virginia, 1994) 296, 307, and 370, n70; Keith E. Whittington, *Constitutional Construction: Divided Powers and Constitutional Meaning* (Cambridge, MA: Harvard University Press, 1999); Whittington, *Constitutional Interpretation: Textual meaning, Original Intent and Judicial Review* (Lawrence: University Press of Kansas, 1999); and H. Jefferson Powell, *A Community Built on Words: The Constitution in History and Politics* (Chicago: University of Chicago Press, 2002).

The proposal and ratification of the Constitution set in course a series of events that allowed Jefferson to continue his exploration of the connection between public opinion and executive discretion. The Constitution included a unitary executive armed with considerable powers, including a veto, and whose selection would be removed from Congress. In *The Federalist*, Hamilton defended unity in the executive on the grounds that unity was conducive to responsibility. Then, in the first Congress, James Madison defended presidential supremacy in the removal power on the grounds that the president completed the link of accountability between administration and the people. Jefferson learned from these two arguments, and it is possible that his opposition to Washington and Hamilton left them open as future paths. Put differently, it is revealing that Hamilton said not only that Jefferson wanted a large construction of executive authority but also that the Virginian was "too much in earnest of his democracy."[6] Instead of choosing between executive power and democracy, Jefferson meant to preserve both.

A National Executive

By the time the flaws of the Articles of Confederation were apparent, Jefferson counted himself among those who believed that an energetic executive was a precondition for a unified and effective – that is to say a useful – national government. Although Jefferson's most famous effort in the early 1780s was writing a plan for the Western territories, he also proposed the creation of a committee to serve in the absence of Congress and to possess what would be delegated by general resolution the executive powers of the general government.[7]

Jefferson must have been proud of his efforts to form a national executive, for his *Autobiography* claims that he was then the first to propose such a committee to serve in the absence of Congress. But Jefferson and others had attempted to organize a similar executive power earlier, in 1775, when Congress formed a committee to create another committee to act during the recesses of Congress. Although the committee's report was never acted on because Congress did not recess, it did become the model for the ninth article in the Articles of Confederation which provided for a "Committee of States" to act when Congress was out of session. In 1775, Jefferson was more willing than others to lodge executive powers in a separate body: the executive powers granted to the committee under Jefferson's draft were significantly narrowed by John Dickinson's draft, the draft that eventually

---

[6] Hamilton to Bayard, *PAH*, 25:319.
[7] Jefferson, *Autobiography*, *TJW*, 49

became the Articles of Confederation. At the urging of Dickinson, the delegates dropped Jefferson's provisions giving the executive committee complete control over the military power as well as the power to commit the nation to war and peace.[8] Again, as a delegate to Congress in 1784, Jefferson's efforts to define the national executive power were complicated by those on both sides of the question of executive power. In an attempt to find more supporters for a stronger executive, he wrote Pendleton that it was "rational and necessary" for the national government to follow New York State's strong executive model by creating an executive branch with some control over legislation by way of a council of revision.[9] Most, however, were reluctant to even create a national executive, and thus Congress failed to appoint a committee to act in its place, leaving the government, in one extreme case, without a head for five weeks. On the opposite extreme, others argued for an executive that could act by its own discretion: James Duane proposed that such a committee be given "general powers" rather than being granted a list of enumerated powers. Jefferson feared both alternatives: a government without a stronger executive would be too weak, yet an executive without defined limits to its powers would be too dangerous. Even though there are textual difficulties with the various plans, it can be said that Jefferson's plan, which closely resembled his 1775 plan, was rejected in favor of a plan that was at once more limited and more general. In 1775 and 1784, members of Congress were unwilling to create a national executive power, but Jefferson was not.[10]

Jefferson argued more explicitly for a separate national executive in early 1786, when Jean-Nicholas Demeunier sent Jefferson questions in order to include an entry on the United States in his *Encyclopedia Methodique*. Here, Jefferson retained his concern for the letter of the law in explaining that laws "made as mild as they should be" would render the pardon power unnecessary: "The principle of Beccaria is sound. Let the legislators be merciful but the executors of the law inexorable."[11] More important, Jefferson noted that the Confederation Congress exercised both executive and legislative powers and recommended that the Congress should create an executive committee: "The legislative business would be better done, because the attention of the members would not be interrupted by the details of execution; and the executive business would be better done, because business of this nature

---

[8] See Boyd's notes, *PTJ*, 6:516–17.

[9] Unfortunately, Pendleton's recommendations in his letter of 17 May 1784, which Jefferson dismissed as too innovative for any "rational man," have been lost. Jefferson to Edmund Pendleton, 25 May 1784, *PTJ*, 7: 292–3.

[10] Roger Sherman, for one, wanted a weak national executive. *PTJ*, 6:522.

[11] Jefferson to Demeunier, 1796, *PTJ*, 10:46–7.

is better adapted to small than great bodies."[12] After beginning with the argument that the legislative branch would be better served by committing the particulars of execution to another body so that it can deliberate on more important objects, Jefferson went on to suggest that legislative deliberation lacked a component of government found under monarchy: "A monarchical head should confide the execution of it's will to departments consisting each of a plurality of hands, who would warp that will as much as possible toward wisdom and moderation, the two qualities it generally wants. But a republican head founding it's decree originally in these two qualities should commit them to a single hand for execution, giving them thereby a promptitude which republican proceedings generally want." More than allowing lawmakers to continue making the law rather than arguing about "details," placing the responsibility for these details in a "single hand" would go some way in curing one defect of republican government by giving it a dose of monarchy. Jefferson went on to soften this rather bold proposal with a compromise: "Congress could not indeed confide their executive business to a smaller number than a committee consisting of a member from each state. This is necessary to ensure the confidence of the Union. But it would be gaining a great deal to reduce the executive head to thirteen, and to debarass themselves of those details." Although Jefferson had not figured out a way to remove the states from the executive committee, he was among those who were trying to create a national executive power separate from congress, and he had learned from the New York Constitution the benefits of the unitary executive. But this was a delicate matter and, as he explained to Demeunier, had "as yet been the subject of private conversations only."

Jefferson had one such conversation with the future central figure of the Constitutional Convention, James Madison. In response to Madison's outline of what would come to be the Virginia Plan, Jefferson responded that he, too, was for more distribution of the powers that were then in the hands of Congress.[13] Having himself tried on numerous occasions to empower the government under the Articles of Confederation, Jefferson explained to Madison that he had recommended that the new constitution should be enabled to exercise its powers "to best advantage" by separating the powers of government into three branches. Creating a separate executive branch was central: "When last with Congress, I often proposed to members to do this by making of the Committee of states, an Executive committee during the recess of Congress, and during it's sessions to appoint a Committee to receive and dispatch all executive business, so that Congress itself should

[12] Ibid., *PTJ*, 10:23.
[13] Madison to Jefferson, 19 March 1787, PTJ, 11:219–25.

meddle only with what should be legislative. But I question if any Congress (much less all successively) can have self-denial enough to go through with this distribution."[14] For Jefferson, but not others in Congress, a national executive was necessary for carrying out the business of the nation. Since Congress did not possess the self-denial to give away some of its power, the "distribution" of executive power "should be imposed on them."[15] When the Federal Convention met in Philadelphia to revise the Articles of Confederation, Jefferson was in France, but he followed the proposal and ratification of the Constitution.[16] When the Convention did create a national executive, Jefferson criticized its lack of a term limit, not its powers.[17]

The Federalist

The Constitution was a central event in the development of Jefferson's plan for executive power, and his understanding of it must have been influenced by the defense of it in *The Federalist*. By November 1787, Jefferson had read the Constitution, and by May 1788, Jefferson had probably received the first volume of *The Federalist*.[18] By November, he had read the second volume and praised the work to Madison: "With respect to the Federalist, the three authors had been named to me. I read it with care, pleasure and improvement, and was satisfied that there was nothing in it by one of those hands, and not a great deal by the second. It does the highest honor to the third, as being, in my opinion, the best commentary on the principles of government which was ever written. In some parts it is discoverable that the author means only to say what may be best said in defense of opinions in which he did not concur. But in general it establishes firmly the plan of government."[19] That Jefferson was writing to his friend might suggest that he overstated his appreciation for the essays defending the Constitution, but Jefferson did indicate his admiration elsewhere. To the correspondent who had sent him

---

14 Jefferson to Madison, 16 December 1786, *PTJ*, 10:603. See also Jefferson to Madison, 20 June 1787, *PTJ*, 11:480–1.

15 Jefferson to Madison, 16 December 1786, *PTJ*, 10:603.

16 He must have been rooting for a new executive, since, as a minister to France, he learned that foreign governments were wary of negotiating treaties and loans with a young country in which the executive power of enforcement rested with the legislative body. Mayer, *Constitutional Thought*, 225.

17 Scholars often fail to notice that Jefferson's first impression to Madison included praise of the veto power *with* the supermajority requirement for an override. Jefferson to Madison, 20 December 1787, *PTJ*, 12:438–43. See, for example, Raymond Tatalovich and Thomas S. Engeman, *The Presidency and Political Science: Two Hundred Years of Constitutional Debate* (Baltimore: Johns Hopkins University Press, 2003), 35–36.

18 Jefferson to William Stephens Smith, 13 November 1787, *PTJ*, 12:355–7; Jefferson to Edward Carrington, 27 May 1788, *PTJ*, 13:208–10;

19 Jefferson to Madison, 18 November 1788, *PTJ*, 14:188.

the first volume of *The Federalist*, Jefferson claimed that "discussion and reflection" had "cleared most" of his first objections to the Constitution.[20] In 1796, Jefferson praised a speech by Gallatin on the treaty power and recommended that it be included in *The Federalist*, as it was "the only rational commentary on the part of the constitution to which it relates."[21] And when Jefferson organized the curriculum for studying the law at the University of Virginia, the *Federalist* was one of only six texts required for instruction. As the "Minutes of the Board of Visitors" put it, "[t]he book known by the title of "The Federalist," being an authority to which appeal is habitually made by all, and rarely declined or denied by any as evidence of the general opinion of those who framed, and of those who accepted the Constitution of the United States, on questions as to its genuine meaning."[22] But it was more than important historical evidence of what Americans at ratification understood the Constitution to be, for Jefferson told Madison in 1788, "it has rectified me in several points."[23] One of these points may have been Hamilton's defense of executive energy.

To be sure, Hamilton's discussion of energy in the executive would have provided points for disagreement. Remarkable for the boldness in pointing to dictators to argue that executive energy was necessary, Hamilton's reference to the Roman dictator in *Federalist* No. 70 would have underscored Hamilton's differences with the famous Virginian.[24] Earlier, in his *Notes*, Jefferson had added to his list of defects in the Virginia constitution the attempt by some Virginians to "create a dictator" in both 1776 and 1781 to protect the state during its most dangerous times.[25] Jefferson blamed this attempt by fellow Virginians to create a benevolent dictator on their being seduced by "the example of an ancient republic," namely, Rome.[26] Hamilton, however, used the example of the Roman dictator to demonstrate to republicans that they needed energy in the executive. Perhaps, then, Hamilton's publishing his praise of Roman dictators on 15 March says something for Hamilton's sense of humor.[27]

[20] Jefferson to Carrington, *PTJ*, 13: 208–210.
[21] Jefferson to Madison, 27 March 1796, *PTJ*, 29:51.
[22] Minutes of the Board of Visitors, 1822–1825, written and signed by Jefferson as Rector. *TJW*, 479.
[23] Jefferson to Madison, *PTJ*, 14:188.
[24] *Federalist*, No. 70, 448.
[25] *Notes*, *TJW*, 252.
[26] Ibid., 254.
[27] According to Jacob E. Cooke, *Federalist* #70 appeared in *The Independent Journal*, March 15, 1788. Jacob E. Cooke, ed., *The Federalist* (Hanover, NH: University Press of New England/Wesleyan University Press, 1961), 471. See William Shakespeare, *Julius Caesar*, act 1, scene ii, as well as act 3, scene i.

Readers may have perceived another possible reference to Jefferson. Hamilton's rhetorical opponents at the time were anti-Federalist writers, but Hamilton's description of his opponents as "enlightened well wishers" – as opposed to the term "plausible," which he used two essays earlier – was meant to draw a distinction.[28] One person might have been his principal partner in writing the *Federalist*: whereas No. 70 listed executive energy as "a leading character in the definition of good government," Madison had presented energy alongside stability as two ingredients that governments of any form must possess, and Madison balanced energy and stability against the necessary ingredient in the republican form, liberty.[29] More likely, Hamilton was referring to the author of the Declaration of Independence: Madison had previously cited Jefferson on the argument that the three powers ought not to be intermixed in order to criticize Jefferson's proposal to appeal to the people whenever two departments of government agreed that the third had exceeded its authority.[30] Furthermore, Jefferson's letters from France might have led some then to believe that he was against ratification. More broadly, even though Jefferson was in Europe, it could be said that Jefferson's reputation was in the air, and some Federalists saw it as an obstacle to ratification.[31] Just one month earlier, for example, Noah Webster had assumed the signatory "Giles Hickory" to argue against the *Notes'* call for a perpetual and unchangeable government.[32] Hamilton may not have then known that Jefferson had written to Madison in December with the confession that he was not "a friend to a very energetic government," but Hamilton must have guessed that anti-Federalists, especially George Mason and Patrick Henry, would interpret Jefferson's *Notes* and relative silence on the Constitution to support their own arguments against ratification.[33]

These differences aside, Jefferson must have been attracted to the Hamilton's explanation of the compatibility between unity of office and

---

[28] *The Federalist* No. 68, p. 434.

[29] *The Federalist* No. 37, p. 224.

[30] *The Federalist* No. 48, p. 318.

[31] Of Washington's selection of Jefferson as Secretary of state in 1789, John Marshall emphasized Jefferson's popular appeal: "His Notes on Virginia, which were read with applause, were believed to evince the soundness of his political opinions; and the Declaration of Independence was universally ascribed to his pen. He had long been placed by America amongst the most eminent of her citizens, and had long been classed by the President with those who were most capable of serving the nation." *Life of George Washington* (Fredericksburg, VA: Citizens' Guild, 1926) 4:320–1.

[32] Noah Webster, "Liberty is never Secured by Paper Declarations," in *The Debate on the Constitution: Federalist and Antifederalist Speeches, Articles and Letters During the Struggle over Ratification*, ed. Bernard Bailyn (New York: Library of America, 1993), 2: 304–15.

[33] Madison to Jefferson, 24 July 1788, *PTJ*, 13: 412–13. See also speeches of Patrick Henry and James Madison on 12 June 1788, in *Debate on the Constitution*, 2: 674, 689.

accountability. By then, Jefferson had already praised the strong executive of the New York Constitution, and he had argued that executive business in a republic should be committed to a "single hand" because republicans tended to elevate deliberation over execution and thus enfeeble the government. And he had long argued that government needed better institutional devices – more proportionate representation as well as special constitutional conventions – to gauge public opinion. As a lawmaker, he had tinkered with vesting clauses for Virginia governors, and, as governor, he had found a way to preserve the law by going outside it during times of necessity and then asking for approval afterward. Throughout, he had attempted to reconcile executive power with public opinion, but he had not yet perfected the institutional connection.

Hamilton's defense of unity in the executive offered one way to do precisely that. As Hamilton put it, not only would a single executive avoid paralysis caused by internal dissent, but a single executive would allow for "responsibility." Importantly, Hamilton extended responsibility beyond legal culpability: "Responsibility is of two kinds – to censure and to punishment. The first is the most important of the two, especially in an elective office. Men, in public trust, will much oftener act in such a manner as to render them unworthy of being any longer trusted, than in such as manner as to make them obnoxious to legal punishment."[34] By censure, Hamilton must have meant failure in reelection rather a formal vote by Congress, for he mentions "public opinion" twice in this capacity – but not Congress – in the remainder of the essay. Moreover, Hamilton connected the next ingredient of energy, duration, to public opinion as expressed in national elections: the president should have an adequate number of years in office so that he may be independent of the public opinion and even firm when he opposes it, but he should be eligible for reelection, so that there would always be before him an incentive to "the positive merit of doing good."[35] Although Jefferson surely disagreed with the point about term limits, he must have been attracted to Hamilton's argument that plurality in the executive would be a "clog" on "good intentions" and a "cloak" to "faults."[36]

A 1791 letter illustrates the point. Archibald Stuart wrote Jefferson to request his and Madison's assistance in forming a new constitution for Virginia, and mentioned that he and others were concerned about the direction of the new national government, particularly the creation of the bank.[37]

---

[34] *The Federalist* No. 70, p. 452.
[35] *The Federalist* No. 72, p. 464.
[36] *The Federalist* No. 70, p. 456.
[37] Archibald Stuart to Jefferson, 22 October 1791, *PTJ*, 22:223–4.

Jefferson agreed that the Constitution needed a better way to preserve the line between state and nation, but his solution is more revealing than his perception of the problem. He explained that the way to ensure that a state would not be so weak that it would "lose ground in every contest" was to create a more powerful executive so that the state would be more equipped to check the national government. The state constitution should harness the executive office to responsibility: "Render the Executive a more desirable post to men of abilities by making it more independent of the legislature. To wit, let him be chosen by other electors, for a longer time, an ineligible for ever after. Let him feel the whole weight of it then by taking away the shelter of his executive council. Experience both ways has already established the superiority of this measure."[38] If the states were to protect liberty, they would have to be strong enough to resist encroachment; and one requirement for a strong government was a unitary executive, an office that would attract able men. If Jefferson's 1791 letter sounds like a primer on the principles enunciated by *The Federalist*, it is because Jefferson had by then read and been persuaded by Publius's essays defending the Constitution.

Removal Power

Hamilton's argument that executive energy was compatible with republican canons was tested in 1789, when the House of Representatives created the State Department.[39] As Madison put it in a letter to Jefferson, a "very interesting constitutional question" had arisen over "by what authority removals from office were to be made."[40] Some Representatives argued that the Constitution meant for the Senate to share the removal power, and others argued that assigning the removal power was a legislative privilege, as the Constitution was silent with regard to the power. Led by Madison, a third group believed that the Constitution left the power to the president alone, and a small fourth group believed that officers could be removed by impeachment alone.[41] In the first two groups, several argued that locating the removal power solely in the president would too closely resemble the former prerogative of the king by rendering officers creatures of the president's will.[42] On the other side of the argument, Madison and others argued that the removal

---

[38] Jefferson to Stuart, 23 December 1791, *TJW*, 984.

[39] Tatalovich and Engeman, *Presidency and Political Science*, 100–101.

[40] Madison to Jefferson, 30 June 1789, *PTJ*, 15:224–9.

[41] Ibid. Madison summarized these opinions in his letter, but see Edward Corwin, *The President's Removal Power Under the Constitution* (New York: National Municipal League, 1927), 12.

[42] Marshall, *Life of Washington*, 4:307–8.

power was executive in nature because the president needed to control his departments if he were to faithfully execute the laws. More than an interesting question, the debate about the removal power also was a debate about tenure of office, presidential power, and accountability to the people.

One problem for Madison in 1789 was that Hamilton in *The Federalist* had argued that the consent of the Senate would "be necessary to displace as well as to appoint."[43] Although it was then known that Madison had participated with Hamilton in writing the already famous defense of the Constitution, the authorship of the individual essays was not; so Madison faced the charge of both arguing against the famous commentary as well as with having engaged in a philosophical flip-flop.[44] One 16 June, William Loughton Smith of South Carolina reminded the House of a "publication of no inconsiderable eminence in the class of political writings, on the constitution," written by authors "of great information."[45] Smith, whom Hamilton often used as a mouthpiece for his own arguments, quoted extensively from Hamilton's argument in *Federalist* No. 77 for the Senate's participation in removal.[46] According to that argument, the Senate's participation in both appointment and removal would ensure that "a change of the chief magistrate" would not "occasion" a "revolution" in the administration of government, that is, because a new president would need the Senate's consent to remove the former president's officers, it would be less likely that a new president could change the tone or ability of administration simply by way of the appointment power.[47] In Smith's hands, the argument from *The Federalist* was meant to undermine Madison's rhetorical position by showing that executive officers needed protection from presidential politics.

The centrality of *The Federalist* to the House debate shows that the role of the presidency within the executive branch was at stake. If the removal power were to be exercised by both the Senate and the president, then a large part of the executive branch would securely rest above the changing

---

[43] *The Federalist* No. 77, p. 489.
[44] Robert Scigliano, introduction to *The Federalist*, xvi.
[45] *Annals of Congress*, House of Representatives, First Cong., 1st Sess., 474–5.
[46] Syrett called Smith a "spokesman for H[amilton] in the House of Representatives," *PAH*, 12:545. This was true throughout the 1790's, and Hamilton wrote of Smith, "I know no man whose loss from the House would be more severely felt by the good cause." Hamilton to Charles Cotesworth Pinckney, 10 October 1792, *PAH* 12:544. Although there is no evidence that Hamilton gave Smith this argument about removal, it is relevant that Smith was also instrumental during the debates over Hamilton's Report on Credit. See *PAH*, 6: 344, n5; and George C. Rogers Jr., *Evolution of a Federalist: William Loughton Smith of Charleston, 1758–1812* (Columbia: University of South Carolina Press, 1962), 189–94.
[47] *The Federalist* No. 77, p. 489.

currents of the electorate.[48] Under Hamilton's formulation in *Federalist* No. 77, any executive officer who "had given satisfactory evidence of his fitness" for the office would be protected against removal by a corrupt or inept president.[49] The consequence of joint removal, however, would be that an officer, once appointed and confirmed, would be irremovable so long as he enjoyed the confidence of the Senate. It would make sense, under such a rule, for executive officials to shield themselves from removal by future presidents by courting the favor of at least half the Senate.[50] Administration would be freed from politics.

Madison must have remembered Hamilton's reflection in *The Federalist* No. 72 on the "intimate connection" between the tenure of the president and the system of administration. In that essay, Hamilton worried that every election of a new president there would be accompanied by a change in the executive branch, because a new president would regard removing his predecessor's officers as "the best proof he can give of his own capacity and desert."[51] For Hamilton, then, the solution was longer presidential tenure; an extended duration of office for the president would help prevent what would otherwise be an ongoing cycle of appointment and removal, occasioning "a disgraceful and ruinous mutability in the administration of the government." As Madison must have perceived, Hamilton's argument was meant to keep one arm of the executive branch from amputating the other: even if presidents were subjected to reelection and therefore subject to the changing fancies of constitutional majorities, executive officers would be able to steady the administration because they would be protected from public opinion, especially if they were on good terms with Senators who were not up for reelection. The result of legislative participation in the removal power would not simply be a move toward legislative oversight of executive duties but also a move toward lifetime tenure for executive officers. That Hamilton had once called for a term of good behavior for senators and the president must have reinforced Madison's resolve to locate the removal firmly within the presidential office.[52]

In the House debates, Madison opened his argument for presidential removal by emphasizing the vesting clause and the "take care" clause. Because the Constitution grants the president the executive power and because the president must "take care" that the laws be executed, the president enjoys

---

[48] *The Federalist* No. 72, pp. 462–3.
[49] *The Federalist* No. 77, p. 489.
[50] Or, one more than one-third if impeachment were required.
[51] *The Federalist* Nos. 71–2, pp. 462–3.
[52] James Madison, *Notes of Debates in the Federal Convention of 1787 Reported by James Madison* (New York: Norton, 1987), 138.

whatever power necessary to his ensuring that the laws be executed that is not explicitly delegated to the legislative or judiciary branch. "In the first section of the first article, it is said, that all legislative powers herein granted shall be vested in a Congress of the United States. In the second article, it is affirmed that the executive power shall be vested in a President of the United States of America. In the third article, it is declared that the judicial power of the United States shall be vested in one Supreme Court, and in such Inferior Courts as Congress may, from time to time, ordain and establish."[53] Madison thus defended the president's right to remove by appealing to inherent executive powers: Because the Constitution "declares that the Executive power shall be vested in a President of the United States," the Senate's participation in the appointment power constituted an "exception" to the "general rule" and, as such, should be "taken strictly." So, for example, the Constitution limits the general grant of executive power to the president by giving the Senate a share in the appointment power, but it does not extend that limitation of the president's power to the removal power. Next, Madison argued that the "take care" clause suggests that the President must be able to control his officers and therefore be able to remove them: "If the duty to see the laws faithfully executed be required at the hands of the Executive Magistrate, it would seem that it was generally intended he should have that species of power which is necessary to accomplish that end. Now, if that officer when once appointed is not to depend upon the President for his official existence, but upon a distinct body, (for where there are two negatives required, either can prevent the removal,) I confess I do not see how the President can take care that the laws be faithfully executed."[54] Under Madison's argument, then, the "take care" clause reinforces the previous argument that the general grant of executive power to the president is to be read broadly. Surprisingly, it was Madison, not Hamilton, who first argued that the difference in the vesting clauses of Articles One and Two implied that the executive power was a general grant of power rather than a collection of enumerated powers.

To be sure, Madison used the vesting clauses not to argue for a new power by implication for the executive but rather to argue against intermixing the three departments. To include the Senate in the removal power would be to "qualify" the executive powers "further than they are qualified by the constitution" and therefore violate the central principle of the Constitution, that which prohibits the intermixture of powers. Because the Constitution itself allows for departures from a strict partition between powers – it includes

---

[53] *Annals of Congress*, 1st Congress, 1st sess., 481.
[54] *Annals of Congress*, 1st Congress, 1st sess., 516.

the president in legislation with the veto, and it includes the Senate in the appointment power – it would be incorrect to argue that the Constitution did not consider whether the Senate should share the removal power. Madison thus concluded, "If the constitution has invested all executive power in the president, I venture to assert that the Legislature has no right to diminish or modify his executive authority."[55] The point is not that the vesting clause makes the president's executive power boundless, for Madison did not address this possibility, but rather that the vesting clause reinforces the larger constitutional proscription against legislative usurpation of executive powers.

But Madison also argued that the president should singly possess the removal power in order to make execution accountable to the public will, and it is this argument that provides the key to understanding Madison's defense of the executive power. For Madison, the problem with giving the Senate part of the removal power was that it would release the president from the responsibility that comes with the unitary office. Borrowing from Hamilton's defense of the Convention's decision to go without an executive council, Madison argued that the president's unity would ensure his accountability to the people and that this accountability would transfer itself to the lower executive officers: "Vest this power in the Senate jointly with the President, and you abolish at once that great principle of unity and responsibility in the executive department, which was intended for the security of liberty and the public good. If the President should possess alone the power of removal from office, those who are employed in the execution of the law will be in their proper situation, and the chain of dependence preserved; the lowest officers, the middle grade, and the highest, will depend on the President, and the President on the community."[56] Empowering the president with the removal power thus ensures popular oversight over the entire executive branch by way of the president's mode of election. Put differently, the president's popular mode of election makes him more trustworthy than the Senate to remove officials. With its members elected by "individual legislatures" and enjoying the longest terms, the Senate was, in Madison's estimation, already a "permanent body." A permanent body would most likely favor a permanent body of executive officers; by checking a president's attempt at removal, the Senate could lengthen the tenure of administrative officers, thus elevating stability over responsibility. Even if the motives of Senators were pure, the practical result would be the same. Because the Senate would not be able to initiate removal, executive officials would not be directly subordinate to either the president or Senate and therefore would exert a will of their own.

---

[55] Ibid.
[56] *Annals of Congress*, 1st Congress, 1st sess., 518.

Without the president possessing the power of removal, the executive would be like a "two-headed monster" so divided against itself that its enterprises could never be wholly accomplished.

Jefferson and Removal

When Madison reported these events to Jefferson, Jefferson passed over the discussion of the removal debate in order to insist on a bill of rights, so it is difficult to determine whether Jefferson then agreed with Madison's defense of the removal power. But there is reason to believe that Jefferson agreed with the assertion of executive power.

By 1789, Jefferson had thought about the appointment and removal powers. In his 1776 constitution, Jefferson distributed the appointment power among the executive and legislative branches. The general rule would be that "all officers, civil and military" would be selected by the executive branch: the administrator would appoint, subject to the council's negative, but the legislature could decide to transfer the appointment power to another official. But there were exceptions: Sheriffs and coroners, for instance, would be selected by voters; the attorney general, the treasurer, and judges on the Court of Appeals would be selected by the House of Representatives.[57] Under Jefferson's 1783 constitution, the appointment power would not be so explicitly shared. In this draft, Jefferson did not mention the appointment power in the section on the executive branch. Rather, the two legislative houses would have the power to appoint the Treasurer, Attorney General, military officers, auditors, officers for their houses "and no other officers, except where in other parts of this constitution such appointment is expressly given them."[58] In the section on the judiciary, Jefferson granted the power to appoint the highest judges to the legislature, but the governor was allowed the power to select the judges of the inferior courts with the advice of council.[59] Whether the executive would hold the power to appoint those "other officers" was not addressed, but Madison later assumed Jefferson's constitution would confer this power on the executive.[60]

---

[57] Jefferson, First and Third Drafts of Virginia Constitution, *PTJ*, 1:343–3, 360–1. Under other plans available to Virginians in 1776, the executive branch had little control over the appointment of offices. John Adams, "Thoughts on Government," *Papers of John Adams*, Robert J. Taylor, ed., (Cambridge, MA: Harvard University Press, Belknap Press, 1977–2004) 4: 86–92. "The Plan of Government as Originally Drawn by George Mason." *PTJ*, 1:367–8. "The Constitution as Adopted by the Convention," *PTJ*, 1:381–2.

[58] Jefferson, Proposed Revision of the Virginia Constitution, *PTJ*, 6:298.

[59] Ibid., 300–2.

[60] In his comments on Jefferson's 1783 Constitution, Madison objected to Jefferson's locating appointments, especially of judges, wholly in either the executive or legislative departments on the grounds that it would encourage corruption. *PTJ*, 6:312.

Although whether the removal power followed from the appointment power was not clear under either of Jefferson's proposed constitutions, his 1780 notes on the removal power reveal that Jefferson thought the matter over privately, if not officially.[61] Although these notes are not complete, they suggest Jefferson's movement toward a strong doctrine of the executive's power to remove. Jefferson began these notes with the clarification that removal would probably not include military officers, as their removal would take the form of court martial. The question of removal, then, "principally affects the Staff, whose rapacity, inattention and means of evasion require energetic superintendence." To this observation, for which Jefferson could have supplied firsthand testimony, Jefferson added the argument that located the superintendence in the executive: "The power of appointing and removing executive officers inherent in Executive. Executive inadequate to every thing. Appoint deputies – qui agit per alterum &c. Ministerial office may be executed by deputy but not judicial. He who appoints may remove." According to Jefferson's notes, then, the power to remove follows from the nature of the executive task. Inherent in this task is the principle of delegation. Since one person cannot carry every law into execution, the executive must appoint deputies. Since such deputies exist in order to help the executive, they must be placed under the executive's supervision, that is, the executive who appoints them should be able to remove them as well. Central to this argument was the distinction between office and estate. As Jefferson put it, "An indefinite conveyance of an estate is for life," whereas "an indefinite appointment to office is during pleasure." The deputy has to be removable or else he would possess the same authority as, and probably more experience than, his principal: If an executive were to "employ a steward indefinitely he [the steward] would have a freehold."[62]

It would not be implausible to suppose that, from Jefferson's low opinion then of executive councils, that he would have been attracted to Madison's argument for a "chain of responsibility" between the people and the president. That his, he probably believed that requiring the consent of the Senate for removal would result in a corrupt relationship between senators and executive officials. Later, he said as much. As Secretary of State, Jefferson advised Washington that the Senate did not have the right to negative the grade of persons appointed as ambassadors. In the first place, the president alone had the power because the "transaction of business with foreign nations is executive altogether. . . . Exceptions are to be construed strictly."[63]

---

[61] Jefferson, "Notes concerning the Right of Removal from Office," *PTJ*, 4:281–2.
[62] Ibid.
[63] Jefferson, "Opinion on the Powers of the Senate," April 24, 1790, *PTJ*, 16:378–81.

But more than just possessing the power to transact business with other governments, the executive is granted by the Constitution control over his own administration: "The Senate is not supposed by the Constitution to be acquainted with the concerns of the executive department." The specifics, perhaps the "special and secret circumstances," of the appointee's duties should not fall under the Senate's review, since the Senate is only "to see that no unfit person be employed." Like Madison's argument for the removal power on the House floor, Jefferson's defense of the president's authority in the appointment power bordered upon relying on a doctrine of inherent powers. Foreign relations were an executive matter, so the Senate's participation in appointing members of the State Department should be limited.

Later, when James Monroe was president, Jefferson objected to a law that required most executive officials to "vacate every four years."[64] Although the policy would appear to be favorable from Jefferson's perspective because it would favor rotation over stability, Jefferson believed that it would give the Senate too many chances to interfere with executive power. Because it would require the Senate to act on "every one nomination" every four years, executive officers would again need to court the Senate's approval: "It will in keep constant excitement all the hungry cormorants for office, render them, as well as those in place, sycophants to their Senators, engage these in eternal intrigue to turn out one and put in another, in cabals to swap work; and to make of them what all executive directories become, mere sinks of corruption and faction." Jefferson further explained that this law was even "more baneful" than "the attempt which failed in the beginning of government to make all officers irremovable but with the consent of the Senate." For Jefferson, the attempts in 1789 and 1820 were alike in that they would have removed the basis for executive accountability by limiting the president's power to control his officers and thus "sap the constitutional and salutary functions of the President." For Jefferson, then, the danger to be avoided was an intimate connection between senator and executive officer because it would separate administration from public opinion. The way to marry administration and public opinion was to give the removal power to the president alone. Jefferson would be the first president to make this case, but, as another chapter shows, he changed Madison's argument.

The President and the Constitution

In Washington's cabinet, there were occasions for agreement between Hamilton and Jefferson. In one of his first jobs as Secretary of State, Jefferson

---

[64] Jefferson to Madison, 29 November 1820, Smith, 1825–6.

proposed two ambitious plans to systemize the nation's weights, measures, and currency.[65] To a question about the president's ability to nominate foreign ministers, Jefferson argued that the Senate's role should be limited since foreign relations were executive in nature.[66] And, although he advised Washington that the veto was "chiefly for cases where they [members of Congress] are clearly misled by error, ambition or interest," he later warned Washington against not using it at all – "The Non-user of his negative begins already to excite a belief that no President will ever venture to use it."[67]

But, as is well known, there were deep differences over whether Congress held the power to incorporate a bank and the president the power to proclaim neutrality. These differences overlapped with partisan ambition, but they also placed before Americans the larger question of how the Constitution should be interpreted. Although the debate between Madison and Hamilton over the Neutrality Proclamation has been studied elsewhere, it is worth revisiting in the context of Jefferson's understanding of presidential power.[68] But in order to understand Jefferson's participation in the debate, which was about the president and the Constitution, Jefferson's well-known contribution to the debate over the constitutionality of the bank, which was about Congress and the Constitution, needs to be summarized.

In 1791, Washington asked members of his cabinet for opinions on whether the Constitution allowed Congress the authority to create a national bank, and Jefferson and Hamilton offered opinions based on opposed interpretations of the Constitution.[69] Hamilton argued, "the power of the government, *as* to the objects intrusted to its management, is in its nature sovereign," and "the right of erecting corporations is one, inherent in & inseparable from the idea of sovereign power." To dispel the notion that the "necessary and proper" clause in Article 1, Section 8, connoted a "restrictive operation," Hamilton explained, "the degree in which a measure is, or is not necessary, cannot be a *test* of constitutional right, but of *expediency* only."[70]

---

65 *PTJ*, 16:602–75.
66 See next chapter.
67 Jefferson, "Opinion on the Constitutionality of the Bill for Establishing a National Bank," *PTJ*, 19:280; Jefferson, "Opinion on Apportionment Bill," *PTJ*, 23:375. Scholars seem unaware of the second statement. See, for example, Raymond S. Tatalovich and Thomas Engeman, *The Presidency and Political Science*, 36.
68 Stanley Elkins and Eric McKitrick, *The Age of Federalism* (New York: Oxford University Press, 1993), 336–365; Marc Landy and Sidney M. Milkis, *Presidential Greatness* (Lawrence: University Press of Kansas, 2000), 29–33.
69 Alexander Hamilton, "Opinion on the Constitutionality of the Bank," *Alexander Hamilton: Writings*, ed. Joanne B. Freeman, (New York: Library of America, 2001), 613–46; Jefferson, "Opinion on the Constitutionality of a National Bank," *TJW*, 416–21.
70 Hamilton, "Opinion on the Constitutionality of the Bank," *Hamilton Writings*, 631.

If Hamilton began his argument with the discussion of what govern-ments must do, Jefferson based his on the question of consent, particu-larly in the Tenth Amendment's reservation of powers not delegated to the national government to the states or the people.[71] According to this argument, if the people did not delegate in the Constitution a particular power to the government, then it should be presumed that they intended to reserve this power to either exercise for themselves or delegate to the government when the need arose. If Congress had a power to incorporate a bank, then, the power would have to be found within the powers dele-gated to it under the Constitution. Jefferson thus divided his argument into two questions. Is the power among those specifically enumerated? Can the power be implied from one of the two general grants of power? Jefferson dis-missed the first question on the grounds that incorporating a bank fell outside the powers to raise money through taxes, to borrow money, or to regulate commerce.

Jefferson's second argument against finding the power among the general powers was more complicated. According to Jefferson, the power to create a bank could not be found "within either of the general phrases," that is, the "general welfare" and the "necessary and proper" clauses. Regarding the first, Jefferson argued that because the Constitution allowed Congress to "lay taxes for *the purpose* of providing for the general welfare" it limited Congress's power to lay taxes to instances that provided for the country's gen-eral welfare. Therefore, Congress could not lay taxes for "any purpose they please," and, likewise, Congress could not do "anything" to provide for the general welfare. Accordingly, when the means and the end are read together, the general grant of power confers limits rather than latitude: to grant the power without requiring the purpose, or to grant any power to effect the purpose, would be to "render all the preceding and subsequent enumera-tions of power completely useless." If the general welfare clause were not understood this way, the Constitution's careful distribution of power would amount to allowing Congress to do "whatever would be for the good of the United States," a construction which Jefferson believed to be as dangerous as it was unworkable: "It is an established rule of construction where a phrase will bear either of two meanings, to give it that which will allow some mean-ing to the other parts of the instrument, and not that which would render all the others useless."[72] For Jefferson, one piece of evidence that confirmed his argument was that the members of the Convention considered allowing Congress the power to institute a bank but voted against it.

[71] Jefferson, "Opinion on the Bank," *TJW*, 416–21.
[72] Ibid., 418.

With the general welfare clause explained, Jefferson used a similar line of reasoning to interpret the necessary and proper clause. Since this clause granted Congress the power to makes laws "necessary and proper" for carrying into execution laws passed under the enumerated powers, the question hinged on whether the power in question was *necessary* for carrying out the enumerated powers. For Jefferson, "necessary" is best understood as an alternative to "convenient." If Congress could exercise its enumerated powers – collecting taxes, and so on – without a bank, then creating a bank was not necessary and therefore not authorized. Like the loose interpretation of the general welfare clause, latitude in the construction of the necessary and proper clause would allow to Congress any power convenient to enacting laws under its enumerated powers. "It would swallow up all the delegated powers," so it must be inferred that the Constitution "restrained" Congress "to the *necessary* means," that is, "to those means without which the grant of power would be nugatory."[73]

These two understandings of the Constitution emerged in the debate over Washington's Proclamation of Neutrality, but this time with regard to presidential power.[74] In April 1793, Americans learned of France's declaration of war against Great Britain and Holland, and a few joined one of the sides in combat or trade.[75] In order to prevent these privateers from embroiling the country in war, Washington needed to find, and set, a foreign policy. The war between France and England made these questions particularly difficult. Was the United States obligated to observe a treaty with France after France's form of government had been changed by revolution? Was it in the interest of the United States to remain neutral even though it was demonstrable that trade with England would be the backbone of the emerging economy? To what extent should the president consider public opinion, especially since "a great majority of the American people," as John Marshall put it, "deemed it criminal to remain unconcerned spectators of a conflict between their ancient enemy and republican France."[76]

On April 12, Washington wrote to Jefferson and Hamilton to ask each to give "mature consideration" as to measures to prevent citizens from "embroiling us" with the warring European nations.[77] On April 18

---

73 Jefferson, "Opinion on the Bank," *TJW*, 419.

74 Perhaps these two understandings were discernible within the pages of *The Federalist*. On this point, it is worth pointing out that Hamilton authorized publishing the *Pacificus* essays in an 1802 edition of the *Federalist*. See Richard Loss, introduction, *The Letters of Pacificus and Helvidius* (Washington, DC: J. and G. S. Gideon, 1845; Delmar, New York: Scholars' Facsimiles & Reprints, 1976), xiv.

75 Marshall, *Life of Washington*, 5:9.

76 Marshall, *Life of Washington*, 5:8.

77 Washington did not then write to the Attorney General or the Secretary of War. Washington to Jefferson, 12 April 1793, *PTJ*, 25:541.

Washington returned to the capital and, on the following day, issued thirteen questions regarding England and France to his cabinet.[78] The first three questions addressed measures which Washington might take:

1. Shall a proclamation issue for the purpose of preventing interferences of the Citizens of the United States in the War between France and Great Britain &ca.? Shall it contain a declaration of Neutrality or not? What shall it contain?
2. Shall a Minister from the Republic of France be received?
3. If received shall it be absolutely or with qualifications–and if with qualifications, of what kind?

The next questions were directed at whether existing treaties with France were still binding, and the final question asked whether it was "necessary or advisable to call together the two Houses of Congress with a view to the present posture of European Affairs." It is worth noting that the most important question for present purposes, whether the president had the power to decide whether the president could declare neutrality, was only indirectly asked in the first and final questions (shall a proclamation issue and should Congress be called). But the respective authority of Congress and the president had been on Jefferson's mind since March, when he had written Madison that he "suppose[d] that Congress would be called" because the "Executive cannot decide the question of war on the affirmative side, neither ought it to do it on the negative side, by preventing the competent body from deliberating on the question."[79]

Washington did not find much consensus within his cabinet. Hamilton counseled that it would be imprudent to observe a treaty with France while a temporary government ruled without a constitution, and he marshaled arguments from writers on natural law to maintain that even though the people of any nation have a right to determine which form of government best secures their happiness it did not follow that other nations must remain involved in the changes which result from that right.[80] Jefferson favored maintaining neutrality but argued that Washington should refrain from formally declaring neutrality, and he suspected that Washington's questions were not neutral. Although the questions were in Washington's "own hand writing," it was "palpable from the style tissu & suite" that the questions were not Washington's but, rather, Hamilton's and "were raised upon a prepared chain of argument," which led to a declaration by the executive that

---

[78] Enclosure, Washington to the Cabinet, 18 April 1793, *PTJ*, 25:569.
[79] Jefferson to Madison, 24 March 1793, *PTJ*, 25:442.
[80] Eclosure, Hamilton and Henry Knox to Washington," 2 May 1793, *PAH*, 14:367–96.

the treaty with France was "void."[81] Jefferson recorded that his suspicions were confirmed when Edmund Randolph told Jefferson that Hamilton had "went with him thro' the whole chain of reasoning of which these questions are the skeleton."[82] On the question of Hamilton's influence on Washington's questions, it is now accepted that Jefferson was right.[83]

Washington issued his proclamation, that the nation was at peace and that any citizen who violated the laws of nations would be prosecuted, on 22 April, but he did not call it a "proclamation of neutrality" in order to satisfy Jefferson.[84] This settled the first and thirteenth questions: a proclamation was issued and Congress was not called. But Washington's proclamation did not end the matter, for there was still the question of receiving the French ambassador without qualification. The answer to this question would determine the state of the existing treaties with France. On 28 April, Jefferson sent his opinion of the French Treaties to Washington, which argued that reason – supported by the writings by Grotius, Puffendorf, Wolff, and Vattel – recommended observing the treaty with France on the grounds that "treaties remain obligatory notwithstanding any change in the form of government, except in the single case where the preservation of that form was the object of the treaty."[85] Washington sided with Jefferson to observe the French treaties and receive Genet without qualification. But even as Genet made himself unwelcome by appealing over Washington to Congress and the people, the diplomatic question with regard to France revealed that the

---

[81] Jefferson, "Notes on Washington's Questions on Neutrality and the Alliance with France," *PTJ*, 25: 665–7. According to Catanzariti, these notes might have been written at a later date, *PTJ*, 25:661.

[82] Jefferson, "Notes on Washington's Questions on Neutrality and the Alliance with France," *PTJ*, 25: 665–7.

[83] *PTJ*, 25:569–70; *PAH*, 14:327. See Hamilton to John Jay, 9 April 1793, *PAH*, 14:297–9. Jefferson submitted his answers to the remaining question on April 30. Catanzariti and Syrett point to an earlier letter from Hamilton to John Jay that included questions similar to Washington's, some even using identical wording. Also, Washington's cabinet journal suggests that the president had received Hamilton's opinion in some form and was not especially interested in the official opinions of Knox. Hamilton and Knox submitted a joint opinion on the third question on 3 May. The date of Hamilton's reply to the remaining questions is uncertain, as the original is missing and John Church Hamilton assigned a date of 2 May 1793. Washington never records Hamilton having turned in a complete reply; Jefferson does but uncharacteristically offers no date. Washington never requested Knox's opinion on the remaining questions, and Jefferson concluded that Knox's opinion "was never thought worth offering or asking for." Dorothy Twohig, ed., *The Journal of the Proceedings of the President, 1793–1797* (Charlottesville: University Press of Virginia, 1981), 124–27; Jefferson, "Notes on Washington's Questions on Neutrality and the Alliance with France," *PTJ*, 25: 665–7; and *PAH*, 14:398, n 2.

[84] Washington, "Proclamation of Neutrality," 22 April 1793, *George Washington: Writings*, ed. John Rhodehamel (New York: Library of America, 1997), 840.

[85] Jefferson to Washington, 28 April 1793, *PTJ*, 25:615.

prior question of executive power had not been settled. By the end of the summer, there would be national examination of the president's authority to direct foreign policy.

The ensuing debate, best represented in the essays written by Hamilton and Madison under the names Pacificus and Helvidius, over the legality and propriety of Washington's decision has been remembered as the first time the growing opposition party could use the people's love of republican France and suspicion of monarchical England as leverage against the previously unassailable Washington, but it was also important as the first instance of a public debate over executive power and the Constitution.[86] Although Jefferson never publicly entered the debate, he persuaded Madison to write a response and advised Madison regarding the particulars. Curiously enough, students of Jefferson's political science, including those who have studied his presidential administrations, have not examined his role in the Pacificus and Helvidius exchange with regard to Jefferson's understanding of executive power.[87]

On the same day he sent Washington his opinion on the French Treaties, Jefferson wrote Madison not to dispute the terms of the proclamation but rather to report an argument that had been proposed within the cabinet: "Would you suppose it possible that it should have been seriously proposed to declare our treaties with France void on the authority of an ill-understood scrap in Vattel?"[88] Madison responded by saying that what most surprised him was that the proposition was even "*discussed*." Sensing, perhaps, his friend's criticism, Jefferson outlined his own position in order to make it clear

---

[86] Marshall, *Life of Washington*, 5:14; Harvey C. Mansfield Jr. notes that such constitutional differences are "characteristically American" in that they arise out of the constitutionalization of executive power. *Taming the Prince: The Ambivalence of Modern Executive Power* (Baltimore: Johns Hopkins University Press, 1989) 275–6. Compare to Rakove, "The Political Presidency" (see note 4), 42.

[87] See, for example, Adams, 516–532; Adrienne Koch, *Jefferson and Madison: The Great Collaboration* (London: Oxford University Press, 1950), 141–147; Robert M. Johnstone Jr., *Jefferson and the Presidency: Leadership in the Young Republic* (Ithaca, NY: Cornell Univ. Press, 1978), 54–57, 80–82.; Forrest McDonald, *The Presidency of Thomas Jefferson* (Lawrence: University Press of Kansas, 1976), 53–55; Mayer, *Constitutional Thought* (see note 5), 232, and Tatalovich and Engeman, *The Presidency and Political Science* (see note 17), 25–42. Gary J. Schmitt does argue that "Jefferson agreed with his cabinet colleagues that the proclamation should be issued," and "nowhere, even in his letters to Madison, suggest[ed] that Washington did not have the authority to make the declaration he did." "Thomas Jefferson and the Presidency," in *Inventing the American Presidency*, ed. Thomas E. Cronin (Lawrence: University Press of Kansas, 1989), 335. But Schmitt misses Jefferson's letter to Madison, in which he claimed that the final proclamation was different than the wording he had authorized in that it made Washington "go out of line to declare things which, tho' true, it was not exactly his province to declare." Jefferson to Madison, 11 August 1793, *PTJ*, 26:650.

[88] Jefferson to Madison, 28 April 1793, *PTJ*, 25:619.

that he was not among those who hoped neutrality would be "mere English neutrality": "A manly neutrality, claiming the liberal rights ascribed to that condition by the very powers at war, was the part we should have taken."[89] In a June letter to Jefferson, Madison elaborated on his own position: although the president had the power to declare the fact that citizens were at peace, a president could not declare that the nation was neutral.[90] Furthermore, Madison indicated that he distrusted Washington's advisors: "I am extremely afraid that the P[resident] may not be sufficiently aware of the snares that may be laid for his good intentions by men whose politics at bottome are very different from his own. As assumption of prerogatives not clearly found in the Constitution and having the appearance of being copied from a Monarchical model, will beget animadversion equally mortifying to him, and disadvantageous to the Government."[91] To ease Madison's doubts, Jefferson explained that he had opposed the declaration on both constitutional and tactical grounds: first, a declaration of neutrality was the same as a declaration that there should be no war, and this was a power "to which the Executive was not competent; second, it "would be better to hold back the declaration of neutrality" in order to increase its value to the warring nations and therefore demand the "*broadest privileges* of neutral nations."[92]

Jefferson's private exchange with Madison was interrupted by Hamilton's going public. On 29 June, Hamilton, using the name "Pacificus," undertook the task of defending Washington's Proclamation against criticisms levied in a series of essays written in *The National Gazette*, signed by "Veritas." Most of Veritas's charges emphasized gratitude toward France and the right of free men to criticize their government, for he was primarily concerned with the merits of neutrality. But Veritas also asked whether Washington was "vested with legal powers to annul treaties by proclamation."[93] There was, and remains, some mystery around these essays: Genet mistakenly believed the author of Veritas to be Jefferson and thus believed that Jefferson would side with his public appeal against Washington, but Jefferson believed that they were the work of a Federalist who meant to sabotage Republicans by feigning to be one of the "exaggerated democrats."[94] And, importantly, the first writer to emphasize *constitutional* authority was "A Friend of the

[89] Madison to Jefferson, 8 May 1793, *PTJ*, 25:688–9; Jefferson to Madison, 13 May 1793, *PTJ*, 26:25–7.

[90] Madison to Jefferson, 13 June 1793, *PTJ*, 26:272–4.

[91] Ibid.

[92] Jefferson to Madison, 23 June 1793, *PTJ*, 26:346.

[93] "Veritas," *National Gazette*, June 1, 5, 8, 12, and 26, 1793. There were others, including "Brutus" who asked whether there was a legal difference between a treaty and a proclamation.

[94] Elkins and McKitrick, *The Age of Federalism* (see note 69), 343, 356, and 821n157; Jefferson, *Anas*, July 12, 1803, L and B, 1:376.

Peace," who wrote to defend Washington against Veritas.[95] Also, Hamilton composed a draft of his Pacificus argument in May, before Veritas published his essays.[96] When Pacificus answered Washington's critics, he charged his opponents with trying to weaken Washington's reputation for partisan gain, but, more important, he used the opportunity to expand the discussion of constitutional authority.[97]

Pacificus offered several arguments for presidential supremacy in foreign policy. First, because the power to declare neutrality can rest with neither the legislative branch (because it is not "the organ of intercourse" with other nations) nor with the judicial branch (because the "province of that department is to decide litigations in particular cases"), it must "of necessity belong to the Executive." Second, because the executive is the organ of intercourse, the president is the agent that must interpret treaties, and the president must determine whether or not an existing treaty applies to his actions as the organ of intercourse. This suggests that the executive's role as organ of intercourse with other nations requires that the executive be connected with the power to declare neutrality. Next, the fact that the vesting clause of Article II lacks a "herein granted" clause means that exceptions to the general grant of executive power were meant to be considered strictly. Under this formulation, even though Congress may have the power to declare war, and though the Senate's two-thirds approval is required to ratify a treaty, the president is free to exercise his right of judgment in order to decide whether he will receive an ambassador, interpret a treaty, or "determine the condition of the Nation" even if acting on his judgment "may establish an antecedent state of things" that would "weigh in" legislative decisions.[98]

But after offering this extended argument, Pacificus added a simpler one that made it unnecessary to "vindicate the authority of the Executive on this broad and comprehensive ground." According to Pacificus, the executive interprets the law by the way he executes it; the executor of the law is by definition more than an errand boy because some errands require judgment. Thus Pacificus used the "take care" clause to argue that execution implies discretion:

The President is the constitutional EXECUTOR of the laws. Our Treaties and the laws of Nations form a part of the law of the land. He who is to execute the laws must first judge for himself of their meaning. In order to the observance of that conduct, which the laws of nations combined with our treaties prescribed to this country, in

---

[95] "Veritas," *National Gazette*, June 15–19, 1793.

[96] Hamilton, "Draft of a Defense of the Neutrality Proclamation," *Hamilton Writings*, 795–800.

[97] Hamilton, "Pacificus" No. 1, in *Hamilton Writings*, 801–809. On Washington's reputation see also Marshall, Life of Washington, 5:14.

[98] Hamilton, "Pacificus" No. 1, in *Hamilton Writings*, 804.

reference to the present War in Europe, it was necessary for the president to judge for himself, whether there was any thing in our treaties incompatible with an adherence to neutrality. Having judged that there was not, he had a right, and if in his opinion the interest of Nation required it, it was his duty as Executor of the laws, to proclaim the neutrality of the Nation, to exhort all persons to observe it, and to warn them of the penalties which would attend its non observance.[99]

The Hamiltonian understanding of presidential power thus relied on two arguments. First, because governments necessarily have the power to preserve themselves against necessity, and because the U.S. government is no more or less than its three branches, any necessary power that does not rest with the legislative or judicial powers must rest with the executive. Just as argument for the constitutionality of the bank supposed that a government, if it is sovereign, must be able to incorporate a bank, the argument for neutrality presupposed that governments must be able to say when they are neutral. The only question is determining which branch holds the power. Or, as Harvey C. Mansfield Jr. puts it, Hamilton's argument implied "that since the government must be able to do anything, if two of the branches do not possess a power, it must reside in the third."[100] Second, because execution necessarily requires interpretation, the difference between the vesting clauses of Articles I and II suggests that framers of the Constitution endorsed the wider view of presidential power. The argument from the vesting clauses joined the argument from sovereignty.

With the advice of Jefferson, Madison replied to Hamilton, under the name Helvidius. According to Helvidius, Pacificus's interpretation was particularly dangerous in its rhetorical scope. Although it was "mingled with a few truths" and seemed to vindicate "an important public act, of a chief magistrate, who enjoys the confidence and love of his country," it simultaneously advanced "principles" which "strike at the vitals" of the Constitution."[101] As Madison noted, Hamilton had changed the stakes of the debate by emphasizing the question whether the president held the authority to issue the Proclamation. To counter Pacificus's redirection or expansion of the question, Helvidius responded with his own strategy: rather than beginning with the question of which branch possessed the power of issuing a proclamation of neutrality, Helvidius began his inquiry with determining the source of Pacificus's constitutional theory. According to this argument, for Pacificus's arguments to be correct, they must have originated somewhere; that is, they must have been derived from "the writers, of authority, on public law," the

[99] Ibid., 809.

[100] Mansfield, *Taming the Prince*, 276.

[101] Madison, "Helvidius" No. 1, *James Madison: Writings*, ed. Jack N. Rakove (New York: Library of America, 1999), 537–8.

"quality and operation" of the powers of war and peace, or the Constitution itself.[102]

Helvidius dismissed the reliability of the first possible source because previous writers on law, especially Locke and Montesquieu, were too influenced by monarchy to offer a better guide than "our own reason and our own constitution."[103] As to the second possible source, the nature and operation of the powers of war and peace, Helvidius maintained a strict definition of execution: because the "natural province of the executive magistrate is to execute laws," executive acts "must pre-suppose the existence of laws to be executed." Because treaties and declarations of war do not constitute executions of law but are like laws in that they need to be executed, the argument that the executive "naturally" possesses these powers incorrectly supposes that the executive naturally has lawmaking, that is legislative, powers. Third, Helvidius asked whether the doctrine resulted from "actual distribution of powers among the several branches of government" according to the Constitution. Here, Helvidius quickly concluded that because Article I places the power to declare war in Congress the power must be naturally legislative. In the case of treaties, the requirement of the Senate's consent by two-thirds and the fact the treaty is said by the Constitution to be the "supreme law of the land" suggests that the president cannot have the power alone.[104]

To counter the possible argument that the president's being the commander in chief implies that he is naturally the branch to make treaties, Helvidius reminded readers that wars were the arena in which it would be safest to leave action and not deliberation to executives: "Those who are to *conduct a war* cannot in the nature of things, be proper or safe judges, whether *a war ought* to be *commenced, continued,* or *concluded.*"[105] "War is in fact the true nurse of executive aggrandizement," for the powers of the sword, public treasures, and patronage gather around the president by virtue of his role as commander in chief. Furthermore, war tempts the passions of the president, because "it is in war, finally, that laurels are to be gathered." "The strongest passions and most dangerous weaknesses of the human breast; ambition, avarice, vanity, the honourable or venial love of fame, are all in conspiracy against the desire and duty of peace." Because the laurels of honor most

---

[102] Ibid., 539.
[103] One might ask how Helvidius could so easily dismiss the commentators on British law whose writings were the very sources for his own theory of the separation of powers. Helvidius perhaps anticipated this difficulty by justifying his move to the next alternative by saying that examining the writers on public law would be "more likely to perplex than to decide."
[104] Madison, "Helvidius" No. 1, *Madison Writings*, 539–43.
[105] Ibid.

likely crown the "executive brow," precautions must be taken to ensure that the "executive will" does not conspire against peace in pursuit of honor.[106]

The reason why Madison wrote a response to Hamilton is not because Hamilton defended the Neutrality Proclamation but rather because Madison and Jefferson objected to Hamilton's particular interpretation of the president's power. Madison wrote only after exchanging a series of letters on the subject with Jefferson, in which Jefferson urged a response, "For god's sake, my dear Sir, take up your pen, select the most striking heresies, and cut him to pieces in the face of the public."[107] Jefferson's fear was that because nobody had challenged Pacificus, that "his doctrine will therefore be taken for confessed," that is, that Pacificus's expansive understanding of executive prerogative would become constitutional gospel. His suspicion that Veritas was actually an agent of Hamilton must have contributed to the urgency of Jefferson's plea. Madison answered the call but told Jefferson that the response would have to both "solid" and "prudent" because the question would be studied by others: "None but intelligent readers will enter into such a controversy, and to their minds it ought principally to be accommodated."[108]

Madison might have hoped that these above average readers would notice the implications for presidential tenure. In *Federalist* No. 75, Hamilton had written that it would be proper to grant a hereditary monarch with the "entire power of making treaties" but that such a grant would be "utterly unsafe and improper" in the hands of an "elective magistrate of four years' duration."[109] The difference between the two was the degree to which tenure of office connected the magistrate's ambition to the interest of his country. Although a hereditary monarch might rule tyrannically, he still "personally has too much stake in the government to be in any material danger of being corrupted by foreign powers." An elected magistrate, on the other hand, would eventually resume his life as "a private citizen" and would therefore be more likely than a king to sacrifice "duty" for "interest" if he possessed the entirety of the treaty power. As Helvidius remembered Hamilton's argument, then, the president's thinness of attachment to office, due to his four-year tenure, was sufficient reason for limiting the president's control over the treaty-power. By implication, Pacificus's argument that the president necessarily enjoys some privilege with regard to the treaty power was to argue that presidential tenure should be lengthened. That Hamilton's plan in the Constitutional

---

[106] Madison, "Helvidius" No. 4, *Writings of James Madison*, ed. Gaillard Hunt (New York: G. P. Putnam's Sons: 1900–1910), 4:174.

[107] Jefferson to Madison, 7 July 1793, *PTJ*, 26:443–4.

[108] Madison to Jefferson, 22 July 1793, *PTJ*, 26:548–9.

[109] *The Federalist* No. 75, pp. 479–480.

Convention called for lifetime tenure for presidents and senators supported such a reading.[110]

At stake was whether the president would be allowed to control matters pertaining to foreign affairs. But, more so than in similar modern debates, also at stake was the question of how the Constitution would be interpreted in resolving this question. Consequently, Jefferson's objection to the Proclamation was not necessarily an example of opposition to presidential power. In short, Jefferson seemed to allow the power to declare the state of the nation to the president: "Upon the whole, my objections to the competence of the Executive to declare neutrality (that being understood to respect the future) were supposed to be got over by avoiding the use of that term. The declaration of the *disposition* of the US can hardly be called illegal, tho' it was certainly officious and improper. The truth of the fact lent it some cover."[111] The problem for Jefferson was that Pacificus's defense of the Proclamation went further than the Proclamation itself in that it articulated the expanded position of presidential privilege in foreign affairs that Hamilton had given within the cabinet meetings: "The right of the *Executive* to declare that we are *not bound to execute the guarantee* was then advanced by him and denied by me. No other opinion expressed in it. . . . The passage beginning with the words 'the answer to this is etc.' is precisely the answer he gave at the time to my objection."[112] More than a personal rivalry, Jefferson's objection stemmed from Pacificus's constitutional argument that the executive had a "similar right of judgment, in the execution of its own functions," which was meant to meet the objection that the legislature's having the power to declare war indicated that the legislature was the appropriate branch to decide whether the nation should be at war or peace.[113] According to Pacificus, by having the duty to preserve peace until a declaration of war is made by Congress, the executive necessarily has a "right of judging what is the nature of the obligations which the treaties of the country impose on the government" and a duty to "enforce the laws incident to the state of the Nation."[114] Jefferson's problem was that Hamilton had crafted Jefferson's compromise into a doctrine.

Because both sides acknowledged that necessity requires the president to act in cases where the law is silent and that sometimes the president and his officers would have to exercise some discretion, what was at stake here was the relationship between presidential power and the law. Just as

---

[110] Madison, *Notes* (see note 53), 138.
[111] Jefferson to Madison, 29 June 1793, *PTJ*, 26:403.
[112] Jefferson to Madison, 30 June 1793. *PTJ*, 26:403.
[113] Hamilton, "Pacificus" No.1, *Hamilton Writings*, 806.
[114] Ibid., 806.

Jefferson believed that the president should not use the word neutrality to describe what existed in fact if not by law, Jefferson believed that executive prerogative, although required in practice, should not be interpreted into the law. But Jefferson soon knew that he lost this fight. Because Genet's attempt to undercut Washington by appealing to the people had the potential to rally public opinion around the president, Jefferson told Madison that the "true wisdom" of the party would be to "abandon" Genet, "approve unequivocally of a state of neutrality" and "to avoid little cavils about who should declare it."[115] As Jefferson noted to Madison, Hamilton had used the affair to urge Washington "in three speeches of $\frac{3}{4}$ of an hour length each" to make his own "appeal to the people" in order to put down the opposition. As Jefferson knew, Washington's prestige, combined with Genet's miscalculation, would force public opinion to side with executive power against constitutional scruples.

Virginia and Kentucky Resolutions

In 1798 Jefferson collaborated with Madison to write and distribute the Virginia and Kentucky Resolutions. Both sets of resolutions protested against Congress's enacting the Alien and Sedition Acts, arguing that the national government had exercised powers it did not have. Together, they emphasized the rights of the states to consider the constitutionality of state laws and thus shoulder some of the burden for later arguments for interposition and nullification. But Jefferson's argument was less moderate than Madison's: Whereas Madison's Virginia Resolutions only invited other states to interpose by calling the Alien and Seditions Acts "unconstitutional," Jefferson's draft of the Kentucky Resolutions outlined a program for nullification.[116] As Jefferson put it, because the Constitution is a "compact," "each party has an equal right to judge for itself, as well of infractions as of the mode and measure of redress," and when the national government "assumes undelegated powers, its acts are unauthoritative, void, and of no force."[117] Although the Kentucky legislature initially opted not to include Jefferson's phrase, "a nullification of the act is the rightful remedy," it did introduce the term into American politics when it adopted the Resolutions again in 1799.[118]

---

[115] Jefferson to Madison, 11 August 1793, *PTJ*, 25:651–2.
[116] Gary Rosen, *American Compact: James Madison and the Problem of Founding* (Lawrence: University Press of Kansas, 1999), 140–41.
[117] Jefferson, "Draft of the Kentucky Resolutions," *TJW*, 449.
[118] Adrienne Koch and Harry Ammon, "The Virginia and Kentucky Resolutions: An Episode in Jefferson's and Madison's Defense of Civil Liberties," *William and Mary Quarterly*, 3rd Series, 5 (1948): 145–176. See Barbara Oberg's notes in *PTJ*, 30: 529–35.

Jefferson began his Kentucky Resolutions with the principle that the states did not combine with each other on the "principle of unlimited submission to the general government" but rather, "constituted the General Government for special purposes." Because the states joined for specific purposes, they reserved "the residuary mass of right to their own self-government," meaning that each state was an equal partner in the compact and therefore held the "equal right to judge for itself" whether the federal government had overstepped the provisions of the compact and what the "measure of redress" would entail. Consequently, the individual states, not Congress or the federal courts, would judge whether the laws would be executed within their respective borders.[119] After outlining Kentucky's right to decide questions of constitutionality, the Resolutions declared the Alien and Sedition Acts void because the Constitution had granted Congress the power to punish certain enumerated crimes, leaving the power to "create, define, and punish" other crimes to the states by the Tenth Amendment.

More than an instance of going beyond enumerated powers, the Alien and Sedition Acts required powers explicitly forbidden to Congress by the Constitution. For example, in the case of the Alien Act, Jefferson argued that removing migrated aliens was equal to prohibiting their migration and therefore violated Article I, Section 9, which explicitly said that Congress could not prohibit the slave trade before 1808. Likewise, the Alien Act's lodging the power to remove aliens in the hands of the president violated the Fifth Amendment's guarantee of due process and thus took power away from the judiciary. And in the case of the Sedition Act, Jefferson argued that the Tenth Amendment and the First Amendment indicated that the states, not Congress, retained "to themselves the right of judging how far the licentiousness of speech and of the press may be abridged without lessening their useful freedom."[120] But Jefferson's final argument addressed the "construction applied by the General Government." In particular, Jefferson referred to the construction of the "general welfare" and "necessary and proper" clauses used to justify not only the Alien and Sedition Acts but also other laws in what he believed to be a trend in Congress. The evidence then was not the specific provisions of the Acts in question but rather "the sundry of their [Congress's] proceedings." Experience proved that these phrases of the Constitution needed "revisal and correction" but "at a time of greater tranquility."[121]

---

[119] Jefferson, "Draft of the Kentucky Resolutions," Resolutions 1 and 2, *TJW*, 449–50.
[120] Ibid., Resolutions 3–6, *TJW*, 450–2.
[121] Ibid., Resolutions 7–8, *TJW*, 452–6.

No state joined Kentucky and Virginia until South Carolina invoked the Resolutions in 1832, and Jefferson's authorship of the Kentucky Resolutions has dealt a considerable blow to his reputation. The extent of the damage to Jefferson has turned on the utilitarian question of whether the argument for states' rights was the political means or the constitutional end.[122] Some scholars have defended Jefferson by arguing that the Resolutions invented the argument from states' rights only to meet the extraordinary, and illegal, challenge to civil liberties in the Alien and Sedition Acts.[123] Even Jefferson's principal biographer defended the Resolutions on the grounds that they were demanded by necessity.[124] As this explanation would have it, the constitutional doctrine is to be forgiven because Jefferson translated the question of constitutional doctrine into political advantage in order to win the Revolution of 1800. Just as he had urged Madison to counter Hamilton's defense of a broad construction as Pacificus, Jefferson enlisted Madison to lead the charge against the Alien and Sedition laws in the newspapers. With Virginia and Kentucky inviting other states to join their protest, the constitutionality of the Alien and Sedition Acts was debated in the House and in the public throughout 1799. Although Republicans lost this constitutional battle, they won the political war.[125]

Even though there are these mitigating factors, Jefferson's Resolutions seem to stand in the way of a strong national government and an energetic president. Leaving the states to decide whether laws were a simple misuse of delegated powers or an assertion of undelegated powers would render the national government to be, as Marshall said of the Constitution in another context, beautiful in appearance but unworkable in practice.[126] Jefferson's draft of the Kentucky Resolutions, for instance, makes no mention of the foreign policy context of the Alien Acts and their possible importance for national defense.[127] And, read through his First Inaugural's praise of the energetic citizen who rises up to defend his country, the Kentucky Resolution's invocation of natural rights bears uncomfortable similarity to Locke's

---

[122] Leonard W. Levy argued that the Virginia and Kentucky Resolutions demonstrate the Jefferson was more concerned with states' rights than with civil liberties. Leonard W. Levy, *Jefferson and Civil Liberties: The Darker Side* (Cambridge, MA: Harvard University Press, Belknap Press, 1963), 46–56.

[123] Koch and Ammon, "The Virginia and Kentucky Resolutions," 174; Koch, *Great Collaboration*, 211; Mayer, *Constitutional Thought*, 206.

[124] Malone, 3:394, 424.

[125] As Jefferson reported to Madison, the House approved, on a 52:48 vote, the "Congressional Report Defending the Alien and Sedition Laws." Jefferson to Madison, 26 February 1799, *PTJ*, 31:62–3. On Madison's writings in the press, see Smith, 1073.

[126] *Gibbons v. Ogden*, 22 U.S. 1 (1824).

[127] I was reminded of this fact by a student.

"appeal to heaven." It is telling that Jefferson never repudiated the revised Virginia Resolutions of 1799, even as the threat of secession loomed during the War of 1812 and slavery grew even more entrenched after 1820.

Jefferson's Kentucky Resolutions are all the more disconcerting because they fit so well with other aspects of Jefferson's constitutional theory. First, because Jefferson believed that the Constitution was a compact among the states, strict construction and states' rights were one and the same. Under this reading, the Tenth Amendment's reservation of powers to the states simply spelled out what the compact theory presumed, while at the same time such a declaration was necessary because of the possibility that some clauses of the Constitution would be too broadly read. It was this connection between the doctrine of enumerated powers and the compact theory of the states that premised his later constitutional scruples over acquiring and incorporating Louisiana. As president, Jefferson persisted in believing that the Louisiana Purchase was unconstitutional, even when some of his advisors gave him arguments to believe otherwise, because it expanded the compact and because the Constitution did not specifically grant the authority for the kind of purchase and incorporation required by the Louisiana Treaty. His solution, a constitutional amendment, would satisfy strict construction *and* the compact theory. Thus, the eighth resolution's call for a "committee of conference & correspondence" to communicate the substance and spirit of the resolutions may have been an attempt to institutionalize an extraconstitutional appeal to the public.

Second, the Kentucky Resolutions also should be understood as Jefferson's first attempt to teach the doctrine of coordinate review. Scholars have commented on Jefferson's "tri-partite doctrine" of separation of powers. Often called coordinate review, or departmentalism, this understanding holds that each department of government is the judge of the constitutionality of actions within its own sphere.[128] As David N. Mayer has noticed, Jefferson arrived at this understanding by 1797, when he protested a federal indictment of Samuel Cabell, and the Kentucky Resolutions pushed the theory of coordinate review to its logical conclusion.[129] Just as the president must be the judge of the constitutionality of executive actions, the states were the only competent judge of the compact they had made with the other states. Although Jefferson had argued against expansive constructions of the Constitution in private letters to Washington, this was the most public (though

---

[128] See Chapter 5.

[129] David N. Mayer, *Constitutional Thought*, 263; Jefferson, "Petition to the Virginia House of Delegates," August, 1797, *PTJ*, 29:491–504; and Rakove, "The Political Presidency" (see note 4), 49. Rakove suggests that Madison's famous account of ambition in Federalist #51 includes departmental interpretations of the Constitution.

still anonymous) of his arguments for strict construction. Its result, that states can interpret some parts of the Constitution, parallels his later argument that each department of government is responsible for deciding the constitutionality of its actions – hence, Jefferson's 1791 recommendation to make the states more able to resist by making the state governorships more attractive to men of ability.[130] Corrected by Madison, Jefferson's 1799 position constitutionalizes the coordinate capacity of the states by relegating nullification to the amendment process.

But did Jefferson's Resolutions close the path to an energetic and national executive? Although Jefferson was willing to leave states the option of protest by amendment, he did not believe that such a protest should necessarily limit presidential power. Rather, the state and the president could act in their separate fields. Indeed, this question, whether a president must refrain from enforcing a law after a state protested the law's constitutionality, was addressed during his administration in a "Memorandum on the Constitution."[131] The author of this unsigned memorandum explained that a state's protest was simply "a qu.[estion] between the State, deeming it unconstitutional, desired to prevent its exercise, and the other states whose cooperation is necessary to affix to the character of unc[onstitutionalit]y." Because the dispute is really a question of whether three-fourths of the states will ratify an amendment, the president need not concern himself: "It is a qu[estion] with the Functionary has nothing to do: the object of his creation is to perform certain functions – under the control of a certain number of the states – his natural state is action." In clear opposition to the view that it "is the duty of the President to desist from enacting the law," the memorandum argued that the president's "functional" duty of execution is primary: "If it were his duty to desist, it could be to only because the State was out of the Union. To consider the State as no longer [consisting][132] part of his Cons[itutional]. field of action, w[oul]d be to decide that she no longer formed part of the Union – to annul the compact as to her – to decide the qu[estion] between the parties to wh[ich] he owed his exec. This he has no manner of authority to do; and the only alternative is continue as if no qu[estion] has arisen to fulfill the purposes of his creation – to perform his duties [and] his field of action to be what the Const. defined them to be and within that field, to persevere in the performing those duties." Thus, Madison's less radical doctrine

---

[130] See p. 125.

[131] Jefferson, Memorandum on the Constitution, MSS 564, Tracy W. McGregor Library of American History, Special Collections, University of Virginia Library. Jefferson's authorship of this document is probable but uncertain; its argument corresponds with the argument of this book.

[132] Or "constituting."

was made compatible with and, even supportive of, executive power, that is, to an energetic unifier of the national will. Because refraining from executing a disputed law in a state would imply that the state existed outside the Union, the president must execute the law as if there were no constitutional dispute. As far as the president is concerned, then, claims by states against the government have no constitutional basis until they take the form of constitutional amendment. Throughout the dispute between a state and the national government, the president takes his bearings from the "purpose of his creation," action. As Chapter 8 shows, Jefferson and his party secured the national basis for presidential selection when they ratified the Twelfth Amendment in 1804 and pointed the president away from the states.

Strict Construction and the Revolution of 1800

By the time he became president, Jefferson had embraced the doctrine of strict construction. Such an interpretation, no doubt, served his interests in opposition, as it allowed him to use the Constitution itself as a way to hold back those in power. And the simplicity of the doctrine – that there is a dangerous slippery slope lurking behind broad construction – must have appealed to those already worried that the Federalists intended to consolidate power for the benefit of the commercial few. Clarity would undermine corruption. Strict construction thus paralleled the argument for a Bill of Rights, in that the people needed a specific text by which they could judge their government. In each case, partisan mobilization was intertwined with constitutional interpretation.

The relationship between strict construction and public opinion was related to the presidency. Rakove is right to note that the foreign policy debates showed early Americans that the presidency was more important than they might have expected, but, as important as it was to decide whether the country would befriend Britain or France, there was more at stake for executive power. The debates over the bank and the neutrality proclamation were, for Jefferson, important for calling attention to the dilemma that he perceived as governor and constitution maker: how can the people be ruled by laws of their own creation when one man must, for their good, sometimes transcend it? Although he admired the strong executive of New York and had proposed empowering the national executive, he was unwilling to embrace a doctrine of inherent executive powers or a construction of the vesting clause that would, as he saw it, undermine popular consent. At the same time, the early question of removals had raised the possibility that there could be a "chain of responsibility" between the people and executive administration. Importantly, the Constitution, and its defense in the *Federalist*, had showed him the way to reconcile necessity with the law while at the same time preserving popular consent, that is, it offered him the chance to institutionalize a democratic form of energy.

As Bruce Ackerman has shown, the democratic presidency became a matter of public debate in 1800, when Republicans argued that the people's intent was the only sure guide to resolving the accidental tie between Jefferson and Burr.[133] More than an accident, this public crisis provided Jefferson with the opportunity to assert and explain the doctrine of democratic energy that he had formulated and revised throughout the 1780s and 1790s. Jefferson presented this understanding in his First Inaugural but, in order to understand that address, it is necessary to appreciate his ambition to change the inaugural address itself. It is therefore time to consider his two objections to the Constitution.

---

[133] Bruce Ackerman, *The Failure of the Fathers: Jefferson, Marshall, and the Rise of Presidential Democracy* (Cambridge, MA: Belknap Press, Harvard University Press, 2005).

4

"To place before mankind the common sense of the subject"

Declarations of Principle

As we have seen, the problem of executive power is that it seems to require violations of the law and thus undermines consent. This is a theoretical problem that calls for a practical solution. As lawgiver and executive, Jefferson struggled with the law's inability to meet the demands of political life. As a writer of constitutions, he formulated and reformulated the vesting clauses for the Virginia governor in order to empower the executive but resisted general grants of authority. As wartime governor, he found that he had to work outside the law in order to defend his state against the British as well as to enforce the laws passed by the Virginia legislature, but he also asked the executive council or the legislative branch for retroactive approval of his extraconstitutional actions. Instead of expanding the law in order to accommodate executive prerogative, Jefferson's understanding of executive power requires that executives defend their actions on the grounds that they acted outside the law to achieve the public good. The means by which executives would throw themselves on the people is by a declaration of principle.

Jefferson believed that declarations of principle would provide the criteria by which the people could judge executives and thus lessen the likelihood that executives would use necessity to act against the public good. Because declarations would show the principles by which executives would be guided, they could be used to demarcate the limits of executive power while at the same time bringing public opinion to a single point. Declarations thus served Jefferson's educational project by preserving a strict construction of the law and by elaborating the principles which comprise the majority will. In short, declarations energize the executive in its directing of the will of the nation while at the same time fortifying the people against the abuse of executive prerogative.

Throughout his political career, Jefferson heard, drafted, wrote, and read declarations. Jefferson made the connection between this form of political expression and public opinion when he drafted the Declaration of Independence, learned the practical usefulness of declarations as wartime governor, and solidified the place of declarations within democratic government when he argued for the Bill of Rights.

Jefferson and Rhetoric

There is evidence that Jefferson's education and early training contributed to lifelong confidence in political speech.[1] As a student, Jefferson worked closely with Dr. William Small, the first professor at William and Mary to use a lecture format, and Jefferson later wrote that Small "fixed the destinies of my life."[2] Small later arranged for Jefferson to be taught by George Wythe, who was also the teacher of other statesman such as John Marshall, James Monroe, and Henry Clay. Jefferson came to admire his teacher, calling him a second father, and he respected Wythe's method of teaching, praising Wythe's instruction to Madison: "Wythe's school is numerous. They hold weekly courts and assemblies in the capitol. The professors join in it; and the young men dispute with elegance, method and learning."[3] Wythe's emphasis on public argument must have made its impression on Jefferson, for he devoted approximately forty percent of the space in his commonplace book to Bolingbroke, with most citations dealing with rules of reasoning and evidence.[4] When he became a mentor for other young men beginning their studies, Jefferson included precise instructions for teaching oneself the "art of speaking and writing correctly."[5]

Additional biographical details illustrate Jefferson's captivation with the art of public persuasion. In his *Autobiography*, Jefferson recorded his admiration as a young man for the oratorical skill of Patrick Henry, saying "He appeared to me to speak as Homer wrote."[6] In his *Notes*, Jefferson praised the oratory of Native Americans and bragged that Logan's speech to

---

[1] This section has benefited from several studies that see rhetoric as central to Jefferson's politics: Robert Dawidoff, "Rhetoric of Democracy," *Jefferson and the Politics of Nature*, ed., Thomas S. Engeman, 99–122 (Notre Dame, IN: Notre Dame University Press); James L. Golden and Alan L. Golden, *Thomas Jefferson and the Rhetoric of Virtue* (Lanham, MD: Rowman and Littlefield, 2002); and Jay Fliegelman, *Declaring Independence: Jefferson, Natural Language, and the Culture of Performance.* (Stanford, CA: Stanford University Press, 1993).

[2] Golden and Golden, *Jefferson and Rhetoric*, 4–5.

[3] Ibid., 5; Jefferson to Madison, 26 July 1780, *PTJ*, 3:507.

[4] Golden and Golden, *Jefferson and Rhetoric*, 47.

[5] Jefferson to Bernard Moore, *TJW*, 1560.

[6] Jefferson, *Autobiography*, *TJW*, 5–6.

Dunmore was superior to the orations of Demosthenes and Cicero.[7] Elsewhere in the *Notes*, Jefferson faulted African Americans for what he believed to be their inability to utter a "thought above the level of plain narration" or to write poetry.[8] His essay, "Thoughts on English Prosody" attempted to show nonnative English speakers that "the accent is not equal; that they are not to be read monotonously" so that these speakers may "form an idea of the degrees of excellence of which this art is capable."[9] Jefferson's large library included books on rhetoric and elocution, including some that theorized on the connections between music and oratory.[10] He recommended the study of the orations of Demosthenes and Cicero, though he preferred those of the former.[11] Moreover, Julian Boyd's discovery of marks above words on a surviving draft of the Declaration indicate that Jefferson meant to emphasize syllables, or pauses, in his own reading of his draft to the Continental Congress, suggesting that Jefferson meant the document to persuade listeners by the way it sounded in addition to how it would persuade readers in the way it was argued.[12]

But Jefferson's faith in declarations did not grow from a mere appreciation for effective public speaking, for Jefferson was critical of several famously good orators, especially Patrick Henry. In his *Autobiography*, Jefferson doubted whether Patrick Henry had read his own "Summary View" because the orator "was the laziest man in reading I ever knew," and, elsewhere, Jefferson said that Henry "read nothing, and had no books."[13] To be sure, Jefferson had a private reason to be critical of Henry, for the political ambitions of the two governors crossed paths several times after the war. Nevertheless, Jefferson's mistrust of Henry grew from a deeper source than personal rivalry. Although Henry's popular oratory reminded him of Homer, Jefferson also believed Henry's talent for speech provided a dangerous example of the sway that demagogues could hold in democratic government. Jefferson provided this impression of Henry to the next generation's greatest orator, Daniel Webster: "His eloquence was peculiar; if indeed it should be called eloquence; for it was impressive & sublime beyond what can be imagined. Although it was difficult when he had spoken to tell what he had said, yet while he was speaking, it always seemed directly to the point.

---

[7] Jefferson, *Notes*, *TJW*, 188.
[8] Ibid., *TJW*, 266–7.
[9] Jefferson, "Thoughts on English Prosody," *TJW*, 612.
[10] Fliegelman, *Declaring Independence*, 14.
[11] Jefferson to John Brazier, 24 August 1819, L&B, 16: 211; Jefferson to Eppes, 17 January 1810, L&B, 12:343.
[12] Fliegelman, *Declaring Independence*, 5–15.
[13] Jefferson, *Autobiography*, *TJW*, 9.

When he had spoken in opposition to my opinion, had produced a great effect, and I myself been highly delighted and moved, I have asked myself when he ceased; 'What the Devil has he said?'."[14] Webster's recording of Jefferson's impression of Henry is best considered alongside of Jefferson's praise for speakers of another sort, Edmund Pendleton and James Madison. Jefferson called Pendleton, not Henry, "the ablest man in debate I have ever met with."[15] Lacking the "poetical fancy" as well as the "lofty and overwhelming diction" of Henry's speech, Pendleton's was "cool, smooth and persuasive;" not vulgar, Pendleton's language was "flowing, chaste & embellished." In addition to being persistent and patient – "you never knew when you were clear of him, but were harassed by his perseverance until the patience was worn down of all who had less of it himself" – Pendleton was persuasive in his gentleness: "Add to this that he was one of the most virtuous & benevolent of men, the kindest friend, the most amiable & pleasant of companions, which ensured a favorable reception to whatever came from him." Jefferson similarly praised the civility of Madison's speech, finding it was indicative of Madison's "habit of self-possession" as well as his "luminous and discriminating mind" – "Never wandering from his subject into vain declamation, but pursuing it closely in language pure, classical and copious, soothing always the feelings of his adversaries by civilities and softness of expression."[16] It is significant that these favorable descriptions of Pendleton and Madison comprise a large portion of his *Autobiography*'s chapter, "Revisals of the Law."

Although Jefferson made it a personal rule to avoid public confrontation and was generally unwilling to flatly contradict anyone, he believed in the persuasive power of public argument.[17] To the young men he mentored, Jefferson recommended the daily practice of public disputation: "If you have any person in your neighborhood engaged in the same study, take each of you different sides of the same cause, and prepare pleadings, according to the custom of the bar, where the pl. opens, the def. answers and the pl. replies."[18] More than honing a tool for the legal trade, these routines in argument were meant to prepare students for public life: "Adapt your language & figures

[14] Daniel Webster, Notes of Mr. Jefferson's Conversation 1824 at Monticello, 1825, *The Papers of Daniel Webster: Correspondence, Volume 1, 1798–1825*, ed. Harold D. Moser (Hanover, NH: University Press of New England, 1974), 372.

[15] Jefferson, *Autobiography*, *TJW*, 33.

[16] Ibid., 37.

[17] Jefferson admired Benjamin Franklin's practice of asking questions or suggesting doubts rather than announcing opinions. Jefferson to Thomas Jefferson Randolph, 24 November 1808, *TJW*, 1195.

[18] Jefferson to Bernard Moore, *TJW*, 1561.

to the several parts of the oration, and suit your arguments to the audience before whom it is supposed to be spoken. This is your last and most importance exercise. No trouble therefore should be spared."[19] By tailoring an argument to the audience, the speaker would be more persuasive in his attempt to command the assent of others. While a young man himself, Jefferson recorded in his commonplace book Locke's rule on the centrality of argument in a commonwealth: "[E]very man has a commission to admonish, exhort, convince another of error."[20]

Declaring Independence

Jefferson first learned the practical usefulness of declarations of principle in his efforts to promote independence from Great Britain.[21] In 1774, Jefferson wrote an essay, later called "A Summary View of the Rights of British America," which argued that the "political relation" between the colonies and England was the same as that between England and Scotland – "having the same Executive chief but no other necessary political connection."[22] In Jefferson's words, it was "approved by many, but thought too bold," and most Virginians "stopped at the half-way house of John Dickinson," which allowed the British parliament to "regulate our commerce" but denied it the right to use that power to raise revenue. Nevertheless, Jefferson's argument was published and "found its way to England," where Edmund Burke popularized it. Carl Becker may have been right to conclude that Jefferson's argument was then "a familiar doctrine to all men," but the point here is that Jefferson put to words a doctrine to which only the most "radical" would assent.[23] Edmund Randolph noted that Jefferson "shook" the "conceded principle" that Americans needed their "mother country": "The young ascended with Mr. Jefferson to the source of those rights, the old required time for consideration before they could tread this lofty ground, which, if it had not been abandoned, at least had not been fully occupied throughout America."[24] At the very least, *A Summary View* took an idea that was

[19] Ibid.

[20] *The Commonplace Book of Jefferson: A Repertory of His Ideas on Government*, ed., Gilbert Chinard (Baltimore: Johns Hopkins University Press, 1926), 378.

[21] No new study of the Declaration of Independence will be offered here. See Carl Becker, *The Declaration of Independence: A Study in the History of Political Ideas* (New York: Vintage, 1958); Garry Wills, *Inventing America*; Michael Zuckert, *The Natural Rights Republic: Studies in the Foundation of the American Political Tradition* (Notre Dame, IN: University of Notre Dame Press, 1996).

[22] Jefferson, *Autobiography*, *TJW*, 9; Becker, *Declaration*, 15–6.

[23] Becker, *Declaration*, 116.

[24] Quoted in ibid., 188.

known to all and used it to point Americans to a new public understanding of American rights.

Although the *Summary View* provided the intellectual step for some Americans, Jefferson changed his argument for independence by forming it into a declaration. Near the end of his life, Jefferson was asked to reflect upon the Declaration of Independence. In response to a letter from Henry Lee asking about the source of the argument of the Declaration, Jefferson offered his explanation of the document's purpose.[25] Although this letter has been quoted often, it has not been sufficiently explained in terms of Jefferson's practice of writing declarations. Jefferson wrote that though "all American whigs thought alike" on the subject of the rights of American colonists, what was lacking was "an appeal to the tribunal of the world" that would explain that independence was the consequence of Britain's denial of these rights. "This was the object of the Declaration of Independence. Not to find out new principles, or new arguments, never before thought of, not merely to say things which had never been said before; but to place before mankind the common sense of the subject in terms so plain and firm as to command their assent, and to justify ourselves in the independent stand we are compelled to take." Under this explanation, the Declaration's originality stems not from its argument but rather from its form. Although American whigs were then in agreement with the Declaration's statement of natural rights, they lacked a statement by which their consensus could be recognized even to themselves. Jefferson reflected elsewhere that people need to have their wills united by a single agent: just as some friends need to be first introduced by another party, public opinion sometimes requires direction.[26] In this letter, Jefferson remarked that the Declaration pointed the public mind toward a single course: "Neither aiming at originality of principle or sentiment, nor yet copied from any particular and previous writing, it was intended to be an expression of the American mind, and to give to that expression the proper tone and spirit called for by the occasion. All its authority rests then on the harmonizing sentiments of the day, whether expressed in conversation, in letters, printed essays, or in the elementary books of public right, as Aristotle, Cicero, Locke, Sidney, &c." Not intended to be an essay in natural right, the Declaration was guided by its purpose – to give Americans the tone and spirit proper to declaring "the causes" which "impel[led" them to "separation." The Declaration's argument in the famous second paragraph was thus more than a summary of an argument commonly held throughout country, for it gathered unexpressed sentiments and crafted them into affirmable sentences. Put somewhat differently, by firmly putting the

[25] Jefferson to Henry Lee, 8 May 1825, *TJW*, 1500–1501.
[26] See Chapter 9.

argument in terms plain enough to gather the assent of the citizenry, the Declaration achieved its rhetorical purpose in detailing the causes by which Americans came to declare independence. Michael Zuckert's metaphor that Jefferson was "scrivener to the American mind" is half-right, for Jefferson was also the molder of it.[27]

As is well known, Jefferson held higher hopes for the document. Just over a year later, Jefferson devoted what would his last letter to detailing what he believed the purpose of the Declaration.[28] To an invitation to participate in the fiftieth anniversary of independence, Jefferson wrote that he hoped that the celebration American independence would occasion the "opening" of "all eyes" to "the rights of man": "May it be to the world, what I believe it will be, (to some parts sooner, to others later, but finally to all) the signal of arousing men to burst the chains under which monkish ignorance and superstition had persuaded them to bind themselves, and to assume the blessings and security of self-government." According to this formulation, the Declaration was meant to be a kind of midwife to democracy throughout the world. Or, to shift the metaphor, the message of the Declaration was more than a summary of American grievances in that the summary preached the sermon of self-government. Furthermore, the self-government advocated in the Declaration would follow from science's departure from antiquity: "The general spread of science has already laid open to every view the palpable truth, that the mass of mankind has not been born with saddles on their backs, nor a favored few booted and spurred, ready to ride them legitimately, by the grace of God." This more radical interpretation of the purpose of the Declaration corresponds with the more modest formulation put in the letter to Lee. Because science had uncovered the palpable truth of equality and had therefore removed the foundation for the argument for privilege, the Declaration's appeal to self-evident truths could unify the argument for rights. Put more directly, the new and public act of uniting the public mind under a particular tone and spirit, aimed toward assent, was itself an argument for equality.[29]

Jefferson as Governor

Jefferson's greatest contribution to his country came in the form of a famous declaration signed by representatives of the states, but Jefferson also included declarations throughout his attempts to govern and reform Virginia. More

---

[27] Zuckert, *The Natural Rights Republic*, 1.
[28] Jefferson to Roger C. Weightman, 24 June 1826, *TJW*, 1516–1517.
[29] Compare to Robert Frost, "The Black Cottage" *The Columbia Book of Civil War Poetry*, Richard Marius, ed. (New York, Columbia University Press, 1994), 450–455.

than routine pronouncements of policy, Jefferson used these declarations to strengthen consent. In 1779, Jefferson authored a bill that guaranteed for citizens "the right" to renounce their citizenship by verbal or written declaration as well as set the procedures by which aliens could become citizens by declaring that "they intend to reside" in and, "give assurance of fidelity to," Virginia.[30] Likewise, Jefferson often attempted to make the Virginia Constitution the fundamental expression of the majority will. Because the document was never ratified by the people or by delegates expressly given the power to ratify the Constitution, it was more like a statute than a constitution – that is, Jefferson believed it would be subject to revision by any legislative majority. It for this reason that Jefferson included a section on ratification in his 1776 constitution: "None of these fundamental laws and principles of government shall be repealed or altered" without the "personal consent" of the people as expressed in the majority in two-thirds of the counties.[31] Likewise, Jefferson's 1783 draft included a section on amending or altering the constitution as well as "a special and temporary provision" for selecting the delegates to ratify and introduce the constitution.[32]

When Jefferson learned that he had been appointed governor by the Virginia legislature, he offered his acceptance in the form of a reply. More than a dutiful gesture of gratitude, the structure of the address was an early form of that used in Jefferson's later inaugural addresses, and, like later addresses, it explored the connection between executive discretion and consent. After giving thanks for his selection, Jefferson pledged that he would be guided by honesty and moderation, that he would observe his duty to office, and would rely on the "wise counsels" of the legislative branch. Jefferson next observed that the selection was made more meaningful by the fact that it occurred in the context of a free polity: "In a virtuous and free state, no rewards can be so pleasing to sensible minds, as those which include the approbation of our fellow citizens." By locating his gratitude for being selected within the context of the larger polity, Jefferson offered a short lesson to his listeners: rather than pretending to be unaware of the opinion of citizens, Jefferson labeled public approval as the most pleasing reward to those who had the sense to understand the power of public opinion in Virginia. Because approbation by fellow citizens is most pleasing, Jefferson's "great pain" would be realized if his "poor endeavors" came "short of the kind expectations"

---

[30] Jefferson, "A Bill Declaring Who Shall be Deemed Citizens of this Commonwealth," *TJW*, 374–5.

[31] Jefferson, Third Draft, *PTJ*, 1:364.

[32] "Jefferson's Proposed Revision of the Virginia Constitution," *PTJ*, 6:304.

of his country. Then, on top of this praise of opinion, Jefferson promised that if he fell short it would be because of his own negligence: "so far as impartiality, assiduous attention, and sincere affection to the great American cause, shall enable me to fulfill the duties of any appointment, so far I may, with confidence undertake." Within this pledge of fidelity and moderation is the implication, perhaps, that errors are necessary, and therefore to be expected, because political life is imperfect and because even the most honest and attentive executive will find that the laws are insufficient to meet every possibility the future might hold.[33]

For duties of his appointment that required more than honesty, attentiveness and patriotism, Jefferson promised to "rely on the wise counsels of the General Assembly, and of those whom they have appointed for my aid in those duties." By promising that he would look to the "counsels" of both the Assembly and Privy Council when his own ability was lacking, Jefferson reformulated the terms of the relationship between the governor and the privy council. Rather than pledging that he would be abide by whatever advice was offered by the majority of the privy council, Jefferson opened the possibility that he would act without resorting to his council's advice, following instead his own fidelity and affection to the "great American cause." Jefferson's acceptance message thus carried within it two important implications. First, he would be honest in his executing his office, but, in explaining the duty of the office, Jefferson offered an expanded definition of what the office would be in practice. Second, Jefferson would uphold the principles of the government, but, in announcing those principles of government, Jefferson slightly modified them.[34]

As Virginia's chief executive, Jefferson often supplemented his relatively weak formal powers by issuing proclamations. For instance, when desertions were weakening Virginia's military, Jefferson wrote to Washington to ask his opinion on the effects of issuing a proclamation to inform deserters that they would be granted amnesty, as Washington had had "experience concerning the efficacy of Proclamations."[35] Similarly, Jefferson used the press to publish a proclamation informing Virginians that military force would be used against them if they settled in territories still in dispute with American Indians.[36]

---

[33] Jefferson, "Message Accepting Election as Governor," 2 June 1779, *PTJ*, 2:277–8.
[34] Ibid.
[35] Jefferson to Washington, 2 August 1780, *PTJ*, 3:524.
[36] Jefferson, "Proclamation Requiring Settlers Northwest of the Ohio to Vacate," *PTJ*, 3:266–7. From "Advice of Council respecting James Haye's Newspaper," in *PTJ*, 5:386, one can see that the executive would contract with newpapers to publish "useful essays and public notification on the part of government."

Jefferson as governor used proclamations to remind citizens of their rights and to define the meaning and scope of their rights. In 1776, Jefferson authored at least one of the two proclamations, issued by the Confederation Congress, inviting mercenary troops serving the British to desert in exchange for some property and the "blessings of peace, liberty, property and mild government."[37] Five years later, Jefferson used his position as governor to renew the offer to foreign mercenaries. In his own proclamation, Jefferson shifted the emphasis of Congress's old proclamation and offered a summary of the revolution: the British had commenced a "cruel and unprovoked war" on a people who were committed to the extension of civil and religious freedom. Jefferson thus added religious liberty to Congress's original offer of fifty acres of land to any foreigner who would leave the British service. But Jefferson's gubernatorial proclamation went even further: any foreigner who would desert would receive two cows, be exempt from taxes and militia duty throughout the war, and be compensated for any "arms or accoutrements" they might bring. Without seeking the approval of the General Assembly, Jefferson used this proclamation to both define the principles of the revolution as well as to counter the tactics of a military adversary.[38]

One of the best examples of Jefferson's using speech to strengthen the military efforts against Great Britain can be found in his "Proclamation Concerning Paroles." In this declaration, which Jefferson drafted carefully while his council was away, Jefferson addressed the British practice of granting paroles to ordinary citizens, and he chose words both to explain the logic of the Revolution as well to counter a British strategy. As Jefferson put it, the British would seize "peaceable citizens" and persuade them to sign a "parole" promising "that they will not on pain of life & fortune be aiding or assisting in any respect to the enemies of Great Britain." For the British, this was a way of disarming Virginians before they were drafted or became militia. For Jefferson, this presented a problem that went deeper than military strategy, as he suspected that some citizens would seek out such paroles "with the wicked designs while they enjoy all the benefits of Government to shift from themselves their just share of its burthens." To make sure that no citizen could proclaim "ignorance of the law either real or pretended," Jefferson issued a proclamation saying that the laws of Virginia prohibited citizens from entering into any "engagements" with a "public enemy" such that their duties to their country would be withdrawn.[39]

---

[37] "Report of a Plan to Invite Foreign Officers in the British Service to Desert." *PTJ*, 1:509–10, 4:506.
[38] "Proclamation Inviting Mercenary Troops in the British Service to Desert." *PTJ*, 4: 505–6.
[39] "Proclamation Concerning Paroles," *PTJ*, 4: 403–405; and H. R. McIlwaine, ed., *Journals of the Council of State of Virginia: Vol. II, October 6, 1777-November 30, 1781* (Richmond: Virginia State Library, 1932), 274–5.

By telling citizens what the laws expected Jefferson accomplished two objects. First, he answered British military strategy with his own: citizens who wanted to preserve the promise to the British, either out of self-interest or a "tender conscience" to an oath taken, would simply be given a "passport" allowing them to cross into the British encampments. By offering a "passport," Jefferson reminded citizens of the coercive power of the executive branch. More important, Jefferson used the proclamation to explain the details of democratic citizenship: having only recently separated from the British Empire, some Virginians did not understand the principles underlying independence. Put another way, Jefferson used the proclamation to tell citizens that they were "incapable by law of contracting engagements which may cancel or supercede the duties they owe to their country while remaining in it."[40] Although Jefferson himself was a lifelong advocate of the private sphere and its liberties, he used this proclamation to teach private-minded citizens the requirements of tacit consent and its obligations and outlined, as he would time and again, the duty of the good and zealous citizen.[41]

Proclamations were therefore doubly useful for Governor Jefferson. They provided the technical means by which he could accommodate emergencies and observe the Virginia Constitution, thus preserving legislative deference even as he carried out the executive duties beyond the competence of any legislative body. At the same time, such proclamations afforded him the chance to give meaning to the law by finding a principled basis for it. By subjecting executive discretion to the public will, the executive could help tell citizens what their public will required.

The Federal Constitution: Two Objections

The Constitution of 1787 and debates over its meaning provided Jefferson with the opportunity to find an institutional foothold for declarations of principle. On 1 November 1787, James Madison sent Jefferson a copy of the recently written Constitution along with "some observations on the subject."[42] Jefferson received Madison's letter in mid-December, and, on 20 December, he replied with his own "few words" on the document.[43] As

[40] Ibid.

[41] John Locke, *Second Treatise*, sections 119–120 in *John Locke: Two Treatises of Government*, student edition, ed. Peter Laslett (Cambridge: Cambridge University Press, 1988), 347–8. Jefferson did not need, as Mayer says, Madison to convince him of this doctrine. Mayer, *Constitutional Thought*, 307; Madison to Jefferson, 4 February 1790, *James Madison: Writings*, ed. Jack N. Rakove (New York: Library of America, 1999), 473–7.

[42] Madison to Jefferson, 24 October and 1 November 1787, *PTJ*, 12:270–86.

[43] Jefferson to Madison, 20 December 1787, *TJW*, 915.

Jefferson put it, he "like[d]" the separation of powers into three departments and the requirement that taxes be levied by the legislature, was "captivated" by the compromise between large and small states, and was "pleased" with the president's qualified veto. But there were provisions that Jefferson did not like – the "omission" of a bill of rights and the permanent eligibility of the president for reelection. Jefferson's two objections to the Constitution were circulated among his contemporaries and, eventually, satisfied: the Bill of Rights was ratified in 1791, and a two-term limit on the president became custom by 1808 and was made constitutional in 1951.[44] Although some scholars have considered each of Jefferson's objections or the reforms arising from Jefferson's criticism, scholars have not yet sufficiently explored whether the two arose out of a common concern with the Constitution.

The scholarly silence on the relationship between a bill of rights and a term limit, perhaps, grows out of a presumption that any connection would be Jefferson's fear of an energetic executive. In the same letter to Madison, the presumption would remind us, Jefferson confessed that he was "not a friend to a very energetic government" on the grounds that an energetic government was "always oppressive."[45] Protecting rights must have been a higher priority for Jefferson than limiting presidential tenure, for during his exchange with Madison, Jefferson conceded that he would abide by the majority's acquiescence to a lack of rotation in the presidential office, but he made no such compromise regarding a declaration of rights. From these undisputed facts the argument seems simple – who else but the chief executive, the highest law enforcement officer, would be the enemy of individual liberties, and what more dangerous executive than one who could rule for life?[46]

But such a conclusion would be only partly true, for Jefferson's prejudice against an executive for life was also based on the doubt that an executive elected numerous times could energetically enough carry out the laws. More precisely, Jefferson's early doctrine of presidential term limits grew out of his larger project to strengthen the presidency by more firmly connecting it to its popular foundations. For Jefferson, a term limit would provide a regular schedule for presidential declaration of principles in the form of an inaugural

---

44 Madison informed Jefferson that George Mason and Patrick Henry cited Jefferson' arguments in the Virginia Ratification debates. Madison to Jefferson, 24 July 1788, *PTJ*, 12: 412.

45 Jefferson to Madison, 20 December 1787, *TJW*, 916.

46 See, for example, Edward S. Corwin, *The President: Office and Powers, 1787–1957*, 4th ed. (New York: New York University Press, 1957), 35; Mayer, *Constitutional* Thought, 225; Adrienne Koch, *Jefferson and Madison: The Great Collaboration* (London: Oxford University Press, 1950), 41–42.

address. Taken together, a declaration of rights and a limit on presidential eligibility would both protect and direct the majority will.

The Argument against a Declaration of Rights

The call for a bill of rights met weighty opposition. The opponents of a bill of rights emphasized the difference between government under the Federal Constitution and government under a king. Under the signatory "Giles Hickory," Noah Webster argued that "declaratory constitutions" were meant to protect the people against powers which existed "independent of their own choice," not as "barriers against the encroachment of our Legislatures."[47] In the Pennsylvania debates over ratification, James Wilson argued that the Constitution's enumeration of powers rendered a bill of rights unnecessary – "every thing which is not given is reserved."[48] Most important, Hamilton argued in *The Federalist* No. 84 that bills of rights were "stipulations between kings and their subjects" and therefore, "according to their primitive signification," have "no application to constitutions, professedly founded upon the power of the people, and executed by their immediate representatives and servants."[49] Following Wilson, Hamilton added that a bill of rights would be redundant – since the people "surrender nothing," they have "no need of particular reservations." More than unnecessary, a declaration of rights would be "dangerous" in that they would be limited and therefore "afford a colorable pretext" for officials to claim more powers than were originally given. If the people would "declare that things shall not be done which there is no power to do," then a government might assume a power to do those things left unmentioned.

Hamilton meant to convince New Yorkers that declarations of principle would prove to be unreliable guarantees against the striving of human ambition. Just as "parchment barriers" could not be trusted to keep one department from encroaching upon another, "those aphorisms" could not be trusted to protect individual liberties and therefore would be more appropriate in "a treatise of ethics than in a constitution of government." Hamilton's disdain for declarations of principle is no more evident than in his final formulation of the argument: "The truth is, after all the declamations we have heard, that the Constitution is itself, in every rational sense, and to every

---

[47] Noah Webster, "On the Absurdity of a Bill of Rights," in *The Debate on the Constitution: Federalist and Antifederalist Speeches, Articles and Letters During the Struggle over Ratification*, ed. Bernard Bailyn (New York: Library of America, 1993), 1:670.
[48] James Wilson, "James Wilson's Speech at a Public Meeting," 6 October 1787, *Debate on the Constitution*, 1: 63–69.
[49] *The Federalist* No. 84, p. 549.

useful purpose, A BILL OF RIGHTS." Because the Constitution's partly federal and partly national distribution of power, along with its organization
of the three departments, would "abridge" the "prerogative" of government
"in favor" of the people's "privilege," there would be no practical difference between the Constitution and a bill of rights. The practical effect of
the Constitution would serve in the place of the declaratory reservation of
liberties to the people. More bluntly, the utility of a declaration had been
rendered obsolete by discoveries in the science of politics: representation,
legislative checks and balances, and an independent judiciary would protect
rights better than all the declarations in the world.[50]

Jefferson disagreed with the argument that a declaration of rights would
jeopardize those rights not specifically enumerated, but, originally, his friend
did not. When Madison wrote Jefferson in October, Madison commented on
the absence of a bill of rights only by reporting that George Mason had left
the convention in "ill humour" because Mason considered the "want of a
Bill of Rights as a fatal objection."[51] Madison also included in his letter a
version of the argument he would soon publish as the tenth essay of the
Federalist – that the principle of "divide et impera" under the "extended
republic," would solve the problem of majority faction. Jefferson passed
over his friend's discussion of the extended republic, but made it clear that
he did not agree with James Wilson's claim powers not specifically granted to
the government would be necessarily reserved by the people. As Jefferson put
it, "A bill of rights is what the people are entitled to against every government
on earth, general or particular, and what no government should refuse, or
rest on inference."[52]

Although he wrote Jefferson often, Madison did not acknowledge his
friend's call for a bill of rights until October 1788, when Madison shifted his
own position.[53] Here, Madison explained to Jefferson that he had always
favored a bill of rights but had never believed that "the omission" was a
material defect. He offered Jefferson four reasons:

1. To "a certain degree" (though not "in the extent" argued by Wilson),
   the rights are reserved because the corresponding powers are not
   granted to the federal government.
2. Since "some essential rights" (especially freedom of "Conscience")
   cannot be "obtained in the requisite latitude," the public is more likely
   to narrow these rights than the government.

[50] Ibid., 549, 551 and No. 9, p. 48.
[51] Madison to Jefferson, 24 October 1788, *PTJ*, 12:280.
[52] Jefferson to Madison, 20 December 1787, *PTJ*, 12: 440.
[53] Madison to Jefferson, 17 October 1788, *PTJ*, 14:16–22.

3. The national government is "limited" in its power, and the state governments will protect against encroachments.
4. Experience proves that "repeated violations" of declarations lessens their efficacy.

After arguing that a bill of rights would be unnecessary within a constitutional framework that would itself control the effects of majority faction, Madison went on to list two ways in which a bill of rights could be useful: first, making "maxims" of the truths of society might limit the influence of interest and passion; second, a bill of rights could provide the grounds for appeal against usurpations of rights by the government. In reply, Jefferson said that he was happy to learn that Madison was "on the whole" a "friend to this amendment," and, importantly, Jefferson confessed that some of Madison's points "had not occurred to me before, but were ackonleged just in the moment they were presented to my mind."[54] He could not, however, refrain answering each of Madison's objections:

1. Although a constitutive act may be "formed as to need no declaration of rights," the Constitution requires a "supplement" because it "leaves some precious articles unnoticed, and raises implications against others."
2. Although a declaration cannot "be obtained" in the "requisite latitude," a declaration should be written to protect what it could: "Half a loaf is better than no bread."
3. Although the powers of the national government are "limited," though the "jealously of the subordinate governments is a precious alliance," governments are "only agents" and therefore require a "text" against which the acts of government may be tried.
4. Although "experience proves the inefficacy of a bill of rights," a bill of rights would "rarely" be "inefficacious": "A brace the more will often keep up the building which would have fallen with that brace the less."

In answering Madison's third objection, Jefferson expanded Madison's utilitarian argument for a bill of rights. Madison had granted that "political truths declared in that solemn manner acquire by degrees the character of fundamental maxims of free Government" and that a declaration of rights could be used by a minority as "grounds for an appeal to the sense of the community" against a dangerous majority.[55] Jefferson agreed that a bill of

---

[54] Jefferson to Madison, 15 March 1789, *PTJ*, 14:659–63.
[55] Madison to Jefferson, 17 October 1788, *PTJ*, 14:20.

rights could serve as a "text" of principles by which the people could instruct their agents, that is, the departments of the state and national governments. Just as the argument from the educative function of a bill of rights was central to Madison's eventual advocacy of a bill of rights as a member of the House, it was critical to Jefferson's transformation of presidential speech.[56]

The Usefulness of Appeals to the Public

To clarify the point on which Madison and Jefferson finally agreed, however, the seriousness of their disagreement requires further consideration. When Madison sent his reply to Jefferson, Jefferson's ideas had been on his mind, for he had just written his own "Observations" on Jefferson's 1783 proposed constitution for Virginia.[57] Curiously, Madison wrote these observations *after* he had, in *The Federalist*, dismantled Jefferson's argument for frequent appeals to the public. In the forty-eighth essay of that work, Madison enlisted Jefferson's *Notes* to illustrate the tendency of legislatures to encroach on the other departments of government, referring to Jefferson as an "authority" (the only instance of that usage of the word in the entire work).[58] But after appealing to Jefferson's argument, Madison disparaged Jefferson's proposal that would have allowed for the Virginia Constitution to be altered in convention whenever two of the branches called for it by two-thirds of their number.[59] According to Madison, rather than protecting the departments of government from each other, these "frequent appeals" to the people would undermine the stability of the Constitution and perhaps seriously upset public tranquility by multiplying experiments so "ticklish" in nature. Having removed the authority who was also the author of the Declaration, Madison was then free to write, famously, that the only way to maintain "in practice" the partitions between the departments was to contrive the "interior structure of government" such that the departments would keep each other in their proper places.[60]

According to Jefferson, Madison's 17 October letter arrived in late February, taking longer than normal to arrive in France.[61] In the meantime,

---

[56] For a study of Madison's advocacy of the Bill of Rights, see Robert A. Goldwin, *From Parchment to Power: How James Madison Used the Bill of Rights to Save the Constitution* (Washington, DC: AEI Press, 1997), 93–95.

[57] Madison, "Observations on the 'Draught of a Constitution for Virginia'," *James Madison: Writings*, ed. Jack N. Rakove (New York: Library of America, 1999), 409–418. Rakove dates this document at October 15, but others have left it simply at October. See Boyd's notes in *PTJ*, 6:316.

[58] *The Federalist* No. 48, p. 318.

[59] *The Federalist* No. 49, pp. 321–6.

[60] *The Federalist* No. 51, p. 330.

[61] Jefferson to Madison, 15 March 1789, *PTJ*, 14:659.

Jefferson had received, from Madison, the second volume of *The Federalist*, which contained Madison's criticism of Jefferson's *Notes*. It would therefore not be too wide a speculation to suppose that Jefferson had, by then, read Madison's criticisms of his argument in the *Notes*. (We also might wonder whether Madison also sent along his recent critique of Jefferson's 1783 proposed constitution for Virginia.) And although Jefferson had by that time already considered his *Notes* flawed and might not have then recommended a frequent recourse to constitutional convention to solve legislative encroachment, it is plausible that Madison's argument in *The Federalist* was on his mind when he sent his reply to Madison.

In his letter, Jefferson argued that declarations of principle were necessary because "governments are only agents," that is, governments "must have principles furnished them."[62] Whereas Madison had written of the way that the extended republic would dilute the danger of majority factions and how the constitutional structure would connect the human interest of the officeholder to the constitutional rights of the office, Jefferson argued that free governments, no matter how perfectly arranged, needed to be motivated by a set of declared principles. Because republics lack an implied governing principle such as honor or fear (what Montesquieu called a "spring"[63]), they needed to declare the principles by which they govern.

The reason why governments, even republics, needed principles furnished them is that the laws must change, both in order to cope with the extraordinary occasions in political life and to remain current with human progress. More than a project to secure rights, Jefferson's defense of a declaration of rights was based on a particular understanding of the law's capacity to meet the demands of necessity. Jefferson's mistrust partly grew out of his reading of the Constitution itself, especially the provision for the suspension of habeas corpus, and, in December 1787, he pointed to "strong inferences from the body of the instrument" which suggested that the suspension of habeas corpus would, in practice, amount to a denial of the right of trial by jury.[64] In July 1788, Jefferson revisited his objection to the provision for suspending habeas corpus by arguing that even though emergencies require

[62] Jefferson to Madison, 15 March 1789, *PTJ*, 14:660. My suggestion that Jefferson was replying to Madison's argument in *The Federalist* would explain why Jefferson announced without transition that "The executive in our governments is not the sole, it is scarcely the principal object of my jealousy." This statement might also have something to do with the date of this letter, as Hamilton had offered his praise of Roman dictators on 15 March of the preceding year.

[63] Montesquieu, *The Sprit of the Laws*, Anne M. Cohler, Basia Carolyn Miller and Harold Samuel Stone trans. and ed. (Cambridge: Cambridge University Press, 1989), 22.

[64] Jefferson to Madison, 20 December 1787, *PTJ*, 12:440.

the government to act swiftly, the Constitution without a bill of rights tacitly encouraged government officials to manufacture emergencies in order to
suspend habeas corpus; without a declaration affirming the people's rights,
suspensions of the right would be frequent, and "the minds of the nation
almost prepared to live under it's constant suspension."[65]

Jefferson's complaint against the provision for the suspension of habeas
corpus did not grow out of an unwillingness to recognize the dangers of
rebellion or invasion. Rather, Jefferson shared Madison's assumption that
emergencies would require special powers by the government. Under Jefferson's plan, even though a jury trial and habeas corpus would be guaranteed
by a declaration of rights, the accused could be arrested "on less probable
testimony" during times of necessity, even if that meant that the accused be
"taken and tried, retaken and retried, while the necessity continues" and
that those falsely accused be allowed "redress against the government for
damages."[66] Suspected insurrectionists or spies could be arrested without
sufficient evidence – and arrested again and again – but not held without a
trial.

The point here is that the difference between the two Virginians over
the necessity of a declaration of rights grew out of their separate solutions
to the difficulties incident to the law's imperfect stance with respect to the
future. The question of the usefulness of a declaration turned on the question whether such a document would be binding once discarded during an
emergency. According to Madison, declarations were only barriers on paper
and were therefore useless in practice: a declaration alone would not protect
minorities against willful majorities because it could never hold up against
"the decided sense of the public." And, for Madison, laws that can be pushed
aside during an emergency would eventually lose their efficacy and therefore
"ought to be avoided."[67] Jefferson, however, disagreed with Madison's use of
the premise that laws should be able to sustain, if not predict, future emergency to conclude that a declaration of rights would insufficiently secure
liberties. Jefferson offered his own solution in the context of his argument
against the Constitution's provision for the suspension of habeas corpus:
"My idea then is, that tho' proper exceptions to these general rules are desirable and probably practical, yet if the exceptions cannot be agreed on, the
establishment of the rules in all cases will do ill in very few. I hope therefore a bill of rights will be formed to guard the people against the federal
government, as they are already guarded against their state governments in

[65] Jefferson to Madison, 31 July 1788, *PTJ*, 13: 443.
[66] Ibid.
[67] Madison to Jefferson, 17 October 1788, *PTJ*, 14:20.

most instances."[68] In place of "exceptions," built into the law because of the law's incompleteness with regard to the future, Jefferson offered declarations, which point the law and its executors toward its most fundamental principles. Like habeas corpus, rights may be denied in fact if not in word during emergencies, but the acknowledgement of those rights in a declaration would help ensure that meeting necessities would not replace securing rights as the end of the Constitution. Jefferson's reliance on declarations of principle to solve the problem of contingency and the law was a crucial component of his democratization of the executive power. As Jefferson explained after he became president, even though such declarations can and would in fact be violated "in moments of passion or delusion," they would furnish a text to which the most "watchful" could appeal in order to lead the public. More simply, declarations were like constitutions in that they would "fix too for the people the principles of their political creed."[69]

Jefferson's position, then, involved more than a calculation that protecting some rights was better than protecting none, for it carried within it a faith in the power of declarations. Jefferson surely found evidence for such faith by his experience in Paris, where he lived and worked around people writing declarations. To Madison, he reported, "Every body here is trying their hands at forming declarations of rights," and he sent copies of declarations written by Lafayette and his physician, Richard Gem.[70] But he was more than a spectator in what he at one time praised as a bloodless revolution by public opinion.[71] Jefferson had, in fact, conferred with Lafayette in drafting Lafayette's declaration, and Lafayette was instrumental in writing the document approved by the French National Assembly that August, "The Declaration of the Rights of Man and the Citizen." According to the preamble of that document, the "representatives of the French people . . . resolved to set forth in a solemn declaration the natural, inalienable, and sacred rights of man."[72] Significantly, the preamble went on to state three reasons for setting

---

[68] Jefferson to Madison, 31 July 1788, *PTJ*, 13:443.

[69] Jefferson to Joseph Priestley, 19 June 1802, Washington, 4:441.

[70] Jefferson to Madison, 12 January 1789, *PTJ*, 14:437.

[71] "The change is this country, since you left it, is such as you can form no idea of. The frivolities of conversation have given way entirely to politicks – men, women, and children talk nothing else: and all you know talk a great deal. The press groans with daily productions, which in point of boldness make an Englishman stare, who hitherto has thought himself the boldest of men. A complete revolution in this government has, within the space of two years (for it began with the Notables of 1787) been effected merely by the force of public opinion, aided indeed by the want of money which the dissipations of the court had brought on. And this revolution has not cost a single life." Jefferson to David Humphreys, 18 March 1789, *PTJ*, 14:676.

[72] "Declaration of the Rights of Man and the Citizen," *The Portable Enlightenment Reader*, ed. Isaac Kramnick (New York: Penguin, 1995), 466–7.

forth these rights in the form of a declaration: first, "continually before all members of the social body," the declaration would be a "perpetual reminder" of rights and duties; second, the declaration would present "the aim of every political institution" and thereby serve as standard by which the acts the legislative and executive powers could be compared; third, the declaration would enable citizens to use its "simple and uncontested principles" to direct their "demands." As Dumas Malone concluded from other phrases in the French document, it is likely that Jefferson spoke "through the mouth of his intimate young friend Lafayette."[73] In a speech honoring Lafayette's 1824 visit to Charlottesville, Jefferson praised Lafayette's role in the "cause" of revolutionary France: "In truth, I only held the nail, he drove it."[74] He would have been more accurate to have added that the method of hammering was his.

The Second Objection: Presidential Reeligibility

Although Jefferson claimed that discussion and reflection changed his mind regarding several of his early objections to the Constitution, he found nothing persuasive enough to concede his point against the reeligibility of the president. In Jefferson's estimation, a president who was allowed by the constitution to be reelected would become an officer for life, making the president a "bad edition of a Polish King."[75] Jefferson's concern over the permanent eligibility of the office derived not simply from a suspicion of foreign intrigue but also from his premonitions about popularly elected executives.[76] As he put it, "Experience concurs with reason in concluding that the

---

73 Malone, 2: 224–5. In 1787, Jefferson wrote Madison that Lafayette could "comprehend perfectly whatever is explained to him" and that the Frenchman's "agency has been very efficacious," Jefferson to Madison, 1787, Washington, 2:108.

74 Jefferson, "Speech on Lafayette," October, 1824, *The Complete Jefferson: Containing His Major Writings, Published and Unpublished, Except his Letters*, ed. Saul K. Padover (New York: Duell, Sloan & Pearce, 1944), 448.

75 Jefferson to John Adams, 13 November 1787, *PTJ*, 12: 351.

76 Under the Polish system of government, voters could elect their monarch, and in practice, Polish voters routinely selected, perhaps through corruption, foreign monarchs over one of their own. Jefferson had probably read Rousseau's "Considerations on the Government of Poland," which argued that the "Nation's Chief" would become its "foremost citizen" rather than its "born enemy" if the constitution would deny eligibility to foreigners and a sitting king's sons. In a puzzling aside, Rosseau writes, "To state my sentiment on this subject in a word, I think than an elective Crown even with absolute power would be preferable for Poland to a hereditary crown with almost no power." Jean Jacques Rousseau, "Considerations on the Government in Poland," in *The Social Contract and Other Late Political Writings*. Victor Gourevitch, trans. and ed. (New York: Cambridge University Press, 1997), 214. Because the U.S. Constitution required that a president be a natural born citizen,

first magistrate will always be re-elected if the Constitution permits it."[77] Jefferson feared a permanently eligible executive because he understood that the people would come to love their presidents.

That other Americans did not follow Jefferson in his fears that the president's permanent eligibility would invite foreign intrigue presented a problem for the advocate of majority will. Indeed, to others, Jefferson confessed astonishment at the fact that, even though so many objected to the absence of a declaration of rights, the eligibility of the president had "scarcely excited an objection in America,"[78] and, to Madison the ambassador to France reflected on whether his objection was misplaced if he was alone in making it – "I readily suppose my opinion wrong, when opposed by the majority," or, as in this case, the "totality."[79] Although Jefferson did acquiesce to the majority's silence on this point, he nevertheless tried to convince others of his argument and later took pleasure in the fact that three states eventually reconsidered the provision.[80]

The key to understanding Jefferson's objection to reeligibility is his assumption that a president who sought reelection would always succeed. Indeed, it might be surprising that the later architect of the Revolution of 1800 lacked Hamilton's faith that regular elections would protect against the dangers of a lifetime executive.[81] More directly, why would the author of the Declaration believe that leaving voters the option of rewarding a president with another term was dangerous? One source for Jefferson's fear was his suspicion of power: "Of the correction of this article however I entertain no present hope, because I find it has scarcely excited an objection in America. And if it does not take place ere long, it assuredly never will. The natural progress of things is for liberty to yield, and government to gain ground. And yet our spirits are free."[82] But this does not adequately answer the question. If Jefferson believed that the people would be able to choose the president,

---

Jefferson's analogy to the Polish king reflected not a fear that foreigners would be elected but that the European powers would try to install an American president on the basis of his expected foreign policy: "It will be of great consequence to France and England to have America governed by a Galloman or Angloman." Jefferson to John Adams, 13 November 1787, *PTJ*, 12:351.

77 Jefferson to Madison, 20 December 1787, *PTJ*, 12:440.
78 Jefferson to Edward Carrington, 27 May 1788, *PTJ*, 13:208–9.
79 Jefferson to Madison, 31 July 1788, *PTJ*, 13:443.
80 Jefferson to James Monroe, 9 August 1788, *PTJ*, 13:488–90; Jefferson to William Short, 20 September 1788, *PTJ*, 13:619–21; Jefferson to Madison, 18 November 1788, *PTJ*, 14:187–90; Jefferson to Humphreys, *PTJ*, 14: 676–9.
81 *The Federalist* No. 72, pp. 463–8.
82 Jefferson to Carrington, *PTJ*, 13:208–9.

why did he also believe that the liberty would "yield" because of the fact that a sitting president would always be eligible for reelection?[83]

The clue is Jefferson's ambivalent stance toward Washington. On the one hand, Jefferson then counted himself among those who believed that Washington's stature was necessary to give the new government strength. In March 1789, for instance, Jefferson confided to David Humphreys that even if the majority did come to agree with him that the president should not be eligible for reelection: "I would wish it to remain uncorrected as long as we can avail ourselves of the services of our great leader, whose talents and whose weight of character I consider as peculiarly necessary to get the government so under way as that it may afterwards be carried on by subordinate characters."[84] In other words, the situation was so dire and the strength of Washington so great that Jefferson was willing to temporarily set aside his fears of a permanent executive. But, on the other hand, Jefferson's faith in Washington's ability "to get the government under way" carried within it a doubt about the safety of Washington's greatness. Even in 1788, before the bank bill and the Neutrality Proclamation, Jefferson contemplated the consequences of Washington on the presidency. To William Carmichael, Jefferson predicted that the perpetual eligibility of the president would not be "cured" while Washington was alive, as Washington's "merit" had "blinded our countrymen to the dangers of making so important an officer reeligible."[85] Jefferson confided similar fears to Edward Carrington: "Our jealousy is only put to sleep by the unlimited confidence we all repose in the person to whom we all look as our president. After him inferior characters may perhaps succeed and awaken us to the danger which his merit has led us into."[86] Washington's greatness, then, was a lullaby that quieted the reality that Washington's successors would not be a great as he.

Jefferson's language indicates that the dilemma caused by Washington's greatness reminded him of Locke's discussion of the "God-like prince." According to Locke, princes who use executive prerogative to promote the public good often inspire the affections of the people.[87] The problem is that such princes are followed by "weak and ill" princes who use executive prerogative for private benefit and thus incite the people to revolution. More

---

[83] To a foreign observer, Jefferson explained that people "choose" their executive since they are themselves not qualified to exercise the office. Jefferson to L'Abbe Arnoux, 19 July 1789, *PTJ*, 15:283.

[84] Jefferson to Humphreys, *PTJ*, 14:676–9.

[85] Jefferson to Carmichael, 12 August 1788, *PTJ*, 13:502.

[86] Jefferson to Carrington, *PTJ*, 13:208–9. Boyd notes that Jefferson had originally written, "inferior characters will succeed."

[87] John Locke, *Second Treatise*, sections 164–6, in *Two Treatises* (see note 44), 377–8.

precisely, Locke left his readers to wonder as to the extent the God-like prince is to blame for cultivating the very trust in the people in which his less trust-worthy successors thrive. If Jefferson was dishonest in his remark to Madison that he was wrong about eligibility because the majority was always right, it was because he sensed a connection between the president and the majority because of the president's peculiar mode of election, a connection amplified by the stature of the man who would first occupy the office. Put differently, if Madison discovered that the extended republic would ensure that majority factions would be too weak to be destructive, Jefferson perceived that a kind of majority would nevertheless gather around the president. It was with this majority in mind that Jefferson planned, in 1791, to "establish principles and examples" which would guard against abuses by Washington's less godlike successors even while he himself was Washington's Secretary of State – hence Jefferson's opposition to Washington's levees and birthday celebrations.[88]

One principle Jefferson had in mind was a term limit for presidents. Jefferson's later decision to seek a second term did not symbolize a retreat from his belief that a president should serve only a single term, for Jefferson had long believed that a single seven year term and two four year terms were practically the same, because presidents seeking reelection would be successful more often than not.[89] As Jefferson wrote in January 1805 of his own decision to seek a second term: "My opinion originally was that the President of the U.S. should have been elected for 7. years, & forever ineligible afterwards. I have long since become sensible that 7. years is too long to be irremovable, and that there should be a peaceable way of withdrawing a man in midway who is doing wrong. The service for 8. years, with a power to remove at the end of the first four, comes nearly to my principle as corrected by experience. And it is in adherence to that that I determined to withdraw at the end of my second term."[90] Written to John Taylor, a principal player in the proposal of the Twelfth Amendment, the statement above reveals Jefferson's continuing project to connect presidential power and political change. Rather than saying that he had been persuaded by Washington's example,

---

[88] Jefferson to Harry Innes, 13 March 1791, Ford, 5: 300. Also, as Vice-President, Jefferson argued that Washington's ceremonial inaugural should not be used as a model because Washington's was more properly the inauguration of the government, not merely a president. Jefferson to Henry Tazewell, 16 January 1797, *PTJ* 29:267.

[89] Leonard D. White, *The Jeffersonians: A Study in Administrative History, 1801–1829* (New York: Macmillan, 1951), 30. For Jefferson's favoring Luther Martin's report that the convention nearly approved a single seven-year term, see Jefferson to William Short, 20 September 1788, *PTJ*, 13:619–21. See also Jefferson to Madison, 20 December 1787, *PTJ*, 12:441.

[90] Jefferson to John Taylor, 6 January 1805, *TJW*, 1153–4.

Jefferson said that the two-term administration reflected his own preference for a single term as modified by practice. The eight-year term is essentially the same as the seven-year term as a sitting president is likely to be reelected, and the election after four years reflects not so much an election but an opportunity to remove an objectionable president.

Jefferson saw the election between terms as a chance to remove a president who was "doing wrong" because he believed that a president's second term would be seen as a continuance of the first. A particularly weak or corrupt president would lose or choose not to seek reelection, while a satisfactory president would win reelection on the execution of the principles of his first administration. Jefferson's description of his rhetorical objective for his inaugural addresses confirms this point: the first was "promise" and the second "performance."[91]

Later, Washington's decision to retire after two terms provided an example to which Jefferson could appeal in order to finally convince Americans that a president should not be perpetually eligible for office. In 1805, Jefferson considered announcing his retirement in the Second Inaugural but was persuaded otherwise by his friends, on the grounds it would be best "not to put a continuance out of my power in defiance of all circumstances."[92] In line with this advice to make "no formal declaration to the public of [his] purpose," Jefferson "freely let" his intent to retire "be understood in private conversation." In December 1807, Jefferson did announce his retirement, and, significantly, he explained his retirement in terms of the presidential office, not his longing for private life. He did so in a reply to the legislature of Vermont, which had urged him thirteen months earlier to seek a third term. In his reply, Jefferson explained that he did not reply to their address in order to avoid "a premature agitation of the public mind."[93] After this apology, Jefferson explained that he "should lay down" his "charge" in order to protect a principle of representative government, "short periods of election." "If some termination to the services of the chief magistrate be not fixed by the constitution, or supplied by practice, his office, nominally for years, will, in fact, become for life; and history shows how easily that turns into an inheritance." To support the term limit in practice, Jefferson invoked Washington. But even though "the sound precedent set by an illustrious predecessor" might have provided sufficient reason for refusing the third term, Jefferson added physical and mental decline as a reason for retiring: "Happy

---

91 Jefferson, Notes of a Draft for a Second Inaugural Address, *TJW*, 1555.
92 Jefferson to Taylor, *TJW*, 1153–4.
93 Jefferson to the Legislature of Vermont, 10 December 1807, *Complete Jefferson*, ed. Padover, 524–5.

if I am the first person to perceive and obey this admonition of nature, and to solicit a retreat from cares too great for the wearied faculties of age."[94] And, "I am sensible of that decline which the advancing years bring on; and feeling their physical, I ought not to doubt their mental effect."[95] With this explanation linking together rotation of office, Washington, and old age, Jefferson announced his retirement.

Jefferson's unflattering portrayal of Washington and other executives suggests that his project to institute a term limit grew out of a concern other than fear that permanently eligible presidents would become tyrannical presidents. The term limit would not only protect against a lifetime president but would also energize the office, as every eighth year could be expected to bring with it a first inaugural, in which the incoming president would take office with his own promise, that is, his own "exposition of the principles" by which he would administer the government.[96] In place, perhaps, of a constitutional convention every generation, there would be a first inaugural every eight years. Paradoxically, the consequence of a president being reelected for life would be weakness not strength: "The danger is that the indulgence & attachments of the people will keep a man in the chair after he becomes a dotard, that reelection through life shall become habitual, & election for life follow that. General Washington set the example of voluntary retirement after 8. years. I shall follow it, and a few more precedents will oppose the obstacle of habit to any one after awhile who shall endeavor too extend his term. Perhaps it may beget a disposition to establish it by an amendment of the Constitution. I believe I am doing right, therefore, in pursuing my principle."[97] Jefferson's insistence that he was right to follow *his* principle is important, for it reveals his efforts to show like-minded republicans that republican principle would be better served by his own stepping down. Because the republican principle required that the majority will be executed, it was necessary to have a president energetic enough to carry out the majority will without muting it by his own popularity. Lifetime tenure is conceivable not because the president will abuse the trust of the people

---

94 See the following responses from *Complete Jefferson*, ed. Padover, 524–528: Jefferson to the Representatives of the People of New Jersey in Their Legislature, 10 December 1807; Jefferson to Messrs Abner Watkins and Bernard Todd, 21 December 1807; and Jefferson to the General Assembly of North Carolina, 10 January 1808. The reason for his initial delay and writing six state legislatures on a single day was surely to allow his party to agree on his successor, but he seized the opportunity to shape Washington's decision into a precedent and ensure that a first inaugural address be given at least every eight years.

95 Jefferson to the General Assembly of North Carolina, 10 January 1808, *Complete Jefferson*, ed. Padover, 529.

96 Ibid.

97 Jefferson to Taylor, *TJW*, 1153.

and retain power but because the people come to be attached to a sitting president and keep reelecting him.

As he characterized it, the consequences of permanent eligibility are senility and apathy. The people's affection for a dotard undermines the existential reason for the executive power in that the executive is meant to be the swift and sometimes terrifying agent of the law. In 1789, Jefferson credited England's decline to the "palsied state" of its executive.[98] The problem would be worse in electoral systems because the people cherish and reelect the aged president partly because, under a moderate and republican government, they might forget the fact that he holds the sword. When wielding the sword is necessary, such a president would fail the people who came to love him because he was safe, or as Jefferson said in 1812, when demurring from a request to return to the presidency, "I was sincere in stating age as one of the reasons of my retirement from office, beginning then to be conscious of its effects, and now much more sensitive of them. Servile inertness is not what is to save our country; the conduct of war requires the vigor and enterprise of younger heads."[99] Even Washington's ability diminished with his time in office, for, as Jefferson saw it, Washington's favoring Hamilton was a result of Washington's mind and body not his heart: although Washington was thoroughly republican in conviction, he had been entangled in the "snares and artifices" laid by others, partly because "age had already begun to relax the firmness of his purposes."[100] In addition to age, Washington's decline was a consequence of his electoral success: to Archibald Stuart, Jefferson wrote of the first president, "His mind had been so long used to unlimited applause that it could not brook contradiction."[101] The consequence of a permanent eligibility would be an executive debilitated by age and numbed by the quadrennial approval of voters.

If the office could become a refuge for dotards, it could also court the ambitions of would-be tyrants. After a Washington might come a Burr, and the latter would possess the power, although not the stature, of the former. Just as the people's affections allow them to continue good presidents even after they had been rendered incompetent by age, their attachments to good presidents would be transferred to the office itself.

Put differently, the office would find strength in the weakness of its once strong occupants. This dilemma of popular leadership explains Jefferson's

---

[98] Jefferson to Humphreys, *PTJ*, 14:677.

[99] Jefferson to Thomas Flourney, 1 October 1812, *Writings of Jefferson*, ed. Washington, 6:82–3.

[100] Jefferson to Madison, 26 November 1795, *PTJ*, 28:539–40; Jefferson to Dr. Walter Jones, 2 January 1814, Ford, 9: 449.

[101] Jefferson to Archibald Stuart, 4 January 1797, *PTJ*, 29:252–3.

peculiar confession to Madison in 1789: "The executive in our governments is not the sole, it is scarcely the principal object of my jealousy. The tyranny of the legislatures is the most formidable dread at present, and will be for long years. That of the executive will come in it's turn, but it will be at a remote period. I know there are some among us who would now establish a monarchy. But they are inconsiderable in number and weight of character. The rising race are all republicans. We were educated in royalism: no wonder if some of us retain that idolatry still. Our young people are educated in republicanism. An apostasy from that to royalism is unprecedented and impossible."[102] In this statement, Jefferson predicted two things: first, some sort of executive tyranny would come, and second, the monarchical principal would lose significance because future generations would be republican. Taken together, the predictions imply that something about republican governance makes executive tyranny more likely. More precisely, they suggest that the tyranny of the executive would come at a time when the people had been so republicanized that they had forgotten about monarchy.

Significantly, this extraordinary passage occurs in the middle of Jefferson's argument that the new Constitution should include a declaration of rights, right after he proclaimed, "The inconveniences of the want of a Declaration are permanent, afflicting & irreparable." A declaration of rights and a term limit were necessary to direct, and therefore tame, a popular president. In summary, the new office of the president is dangerous because of its power, but not all of its power lies in the fact that it is the chief executive. This executive is peculiarly democratic and therefore finds some of its power in its democratic sources. Consequently, government by majority rule adds to executive power a dimension previously unavailable to kings.

The Return to the United States

When Jefferson returned to Virginia he was met by an escalating political problem. From Madison, he learned that Washington had asked him to join his administration as the nation's first Secretary of State. That Madison was Washington's emissary suggests that even Washington feared that the author of the Declaration would coolly turn down the appointment and ask to return to Paris. A refusal by Jefferson would be particularly harmful to the new government, not only because Jefferson was an important political figure but also because Patrick Henry had by then called for a second ratifying convention so that Virginia might reconsider its ties with the national government. Madison, it seems, especially worried that Jefferson would refuse

[102] Jefferson to Madison, 15 March 1789, *PTJ*, 14:661.

Washington's nomination, and it is plausible that Madison enlisted other Virginians to persuade Jefferson to accept the position. Thus, as Julian Boyd concludes, the welcome address by the citizens of Albemarle – which was signed by James Monroe, John Breckinridge, Wilson Carey Nicholas, and others – should be seen as part of Madison's larger campaign of persuasion.[103]

In its form, the address by the citizens of Albemarle was both a formal statement of welcome to one of the county's favorite sons but also an endorsement of Jefferson's conduct in the past. Although the signers of the welcome did not list every one of Jefferson's accomplishments and services, they were "particularly happy to observe, the strong attachment you [Jefferson] have always shewn to the rights of mankind, and to those institutions[s] that were best calculated to preserve them." But, although they would always approve of Jefferson's devotion to securing rights, they wrote in order to ask Jefferson to accept Washington's nomination.[104] Given the stakes of his decision to work under Washington, Jefferson viewed his reply to the citizens of Albemarle an opportunity to not only align himself with the fledgling government and Washington's administration but to shape the definition of democratic government. Jefferson received the welcome on 16 January 1790, but postponed the formal reception of the welcome for more than three weeks so that he could respond with a proper reply, and the existing copy of Jefferson's response reveals that he altered the text several times in the three weeks before delivery on 12 February.[105]

The immediate political ambition of Jefferson's reply can be discerned only by comparing it to an earlier draft. In the original, Jefferson recommended that he and his neighbors join the union because separation would be more harmful than imperfect union: "Let us never forget, my friends, that while we go together, even were it to be in error, we are safe and may return again to the right way: but that if we separate for a moment, we are undone. Let us then one and all lay our hands to the machine of government which we have erected for ourselves, and if we find, after due trial, that it does not work well, we will join in concord with our brethren of the whole union to amend the defects which time and trial shall have pointed out. The liberality with which you are pleased to approve the attachment of an individual to the general rights of mankind assures your approbation of this it's kindred sentiment."[106] In this form, Jefferson's reply implied that the

[103] *PTJ*, 16:171, 178.
[104] Address of Welcome by the Citizens of Albemarle and Jefferson's Response, *PTJ*, 16:177–8.
[105] See Boyd's notes, *PTJ*, 16:173.
[106] Address of Welcome by the Citizens of Albemarle and Jefferson's Response *PTJ*, 16:173–4.

general government was possibly flawed, yet at the same time emphasized that the benefits of union should trump attempts to remain separated because of objections to the particular form of union. Furthermore, it recommended union as a means by which the general government could be improved. But Jefferson changed his address from appealing to the local concerns of Albemarle County to a defense of the rightfulness of majority rule, universal in its applications.[107] Boyd writes that the "drastic dislocation in the center of a formal response" suggests that some occasion prompted Jefferson to revise his response, and he points to Jefferson's reading *Decius's Letters*, an attack on Patrick Henry written by Wilson Carey Nicholas. In this work, Nicholas criticized Henry's recommendations that Virginia reevaluate its relationship with the general government, warned against separation, and labeled Henry a dangerous demagogue – all characteristics of Jefferson's original draft. Boyd conjectures that Jefferson had written his first draft before having read *Decius's Letters*, and then, upon reading *Decius* and receiving Washington's request to join his administration, he "paused for reflection." Rather than addressing the immediate dangers represented by Henry, the response, for Jefferson, called for something more permanent.

Freed from the dilemma of Henry, the new section was the central passage in which Jefferson wrote what Dumas Malone later considered the best summation of the "philosophy by which his [Jefferson's] feet were guided":

It rests now with ourselves alone to enjoy in peace and concord the blessings of self-government, so long denied to mankind: to shew by example the sufficiency of human reason for the care of human affairs and that the will of the majority, the Natural law of every society, is the only sure guardian of the rights of man. Perhaps even this may sometimes err. But it's errors are honest, solitary, and short lived. – Let us then, my dear friends, forever bow down to the general reason of the society. We are safe with that, even in it's deviations, for it soon returns again to the right way. These are lessons we have learnt together. We have prospered in their practice, and the liberality with which you are pleased to approve my attachment to the general rights of mankind assures we are still together in these it's kindred sentiments.[108]

In this statement, replacing the praise of union over imperfection, Jefferson offered one of his many defenses of majority rule and the belief that that the conduct of the citizens of Albemarle was in some way a test for the universal applicability of republican government. That is, the passage on the Constitution's difficulties was replaced with a reflection on republican difficulties. Taken together, the two passages show Jefferson's concern over the relationship between the law and the people. Here, it should be noted, Jefferson

---

[107] Ibid.
[108] Address of Welcome by the Citizens of Albemarle and Jefferson's Response, *PTJ*, 16:179.

opened the possibility that majority rule is flawed in that the majority will can sometimes err but recommended the majority will as the surest guardian of rights on the basis that the majority will always returns to truth after its error. What this passed over, however, is the question whether the majority will returns by its own accord to the "right way" or whether it must be guided there. As Washington's Secretary of State, not himself holder of the executive power, Jefferson could pose the question without answering it. In his First Inaugural, Jefferson would again take up this question, and would suggest that the majority needed to be guided.

Declarations and the Constitution

Because of the problem of necessity and the law, declarations are intimately connected with executive power. Like *the* Declaration, the Bill of Rights serves as a standard by which the president's actions can be judged, loosening the tension between the president's job to execute the laws and his job as the people's officer. Furthermore, as the list of grievances against George III in Jefferson's constitution for Virginia indicates, a statement of principles such as the Bill of Rights can be used to judge an executive's weakness as well as his strength. Securing rights, after all, requires that the government be energetic enough.

It is Jefferson's belief in declarations of principle, rather than his assertion states' rights, that reveals how radical the Kentucky Resolutions really were. Because the Alien and Sedition Acts were, for Jefferson, obvious violations of other liberties, they confirmed his previous warnings of the danger of implied powers. But, as suggested by the repeated formulation that the Alien and Sedition Acts violated the "general principle" and "express declaration" of reserved powers, the Kentucky Resolutions must have been about defending the usefulness of declarations, such as that in the First and Tenth Amendments, as much as they were about the rights declared protected in them. If the "general clauses" of the Constitution conferred the government the power to transcend the protections declared in the Bill of Rights, the people would have little chance of determining exactly what their rights were. Jefferson must have believed that it was then the time to test whether a bill of rights would be useless in practice or whether it could be used to prick the people into opposition.[109]

---

[109] Interpretations of the Resolutions as "party propaganda" do not quite get this point. See, for example, Stanley Elkins and Eric McKitrick, *The Age of Federalism* (New York: Oxford University Press, 1993), 721.

There is therefore a bit of irony in the fact that the Resolutions were clearly meant to sway public opinion to the Republican opposition. In obvious rhetorical excess, they denigrated public opinion when they proclaimed that "confidence is everywhere the parent of despotism" and "free government is founded in jealousy, and not in confidence." Although there was a Jeffersonian ring to the praise of jealousy and the criticism of confidence, it contradicted Jefferson's larger attempt to connect executive power with the public's opinion. Even in 1784, as a delegate to the Congress under the Articles, Jefferson had attempted to strengthen the executive in order to ensure the "confidence" of the Union. As president, he often defended his actions on the grounds that he spoke for the national will, that is, that his extraordinary actions were meant to unify the presidency in the confidence – not the jealousy – of the people.

But declarations can take other forms, and no officer can more conveniently, or more authoritatively, offer them as the president. Recall that Jefferson advised Republicans to silence their scruples over the Neutrality Proclamation when Hamilton urged Washington to denounce Republicans in an appeal to the public. Implicit in both Hamilton's and Jefferson's advice is that an extraordinary act of executive power – crushing the opposition – would find support in the appeal to the people. Thus, of the French Declaration of Rights, Jefferson suggested that the king's authority could be harnessed in the service of limiting the king's powers: "all this shall be fixed by a convention so solemn as that his successor shall not be free to infringe it, that is that he will concur in a Declaration of rights."[110] When he himself became president, Jefferson used the Election of 1800 to transform the inaugural address from a procedural formality to a regular announcement of the will of the nation. And, as Chapter 9 shows, Jefferson used the various forms of presidential speech – the annual address, the special message to Congress, the presidential proclamation, the open letter, and the reply to address – to report and defend the executive privilege taken by himself and others while at the same time subjecting that privilege to public judgment, to shape the electorate's constitutional understanding, and to defend partisan policies. For Jefferson, a declaration of principle would limit executive power even as it presupposed it.

[110] Jefferson to Adams, 14 January 1789, Cappon, 236.

5

The Real Revolution of 1800

Jefferson's Transformation of the Inaugural Address

Of his own election in 1800, Thomas Jefferson famously said, it "was as real a revolution in the principles of our government as that of 1776 was in its form."[1] By this interpretation, the partisan contest of 1800 was the culmination of the disputes of the 1790s in that it was as much a contest over the meaning of the new Constitution as a fight over who would rule. When, as he put it, the "mighty wave of public opinion" had rolled, Jefferson's Republican Party was proven to be the people's party, just as the Revolution of 1776 had declared the people's opposition to England's form of government.[2] "The nation declared its will by dismissing functionaries of one principle, and electing those of another."[3] As certain as he was that there were two parties in nature, and that one party was for the people and the other against the people, Jefferson believed the Revolution of 1800 was a victory for a reading of the Constitution that would be more favorable to popular government.

Central to this transformation of executive power was changing the form of the inaugural address in order to meet the educative requirement of democratic leadership. Although democratic government is government by the majority will, majorities are comprised of citizens who need to have those very principles explained to them. One reason why governments needed principles furnished to them is that the laws must change, both in order to cope with the extraordinary occasions in political life and to remain current with human progress. As has been argued, Jefferson's understanding of the prerogative power allowed him to advocate a strict construction of the Constitution

[1] Jefferson to Spencer Roane, 6 September 1819, *TJW*, 1425.
[2] Jefferson to Joseph Priestly, 21 March 1801, *TJW*, 1086.
[3] Jefferson to Roane, *TJW*, 1425.

and simultaneously recommend that presidents achieve the public good during "great occasions," even if the public good requires temporarily setting the Constitution aside. Because the condition for such extraordinary prerogative is that the president must "throw himself" on the public for justification, declarations serve as the standard by which the public may try the president and afford the president the very rhetorical form by which his appeal to the public might take.

Another reason why majorities need declarations of principles is that they sometimes fail to understand the nature of their majority status. Although the majority will is both imprecise and malleable, Jefferson believed that the president could enlighten and direct the majority will because he alone could claim to represent it. In line with his perception that the president could energize the government by gathering public opinion around the administration of the laws, Jefferson used the inaugural address to transform public opinion. At the same time, by embodying public opinion the president would give it shape, enabling it in turn to control executive power.

More than a victory for the people's party, the botched election of 1800 provided Jefferson with the opportunity to demonstrate and institutionalize his understanding of executive power. Even as he used the First Inaugural to extend an olive branch to the losers of the election, he offered a justification for the democratic executive and a promise that government under his watch would not only have the "energy to preserve itself" but would also be "the strongest Government on earth."[4] Jefferson used the inaugural address to connect constitutional change by way of presidential selection with declarations of principle. Understood as a statement on the presidency and not simply the parties, Jefferson's First Inaugural was more revolutionary than scholars have recognized. To assert the president as the caretaker of the will of the nation, and to gather the national will around a set of declared principles, Jefferson deliberately transformed the inaugural address into a regular opportunity for announcing change. Just as Jefferson spent most of his life crafting a philosophy of enlightenment, the lifelong politician spent most of his career connecting the project of education to executive power.

Vice President

When Jefferson was elected Adams's vice president, he set out to change the way vice presidents assume office. Just as he would later change the "forms" surrounding the presidential office, Jefferson took measures to prevent the previous ceremony honoring Adam's election as vice president from

---

[4] Jefferson, "First Inaugural Address," 4 March 1801, *TJW*, 493.

becoming precedent. In the first place, Jefferson believed that the vice president should not deflect attention from the president, so he gave Madison
instructions urging other Republicans to refrain from honoring Jefferson
instead of Adams.[5] By honoring Jefferson, Republicans would exacerbate
the division between Jefferson and Adams, a division Jefferson was des-
perately trying to understate.[6] More important, Jefferson wished to cur-
tail the precedent set by Washington and Adams by drawing a distinction between inaugurating the Constitution and inaugurating a president:
"But this was the inauguration of our new government, and ought not to
drawn into example." By characterizing the fanfare of 1789 as celebrating
the Constitution rather than the election of Washington and Adams, Jefferson was already trying to change the way the public would understand its
presidents.

If Jefferson aimed to prevent the ceremonial acknowledgement of becoming vice president, he also sought to shape the office in his acceptance speech.
Indeed, one could even say that Jefferson presented his first inaugural address
not as the nation's third president but rather as the nation's second vice president. In the latter address, delivered to the Senate, Jefferson apologized for
his lack of recent legislative experience, promised that he would place the
rules of the Senate above his own opinion, pledged his allegiance to union,
and praised the selection of John Adams as president.[7] The second and third
themes are the most important, for in them Jefferson presented his understanding of the two constitutional duties of the vice president: presiding over
the Senate and ensuring the constitutional succession of the chief executive.
In the first case, Jefferson assured senators that he would be guided by Senate
rules, not political preference:

If a diligent attention, however, will enable me to fulfill the functions now assigned
me, I may promise that diligence and attention shall be sedulously employed. For
one portion of my duty I shall engage with more confidence, because it will depend
on my will and not on my capacity. The rules which are to govern the proceedings of
this House, so far as they shall depend on me for their application, shall be applied
with the most rigorous and inflexible impartiality, regarding neither persons, their
views, or principles, and seeing only the abstract proposition subject to my decision.
If, in forming that decision, I concur with some and differ from others, as must of
necessity happen, I shall rely on the liberality and candor of those from whom I differ,
to believe that I do it on pure motives.[8]

---

[5] Jefferson to Madison, 16 January 1797, 958–9.

[6] Jefferson to John Adams, 28 December 1796, Cappon, 286.

[7] Jefferson, "vice presidential Inaugural Address, in the Senate," 4 March 1797, *The Complete Jefferson: Containing His Major Writings, Published and Unpublished, Except his Letters*, ed. Saul K. Padover (New York: Duell, Sloan & Pearce, 1944), 381–2.

[8] Ibid.

In place of political experience, which itself may be too vulnerable to the influence of political opinion, Jefferson offered his determination to be guided strictly by the inflexible rules governing the Senate. When differences of opinion in interpreting those rules arise, as they must, good will suggests that each side give the other the benefit of the doubt. But "liberality and candor" alone seem to be insufficient, for Jefferson next offered a declaration of his "zealous attachment to the Constitution of the United States." Lest any Senator worry that Jefferson was ambivalent toward the federal union, Jefferson labeled "union" as the "first of blessings" and the "preservation of that Constitution which secures it" as "the first of duties." But after offering his own oath of office as vice president, Jefferson backed away from claiming that the principle of "union" would guide him in his job: "But I suppose these declarations not pertinent to the occasion of entering into an office whose primary business is merely to preside over the forms of this House, and no one more sincerely prays that no accident may call me to the higher and more important functions which the Constitution eventually devolves on this office." The two functions of his new office were to preside over the Senate and to assume the power of the presidency if Adams were to be incapacitated. As Jefferson's address put it, he would be competent for the first because of his attachment to following the rules, guided by his allegiance to the Union. But even declarations of allegiance to Union become impertinent when given by an officer whose primary duty is to merely ensure that the rules be followed.[9]

Jefferson's statement of allegiance to Union and confession of impertinence make sense only in the secondary duty of the vice president to protect the constitutional succession of the office. By alluding to the possibility of disagreement in the context of the two role of the vice president, Jefferson blurred the difference between those very job descriptions: his "merely" presiding over the Senate by its rules would be guided, to some extent, by the more serious fact that "higher and more serious functions" might be required of him. His pledge of devotion to Union, then, was meant to assure those Federalists worried that a closet anti-Federalist was what is now called "a heart-beat away" from heading the executive branch, just as it was meant to assure Senators that he would be guided by a principle over and beyond the Senate rules. Ironically, it was devotion to his understanding of Union that allowed him to manipulate Senate rules during the crisis of 1800 to keep open his path to the presidency.[10] More to the point, in contrast to Adams

---

[9] Ibid.

[10] Bruce Ackerman, *The Failure of the Founding Fathers: Jefferson, Marshall, and the Rise of Presidential Democracy* (Cambridge, MA: Belknap Press, Harvard University Press, 2005), 55–76.

who used the occasion to preside over a ceremony and praise Washington, Jefferson used the speech, as he did in every acceptance speech throughout his long career, to define and expand the powers of his office.[11] And, using the speech to reconstruct his office, he alluded to another occasion when it would be pertinent to make declarations about the principles of government.

Washington and Adams

For his first inaugural address, George Washington considered offering a statement of the purpose of the presidency and making policy recommendations to Congress but chose otherwise.[12] Consequently, in John Marshall's description of Washington's inauguration, Marshall described the ceremonies of the event and presented the text of Washington's address, but he offered no comment upon the content of the address. Marshall wrote, Washington took the oath in an "open gallery adjoining the senate chamber" in order "to gratify the public curiosity" but delivered his address in the privacy of the Senate chamber after "having taken it[the oath] in the view of an immense concourse of people, whose loud and repeated acclamations attested the joy with his being proclaimed President of the United States inspired them."[13] For Washington and his audience, then, the oath met the demand for the formal occupation of the office of the president, but the address was merely something to be delivered and replied to in private.

But it is equally important that both the Senate and the House passed over the content of Washington's speech. Rather than responding or even acknowledging the substance of Washington's address, each house praised the former general's reputation and thanked Washington for once again heeding the call of his country. The Senate saw in Washington's character a unifying quality: "In you all parties confide; in you all interests unite." The House declared the election proof of the nation's gratitude: "You enjoy the highest, because the truest honour, of being the first magistrate, by the unanimous choice of the freest people on the face of the earth."[14] Washington's reputation and decision to hold office, not Washington's words, mattered most to members of Congress. Why?

---

[11] John Marshall, *Life of George Washington*, (Fredericksburg, VA: Citizens' Guild, 1926), 4: 272–3.
[12] George Washington, "Fragments of a Draft of the First Inaugural Address," *George Washington: Writings*, ed. John Rhodehamel (New York: Library of America, 1997), 702–716; Jeffrey K. Tulis, *The Rhetorical Presidency* (Princeton, NJ: Princeton University Press, 1987), 48.
[13] Marshall, *Life of Washington*, 4: 278–286.
[14] Ibid., 4: 285–6.

Washington divided his address into six paragraphs. In the introductory paragraph, Washington reflected on his decision to leave the "retreat" he had "chosen with the fondest predilection" to answer the "voice" of his "Country," which he would hear only "with veneration and love." In the second paragraph, Washington gave homage to the "Almighty Being who rules over the Universe" and reflected that the people of the United States were uniquely "bound to acknowledge and adore the invisible hand, which conducts the Affairs of men." It was not until the third paragraph that Washington spoke of politics, but even then, the new president avoided commenting how his administration would be run. After citing the constitutional power to "recommend" measures to Congress Washington explicitly refrained from using his address to make such a recommendation: "The circumstances under which I now meet you, will acquit me from entering into that subject, farther than to refer to that Great Constitutional Charter under which you are assembled." Rather than using the ceremony to offer a specific recommendation, Washington praised his audience. "It will be more consistent with those circumstances, and far more congenial with the feelings which actuate me, to substitute, in place of a recommendation of particular measures, the tribute that is due to the talents, the rectitude, and the patriotism which adorn the characters selected to devise and adopt them." After making this connection between the first two paragraphs – that choosing love of country over personal happiness would be a choice rewarded by the divine plan in nature – Washington devoted the next paragraph to one particular political question, the adoption of a bill of rights. Here, Washington turned his audience's attention to the "objections" against the Constitution, but, again, "instead of undertaking particular recommendations on the subject," Washington declared that he would "give way" to Congress's "discernment and pursuit of public good." Furthermore, Washington said that he was assured that moderation would guide the question involving "a reverence for the characteristic rights of freemen, and a regard for the public harmony." In the fifth paragraph, Washington told the House that he would decline receiving any pay for his service, and, in the sixth, Washington again thanked the "benign Parent of the human race" for the blessings of tranquility, security, and unanimity upon the United States.[15]

One conspicuous feature of Washington's address is that the intended audience was the "Fellow Citizens of the Senate and of the House of Representatives."[16] More than a detail of ceremony, the salutation to the members of Congress foreshadowed the thematic content of the inaugural – public

---

[15] George Washington, "First Inaugural Address," 30 April 1789, *Washington Writings*, 730–4.
[16] Ibid., 730.

service over private pursuit, divine favor on those who obey the call to public service, the president's duty to recommend measures to Congress, the adjudication of the wide and various demands for amendments protecting rights, and the president's salary. Washington provided the model for what Jeffrey K. Tulis has described as the Founder's presidency: rather than speaking to the wider citizenry, Washington deliberately spoke only to those elected to represent the general public.[17] Indeed, his only mention of "the people," save gracious references to being called by the "voice of my country" and being elected by "fellow citizens," referred to the American people as "a people," that is, as a particular community continuing through history.

True to his reputation for loquaciousness, Adams delivered a longer address than did his predecessor.[18] Compared to Washington's address, it is difficult to determine the intended audience.[19] Lacking a salutation, the address consisted of fourteen paragraphs and treated the history of the revolution and government under the Articles of Confederation, offered an account of Adams's service to the country, praised the Constitution, urged vigilance against corruption in elections, praised Washington, listed Adams's own beliefs and promises, and asked for blessing from "that Being who is supreme over all." Adams did, however briefly, allude to his being representative of the people by virtue of his being an elected official: in giving praise for the Constitution's principle that those who hold the government's authority be "exercised by citizens selected at regular periods by their neighbors to make and execute laws for the general good," Adams asserted that government chosen by an "honest and enlightened people" was "more amiable and respectable" than a government instituted by accident or retained from antiquity. To support this claim, Adams appealed to the "people": "For it is the people only that are represented." Although Adams explicitly referred to the "people," he did not go on to assert that the president was peculiarly representative of the people. Rather, Adams went on to suggest that the "people" could be represented in other constitutional arrangements: "It is their power and majesty that is reflected, and only for their good, in every legitimate government, under whatever form it may appear."[20]

---

[17] Tulis, *Rhetorical Presidency*, 48.

[18] John Adams, "Inaugural Address," 4 March 1797, *The Inaugural Addresses of the Presidents*, ed. John Gabriel Hunt (New York: Gramercy, 1995) 13–20.

[19] Tulis writes that Adams was the last president to refrain from addressing "the people at large." *Rhetorical Presidency*, 48.

[20] John Adams, "Inaugural Address," 16.

Jefferson's Statement of Promise

Unlike those of his predecessors, Jefferson's first inaugural address presented a public lesson in presidential power. After the extended election of 1800 and the first opposition victory in the nation, Jefferson offered an address that has been remembered for its attempt to unite rather than divide its listeners. The gentle message of the address would have first been noticeable in the speech's presentation. Previously, Washington and Adams had ridden in carriages to their inaugurations, and each, emphasizing the president's role as commander in chief, had worn a sword. Jefferson, however, dressed in what some considered the habit of a plain citizen, walked without cavalcade from his temporary residence, and wore no sword.[21] It was the mild resolution of the Revolution of 1800 that later most impressed the greatest student of Jefferson's presidency, Henry Adams – "Hence arose a sense of disappointment for future students of the Inaugural Address. A revolution had taken place; but the new President seemed anxious to prove that there had been no revolution at all."[22]

But Adams's ascription of disappointment to future scholars reveals something about Jefferson's audience that the great historian missed. Jefferson's listeners probably would not have been disappointed because their expectations would have been remarkably different from an inaugural audience in Adams's day or our own. Because each previous inaugural address had been more a ceremonial observance of the oath of office than a fresh statement of principle, few in Jefferson's audience would have expected his inaugural address to include anything more than a statement of gratitude, an acknowledgment of the oath of office, and, perhaps, an offering of thanks to a supreme being. Had members of Jefferson's audience expected that the new president would initiate a revolution, they had little reason to expect that the president would signal that revolution by announcing it that day.

The First Inaugural's message of moderation notwithstanding, Jefferson approached the occasion with considerable ambition. As was the case when he drafted the Declaration of Independence, Jefferson had just over two weeks to write the address, worked without a secretary, and, probably, consulted no books.[23] Unlike 1776, when he submitted his draft to John Adams, Benjamin Franklin, and others, Jefferson probably did not ask others to revise

---

[21] Adams, 134–5; Malone, 4:3; Noble E. Cunningham Jr., *The Inaugural Addresses of President Thomas Jefferson, 1801 and 1805* (Columbia: University of Missouri Press, 2001), 1.
[22] Adams, 141.
[23] Malone, 4: 17.

the Inaugural.[24] Just as he used the Declaration to unite revolutionary sentiment under a single argument, Jefferson used the Inaugural to create an occasion in which presidents would declare the principles by which their administration will be guided. Alongside the formal oath of office, which the Constitution prescribed as the signification of a president's assumption to office, Jefferson used the address to teach his understanding of presidential power and to interpret the consequences of the recent election. Part of Jefferson's project was surely pedagogical, for the president believed himself to be an agent in the spreading enlightenment. The method, however, was at least as important: Jefferson invented a new presidential tradition simply by stating how he would be president. While moderation would serve in the place of retaliation, the Election in 1800 signified a second Revolution, and his First Inaugural would be the founding document for the new government. The famous call to conciliation between the two parties was thus part of a larger project to establish the inaugural address as the space in which such calls could be offered. The first inaugural address to be delivered in Washington, Jefferson's would be the model for the rest.

Unlike Washington and Adams, Jefferson directed his address to "Friends and Fellow Citizens."[25] Like Washington, Jefferson divided his address into six paragraphs. But if Washington used the address to mark the occasion of the former military commander taking the oath to support the Constitution, then Jefferson used the address as he had in previous addresses for lesser jobs, to redefine and expand his office. Jefferson opened the first paragraph with a reflection on his being "called upon to undertake the duties of the first executive office." After offering thanks, Jefferson warned that "the greatness of the charge" would be "above" his "talents," partly because the "transcendent objects" of the future would be impossible to predict and partly because the future would find the country involved with nations governed by "might" instead of "right." Rather than ending the paragraph with these doubts, Jefferson then reassured his audience that he would look to the members of Congress on which he could "rely under all difficulties." "To you, then, gentlemen, who are charged with the sovereign functions of legislation, and to those associated with you, I look with encouragement for that guidance and support which may enable us to steer with safety the vessel in which we are all embarked amidst the conflicting elements of a troubled world."[26]

---

[24] This would be a worthy historical study. Jefferson's letters to Madison, for instance, end with news of Jefferson's selection and begin again after the inauguration.

[25] Jefferson, "First Inaugural Address," 4 March 1801, *TJW*, 492–6.

[26] Jefferson, "First Inaugural," *TJW*, 492.

The implied question of the introductory paragraph lays out the thematic structure of the address – why should Jefferson "despair" at the "undertaking" of assuming new office? Because even the "sovereign function of legislation" may be inadequate to the hopes and necessities contained in the future, the supporting premise for this claim of despair is that the president would not always be bound by the legislative will during the extraordinary occasions brought about by the nation's transcendent hopes or the meddling of nations "who feel power but forget right." By assuring readers that he would look to the guidance of legislators during emergencies, or when the opportunity arose to achieve the transcendent objects of the nation, Jefferson reminded readers that he would decide whether it was appropriate to consult Congress. As his audience might have remembered, Jefferson had once sided with Washington in refusing to consult with the Senate regarding the power to advise the president in nominating ambassadors on the grounds that "the transaction of business with foreign nations is Executive altogether."[27] Jefferson expanded on this early statement of presidential privilege in foreign relations by letting the public (including other governments) know that he would be the one steering the ship of state in the uncharted waters of aspirations and dangers.

After raising the question of executive leadership in a world of contingency, Jefferson offered his famous call for conciliation. Republicans and Federalists might have expected Jefferson's address to announce a Republican program of retribution for three Federalist administrations, beginning with repeals of the Jay Treaty and the Judiciary Act. Furthermore, Republicans and Federalists might have believed that Jefferson would announce a radical agenda, including policies aimed at redistributing property and further disestablishing religion. But these hopes and anxieties proved premature, for Jefferson announced no such program but, instead, offered a call to unity under the banner of preserving the Constitution. The often-quoted phrase of Jefferson's First Inaugural, "We are all republicans; we are all federalists," then, might have been at least as surprising for those who were alive when it was first given as it is memorable today.

As Dumas Malone has noted, the message of comity was timely.[28] Assuming office only after the prolonged election, Jefferson took the occasion to mark the unity in the country rather than the divisions. The second paragraph of the address thus directed listeners to the rules of the Constitution, not the programmatic demands of the victorious majority – "all will, of,

---

[27] Jefferson, "Opinion on the Power of the Senate Respecting Diplomatic Appointments," 24 April 1790, *PTJ*, 16:378–82.

[28] Malone, 4:7–22.

course, arrange themselves under the will of the law, and unite in common efforts for the common good." The will of the law would require that the minority abide by the results of the election, as it would require that the majority respect the rights of the minority. "All, too, will bear in mind this sacred principle, that though the will of the majority is in all cases to prevail, that will to be rightful must be reasonable; that the minority possess their equal rights, which equal law must protect, and to violate would be oppression." In order to be reasonable, the majority must respect the rights of the minority, partly because reasoned self-interest would remind members of the majority that they might one day find themselves on the losing side of a presidential election. More than mastering the arithmetic of self-interest, the reasonable majority would recognize that the differences between it and the minority were not so great. Because "religious intolerance" had been "banished" and because the "throes and convulsions of the ancient world" were felt only faintly, reasonable people would know that Americans were united under the Revolution. Consequently, members of the majority and members of the minority could discern the distinction between "difference of opinion" and "difference of principle."[29]

By not announcing a partisan program, Jefferson's First Inaugural demarcated a limit on the power of a newly elected president. Rather than using the election to harden the majority and to banish the opposition, Jefferson used the victory to understate the differences dividing the country. And instead of calling for the revolution he had written about to friends, the president consolidated the change of power under the process laid out by the formal guarantees of the Constitution.

But the call for unity only set the stage for the larger argument to come.[30] After the introduction set forth the suggestion that the president was responsible for guiding the country to its aspirations in a world made dangerous by other governments, and the second and third paragraphs reminded listeners that the traditional obstacles to good government were absent in the United States, the fourth and fifth paragraph explicitly set out the method by which Jefferson would lead. Here, Jefferson began by stating that he would list what he deemed "the essential principles" of the government, "those which

[29] Jefferson, "First Inaugural," *TJW*, 492–3.
[30] Scholars have made much of the partisan implications of the middle paragraphs of the First Inaugural, but they have largely ignored the introductory and closing paragraphs and have thus missed the larger point about parties. See, for example, Adams, 135–6; David N. Mayer, *Constitutional Thought of Thomas Jefferson* (Charlottesville: University Press of Virginia, 1994), 120–2; Stephen Skowronek, *The Politics Presidents Make: Leadership from John Adams to George Bush* (Cambridge, MA: Belknap Press, Harvard University Press, 1993), 171; Stephen Howard Browne, *Jefferson's Call for Nationhood: The First Inaugural Address* (College Station: Texas A&M University Press, 2003).

ought to shape its administration."[31] As he had written to Madison during their famous argument about the effectiveness of a declaration of rights and as he would later write to John Colvin in order to explain executive prerogative, Jefferson appealed here to a statement of principle even though the principle would necessarily have exceptions: "I will compress them within the narrowest compass they will bear, stating the general principle, but not all its limitations." Put differently, even though the principles of government carry exceptions within themselves, he would summarize, as neatly as possible, the principles of government without speaking of their exceptions. The principles were the following:

1. Equal and exact justice to all men, of whatever state or persuasion, religious or political:
2. peace, commerce, and honest friendship with all nations, entangling alliances with none:
3. the support of the State governments in all their rights, as the most competent administrations for our domestic concerns and the surest bulwarks against antirepublican tendencies:
4. the preservation of the General government in its whole constitutional vigor, as the sheet anchor of our peace at home and safety abroad:
5. a jealous care of the right of election by the people – a mild and safe corrective of abuses which are lopped by the sword of revolution where peaceable remedies are unprovided:
6. absolute acquiescence in the decisions of the majority, the vital principle of republics, from which there is no appeal but to force, the vital principle and immediate parent of despotism:
7. a well-disciplined militia, our best reliance in peace and for the first moments of war till regulars may relieve them:
8. the supremacy of the civil over the military authority:
9. economy in the public expense, that labor might be lightly burthened:
10. the honest payment of our debts and sacred preservation of the public faith:
11. encouragement of agriculture; and of commerce as its handmaid:
12. the diffusion of information and arraignment of all abuses at the bar of the public reason:
13. freedom of religion; freedom of the press, and freedom of person under the protection of the habeas corpus:
14. and trial by juries impartially elected.[32]

---

[31] Jefferson, "First Inaugural," *TJW*, 494.
[32] Jefferson, "First Inaugural," *TJW*, 494–5. The numbers correspond to breaks indicated by a "–" in Jefferson's final draft. See Noble E. Cunningham Jr., *Inaugural Addresses*, 7–15.

To some extent, Jefferson's promise to "compress" the principles by which he would govern was an improvement upon Adams' inaugural address. Toward the end of that address, Adams assured his listeners that he would be up to the task of replacing Washington and, for evidence, offered a list of his own beliefs.[33] Adams's list was long, for it included general affirmations of "attachment to the Constitution" and respect for the state constitutions, specific reassurances of "personal esteem for the French nation" and a "spirit of equity and humanity to the aboriginal nations of America," and personal testaments to his own "elevated ideas of the high destinies of this country" and "veneration for the religion of a people who profess and call themselves Christians" – just to name a few. Not exactly a statement of principles by which to guide his administration, the list of personal beliefs was meant to reassure those who might have suspected that Adams preferred a government less republican. The list, then, fit the larger purpose of Adams's inaugural address, namely, to praise Washington and to pledge his support for the republican system laid out in the Constitution.[34]

In place of a statement of personal beliefs, Jefferson's principles were meant to summarize the essential principles of the government. As Jefferson put it, these principles would direct the nation in the future just as they had previously guided the nation through revolution and ratification: "These principles form the bright constellation which has gone before us and guided our steps through an age of revolution and reformation."[35] By informing both revolution and reformation, the principles testified to both theory and action – "The wisdom of our sages and the blood of our heroes have been devoted to their attainment." More than Jefferson's own recipe for good government, the principles were both descriptive and prescriptive in that they revealed the will of the nation while at the same time guiding it: "They should be the creed of our political faith, the text of civic instruction, the touchstone by which to try the services of those we trust; and should we wander from them in moments of error or alarm, let us hasten to retrace our steps and to regain the road which alone leads to peace, liberty, and safety."[36] But Jefferson's claim that his list of principles was the same as those of revolution and ratification was, at best, arguable. Indeed, the second, third, ninth, eleventh, and twelfth principles would have been flatly contradicted by Alexander Hamilton and others; the sixth principle's characterization of a republic differed from that given in *Federalist* #10, and the tenth, thirteenth,

---

[33] John Adams, "Inaugural Address," Hunt, ed., 17–19.
[34] Tulis emphasizes the awkwardness of Adams's address. *Rhetorical Presidency*, 49.
[35] Jefferson, "First Inaugural," *TJW*, 495.
[36] Jefferson, "First Inaugural," *TJW*, 495.

and fourteenth principles were partisan stabs at the Alien and Sedition Acts. More important, members of his audience might have asked why the new president was offering these principles at all.

Alone, Jefferson's declaration of principles would have begged the question why a losing party turn should over the reigns of power and cooperate with the party that defeated it. The first president to lead a change of party, Jefferson answered this question by establishing once and for all the president as the principal definer of the republican principle. The occasion to remind both groups of partisans of election rules under the Constitution became, in Jefferson hands, an occasion to declare the sacred principle underlying those rules. In laying out the doctrine of majority rule and then qualifying it with the proviso that the majority must be reasonable in order to be just, Jefferson placed his office, and the inaugural address itself, as the standard by which the majority's rightfulness would be judged. To guide the majority that elected him, then, Jefferson set forth an explanation of what would be the essential principles of his administration. As his friend Benjamin Rush put it, Jefferson's inaugural address "had concentrated whole chapters into a few aphorisms in defense of the principles and form of our government."[37]

But why would a new president list the principles of the government and the rights of the people after the Constitution and Bill of Rights had already been affirmed by the formal process of ratification? And why did this list of principles not resemble the formal distribution of powers set out in the Constitution or reveal confidence in Madison's theory that the extended republic would solve the problem of majority faction? The answer reveals Jefferson's growing faith in the utility of written declarations to both empower and constrain the executive. By using his inaugural address to enunciate what he thought to be the "essential principles of our government," Jefferson placed the president as the exponent and protector of the majority will. Previously, as Secretary of State, he had instructed a diplomat to consider the "will of the nation" as his "polar star."[38] Here, as president, he offered a way for citizens to find the "bright constellation" guiding the republic through both revolution and reformation, and these principles, to mix metaphors, would serve as the "touchstone" by which officers in high trust would be judged. Although political practice might require that the government bow to the demand of necessity – that Jefferson and his audience wander in moments of error or alarm – the president would be responsible for leading the people and their representatives back to the "creed of our political faith."[39]

---

[37] Benjamin Rush to Jefferson, 12 March 1801, as quoted in Malone, 4: 24.
[38] Jefferson to Thomas Pinckney, 30 December 1792, *PTJ*, 24: 803.
[39] Jefferson, "First Inaugural," *TJW*, 495.

After enumerating the principles that would guide the government, Jefferson returned in the fifth paragraph to the theme of the task being too great for his efforts. At one level, Jefferson's reflecting on his future failures was simply an affirmation of human imperfection in political office. As Jefferson noted, he himself had learned throughout his political life in "subordinate offices" that one rarely holds as high a reputation upon leaving office as that held upon entering it. This truth was complicated and confirmed by Washington, the "country's first and greatest revolutionary character": Washington's greatness might empower the executive office by connecting it to Washington's reputation, or it might limit the office by overshadowing successors while binding them to Washington's precedent. Notwithstanding, or perhaps because of, his greatness, even Washington did not enjoy the same prestige after retirement as when he entered office.[40]

Even more than a cautious reflection on the limits of human achievement, the fifth paragraph acknowledged the possibility of error in order to expand presidential power, not to limit it. As in his previous acceptance speeches, Jefferson noted that he would sometimes make unintentional mistakes even though he would resist the temptations of corruption or partiality: "I shall often go wrong through defect of judgment." But, unlike his address as vice president when he posited strict construction and fidelity to union as assurance that he would do his best, Jefferson this time added that others would likewise make mistakes when he himself was right: "When right, I shall often be thought wrong by those whose positions will not command a view of the whole ground."[41]

By a view of the whole ground, Jefferson might have meant that as president he would be responsible for overseeing the entirety of the executive branch throughout the nation rather than one particular department in one particular state; and he probably meant that as president he could uniquely determine the national interest, as opposed to the more particularized interests represented by members of the House and Senate. In his introduction, Jefferson had spoken of the country's rapid advance to a destiny beyond human imagination and of its overcoming the obstacles set by foreign nations wishing to extend their empires. And, in the fourth paragraph, Jefferson had summarized the principles of the government in order that they might provide a "touchstone" against which leadership could be tried during "moments of error or alarm." But, in the fifth, Jefferson reminded his listeners that others in the government would make mistakes because their own perspective would be limited: "I ask your indulgence for my own errors, which will never

40 Ibid., 495–6.
41 Ibid., 495.

be intentional, and your support against the errors of others, who may condemn what they would not if seen in all its parts." By the "whole ground," then, Jefferson must have also meant those "great occasions," during which the president would possess better information than others.[42]

With this claim to the high ground, a president would be able to defend those occasions in which he might have to act according to his best discretion possessing particular or incomplete information. Throughout his presidency, Jefferson would use the "Special Message" to report acts of executive discretion. In his "Special Message on the Burr Conspiracy," for example, Jefferson urged members of Congress to judge his delay in taking preventative measures against Burr according to the information he possessed at the time of his inaction.[43] Jefferson explained that he possessed only imperfect evidence found in letters "often containing such a mixture of rumors, conjectures, and suspicions" and therefore found it "difficult to sift out the real facts," relying instead on "general outlines." And, to the governor of Louisiana, Jefferson sent his message on the Burr Conspiracy and wrote with language similar to that used in his special message to Congress regarding Eaton's taking Tripoli: "Your situations have been difficult, and we judge of the merits of our agents there by the magnitude of the danger as it appeared to them, not as it was known to us."[44] As Jefferson would later write Colvin, he told Claiborne that during "great occasions" "every good officer must be ready to risk himself in going beyond the strict line of the law."[45] Rather than information gathered after the fact, the officer's "motives" would "be a justification as far as" there might be "any discretion in his extralegal proceedings." Just as Wilkinson, who violated habeas corpus to prevent a conspiracy that never fully materialized, and Jefferson, who was slow to act to prevent that conspiracy when its threat was very real, would be judged according to his understanding of the events as they unfolded, so too would presidents be judged in their attempts to lead the nation through the "great occasions" standing in the way of its achieving its "transcendent objects."

But if the president must steer the state, who decides its destination? The thrust of Jefferson's reasoning about the president alone seeing the whole ground was to preempt conflicts with the other branches of government by reminding his audience that he alone was nationally elected. His election, like every election, served two purposes: it decided a "contest of opinion," and it implied "approbation" for Jefferson's service in the past. Announced

[42] Ibid., 495–6.
[43] Jefferson, "Special Message on the Burr Conspiracy," 22 January 1807, *TJW*, 532.
[44] Jefferson to Governor W. C. C. Claiborne, 3 February 1807, Washington, 5:40–1.
[45] Jefferson to John Colvin, 20 September 1810, *TJW*, 1232.

as the "voice of the nation," "according to the rules of the Constitution," Jefferson's victory defined the "will of the law" under which both Federalists and Republicans were obliged to unite.[46] By claiming the whole ground, Jefferson combined the argument for executive prerogative with the argument for the presidential mandate.

In a study of Jefferson's influence on the American character, Jean M. Yarbrough has written that part of the Virginian's "enduring appeal" can be traced to Jefferson's redirecting the Christian virtue of hope to the dream of continuing success on earth. "It is part of the American character to believe that the best days are still to come, and Jefferson, more than any other Founder, speaks to this longing."[47] It was to this hope for better days that Jefferson hitched the presidency. Rather than confining the office to the dutiful carrying out of the legislature's will, the president could find discretion in and because of the people's expectancy that great occasions would bring good. Lacking the capacity to see the whole of the democratic experiment, and lacking, perhaps, the will to see beyond ancient attachments, legislators would occasionally need to be directed to the fundamental principles of the government. Put simply, "the world's best hope" needed democratic energy in the form of a new presidency.

The First Inaugural provides a working summary of Jefferson's theory of presidential power. The president can be energetic, and he must, because he alone is nationally elected. And being nationally elected confirms the president's responsibility as an executive officer to occasionally move outside the law when necessity demands it, but a respect for the majority will forbids concealing such actions under loose constitutional interpretation. To more clearly mark the bounds of the president's departures from the law, the president offers statements of principles by which the public can judge, as well as support, presidential action. For Jefferson, the question whether a government could be both free and sufficiently energetic hinged on the people's confidence in the president.

Jefferson famously wrote his epitaph to include his authoring of a declaration, a statute, and his founding of the University of Virginia – not his serving two terms as president. This detail of Jefferson's biography correctly reminds those who study Jefferson's presidency that education rather than politics was this president's passion. But Jefferson changed the presidency by forcing presidents to connect in speech approval of their behavior to electoral revolution. Part of this project was similar to that of the Declaration

---

[46] Jefferson, "First Inaugural," *TJW*, 492.
[47] Jean M. Yarbrough, *American Virtues: Thomas Jefferson on the Character of a Free People* (Lawrence: University Press of Kansas, 1998), 194.

of Independence: just as Americans in 1776 needed someone to unite their sentiments under a proper tone and spirit, Americans in 1800 needed the president to distinguish differences of opinion from differences of principle. Part of this project was similar to that of the Bill of Rights: just as Americans in 1789 needed a text of liberties by which they could test the powers of the national government, Americans in 1800 needed the president to state principles by which they could test his extraordinary and expansive acts of nation-building.

Confirmation of the Revolution

Although Jefferson used a reading copy with abbreviations to deliver the address on 4 March, Samuel Harrison Smith had been given a complete copy to be published on that morning in the *National Intelligencer*, and Smith had copies printed for attendees of the ceremony. As Noble S. Cunningham has documented, the address quickly reached a wide audience.[48] More important, Jefferson's transformation of the Inaugural Address was not missed by readers, and Federalists found much to criticize. The London *Monthly Magazine* noted the novelty of the address's style, commenting on the "language which the members of Congress [had] not been accustomed to hear from the Chair." Gouverneur Morris objected to the speech's length, saying that it was "too long by half," and John Marshall wrote that the speech was "strongly characteristic of the general cast of his political theory." Marshall may have had in mind something similar to what Alexander Baring reported to his father: "I recommend your reading [the speech] as it is the manifesto of the party and a declaration (I believe a just one) of his political creed. It is here much admired though I confess it confirms my invariable opinion of the man, that he is a visionary theorist." The U.S. minister to Portugal, William Loughton Smith, disapproved of the speech's rhetorical structure: "I don't like the language of the Speech – its too much of an oration and was more adapted to a 4th July Declaration by a younger spouter hot from Princeton than to a solemn discourse delivered by the President to the Nation on such an occasion." Other unfriendly partisans complained of Jefferson's use of metaphor and laxity of grammar.[49]

As Cunningham has shown, those on the victorious side of the Election of 1800 applauded the speech's ambition. *The American Citizen* called it "the first speech of the first magistrate of a free and enlightened people" and praised it as "the solemn declaration of the first republican officer of

[48] Cunningham, *Inaugural Addresses*, 39–72. Quotations below are from Cunningham.
[49] Ibid., 39–53.

an executive capacity that ever adorned the annals of history." In letters to Madison, Dr. William Thornton wrote that the speech proved that the nation finally had a "philosopher" at its "head," a philosopher "whose heart appears in every action," and Ralph Bowie predicted that the speech would be regarded as a success: "It might indeed naturally be expected that candid men of all descriptions, would cordially approve of the Principles so pure and Sentiments so just and liberal, delivered in Language so elegant and impressive." William Branch Giles complimented the president on his choice of words, remarking that the address was "the only American language" he had "ever heard from the Presidential chair." To Jefferson, Rush wrote that the speech had "opened a new era" because never before had "the public mind more generally or agreeably affected by any publication." In the *National Intelligencer*, Samuel Harrison Smith praised Jefferson's use of the address to announce the principles of government: "To such a People, it became the man of the people to speak with respectful truth" and "to declare the general principles by which he was actuated, and by an adherence to which he was willing to be judged." In a pseudonymous preface to a pamphlet published in London, the address was praised on grounds of its encouraging the "wavering patriot on this side of the ocean" and went as far as to say that it could "have a good effect on the great Bonaparte himself." Furthermore, the speech would be used as a blueprint for the new government, which would be especially useful because the "new confirmed Government of America will be perhaps, to the framers of constitutions, hence-forward, a normal school, a model for statesman to work by." That an American language was enunciated from the chief executive office was not missed on others, whether domestic or abroad.[50]

As the president and his contemporaries were well aware, the arrival of the Revolution of 1800 was trumpeted in the form and style of a new inaugural address. By gathering the sentiment of public opinion into the aphorisms of democratic government, the Inaugural was more a testament of presidential ambition than political conciliation. In lifting the inaugural address above the oath, Jefferson not so quietly achieved the constitutional revolution Henry Adams expected but could not recognize.

[50] Ibid., 41–63.

6

To "produce a union of the powers of the whole"

Jefferson's Transformation of the Appointment and Removal Powers

Jefferson described his election as a revolution, but his First Inaugural showed that elections, in place of revolutions, would provide the means for determining the majority will. More than any of his contemporaries, Jefferson perceived that the president would come to embody the majority by way of the presidential election. Thus Jefferson advocated a term limit for presidents in order to maximize the opportunities for presidents to lead constitutional majorities. And thus Jefferson invented the inaugural address as a practical means by which the principles of constitutional majorities may be enunciated.

The first test of Jefferson's declaration of principles was the appointment and removal powers. Because 1800 was the first transfer of power, the meaning of that election would most immediately turn on the way Jefferson distributed executive offices. Scholars have long recognized that Jefferson should share some of the credit, normally reserved for Andrew Jackson, for inventing the spoils system, in which the victorious party distributes offices to its members.[1] By refusing to acknowledge John Adams's

---

[1] Carl E. Prince, "The Passing of the Aristocracy: Jefferson's Removal of the Federalists, 1801–1805," *Journal of American History* 57 (1970): 563–75. Stephen Skowronek, *The Politics Presidents Make: Leadership from John Adams to George Bush* (Cambridge, MA: Harvard University Press, Belknap Press, 1993), 72; Robert M. Johnstone Jr., *Jefferson and the Presidency: Leadership in the Young Republic* (Ithaca, NY: Cornell University Press, 1978), 104; Marc Landy and Sidney M. Milkis, *Presidential Greatness* (Lawrence: University Press of Kansas, 2000), 65. Merril D. Peterson *Thomas Jefferson and the New Nation: A Biography* (New York: Oxford University Press, 1970), 680; Merril D. Peterson, *The Jeffersonian Image in the American Mind* (New York: Oxford University Press, 1962), 82–3; and Susan Dunn, *Jefferson's Second Revolution: The Election Crisis of 1800 and the Triumph of Republicanism* (Boston: Houghton Mifflin, 2004), 246. Others, however, conclude that Jefferson's removals were moderate and therefore predated the spoils system: Leonard D White, *The*

"midnight appointments," eliminating offices in the military and judiciary, forcing resignations, removing those who would not resign, and by appointing fellow partisans to theses offices, Jefferson brought the Revolution of 1800 to the bureaucracy. Again, instead of shunning executive power, Jefferson embraced it.

What scholars have not appreciated fully enough, however, is the extent to which Jefferson's argument for the removal power was based on his plan for executive power. Jefferson used the appointment power and fortified the removal power to further gather what he called "confidence" around the president. When he was elected president, however, the president's power with regard to appointments and removals was still unsettled. So Jefferson's embrace came with an explanation: a strong executive with regard to appointments and removals was beneficial to, and even necessary for, republican government. This explanation surely provided a rationale for his actions as president and party leader, but it also completed Madison's 1789 argument for a connection – a "chain of responsibility" – between public opinion and executive power. By attaching "public confidence" to the president, a vigorous use of appointments and removals would provide the "unity of object and action" to the everyday affairs of the national government as well as to the larger aspirations of the national electorate. For Jefferson, the president's power to remove officers from previous administrations could not just be asserted – it had to be defended.

Organizing the Cabinet

In 1800, the relationship between the president and the cabinet was uncertain. Although Washington believed that his own administration would be a precedent for future presidents, he did not prescribe a set of rules for the cabinet, did not hold a formal cabinet meeting until near the end of his first term, and did not even use the word "cabinet" until April 1793.[2] Instead, his contribution to the development of the cabinet lies chiefly in the men he appointed.[3] Furthermore, Washington consulted his cabinet through

Jeffersonians: A Study in Administrative History, 1801–1829 (New York: Macmillan, 1951), 379; Forrest McDonald, *The Presidency of Thomas Jefferson* (Lawrence: University Press of Kansas, 1976), 35–36.

[2] Sidney M. Milkis and Michael Nelson, *The American Presidency: Origins and Development 1776–2002*, 4th ed. (Washington, DC: CQ Press, 2003), 72–3.

[3] Marshall, *Life of Washington*, 4:320; Glenn A. Phelps, "George Washington and the Founding of the Presidency," in "Origins and Inventions of the American Presidency," ed. Thomas E. Cronin, special issue, *Presidential Studies Quarterly* 17 (1987): 356–7.

requests for opinions, and questions of foreign policy were as likely to be sent to the Treasury as they were to the State Department.[4] And there was nothing special about his cabinet: in addition to requesting written opinions from his own executive officers, Washington sought the counsel of the Supreme Court and the Senate.

One reason for Washington's informal method was to avoid discord. By receiving the opinions of his cabinet members in writing, Washington kept disagreements private and therefore retained control – one member could never really know whether his own advice was in the majority or alone in dissent, thus narrowing the room for criticism of Washington's ultimate decisions. But Washington's method begot two types of conflict. First, cabinet members feuded when the President was out of the office. With Washington home during the Genet Affair, his cabinet had to decide what to with *The Little Sarah*, an English ship that was captured by the French, brought into Philadelphia, and outfitted as the privateer, *le petit Democrat*. The Secretaries of War and Treasury wanted to establish a military battery with militia to keep the ship at port, whereas the Secretary of State argued that military force should not be yet employed without the president's approval. The governor of Pennsylvania disbanded the militia on Jefferson's advice, and the ship set sail before Washington returned, setting up Genet's threat to appeal to the people over Washington.[5] The disagreement over the use of military force grew out of the lack of harmony and unity of action within Washington's cabinet: when Washington away, his cabinet was simply supposed to superintend, in Marshall's words, "the execution of those rules as previously established," but it was the interpretation of those rules under the Constitution which rendered execution so difficult in Washington's absence. Second, Washington's method of receiving opinions in private led cabinet members to wonder whether the president was playing one opinion off the other: Jefferson came to believe that Hamilton had Washington's ear in person, whereas Jefferson was made vulnerable by his stating his opinions in formal letters.[6]

If Washington's informality contributed to growing internal dissension, John Adams's unwillingness to select his own cabinet led directly to open struggles for control. By the end of his administration Adams came to believe that Hamilton was conspiring to wrest control of his administration from

---

[4] See especially Dorothy Twohig, ed., *The Journal of the Proceedings of the President, 1793–1797* (Charlottesville: University Press of Virginia, 1981), 108–20. See also the discussion of the Neutrality Proclamation in Chapter 3.

[5] Marshall, *Life of Washington*, 5:36–40.

[6] See Chapter 3.

him, and he spurned the advice of his cabinet on both foreign and domestic questions, and eventually forced the resignation of his Secretary of War and fired his Secretary of State. Adams himself was to blame for his department heads being closer to Hamilton than to himself, for he had balked from appointing his own cabinet, retaining instead those serving at the end of Washington's second administration. Lacking a precedent and unwilling to set one, Adams chose to make as few removals as possible and considered skill and experience over friendship and party affiliation. The conflict over his assertion of the removal power, discussed later, grew out of his unwillingness to assert his control over appointments.[7]

Jefferson looked to Washington's example rather than Adams's in receiving advice from his cabinet. Several months after his inauguration, Jefferson distributed his "Circular to the Heads of the Departments." In that document, Jefferson noted that the communication between the president and his cabinet was lacking uniformity, that is, some cabinet members were submitting more matters for his approval than others. Accordingly, Jefferson proposed that a "uniform course of proceeding as to manner & degree, should be observed," and for his model, Jefferson explicitly selected Washington's administration over Adams's: "Having been a member of the first administration of Washington, I can state with exactness what our course then was." All letters addressed to the departments eventually went through Washington; if a letter required no answer, it was sent to Washington for his own information, and if it required an answer it was sent to Washington with the department head's proposed answer. "By this means, he was always in accurate possession of all facts and proceedings in every part of the Union, and to whatsoever department they related; he formed a central point for the different branches; preserved a unity of object and action among them; exercised that participation in the suggestion of affairs which his office made incumbent on him; and met himself the due responsibility for whatever was done." For Jefferson, Washington was the opposite of his immediate predecessor Adams, whose "long and habitual absences from the seat of government" resulted in a kind of cabinet rule. Lacking unity of execution, Adams's administration was ineffective because his absences had "parcelled out the government, in fact, among four independent heads, drawing sometimes in opposite directions." Jefferson, by contrast, would

---

[7] In 1809 Adams said that he risked a "dead negative in the Senate" without Hamilton's approval. See Syrett's introduction to *Letter from Alexander Hamilton, Concerning the Public Conduct and Character of John Adams*, PAH, 25:184; John Ferling, *John Adams: A Life* (New York: Henry Holt, 1996), 333, 390–1; and Ralph Adams Brown, *The Presidency of John Adams* (Lawrence: University of Kansas Press, 1975), 27.

aim to be the "central point" from which the different departments would carry out the laws.[8]

But Jefferson parted with Washington on one crucial point. Rather than following Washington's practice of selecting the "best available man," Jefferson selected his officers with loyalty to his program in mind.[9] More precisely, as Landy and Milkis show, Jefferson raised the requirement of loyalty to friendship for appointments at the highest level, selecting Madison as Secretary of State and Albert Gallatin as Secretary of Treasury.[10] As a result, Jefferson's cabinet was political as much as it was administrative: when Jefferson met with the entirety of his cabinet, it was to discuss constitutional questions, partisan strategy, or foreign affairs, not to address departmental business.[11] As a result of his lifting politics over merit, Jefferson's leadership went unchallenged, and his cabinet presented a picture of unity to Congress and the public. For example, Malone's examination of the "surviving record" found "instances of dissent" but concluded that "as a rule he and his counselors were so successful in arriving at a consensus that there was no need to take a formal vote."[12] To be sure, there were disagreements, for, as Leonard White wrote, Gallatin "opposed Jefferson on his removal policy, on the building of dry docks, on the need for a constitutional amendment to justify the purchase of Louisiana, and the embargo of 1807, and tempered Jefferson's views on other matters."[13] But, according to Jefferson, the unanimity among members of his own cabinet rested on the fact that each member knew that the president's decision was final: "[A]ble and amicable as these members were, I am not certain this [unanimity] would have been the case, had each possessed equal and independent powers."[14] As Leonard White observed, in 1801 the cabinet might have become an executive council, but it did not.[15]

Appointments and Public Respect

As was argued in Chapter 3, one concern for Jefferson as Secretary of State was that the Senate would use its power to confirm nominees to interfere with executive administration. Once president, Jefferson repeated his position that the Senate was not authorized to use its power to confirm in ways

---

[8] Jefferson, "Circular to the Heads of the Departments," Ford, 8:99–100; on the problem, see Malone, 4:62–3.

[9] McDonald, *Presidency of Jefferson*, 37.

[10] Landy and Milkis, *Presidential Greatness*, 51–52.

[11] White, *Jeffersonians*, 83.

[12] Malone, 4: 62.

[13] White, *Jeffersonians*, 136.

[14] Jefferson to Destutt de Tracy, 16 January 1811, *TJW*, 1241–1247.

[15] White, *Jeffersonians*, 77.

that would interfere with the president's plan for administration: "I have always considered the control of the Senate as meant to prevent any bias or favoritism in the President toward his own relations, his own religion, toward particular states &c. and perhaps to keep very abnoxious persons out of offices of the first grade. But in all subordinate cases I have ever thought that the selection made by the President ought to inspire a general confidence that it has been made on due inquiry and investigation of character, and that the Senate should interpose their negative only in those particular cases where something happens to be within their knowlege, against the character of the person and unfitting him for the appointment."[16] Again, the Senate's participation in the appointment power was meant to be limited to preventing corrupt or obviously poor appointments and would not include general rules for the kinds of persons appointed. At the same time, Jefferson argued that the Senate's rather narrow role in appointments was meant to assist the president in finding officers who would have the confidence of the people. In this statement and many others like it, Jefferson included an estimation of the "confidence" in administration brought about by removals and appointments. His transformation of the appointment power as president would rest on his calculation of the relationship between execution and public opinion.

Jefferson the president courted public respect in two ways. First, Jefferson perceived that a "geographical equilibrium [was] to a certain degree expected," so the president conducted appointments according to the temper he perceived in each state.[17] "The temper of some states requires a stronger procedure, that of others would be more alienated even by a milder course."[18] "Some states require a different regiment than others. What is done in one state very often shocks another, though where it is done it is wholesome."[19] In considering the peculiar characteristics of each state, Jefferson also had to assess the differences among the states governed by his own party. Because of the "moderation" in most states, Jefferson would make no removal except for "malversation," but "in the middle States the contention had been higher, spirits were more sharpened & less accommodating."[20] Thus, in the middle states, Jefferson found it necessary "to practice a different treatment, and to make a few changes to tranquilize the injured party."

[16] Jefferson to Albert Gallatin, 10 February 1803, Ford, 8:210–1.
[17] Jefferson to Horatio Gates, 8 March 1801, Ford, 8:11. Jefferson took special care regarding appointing Virginians. See Jefferson to Samuel Smith, 24 March 1801, Ford, 8:28–9.
[18] Jefferson to William Findley, 24 March 1801, Ford, 8:27.
[19] Jefferson to Thomas McKean, 24 July 1801, Ford, 8: 78.
[20] Jefferson to William Short, 3 October 1801, Ford, 8:97.

Another way Jefferson sought to maintain public respect was by appointing officers with good reputations among citizens. This is not to say that Jefferson was the first president to use appointments to cultivate public opinion. For instance, of George Washington's first cabinet, John Marshall wrote, "In its composition, public opinion as well as intrinsic worth had been consulted, and a high degree of character had been combined with real talent."[21] As Johnstone and McDonald have written, Jefferson most often drew from the aristocratic class to find appointees.[22] But more than just being a child of his time who assumed that government was the playground for elites, Jefferson perceived the disjunction between the cares of citizens and the duties of public servants. To Benjamin Hawkins, the president noted that "there would always be a greater proportion" of "aristocratic" representatives than the "standard of the people," although he did not say whether it was because the electorate preferred to be represented by aristocrats or whether aristocrats were especially good at being elected.[23] Even if Jefferson believed that he "had a preferable right to name agents for [his] own administration," he was also careful to make no appointment that would be disapproved by the public: "There is nothing I am so anxious about as good nominations, conscious that the merit as well as the reputation of an administration depends as much on that as on it's measures."[24] Furthermore, when Jefferson solicited recommendations for potential officers, he often charged his friends to balance state and national concerns: "I pray you to take a broad view of this subject, consider it in all its bearings, local and general, and communicate to me your opinion."[25] Later, Jefferson advised President Monroe to dismiss an appointee whose qualifications Jefferson believed to be adequate but whose "temper and prudence" were "questionable" and therefore "defective" in the public's opinion.[26] As he put it, "this latter circumstance is always important, because it is not wisdom alone, but public confidence in that wisdom which can support an adm[inistration]."

Removals

Jefferson's use of the removal power has yet to be fully understood because scholars have concentrated on the question of whether Jefferson was the

[21] John Marshall, *Life of George Washington* (Fredericksburg, VA: Citizens' Guild, 1926), 4: 324.

[22] Johnstone, *Jefferson and the Presidency*, 111; McDonald, *Presidency of Jefferson*, 36.

[23] Jefferson to Benjamin Hawkins, 18 February 1803. Ford, ed., 8: 212.

[24] Jefferson to Archibald Stuart, 8 April 1801. Ford, ed., 8:47.

[25] Jefferson to the Postmaster General and Jefferson to Pierrepont Edwards, 29 March 1801, Ford, 8:45.

[26] Jefferson to James Monroe, 1824, Ford, 10:316.

inventor of the spoils system rather than on the extent to which Jefferson connected the removal power to public opinion.[27] A possible explanation for this oversight is that scholars have missed the presidential connection. It has not been fully appreciated that the president's removal power had not yet been settled firmly as a matter of constitutional authority. More precisely, Jefferson defended the appointment and removal power while others were trying to limit the president's influence over executive officers. Jefferson's position on this constitutional question demonstrated his belief that for the executive branch to be energetic the president must harness the presidency's peculiar source of energy, public opinion. Put differently, "public confidence," the term he used most often, in executive officers would guarantee that administration would be both vigorous and popular.

To be sure, Madison's victory in the House Debate of 1789 set the important precedent that the president would have the power to remove, but Madison's victory was narrow, and later events suggested that others would attempt to undo it. Consider Adams's removal of members of his cabinet. Many Federalists were angry with Adams, and some believed that Adams had executed the purge in order to fulfill some bargain with Jefferson.[28] Moreover, Hamilton used the occasion to publicly argue that Adams had been wrong to disregard the advice of his cabinet regarding foreign relations. According to Hamilton, who had written in *The Federalist* that the power to require the opinion of cabinet members in writing was "a mere redundancy," Adams had transgressed constitutional design by not consulting his cabinet: even though a president is under "no positive injunction to ask or require" the opinion of his cabinet members, "the Constitution presumes that he will consult them; and the genius of our government and the public good recommend the practice."[29] Furthermore, the president who does not consult his cabinet presumes himself infallible. If the president refuses to consult, then he would "tend to exclude from places of primary trust, the men most fit to occupy them."[30] As has been argued, Hamilton noted in *The Federalist* that the Senate would "of course" participate in presidential removals, and it is possible that he instructed his lieutenants to argue against

[27] Adams, 152 and 200; Johnstone, *Jefferson and the Presidency*, 104; Skowronek, *Politics Presidents Make*, 72; Peterson, *Jefferson and the New Nation*, 680 and *Jeffersonian Image in the American Mind*, 82–3; Landy and Milkis, *Presidential Greatness*, 65; McDonald, *Jefferson and the Presidency*, 35–36.

[28] Theodore Sedgwick to Hamilton, 13 May 1800, PAH, 24:482. See Syrett's notes on pp. 483–5.

[29] *The Federalist*, No. 74, p. 475; Hamilton, *Letter*, PAH, 25:214.

[30] Hamilton, *Letter*, PAH, 15:215.

presidential removals in the 1789 House debate.[31] Hamilton's 1800 letter against Adams thus continued his assault on presidential removal powers and raised the question of whether the presidential system was capable of running the executive branch and carrying out the laws. Thanks to Hamilton, presidents after Adams may have been reluctant to assert the removal power that Madison had won for them in 1789.

It is therefore probably no accident that a subplot of the Election of 1800 was the distribution of offices. Consider the events. First, during the standoff in the House, Federalist dealmakers approached both Aaron Burr and Jefferson to extract a promise to leave in place Federalist officeholders. Although Jefferson claimed to have made no such deal, the possibility is important because it again suggests a rather brazen attempt to temper the president's removal powers.[32] Second, in John Marshall's famous assertion of judicial review in *Marbury v. Madison* (1803), the argument for judicial review was but one-third of the opinion, whereas the other two-thirds advanced the argument that the president's discretion in his appointment power was limited by a distinction between political officers and legal officers. That is, as Marbury was not a political officer, and therefore not subject to presidential removal, Jefferson had to deliver the commission executed under Adams. Indeed, it was Marshall's argument that the courts could force the executive branch to issue the appointment to Marbury, not Marshall's assertion of judicial review, to which Jefferson most objected. Combined with the Supreme Court's near simultaneous deference in *Stuart v. Laird* (1803) to Congress's power to repeal the Judiciary Act, *Marbury* caused Jefferson to believe that the presidential removal power was under attack. In short, Jefferson and his contemporaries knew that the third president's appointments and removals would be important for the parties but also for the presidency.[33]

Instead of allowing the removal power to be relocated to Congress or become dormant, Jefferson asserted the president's removal power, and, rather than maintaining public silence regarding this power, he publicly defended it. Because the appointment and removal powers were meant to allow the president to cultivate public confidence, the removal power would

---

[31] Chapter 3.

[32] On the deal see Malone, 4: 13–14; Garry Wills, *Negro President: Thomas Jefferson and the Slave Power* (Boston: Houghton Mifflin, 2003), 86–88; and Bruce Ackerman, *The Failure of the Founding Fathers: Jefferson, Marshall, and the Rise of Presidential Democracy* (Cambridge, MA: Belknap Press, Harvard University Press, 2005), 104–7.

[33] Dumas Malone, 4: 117; Richard E. Ellis, *The Jeffersonian Crisis: Courts and Politics in the Young Republic* (New York: Oxford University Press, 1971), 65; and Christopher Wolfe, *The Rise of Modern Judicial Review: From Constitutional Interpretation to Judge-Made Law* (New York: Basic Books, 1986), 98.

be practiced frequently, if not vigorously. Over time, his policy shifted, and he eventually elaborated three grounds for removal: an officer could be removed because of corruption or abuse of office, because his absence was needed in order to restore a proper proportion of Republicans, or in order to strengthen the administration by replacing executives in office with others who were better respected by the public.

The problem was that his First Inaugural stood in the way of removals. In that address, Jefferson declared famously that differences in opinion were not the same thing as differences in principle, and, early into his administration, Jefferson let it be known that he would not remove Adams's appointees simply on the grounds they held different political opinions. From this principle of toleration, however, Jefferson excepted Adams's so-called midnight appointments. Those appointments would be treated as "nullities," as even Adams's friends agreed with Jefferson that those appointments were an "outrage on decency" and should not take effect. More important, however, is that Jefferson considered null all appointments Adams made after Adams knew that he had not been elected for second term, that is, on 12 December 1800. As Jefferson saw it, the outrage was not merely that Adams had issued appointments up to three hours before leaving office but that Adams had appointed officers to work in the administration of someone other than himself. The time or date did not matter as much as the fact that Adams had made appointments for another presidential administration.[34]

Subject to actual removal, at first, would be only officers guilty of "gross abuses of office."[35] According to Jefferson, such removals would be few in number, but they would be vigorously executed. By promptly and consistently removing corrupt officers, Jefferson would avoid the appearance of removing an official on the grounds of difference of opinion: "Those who have acted well have nothing to fear, however they may have differed from me in opinion: those who have done ill, however, have nothing to hope; nor shall I fail to do justice lest it be should be ascribed to that difference of opinion."[36] The Revolution of 1800, at least as he saw it a few months into his first term, would not lead to a tide of removals, that is, it would not occasion the "disgraceful and ruinous mutability in the administration of the government" of which Hamilton warned in *The Federalist*.[37] In Jefferson's estimation,

---

[34] Jefferson to William Findley, 21 March 1801, Ford, 8:26–7; and Jefferson to Henry Knox, 27 March 1801, Ford, 8:35–38. Later, to Abigail Adams, Jefferson claimed that he considered Adams's last appointments as meant to be "personally unkind," since they included Jefferson's enemies. Jefferson to Abigail Adams, 13 June 1804, Cappon, 270.

[35] Jefferson to Elbridge Gerry, 29 March 1801, Ford, 8:42.

[36] *Ibid.*

[37] *The Federalist* No. 72, p. 463.

removal would be rare: "After the first unfavorable impression of doing too much in the opinion of some, & too little in that of others, shall be got over, I should hope a steady line of conciliation very practicable."[38] Although Jefferson had reassured officeholders that no officer would be removed on the grounds of political opinion alone, he eventually declared that grounds for removal would include considerations of the proper proportion of Republicans and Federalists as well as attentiveness to the administration's standing in public opinion.

Removing a man from his post was no easy decision, but Jefferson did it. It must have been difficult for a man who famously preferred avoiding confrontation to meeting it, and Jefferson described executing the removals as a "painful office," but a necessary duty, like the "office of the hangman."[39] Nevertheless, As Carl Prince documents, Jefferson used a broad definition of misconduct – including a loose notion of alcohol abuse – to carry out what can fairly be called a purge of the young Federalists who posed a threat to his Republican administration.[40] As a "public executioner" might justify his calling on the grounds that "the public voice call[s] for it," Jefferson extended his removal policy beyond officials guilty of misconduct.[41] In his arithmetic, a fair proportion would leave Republicans with roughly three out of four offices, and, as Skowronek summarizes, "Within two years of his inauguration, the President himself calculated that only 130 of the 316 offices subject to his appointment power were still held by Federalists."[42]

Only a few months after the First Inaugural, Jefferson told advisors that he would be more aggressive in Connecticut. In that state, Jefferson believed "a general sweep seem[ed] to be called for on principles of justice and policy." Because Connecticut's legislature had removed "every republican even from the commissions of the peace and the lowest offices," Jefferson employed removal to install displaced Republicans and to "retaliate" against the Federalist stronghold.[43] To his attorney general, Jefferson characterized this retaliation as punishing "intolerance": "Their late session of legislature has been more intolerant than all others. We must meet them with equal intolerance. When they will give a share in the state offices, they shall be replaced in

---

[38] Jefferson to Benjamin Rush, 24 March 1801, Ford, 8:32.

[39] Jefferson to Elias Shipman and Others, A Committee of the Merchants of New Haven, 12 July 1801, *TJW*, 497–500; and Jefferson to Larkin Smith, 26 November 1804, Ford, 8:336–7. Henry Adams wrote that Jefferson exhibited a "dislike for whatever might seem harsh or disobliging." Adams, 222.

[40] Prince, "Passing of the Aristocracy" (see note 1), 573–5.

[41] Jefferson to William Short, 19 May 1807, Ford, 9: 50–1.

[42] Skowronek, *Politics Presidents Make*, 72.

[43] Jefferson to Wilson Cary Nicholas, 11 June 1801, Ford, 8:64.

a share of the General offices. Till then we must follow their example."[44] But more than just using removals as a recriminatory measure against what he believed to close-mindedness within the Connecticut state government, Jefferson used the removal power to ensure that Republicans held a proportionate share of offices. By placing Republicans in Connecticut's offices the president would see more of his own administration enacted. As he put it, considerations of "justice" and "policy," then, guided his aggressive removal policy in the opposition's stronghold.

To protest the removal of Federalists in their state, several New Haven Merchants addressed a remonstrance to Jefferson, protesting the president's departure from the Inaugural's declaration of political tolerance. To counter what he believed to be a misinterpretation of the inaugural's call to conciliation, Jefferson responded to the merchants in an open letter.[45] Jefferson believed his reply would offer a unique opportunity for him to state his policy, to correct a popular misunderstanding of his inaugural address, to rally his party, and to mobilize support among the general public. As he put it, the Connecticut remonstrance was timely in that it provided him with an opportunity to explain the principles of his administration, and, specifically, the meaning of his declaration in the First Inaugural: "An opportunity was also wanting to come forward and disavow the sophistical construction on what I had declared on the 4th of March, to declare the justice of some participation by the republicans in the management of public affairs, and the principles on which vacancies would be created. I verily believe here will be a general approbation of what has been avowed in answer to the remonstrance, and that we may now proceed in our duty with a firmer step. I certainly feel more confident since an opportunity has been furnished me of explaining my proceedings."[46] By replying to the New Haven merchants, Jefferson could both interpret his own Inaugural as well as establish a new understanding of the purpose of the power to appoint and remove. Furthermore, the letter would rally both partisan and public support, thereby energizing his administration by giving it a firmer step. Because this declaration required "a peculiar mixture of energy and delicacy," Jefferson crafted it with care.[47]

In this reply, Jefferson first argued that his Inaugural's "exhortations to *harmony*" had been "quoted and misconstrued into assurances that the tenure of offices was to be undisturbed." In that message, Jefferson famously implied that there was but one party in America, as all believed

44 Jefferson to Levi Lincoln, 11 July 1801, Ford, 8:67.
45 Jefferson to Shipman and Others, *TJW*, 497–500.
46 Jefferson to Pierpont Edwards, 21 July 1801, Ford, 8:74.
47 Madison to Jefferson, 10 July 1801, quoted in Adams, 152.

in a republican form of government. In other words, as Americans were members of the one party which cherished the people, a just distribution of offices would have to ignore party labels. But to the New Haven merchants, Jefferson explained that those Republicans who had been previously denied office in fact had "equal rights" and therefore should be given their just share of offices after the "public sentiment at length declared itself" – "Is it *political intolerance* to claim a proportionate share in the direction of the public affairs?" With this argument, Jefferson appealed to the principle of correcting the disproportionate distribution of offices, implying that there was a correct proportion that could be determined. So, with his reply, Jefferson must have meant to acknowledge that he had previously exaggerated the sameness between the two parties, for proportionality would mirror what he believed to be, as he put it elsewhere, the occurrence of the two parties occurring "of nature" and existing "in all countries." Parties could be characterized by whether they "fear" or "cherish" "the people," and, the First Inaugural to the contrary, partisans who tipped the balance of proportionality would be subject to removal.[48]

But Jefferson did not stop with the argument for party spoils, for he offered another standard by which the just distribution of offices could be determined. In addition to the argument about representative proportionality, Jefferson offered an argument connecting administration and the distribution of offices with the presidential election: "If the will of the nation, manifested by their various elections, calls for an administration of government according with the opinions of those elected; if, for the fulfillment of that will displacements are necessary, with whom can they so justly begin as with persons appointed in the last moments of an administration, not for its own aid, but to begin a career at the same time with their successors, by whom they had never been approved, and who could scarcely expect from them a cordial cooperation?" Under this understanding, removals are necessary in order for the president to effect his administration, which is itself a manifestation of the public will as evidenced by the election. The president, then, not only has the authority to remove political opponents and appoint fellow partisans but is obliged to do so if he is to administer the public will. More than a check on corruption or a thumb on the scales of party equality, the removal power, as reconstructed by Jefferson, would further connect

---

[48] Jefferson to Shipman and Others, *TJW*, 498–500. On Jefferson and parties in nature, see: Jefferson to Lafayette, 4 November 1823, *The Life and Selected Writings of Thomas Jefferson*, ed. Adrienne Koch and William Peden (New York: Modern Library, 1944), 712–3, and Harvey Mansfield Jr., "Thomas Jefferson," in *American Political Thought: The Philosophic Dimension of American Statesmanship*, ed. Morton J. Frisch and Richard G. Stevens (Itasca, IL: F.E. Peacock, 1983), 44–50.

presidential administration to the "will of the nation." This is the energy that had to be made delicate.[49]

Henry Adams characterized Jefferson's argument from proportions as a convenient way for Jefferson to part with his Inaugural's call to political harmony in order to do "justice to his friends." Thus, Adams concluded, "without going so far as to assert that to the victors belonged the spoils, he [Jefferson] contented himself with claiming that to the victors belonged half the spoils."[50] But Adams missed the point of the letter to the New Haven merchants. Taken together, the argument from proportion and the argument from administration show that a strong executive removal power would "effect the purposes of justice and public utility."[51] The majority may with reason demand a proportionate share of the public offices because it is just for the majority to determine the administration of the laws, and public utility would be served because executive officials would cooperate with the will of the nation. Because the electorate would believe the laws were justly executed, presidential administration would be invigorated by the public confidence. Put differently, Jefferson believed that a "rigorous" adherence to justice would require removing at least one-half of the Federalists in office, as "it was known that these [republicans] composed a very great majority of the nation," but the majority of the nation also was so "moderate" that it did not demand that justice be so rigorously enforced.[52] Public confidence, then, would guide the sorting between too much or too little justice in removals.

In addition to proportionality, the letter to the New Haven Merchants suggested another reason for removing Federalists to make room for Republicans – executive officials could be removed on the grounds that replacing them would more likely stimulate public confidence and thus empower the administration. According to this argument, administering the public will involved maintaining the public respect. As he wrote elsewhere, Jefferson's concern with the "reputation of an administration," as it related to nominations, revealed not an attempt to cultivate a legacy inasmuch as it reflected Jefferson's belief that connecting public "respect" to appointments would energize the government, since, as he explained elsewhere, the "public respect alone can give strength to government."[53] Not only was the majority will a guide to the question as to which officers should rule, for it also ensured that those officers would more effectively rule. On these grounds, Jefferson could

---

49 Jefferson to Shipman and Others, *TJW*, 499.

50 Adams, 153.

51 Jefferson to Elias Shipman and Others, 12 July 1801, *TJW*, 497–500.

52 Jefferson to William Short, 3 October 1801, Ford, 8:97.

53 Jefferson to Archibald Stuart, 8 April 1801, Ford, 8: 46–7; Jefferson to Archibald Stuart, 25 April 1801, Ford, 8:47.

find the justification for rewarding partisans with petty offices, the offices he considered to be of "mere profit." Jefferson used these lower offices to reward the veterans of the Revolution and participants in what he believed the republic's second revolution, his own election, as "appointments on that principle would gratify the public, and strengthen the confidence so necessary to enable the executive to direct the whole public force to the best advantage of the nation."[54] Party spoils, like the party itself, would serve low and high purposes.

In 1803, Jefferson enunciated an even more aggressive position in a pseudonymous response to a reply to his open letter to New Haven merchants. Although Jefferson later claimed that he never entered public disputes without signing his name, he did, according to Ford, write the essay "Fair Play" under the signatory of "a Massachusetts citizen." In this essay, Jefferson outlined the ways by which a just proportion of offices might be determined: "They can now bear to talk themselves of an *equal number*, instead of a monopoly of offices. This is well, as a first system; & we hope, in the progress of convalescence, they will become able to bear the idea of a *due proportion*. On this ground we are ready to compromise with them: and I ask what is their due proportion? I suppose the relative number of the two parties will be thought to fix it; and that, judging from the elections, we over-rate the Federalists at one-third or fourth of the whole mass of our citizens." One problem with elections under the federal system was determining whether to count them within each state or by the state together, that is, nationally. Here, Jefferson sided with the nation over the states as the measure of the majority will, at least on the grounds that determining a majority will from the states would be too complicated. The question, again, was whether to effect these changes by removing Federalist officeholders or by waiting for them to retire. Jefferson's "Massachusetts citizen" confessed impatience – "they proceeded slower than I expected" – but also stated that he was willing to trust the "constitutional authorities," as the slower pace might "allay the passions which so unpleasantly divide & disquiet us." Having discarded the extreme positions taken by Republicans and Federalists, Jefferson's "Massachusetts citizen" closed with the assurance of a "fair compromise" arrived at by a president bound to "modify jarring principles." The proportionality required by nature would have to be softened by executive judgment.[55]

But there was one exception to the proportionate distribution of offices, that is, one jarring principle that could not enter into the compromise.

---

[54] Jefferson to John Page, 17 July 1807, Ford, 9:117–9.
[55] Jefferson, "Fair Play," Ford, 8:234–9.

According to the author of "Fair Play," the president could not allow a "monarchist," someone who opposed the republican form of government, to hold office. Put somewhat differently, as member of the other party in nature, to which Jefferson only alluded in his inaugural, monarchists could expect toleration from the executive but not an office in its administration: "These men have no right to office. If a monarchist be in office anywhere, and it be known to the President, the oath he has taken to support the constitution imperiously requires the instantaneous dismission of such an officer and I should hold the President highly criminal if he permitted such to remain." Here, Jefferson alluded to a problem with distributing offices in democracy. Under the argument from proportion it would seem that monarchists would hold a special claim to office, as they represented one portion of the people. But here Jefferson denied any share in the government to persons who preferred monarchy to republicanism on the grounds that the president's oath, to execute his office and to protect the Constitution, required their removal. Significantly, Washington had referred to his oath to defend his use of the military to put down riotous settlers in Western Pennsylvania, but it was Lincoln who deliberately transformed the oath into a source for, rather than a constraint on, presidential discretion.[56] Following Washington, and anticipating Lincoln, the "Massachusetts Citizen" used the oath to argue for a wider presidential privilege, and, in this case, the oath required, or allowed, the president to more vigorously assert a hitherto contested removal power.[57]

The Transformation

Again, Jefferson extended executive power instead of distancing himself from it, but there were alternative paths. Public opinion, always on the president's mind, was scattered. A few days after taking office, for instance, Jefferson noted that public opinion was no sure guide regarding the question: Federalists would "cry out on the first touch on their monopoly," while Republicans would "clamor for universal removal."[58] "My idea is that where two measures are equally right, it is a duty to the people to adopt that one is most agreeable to them.... But as to removals from office, great differences of opinion exist. That some ought to be removed all will agree. That all should, nobody will say: And no two will probably draw the same line between these two extremes; consequently nothing like general approbation can be

---

[56] See Chapter 10.
[57] Jefferson, "Fair Play," Ford, 8:238.
[58] Jefferson to John Dickinson, 23 July 1801, Ford, 8:76.

expected."[59] Moreover, instead of leaving the power to his party in Congress, he unequivocally asserted the president as the caretaker of executive administration. Removal of executive officials was thus different from removal of judges by virtue of the repeal of the Judiciary Act. In the case of the latter, Congress asserted its power to remove judges by repealing the act which created their offices. To be sure, they employed Jefferson's statistics that the new judges were not needed, and they extended the distinction between freehold and office, also used by Jefferson in his 1780 observations on removal, to argue that judges served at the pleasure of the people.[60] The point here is that the repeal was known as "the president's measure," but it turned on congressional rather than executive power. Jefferson might have opted for this method with regard to executive officers, but he did not.[61]

It is also important to notice that Jefferson did not continue along another path left open by Madison. Recall that in the 1789 debate Madison had argued that the presidential removal power forged of "chain of responsibility" between administration and the people, but he also argued that the difference in the vesting clauses of Articles One and Two revealed an expansive grant of executive authority to the president. The reason what Jefferson embraced Madison's first argument but spurned the latter is because Jefferson had serious reservations about undefined grants of authority in written constitutions. Like Hamilton's claim as Pacificus that the Constitution silently authorized the president to determine whether treaties were still binding, Madison's claim for inherent executive authority raised dangerous questions about the illimitable nature of executive power. Rather than following Madison's constitutional argument, Jefferson emphasized Madison's functional argument, which preserved public opinion as an extraconstitutional check on power. Jefferson's remarkably public defense marked an expansion of presidential power, but it also suggested a way to dismantle it.

Jefferson was well aware that his use of the appointment and removal power marked a departure from the path charted by his predecessors. As he explained to Horatio Turpin near the end of his own administration, the model for the use of the appointment power was not to be found in earlier administrations but rather in the "nature of our government": "Its energy depending mainly on the confidence of the people in the chief magistrate, makes it his duty to spare nothing which can strengthen him with that confidence."[62] After he retired, Jefferson explained to a family member that he

[59] Jefferson to William Findley, 24 March 1801, Ford, 8:26–7.
[60] Jefferson, "First Annual Message," *TJW*, 507; Adams, 195.
[61] Ellis, *Jeffersonian Crisis*, 44–45.
[62] Jefferson to Horatio Turpin, 10 June 1807, Washington, 5:90.

could not assist him in securing an appointment because it would undermine the public's confidence in the administration: "In a government like ours, it is the duty of the Chief Magistrate . . . to unite himself in the confidence of the whole people."[63] This union with people's confidence "alone" could gather together the potential energy of the government, that is, "produce a union of the powers of the whole, and point them in a single direction." Here, Jefferson made the connection between executive energy and popular leadership clear: rather than being antithetical to executive power, democracy was part and parcel of it.

In summary, Jefferson's public defenses of the removal power pointed to a theory of administration. Government offices should be divided between the parties that Jefferson believed to be natural – the Whigs and the Tories. The proportion awarded to each should reflect the public will, as determined by the national elections, especially the presidential election. Because the people would have more confidence in an administration that resembled itself, the removal power would use the means of justice to serve the ends of effectiveness. Rejecting Hamilton's position in the *Federalist* that the Senate should have a share in administration by way of appointment and removal, Jefferson firmly reestablished Washington's precedent of presidential removal while at the same time changing it by connecting the power to the public will. Even before he became president, Jefferson combined his understanding of party with his concern for elections – interfering with elections would be grounds for removal, "because the constitutional remedy by the elective principle becomes nothing, if it may be smothered by the enormous patronage of the general gov[ern]me[n]t."[64] Once he was elected president, he was lucky that the outgoing Federalists had forced his hand, allowing him to explain that his election conferred on him the painful duty to be executioner on behalf of the public will.

When Jefferson settled this question of authority, he added the point that the president ought to be a kind of custodian of public opinion. By offering alongside the practice of actual removals the argument that a president may remove officers because the president represents the constitutional majority, Jefferson connected the removal power to his larger doctrine of presidential power. This doctrine included public confidence as a source for energy in the unitary executive.

It is useful, then, to note the parallels with other aspects of Jefferson's plan for executive power. When Jefferson told Garland that public confidence required him to "spare nothing" which would strengthen that confidence,

[63] Jefferson to J. Garland Jefferson, 1810, Ford, 9:270.
[64] Jefferson to Thomas M'Kean, 2 February 1801, Ford, ed., 7: 487.

he seemed to allude to his understanding of presidential prerogative. Under that doctrine, presidents must step outside the law even in cases not required by necessity. Accordingly, Jefferson's manipulation of the law – manifested in slander campaigns, refusals to deliver commissions, and mathematical sleights of hand – was a war on the law itself, waged on behalf of the public will. But there is also a difference: because Jefferson believed that executive appointments and removals were, under the Constitution, an executive matter, he did not believe that removals were, properly speaking, unconstitutional. Here, perhaps lies an explanation for Jefferson's recourse to the oath of office. On the one hand, he believed that removing Federalists was well within his constitutional powers, but, on the other, he had misgivings about using the oath for expanding presidential power, and using removals for partisan purposes was certainly an expansion. As a result, he referred to the oath, but only under pseudonym.

Just as his position on removals was related to his understanding of prerogative, it tested his reliance on presidential declarations to both direct the majority will and to mark the limits of presidential power. Indeed, the most striking aspect of the open letter to the New Haven Federalists is Jefferson's observation that he wanted an opportunity to correct what he characterized as a misinterpretation of the First Inaugural. Put differently, the Inaugural, more than the offices, was at stake. If Federalists succeeded in elevating the party unity theme of the Inaugural over the majority will theme, then the Revolution of 1800 would be a matter of politics but not administration – declarations of principle could come and go, but the execution of the laws would be stable and separate. At the same time, if the Inaugural was proven to be mere rhetoric, distinct from and even masking over the real twists and turns of politicians contending for power, then the people would come to expect presidents to offer declarations of principle but depart from them whenever it was in their interest. Jefferson recognized that the remonstrance from New Haven was timely because he needed a chance to explain how principle could be put to practice.

Combined, prerogative and declarations strengthen executive power by refashioning the majority will. Because the majority will is dispersed and imprecise, appointments and removals should be directed at gathering confidence around the president, which is to say that appointments and removals give form and meaning to ideas that would otherwise remain abstract and tentative. Just as action brings clarity to thought, appointments and removals would provide the bodies to carry out public opinion. For consent to work, the public had to have confidence – not jealousy – in its executives.

But if the presidential election produces a change of the offices, what would prevent the administration of the laws from becoming, as Hamilton worried, "ruinous and mutable"? Jefferson avoided answering this question directly, saying that had there been a proportionate share of offices in the first place, not that many changes would be necessary. At the same time, his argument for confidence in the executive corresponds to his statements in republican government. By allowing presidents to gather the will of the nation around administration, appointments and removals would keep the government in line with what Jefferson later called the "mother principle" of republicanism – that "governments are republican only in proportion as they embody the will of the people, and execute it."[65]

Indeed, when contrasted to Jefferson's argument that public confidence derives from proportionality, Hamilton's concern for steady and immutable administration suggests that removals might have traveled along other paths. The participation of the Senate in the removal power would have moved the bureaucracy closer to a civil service based on merit and holding office for life, because Senators would find that a longer tenure for executive officers would separate them presidential ambition and insulate them from the currents of national politics. The possibility that appointees would serve longer than the executive who had appointed them, if not for life, was real. Merit would, perhaps, come to trump affiliation with a principle and thus become the new standard of public confidence. Even without the participation of the Senate, had Jefferson not asserted his power to dismantle the lame-duck creation of a defeated party, elections and offices would be separated. This explains Jefferson's emphasis on the word confidence: if the officers who execute the laws are unrelated to the presidential election, then the people might come to believe that presidential elections were meaningless. In short, when Jacksonians made the less elegant claim that the spoils belonged to the victors, they were putting into practice what Jefferson had made possible in theory.

[65] Jefferson to Samuel Kercheval, 12 July 1816, *TJW*, 1396.

7

The Louisiana Purchase

By the time Jefferson was elected president, he was an experienced law-maker as well as a seasoned executive. As two-term governor during wartime, ambassador, secretary of state, and vice president, Jefferson was well aware that necessity sometimes required extraordinary acts of executive discretion. As representative of his state, participant in the formation of his state's constitution, reformer of his state's laws, discussant with Madison, and cofounder of his party, Jefferson also understood the sometimes strained relationship of executive prerogative and consent. Throughout his career, he attempted to preserve the law by interpreting it strictly while at the same time explaining that a strict construction of the law would require that the law be set aside during times of necessity or enterprise, on the condition that the executive submit to political judgment by announcing his extralegal activity. His transformation of the prerogative power turned on what he believed to be the connection between executive power and majority rule.

The Louisiana Purchase has been considered the greatest achievement of Jefferson's administration but also an example of political principle yielding to practical necessity. Henry Adams called the event "so momentous" that it "defied measurement" and speculated that the purchase "ranked in historical importance next to the Declaration of Independence and the adoption of the Constitution." But, in Adams's view, the Purchase's importance derived as much from its constitutional legacy as from its size, for Jefferson's purchasing and incorporating Louisiana was the fatal blow to the strict construction of the Constitution.[1] Scholars have similarly pointed to the Louisiana Purchase as an example of Jefferson's abandoning his constitutional scruples

---

[1] Adams, 334, 386–7.

when confronted by political difficulty.[2] Some have gone so far as to label Jefferson's handling of the Louisiana Purchase as an example of the prerogative power.[3] As the central event of Jefferson's presidency, and the most obvious illustration of the tension between executive power and consent, the Louisiana Purchase requires more investigation.

Louisiana

As Jefferson understood the Constitution, there was no grant of authority that would allow the national government to incorporate new territory into the Union. The question of the constitutionality of the Purchase thus resembled the debate over the bank: does the treaty power contain an implied power to enlarge the country? But, as even the most casual reading of the Convention debates reveals, changing the size of the country raises questions about the relationship of the states to one another and of each state to the union. For Jefferson, the Purchase was unconstitutional because it would reconstruct the Union.[4] Changing the terms of the contract between the states, then, would require an amendment to the Constitution.

Jefferson's difficulty in finding a defense for the Purchase grew from a problem fundamental to his doctrine of strict construction. It is very difficult to argue for strict construction of a document that includes political compromises, some of which its chief proponents believed contradicted its own spirit and design.[5] In the case of incorporating new territory, the Northwest Ordinance as well as the Articles of Confederation implied that Americans at the time of the Founding believed that new territories would join the

---

[2] Stephen Skowronek, *The Politics Presidents Make: Leadership from John Adams to George Bush* (Cambridge, MA: Harvard University Press/Belknap Press, 1993), 79; Joseph J. Ellis, *American Sphinx: The Character of Jefferson* (New York: Knopf, 1996), 210–12 (Page references are to the 1998 edition); and Marc Landy and Sidney M. Milkis, *Presidential Greatness* (Lawrence: University Press of Kansas, 2000), 78.

[3] Arthur M. Schlesinger Jr., *The Imperial Presidency* (Boston: Houghton Mifflin, 1973), 23–25; Robert M. Johnstone Jr., *Jefferson and the Presidency: Leadership in the Young Republic* (Ithaca, NY: Cornell University Press, 1978), 71–4; David N. Mayer, *Constitutional Thought of Thomas Jefferson* (Charlottesville, VA: University Press of Virginia, 1994), 253; Paul A. Rahe, "Jefferson's Machiavellian Moment," in *Reason and Republicanism: Thomas Jefferson's Legacy of Liberty*, ed. Gary L. McDowell and Sharon L. Noble (Lanham, MD: Rowman and Littlefield, 1997), 65–6; Gary J. Schmitt, "Thomas Jefferson and the Presidency," in *Inventing the American Presidency*, ed., Thomas E. Cronin (Lawrence: University Press of Kansas, 1989), 337–8; Raymond Tatalovich and Thomas S. Engeman, *The Presidency and Political Science* (Baltimore: Johns Hopkins University Press, 2003), 36; and Clement Fatovic, "Constitutionalism and Presidential Prerogative," *American Journal of Political Science* 48 (2004): 434–5.

[4] Peter S. Onuf, "The Revolution of 1803," *The Wilson Quarterly* 27(2003): 22–9.

[5] *The Federalist* Nos. 37 and 54, pp. 221–29, 348–53.

Union and their inhabitants admitted as citizens. Nevertheless, this assumption was blurred by the wording of the Constitution, which Gouverneur Morris deliberately crafted in order to avoid the possibility that new territory would be granted political representation.[6] To get around the paradoxes of strict construction, Jefferson implemented his unique doctrine of presidential strength.

The Diplomatic Mission

Spain's cession of Louisiana to France was not welcomed by Jefferson. After learning of the deal in April 1802, he wrote to the ambassador to France, Robert Livingston, to express concern.[7] In the president's estimation, the cession "completely reverse[d] all the political relations of the US" and therefore would "form a new epoch" in America's "political course." Formerly an ally and a symbolic counterpart to Jefferson's party, republican France had made itself an enemy to the United States by acquiring New Orleans from Spain. "There is on the globe one single spot, the possessor of which is our natural and habitual enemy. It is New Orleans, through which the produce of three-eighths of our territory must pass to market, and from its fertility it will ere long yield more than half our whole produce and contain more than half our inhabitants." Spain might have been a less dangerous power to continue its hold on the city, for, with its waning influence in the region, it had allowed the United States the right of deposit, that is, the ability to use the port of the river of which the Americans had already laid claim. France, by contrast, had too much to gain by keeping New Orleans closed to the United States: the "impetuosity of her temper, the energy and restlessness of her character" would forever bump against the national aspirations of the American republic, "which though quiet, and loving peace and the pursuit of wealth," was as "enterprising and energetic as any nation on earth." If France were to assert control over New Orleans, then the United States would have to "marry" itself to its former enemy, the British navy. As Jefferson put it, the mounting crisis in foreign policy was not lost on public opinion. "Every eye" in the nation was "fixed on this affair of Louisiana," for it had "produced more uneasy sensations through the body of the nation" than any

---

[6] Morris to Henry W. Livingston, 4 December 1803, quoted in Everett Somerville Brown, *Constitutional History of the Louisiana Purchase, 1803–1812* (Berkeley: University of California Press, 1920), 44.

[7] Jefferson to Robert Livingston, 18 April 1802, *TJW*, 1104–7. See also "The Cession of Louisiana" in *Old South Leaflets*, Vol. 6 (Boston: Directors of the Old South Work, Old South Meeting House, 1906).

event since the revolutionary war.[8] Hamilton, who had in 1799 argued that
Congress should declare war on France so that "the Executive should be
clothed with power" to secure Louisiana and Florida against France and her
allies, believed that the cession presented an emergency for national security
and a dilemma for the Republican Party.[9] And although Jefferson did not
say it, the uneasiness was most pronounced in the South: if Henry Adams
is to be trusted, southerners "looked to the military occupation of Mobile,
Pensacola, and New Orleans as a future political necessity."[10]

To resolve the foreign policy dilemma and to settle public opinion, Jefferson asked James Monroe to serve as special minister to France.[11] Appointing
someone as devoted to Jefferson as Monroe would signal to Napoleon that
the nation's representative was speaking for the administration and, perhaps
just as important, also would quiet mounting anxiety in the South and West,
regions in which Monroe was particularly respected. As Jefferson reminded
Monroe, "remonstrances" and "memorials" had been "circulating through
the whole of the western country," partly because the people were not privy
to what Jefferson had hitherto done in secret. Nevertheless, Monroe's task
would be difficult – he would have to purchase New Orleans, secure a right
of deposit, or go to London to form a new alliance. Because no one set of
instructions could be given that would meet every possible combination of
these three alternatives, Monroe would be allowed special latitude: "Something sensible therefore was become necessary; and indeed our object of
purchasing N. Orleans and the Floridas is a measure liable to assume so
many shapes, that no instructions could be squared to fit them, it was essential then to send a minister extraordinary to be joined with the ordinary one,
with discretionary powers, first however well impressed with our views and
therefore qualified to meet and modify to these every form of proposition
which could come from the other party." Because the difficulty of the task
was not lost on Monroe, Jefferson appealed to the Virginian's sense of public
honor – "All eyes, all hopes, are now fixed on you" – and warned that if
Monroe were to decline the nomination, "the chagrin would be universal,
and would shake under your feet the high ground on which you stand with
the public."

But on what authority would Monroe stand in venturing to broker a deal
which would decide whether the nation would remain at peace? Absent from

---

[8] Jefferson to Livingston, *TJW*, 1105.
[9] Hamilton to Harrison Gray Otis, 26 January 1799, *PAH*, 22:441; and Hamilton to General
    Charles Cotesworth Pinckney, 29 December 1802, *PAH*, 26:71–3.
[10] Adams, 229.
[11] Jefferson to James Monroe, 13 January 1803, *TJW*, 1111–13.

Jefferson's appealing to Monroe's ambition was any reminder or explanation of the source or limits of Monroe's constitutional authority. Jefferson never mentioned to Monroe that the deal he would broker might lie outside the authority granted the general government by the Constitution. In fact, Jefferson's reminder of Monroe's ambition for public life suggests that that the president had already pushed aside his constitutional scruples, even in advance of his learning of the vastness of the territory acquired in the purchase of Louisiana. "I am sensible after the measures you have taken for getting into a different line business, that it will be a great sacrifice on your part, and presents from the season and other circumstances serious difficulties. But some men are born for the public. Nature by fitting them for the service of the human race on a broad scale, has stamped with the evidences of her destination and their duty."[12] By serious difficulties Jefferson must have meant the financial hardship caused by the expenses and low salary of public service – no small matter consideration for Monroe, who was less wealthy than Jefferson. But in addition to the costliness of the mission, Jefferson must have meant the painful and politically risky task of negotiating a controversial and complicated treaty. To fortify Monroe with regard to the latter, Jefferson appealed to his argument for a natural aristocracy.[13]

As is well known, Napoleon offered to sell more than Jefferson could have imagined. Consequently, Adams questioned whether Jefferson deserved the credit for what turned out to be the greatest achievement of Jefferson's presidency.[14] What has not been sufficiently considered, however, is the fact that Monroe and Livingston went outside their official instructions by purchasing such a large extent of territory and spending fifty percent more than they were allotted. Monroe's official instructions provided for three scenarios. If Napoleon were willing to sell New Orleans and the Floridas, then Monroe and Livingston were authorized to spend up to $10 million to purchase as much as Napoleon would sell. If Napoleon refused to sell, then Monroe and Livingston were to secure the right of deposit. In the event that Napoleon refused to either sell or allow the right of deposit, then Monroe and Livingston were to act according to another set of instructions.[15] Although Monroe's instructions were written by Madison, Jefferson had read them and, with one minor exception, had called them "entirely right."[16]

[12] Ibid.
[13] Jefferson to John Adams, 28 October 1813, Cappon, 387–9.
[14] See, for example, Adams 285–335.
[15] Adams, 297–8.
[16] Jefferson to Madison, 22 February 1803, Smith, 1262.

The Constitutional Question

Although Jefferson passed over the constitutional question in his letter to Monroe, he did consider it. On the same day that Jefferson wrote to Monroe, Gallatin wrote Jefferson to offer his own opinion on this constitutional question. Gallatin's letter was written in reply to Attorney General Levi Lincoln's recommendation that the administration dodge possible constitutional objections by annexing the territory to an existing state or states. According to Gallatin, such a policy would not answer the proposed constitutional argument that the government did not have the power to acquire territory: under Lincoln's argument, Massachusetts could acquire Cuba whenever the national government was in a colonial mood. More important, Gallatin argued that there was no such constitutional problem, as "the existence of the United States as a nation presupposes the power enjoyed by every nation of extending their territories by treaties." Therefore, the organs by which the government may make treaties, the president and the Senate, were authorized by the Constitution to acquire territories, and Congress had the power to govern territories once acquired. Gallatin noted that if there were a constitutional difficulty, it would arise from the Tenth Amendment. One could argue that because all powers not delegated to the government are reserved to the states or to the people, the national government would have to acquire authority in this case from the states or the people. Gallatin's advice, given to the very person who had used similar reasoning against the bank, was that such an argument would be forced: "If that be the true construction of the Constitution, it substantially amounts to this: that the United States are precluded from, and renounce altogether, the enlargement of territory, a provision sufficiently important and singular to have deserved to be expressly enacted. Is it not a more natural construction to say that the power of acquiring territory is delegated to the United States by the several provisions which authorize the several branches of government to make war, to make treaties, and to govern the territory of the Union." As Gallatin explained, the argument from construction would not apply in this case because such an obvious implied power would have been expressly denied rather than simply omitted.[17]

Jefferson agreed with Gallatin's rejection of the argument that the government could add territory to existing states, but the president retained the distinction between the Union acquiring territory and incorporating that territory into the Union. "You are right, in my opinion, as to Mr. L's proposition

---

[17] Albert Gallatin to Jefferson, 13 January 1803, *Writings of Albert Gallatin*, ed. Henry Adams (Philadelphia: J. B. Lippincott & Co., 1879), 1: 212–5.

that there is no constitutional difficulty as to the acquisition of territory, and whether, when acquired, it may be taken into the Union by the Constitution as it now stands, will become a question of expediency. I think it will be safer not to permit, the enlargement of the Union but by an amendment of the Constitution."[18] Constitutional interpretation aside, Jefferson and his cabinet then made preparations for making an alliance with Great Britain, in the event that Napoleon refused to sell or grant right of deposit.[19] So set was Jefferson on acquiring New Orleans, that the plan for treating with Great Britain included a strategy for eventually gaining New Orleans by military means.

From the time of his letters to Monroe and Gallatin until the arrival of news of the treaty, Jefferson seems to have spent little time thinking over the constitutional difficulties of the purchase. Indeed, the most striking thing about the correspondence between Jefferson and Madison between January 1803 and July 1803 is that the two friends who had so often exchanged views on constitutional interpretation rarely wrote each other about Louisiana. Rather than discussing whether the power to incorporate territory was an implied power of every government, the president and Secretary of State devoted their attention to other occasions where other executive officials were far away from Washington: the Lewis and Clark expedition, payment to a Danish captain who had goods taken from him, and the escalating conflict in Tripoli. Events had directed Jefferson's thoughts away from constitutional questions.[20]

After news of the treaty arrived on 3 July 1803, Jefferson backed away from Gallatin's argument that acquiring territory was an implied power of the government. The president's change in heart grew out of the fact that Monroe and Livingston had signed a treaty for which they had been given insufficient authority. First, the enormity of the territory was beyond the scope of the instructions and budget. Second, the treaty stipulated that the inhabitants of the territory be given the rights of citizens and admitted, eventually, as citizens. Even though Madison had written Monroe with a draft model for a treaty that included a provision to "incorporate the inhabitants of the hereby ceded territory with the citizens of the United States on an equal footing,"[21] the extension of this stipulation to inhabitants of

---

[18] Jefferson to Albert Gallatin, January, 1803, Ford, 8:241.

[19] Jefferson, *Anas*, in Paul Leicester Ford, ed., *The Works of Thomas Jefferson*, 12 volumes (New York: GP Putnam's Sons, 1904–05), 1: 372.

[20] Jefferson to Thomas Paine, 13 January 1803, Ford, 8:189; Jefferson, "Confidential Message on Expedition to the Pacific," 18 January 1803, Ford, 8:192–202.

[21] Madison to James Monroe, 2 March 1803, Quoted in Brown, *Constitutional History*, 66–7. Monroe set sail on March 8, 1803.

the larger Louisiana Territory was beyond Monroe's instructions and would significantly change the shape of the United States. To solve the problem of incorporation, which was made more difficult by the requirement of citizenship, Jefferson and Madison worked on an amendment to the Constitution authorizing the incorporation of the territory and guaranteeing white inhabitants of Louisiana basic rights.[22] Meanwhile, Jefferson and his cabinet resolved that the "substance of the treaty" would be "made public," but "not the treaty itself."[23]

After exchanging drafts with Madison, Jefferson wrote Republican leaders in Congress to tell them that an amendment would be necessary even after the treaty was ratified and money appropriated. In August, he informed Breckinridge that the treaty would be laid before "both Houses" so that the Senate could ratify it and that the House could make the necessary appropriations. And he seemed confident that Congressmen would recognize the opportunity the situation presented and would approve the treaty: "They, I presume, will see their duty to their country in ratifying & paying for it, so as to secure a good which would otherwise probably be never again in their power." But their approval of the treaty would have to be expressed by proposing a constitutional amendment. To convince Breckinridge that this more difficult task was necessary, Jefferson employed the formula he had crafted over the years: "The constitution has made no provision for our holding foreign territory, still less for incorporating foreign nations into our Union. The Executive in seizing the fugitive occurrence which so much advances the good of their country, have done an act beyond the Constitution." Because the president and his ministers had gone outside the Constitution to negotiate a treaty, the Senate would need to ratify the treaty and then recommend an amendment to the Constitution. Just as in 1781 he had called members of the Virginia Assembly into an early session with the instructions to give sanction to officials who had executed an expired impress, Jefferson asked Senators to assume the risk incurred by the executive branch: "The Legislature in casting behind them metaphysical subtleties, and risking themselves like faithful servants, must ratify & pay for it, and throw themselves on their country for doing for them unauthorized what we know they would have done for themselves had they been in a situation to do it." Worth noting in Jefferson's plan is that the amendment would not simply exonerate the executive branch from acting without authority but would also justify Senators and members of the House who approved of the treaty. Put differently, Jefferson's letter to the Senator from Kentucky was meant to stiffen

[22] Jefferson to Madison, July 1803 and 24 August 1803, Smith, 1269–71.
[23] Jefferson, *Anas*, 374.

the resolve of legislators for whom constitutional words might have gotten in the way of action. To explain and persuade, Jefferson added the following example: "It is the case of a guardian, investing the money of his ward in purchasing an important adjacent territory; & saying to him when of age, I did this for your good; I pretend no right to bind you: you may disavow me, and I must get out of the scrape as I can: I thought it my duty to risk myself for you." By illustrating the purchase in terms of the guardian and the ward, Jefferson meant to persuade the Senator that ratification would be appropriate and praiseworthy even while expecting constitutional amendment: although the ward might in theory disavow the guardian, Senators who followed the administration "would not be disavowed by the nation."[24]

In line with his expansion of Locke's "always in being" to "constant agency," Jefferson's ward example broadened the application of the prerogative power, for it suggested, unlike Locke's example of pulling down an innocent man's house to stop a fire, that the prerogative could be used as an investment.[25] Less of a necessity than self-preservation, investment affords more room to those who act out of the course of law for the public good. Seen from the viewpoint of investment, the president's prerogative power is required by the people for whom the president acts as agent. Educated under this understanding, the people extend credit to their presidents, expecting them to invest for their good.

As is well known, Jefferson's recommendation of the amendment was complicated by the circumstance that his French counterpart cared little for constitutional argument. This point is best illustrated by a story relayed by Henry Adams: when his brother said that it would violate the French constitution to sell Louisiana without the consent of the Chambers, Napoleon scoffed, "Constitution! Unconstitutional! republic! national sovereignty! – big words! great phrases! Do you think yourself still in the club of St. Maximin?"[26] Although Adams must have meant for some of this account's color to rub off on Jefferson, the point here is that the president knew that the opportunity to purchase the territory was subject to Napoleon's will, not French law. Accordingly, Jefferson stopped recommending an amendment to the Constitution after hearing reports that Napoleon had second thoughts about following through on the deal. On 17 August, Jefferson received a letter from Livingston that said Napoleon had expressed regrets in selling

---

[24] Jefferson to John C. Breckinridge, 12 August 1803, Ford, 8:242–5.

[25] For "constant agency," see p. 41. For Locke's example, see *Second Treatise*, sections 159–60 in *John Locke: Two Treatises of Government*, student edition, ed. Peter Laslett (Cambridge: Cambridge University Press, 1988), 375.

[26] Adams, 326–7. Adams also reports that Napoleon said that, as the treaty was "conceived by me, negotiated by me," it would also be "ratified and executed by me alone."

Louisiana and was making preparations to protest the deal if the Americans were tardy in ratifying the treaty. On 18 August, Jefferson forwarded Livingston's letter to Madison and included a change in the direction of the administration: "I infer that the less we say about constitutional difficulties respecting Louisiana the better, and that what is necessary for surmounting them be done sub silentio."[27] On the same day, Jefferson wrote Breckinridge to inform the senator of the new strategy: "A letter received yesterday shews that nothing must be said on that subject which may give a pretext for retracting; but that we should do sub-silentio what shall be found necessary. Be so good therefore as to consider that part of my letter as confidential." In place of public declaration, the Senate should rely on organization, speed, and, most important, secrecy. "It strengthens the reasons for desiring the presence of every friend to the treaty on the first day of the session. Perhaps you can impress this necessity on the Senators of the western states by private letter." Breckinridge seems to have been persuaded by the president. In his reply of mid-September, the Senator worried that "our Atlantic Brethern of *both* parties" would be alarmed that the "empire" would be so greatly expanded in "one quarter of the union." But he assured Jefferson that he would work to have the treaty ratified: "We certainly discharge the duty imposed on us, and I am willing to answer to our posterity, by seizing every occasion to advance the present prosperity of our country." The timely arrival of friendly Senators proved was crucial to ratification of the Louisiana Purchase.[28]

About a week later, Jefferson wrote a similar message to Wilson Carey Nicholas, enclosing a letter from Monroe which contained the hint that Napoleon was considering changing his mind. In this letter, Jefferson explained that "in the opinion of our ministers" Napoleon would not have sold the territory "if the things were to do over again" and that if the United States gave "the least opening, they [France] will declare the treaty void." Further, Jefferson told Nicholas that "a warning amounting" to the threat that France would void the treaty was "written by their minister to our Secretary of Sate, direct." The president then gave the Senator from Virginia instructions much like those given to Judas Iscariot: "Whatever Congress shall think it necessary to do, should be done with as little debate as possible, & particularly so far as respects the constitutional difficulty."[29]

---

[27] Jefferson to Madison, 18 August 1803, Smith, 1278.
[28] Jefferson to Breckinridge, 18 August 1803, Ford, 8:244–5; John C. Breckinridge to Jefferson, 10 September 1810, *The Thomas Jefferson Papers, Series 1, General Correspondence, 1651–1827*, Library of Congress.
[29] Jefferson to Wilson Carey Nicholas, 7 September 1803, *TJW*, 1139–41; and John 13: 27.

Jefferson's letter to Nicholas was actually written in reply to the Senator's unsolicited letter of advice to the president. In that letter, Nicholas argued for an expansive interpretation of the treaty power in order to justify the acquisition of Louisiana. According to Nicholas, the only limit to the power to acquire territory was that "new states" could not "be formed out of the old ones without the consent of the *State* to be dismembered." This exception, according to Nicholas, proved that "it was not intended to confine the congress in the admission of new States to what was then the territory of the U.S." After giving his opinion on the treaty power, Nicholas gave his opinion on the domestic implications of the president's choice of action. Without knowing that Jefferson then believed Napoleon was looking for a way out of the treaty, Nicholas urged Jefferson to refrain from making public his opinion that the treaty required an amendment: "By giving an opinion before the Senate act upon it, you wou'd take the whole responsibility of that opinion upon yourself in the public estimation, whereas if the Senate act before your opinion is known they will at least divide the responsibility with you." Behind Nicholas's advice for dividing the responsibility of negotiating a treaty beyond the power of the Constitution was a threat which Jefferson might have regarded as more serious than that sent by the French minister: "I shou'd think it very probable if the treaty shou'd be by you declared to exceed the constitutional authority of the treaty making power, that it would be rejected by the Senate, and if that should not happen, that great use wou'd be made with the people, of a wilful breach of the constitution." Nicholas's advice pitted constitutional scruples against public opinion and therefore placed before Jefferson a peculiar dilemma: if the president admitted that he doubted the Constitution provided for the terms of the Louisiana treaty, the president would either guarantee the failure of the treaty in the Senate or, at least, risk being blamed with trying to persuade the Senate to ratify an unconstitutional treaty. By remaining silent, the treaty would likely pass and the president could share whatever criticism regarding the Constitution with the Senate.[30]

What is curious about Jefferson's reply is that the president sidestepped Nicholas's threat that the Senate would probably reject the treaty if Jefferson voiced his scruples. Rather than assuring Nicholas that he possessed the requisite votes in the Senate, Jefferson responded with a lesson on the treaty power and constitutional interpretation. According to Jefferson, the Constitution limited the government to the territory "precisely fixed by the treaty of 1783" because the Constitution's declaration that it was "made for the

---

[30] Wilson Carey Nicholas to Jefferson, 3 September 1803, quoted in Brown, *Constitutional History*, 26–27.

US" suggests that Congress was given the authority to admit new states out of "the territory for which, & under whose authority alone, they were then acting." By contrast, Nicholas's broad interpretation of the treaty power would allow for Congress to admit "England, Ireland, Holland, &c" into the United States. "When an instrument admits two constructions, the one safe, the other dangerous, the one precise, the other indefinite, I prefer that which is safe & precise. I had rather ask an enlargement of power from the nation, where it is found necessary, than to assume it by a construction which would make our powers boundless. Our peculiar security is in possession of a written Constitution. Let us not make it a blank paper by construction." The argument that the treaty power was "boundless" was more dangerous than incorrect in that it jeopardized the limitations of power under the Constitution.[31]

Jefferson's concern for the Constitution, however, did not indicate any attachment to the particular document. Rather, Jefferson's argument presumed that the distribution of powers set forth in the Constitution was "defective," which "is the ordinary case of all human works," but was worth preserving as a starting point: "Let us go then perfecting it, by adding, by way of amendment to the Constitution, those powers which time & trial show are still wanting." The Louisiana treaty, then, illustrated that the Constitution was defective in that it did not provide for incorporating new territory, and an appeal to the people in the form of amendment would "set an example against broad construction." By advocating an amendment, Jefferson and his followers in Congress would give public opinion a lesson on constitutional scruples.[32]

But Jefferson did not end his reply with a demand for the amendment, for he closed this lesson on construction with a confession of compromise. If "our friends shall think differently," then he would "acquiesce," with the qualifying hope that "the good sense of the people" would "correct the evil of construction."[33] Another of Jefferson's "friends," Thomas Paine, did think differently, for the author of *Common Sense* wrote the president with the reminder that constitutional questions were less important than republican ones. For Paine, the Purchase would "extend the principles of it over a larger territory, and this certainly is within the morality of the Constitution."[34] Whether Jefferson would have agreed that the situation could be judged only by "the circumstances of the times," it is probable,

---

[31] Jefferson to Wilson Carey Nicholas, *TJW*, 1139–41.
[32] Ibid.
[33] Ibid.
[34] Thomas Paine to Jefferson, 23 September 1803, quoted in Malone, 4: 321.

as Mayer notes, that Jefferson saw in Paine's "a refreshing bit of common sense": the larger the country, the larger the application of the Constitution's principles.[35] Conveniently, Jefferson himself had spoken of "the Empire of liberty" when he was the governor of Virginia, and Madison had argued in 1787 that the "extended republic" would be beneficial to republican government. Moreover, Paine's emphasis on the principles of the Constitution must have reminded Jefferson of his own praise of "faithful citizens" who did not allow "legal scruples" to interfere with their executing the "substance" of the law.[36] Jefferson never publicly recommended constitutional amendment, and, persuaded by his friends, the president did not inform the Senate that he believed he had acted outside his own constitutional authority.[37]

Breckinridge seems to have executed Jefferson's request that "friends of the treaty" arrive on time. On 17 October, the Eighth Congress began its first session, "three weeks sooner than the time established by a law of last session," according to William Plumer.[38] Because Jefferson delivered his addresses by writing rather than in person, Senators assembled with their counterparts from the House to receive the president's "Third Annual Address," in which Jefferson reported the Purchase, and without defending or questioning its constitutionality, stated that the Senate would ratify the treaty.[39] Jefferson's wishes for a speedy and secret ratification were obeyed: Although Plumer (F-NH) recorded the debate in his memoirs, the injunction of secrecy must have prevented public accounts of debate, for the *Annals of Congress*, which were compiled later, recorded none ("The Senate assembled, and, after the consideration of Executive business, adjourned"). In the quick ratification of the treaty, Plumer discerned an objectionable party spirit that had undermined the Senate's power to ratify treaties: "As far as his influence can extend this is destroying the freedom of opinion in the Senate on that subject."[40] For Plumer, who would not have read Jefferson's letter to Breckinridge, one leading Republican's argument presumed that the Purchase was unconstitutional. Even so, no Republican was concerned enough about constitutional propriety to vote against the treaty, and the Senate ratified the

---

[35] Mayer, *Constitutional Thought*, 250–1.

[36] See Chapter Two.

[37] Malone, 4: 325–6.

[38] William Plumer, *William Plumer's Memorandum of the United States Senate, 1803–1807*, ed. Everett Somerville Brown (New York: Macmillan, 1923), 1.

[39] Jefferson, "Third Annual Message," 17 October 1803, *TJW*, 511–17. Clement Fatovic overstates this point when he asserts that Jefferson raised "constitutional questions" in this address. "Constitutionalism and Presidential Prerogative" (see note 3), 434.

[40] Plumer, *Memorandum*, 2.

treaty, twenty-four to seven (24:7), on 20 October.[41] Plumer noted that the Senate had "taken less time to deliberate on this important treaty, than they allowed themselves on the most trivial Indian contract."[42] At least one Senator who was not a friend to the treaty, John Quincy Adams (F-MA), arrived after the treaty had been ratified.

Jefferson might have used Republican arguments to defend the constitutionality of the Purchase. On the Senate floor, John Taylor (R-VA) argued that because each state was sovereign before formation of the Confederation, each state once possessed the power to acquire territory and therefore either retained or forfeited that power on joining the Confederation.[43] But because states had surrendered their respective powers to wage ware or to make compacts, Taylor argued, they must have forfeited too their rights to acquire territory. Because no other means of acquiring territory existed, that power must have been surrendered to the Confederacy, as supported by the fact that the Constitution did not prohibit the national government from exercising this power. In the House, John Randolph (R-VA) defended the Purchase by asserting presidential supremacy in foreign affairs. Becuase the executive was the "organ by which we communicate with such [foreign] States," the president "must be the prime agent" in negotiating treaties; and, as the treaty was laid before the Senate for ratification, the "initiative" taken by Jefferson was wholly constitutional.[44] Furthermore, Randolph asserted that the opposing position wrongly presumed an implied limit to the nation's expansion: "That the Constitution should tie us down to particular limits, without expressing those limits; that we should be restrained to the then boundaries of the United States, when it is in proof . . . that no such bounds existed, or do now exist, was altogether uncomprehensible and inadmissible."[45] The arguments of Taylor and Randolph resembled that formulated by Gallatin in January: the nation can acquire territory because all nations can extend their territories by treaty; if the framers of Constitution supposed

---

[41] *Annals of Congress*, 8th Cong., 1st sess., 15. The Senate's vote on the treaty was recorded in the *Journal of the executive proceedings of the Senate of the United States of America, 1789–1805*, which was, at the time, to be kept secret. U.S. Congress, *Senate Exec. Journal*. 8st Cong., 1st sess., 20 October 1803.

[42] Plumer, *Memorandum*, 13.

[43] *Annals of Congress*, 8th Cong., 1st sess., 51. Plumer recorded that Taylor also defended the treaty on grounds like those Jefferson initially gave to Breckinridge, indicating that "he would, like an attorney who exceeded the authority delegated to him by his client, vote to ratify the treaty, *& throw himself upon the people*, & request the States so to amend the Constitution." Plumer, *Memorandum*, 12.

[44] Brown, *Constitutional History*, 53.

[45] Ibid., 63.

that the boundaries of the United States were fixed, than they would have explicitly said so; by inference, the organs authorized to make treaties were competent to acquire territory.

Also in the House, Caesar Rodney (R-DE) claimed the broadest amount of authority for the national government to make the Purchase.[46] Like Gallatin, Taylor, and Randolph, he argued that the power to acquire territory, unless specifically forbidden by the Constitution, was provided to Congress. Going further than the others, Rodney grounded his argument on the clauses authorizing Congress to makes laws providing for the general welfare and the common defense as the source for this authority: "Have we not also vested in us every power necessary for carrying such a treaty into effect, in the words of the Constitution which give Congress the authority make all laws which shall be necessary and proper for carrying into execution the foregoing powers, and all other powers vested by this Constitution in the government if the United States or in any department or officer thereof?" Rodney's argument resembled Hamilton's argument for the constitutionality of the bank in that it found in the general welfare clause the authority to purchase and acquire territory. Similarly, by bringing presidential discretion within the Constitution, Rodney followed the example set by Hamilton's defense of the Neutrality Proclamation. Significantly, neither Jefferson nor the Republican leadership embraced Rodney's wider argument from the general welfare clause.[47]

But the Republican leadership's argument also relied on a clever use of the argument for implied powers. The Gallatin/Randolph position rested on the assumption that if the Constitution meant to forbid expansion it would have said so without leaving it to implication: since the government is not forbidden the power to acquire territory, the only question is determining which department of government holds the power. Although they would not have granted Hamilton's premise that "the Constitution must be construed so as to make its own survival possible" because "Energy is Wisdom," they borrowed a feature of it to argue that the Constitution must be construed so as to make (territorial) change possible.[48] Like those who argue that prerogative is constitutional, Republican members of Congress attempted to make the Constitution compatible with their good fortune.

[46] Adams, 373–4.

[47] Adams characteristically explained this by way of geography: since Rodney was "a Northern democrat," his opinion on the Constitution "carried little weight." Adams, 372.

[48] Landy and Milkis, *Presidential Greatness*, 32. The statement on energy is from Hamilton to C. C. Pinckney, 29 December 1802, *PAH* 26:72.

The Political Question

Robert W. Tucker and Alan Hendrickson have disputed the basis for Jefferson's belief that Napoleon seriously considered changing his mind. These scholars detect a "sense of urgency" in Jefferson's communications after Livingston and Monroe had written that Napoleon was worried that he would not receive the money and was regretting his decision. But they argue that Jefferson's fear was premature, and, pointing to the fact that Madison and Gallatin did not believe the treaty was at risk, they conclude that Napoleon would probably have not canceled the treaty. Consequently, they emphasize what they believe to be Jefferson's sacrificing his central political principle: "Jefferson did not think of strict construction as something that was *his* in the sense that it represented his preference – even his strong preference. Instead, it was seen as the way of truth in matters political. Yet Jefferson had departed from the way. Why?" For these scholars, the only explanation for Jefferson's abandoning strict construction was that he believed the risk of losing the treaty was too great for asking for amendment. But, as Jefferson's Republicans controlled the Senate with a twenty-five to nine advantage, the defeat of the treaty was unlikely. Accordingly, they conclude "that in order not to run *any* risk Jefferson put aside his constitutional scruples in the case of Louisiana."[49]

By putting the question of Napoleon's course of action aside, Tucker and Hendrickson are right to redirect attention to the Senate, but they do not appreciate seriously enough the risk that the Senate would have rejected or delayed ratification. Specifically, they underestimate the dilemma posed by the distinction between acquisition and incorporation. As Nicholas and others would have told Jefferson, Senators could have taken one of three positions regarding the constitutionality of the treaty. First, both the purchase and incorporation were constitutional – the position taken by the Republican leadership. Second, although the purchase was constitutional, incorporation was not – the position taken by Timothy Pickering (F-MA). Last, the national government possessed neither the power to buy Louisiana nor the power to add it into the Union – the position once held by Jefferson but elaborated by John Quincy Adams (F-MA).[50]

But Jefferson's supporters in the Senate quickly put this theoretical distinction to rest when they ratified the treaty without significant debate.

---

[49] Robert W. Tucker and David C. Hendrickson, *Empire of Liberty: The Statecraft of Thomas Jefferson* (New York: Oxford University Press, 1990), 168, 171.

[50] Roger Griswold asserted that incorporation would obliterate the "perfect union of the States" and that the treaty was void since a guarantee of incorporation was in principle the same as incorporation. Brown, *Constitutional History*, 71.

	Power to Incorporate	No Power to Incorporate
Power to Acquire:	Republican Leadership	Pickering
No Power to Acquire:		J. Q. Adams

FIGURE 1. Possible Constitutional Positions Regarding Ratification of Louisiana Treaty

Accordingly, most of the debate on the treaty was actually debate on the votes allowing the president to take possession and appropriate funds for the purchase. With ratification of the treaty, the question of the constitutionality of incorporation was made chronologically irrelevant.

Nevertheless, the question whether the government held the authority to incorporate territory was addressed in the context of an appropriations bill. As Breckinridge (R-KY) noted with some impatience on November 3, some Senators had used debate on the appropriations bill for a "re-discussion of the merits of the treaty."[51] In reconsidering the merits, opposition arguments varied: Samuel White (F-DE) asked for more time to consider the treaty and cautioned that United States citizens in large numbers would leave the East to cross the Mississippi; William Hill Wells (F-DE) argued that the Senate should wait to make appropriations until France had carried out its obligations; Uriah Tracy (F-CT) asserted that even though the Constitution allowed for Congress to admit new states in the Union, it did not allow the president and the Senate to force foreign territories into the Union by way of treaty; Timothy Pickering (F-MA) asserted that the authority to admit new territories into the union required the assent of each state, but he did allow that the United States could "acquire new territory, either by purchase or conquest, and to govern the territory so acquired as a dependent province." Opponents to the treaty, however, did not have a discernible strategy: as Breckinridge noted, the opposition's "lesser objections" indicated that its members were "at war among themselves on the greater one."[52]

Breckinridge defended the treaty by comparing its opponents to those who had once argued that a republic had to be small. Because the country's boundaries were "already extensive," the country had proven that the "extended republic" could successfully remedy the causes of the republican form of government. Because the "extended republic" had already proven

---

[51] *Annals of Congress*, 8th Cong., 1st sess., 58.
[52] Ibid., 31–59.

	For Appropriation	Against Appropriation
For Purchase:	Republican Leadership	
Against Purchase:	Plumer	Pickering

FIGURE 2. Policy Questions after Ratification of Louisiana Treaty

itself, and because it was agreed that Americans from the East would settle the territory, the question, according to Breckinridge, was whether the territory would be populated by "American people under American jurisdiction" or by Americans "under the control of some foreign, powerful, and rival nation."[53]

Breckinridge's impatience with those who wished to reconsider the merits of the treaty was meant to create another position and draw some to the side of the appropriations. This position, most famously taken by Plumer (F-NH), held that even though the government lacked the authority to acquire Louisiana, the power to incorporate territories resulted from the ratified acquisition, so debate about incorporation was futile.[54] With the ratified treaty in hand, the 3 November appropriations vote was easily won by the Republicans, joined by Plumer (F-NH), Simeon Olcott (F-NH), and Adams (F-MA).

But there was another vote. The secret Senate Executive Journal records a 4 November vote on the 20 October motion to modify the third article of the Treaty to leave the United States "at liberty" to "make future arrangements" to "best promote the general interest" of the "free inhabitants" of Louisiana, that is, to relax the treaty's requirement of incorporation and rights of citizenship. Curiously, the only members of the opposition who voted in the affirmative were Wells (F-DE), White (F-DE), and Dayton (F-NJ). Even more curious, six others joined this group – that is, six Senators who voted for the treaty also later voted to modify its provision for incorporation. This vote indicates that the constitutional question lingered in the minds of some Senators after ratification.

By comparing Senate debates with the Senate Executive Journal, it becomes clear that from 20 October (the date of the ratification of the treaty) onward, there was a silent minority who held reservations about the third

[53] Ibid., 59–61.
[54] Plumer, *Memorandum*, 31.

	For Incorporation	Against Incorporation
For Treaty:	Republican Leadership	Six senators
Against Treaty:	Plumer	Wells, White, and Dayton

FIGURE 3. Constitutional Questions after Ratification of Louisiana Treaty

article's rigid requirement of incorporation. Put another way, even though there was a chronological problem with voting for ratification and then being against incorporation, one-fifth of the senators in attendance held that position. Although Pickering (F-MA) himself defended the position that one could acquire territory but not incorporate it, he failed to discern quickly enough that some supporters of the treaty were similarly reluctant to grant incorporation; Jefferson and Breckinridge had moved too quickly for the opposition to mold its lesser arguments into a great one.

What was the "risk," then, that the treaty would falter in the Senate? More accurately, why did Senator Wilson Carey Nicholas, one of Jefferson's most trusted lieutenants, advise Jefferson to remain silent? If all thirty-four Senators voted, then ratification would require twenty-three votes – easily within the Republican majority. Nevertheless, the Senate's voting record in the fall of 1803 suggests that the vote on ratification could have been closer. During the crucial period of ratifying the treaty, there were four different occasions to vote on the Louisiana Purchase and two on unrelated subjects: on 20 October, the Senate ratified the treaty, 24:7; on 26 October, the Senate voted to allow the president to "take possession" of the territory, 26:6; on 31 October, the Senate passed a resolution honoring Samuel Adams and Edmund Pendleton, 21:10; on 3 November, the Senate approved creation of stock to pay for the purchase, 26:5; on 4 November, a resolution to modify the third article of the treaty failed, 9: 22; and on 4 November a motion to consider what became the Twelfth Amendment failed, 12:19. As Table 1 shows, the minority shifted.

As Table 1 illustrates, consistent opposition was small, and it consisted of James Hillhouse (F-CT), Pickering (F-MA), Olcott (F-NH), Plumer (F-NH), Uriah Tracy (F-CT), William Hill Wells (DE), and Samuel White (F-DE). They were sometimes joined by Jonathan Dayton (F-NJ) and John Quincy Adams (F-MA). But of the remaining twenty-two voting members (in one case twenty-three), six joined Wells, White and Dayton on the vote to modify the third article of the treaty, and three defected from the Republican leadership on the vote to consider the Twelfth Amendment (more on that

TABLE I. *Senators Voting in the Minority during Debate on the Louisiana Treaty*

October 20 (Ratify)	October 26 (Take Possession)	October 31 (Honor Adams and Pendleton)	November 3 (Appropriations for Purchase)	November 4 (Modify Article #3)	November 4 (Consider 12th Amendment)
Hillhouse	Hillhouse	Hillhouse	Hillhouse	Wells	Hillhouse
Pickering	Pickering	Pickering	Pickering	White	Pickering
Olcott	Olcott	Olcott	Tracy	Dayton	Olcott
Plumer	Plumer	Plumer	Wells	Anderson	Plumer
Tracy	Tracy	Tracy	White	Butler	Tracy
Wells	Adams	Wells		Baldwin	Wells
White		Adams		Potter	White
		Dayton		Jackson	Adams
		Bradley		Logan	Dayton
		John Smith			Anderson
					Butler
					Maclay

vote later). Two senators, Joseph Anderson (R-TN) and Pierce Butler (R-SC), were in both groups. Although each of these six votes differed in degree of importance, we can conclude that the Republican leadership controlled a voting block of fifteen Senators, six short of the twenty-one members needed for a two-thirds majority.[55]

For the treaty to have been defeated, then, the seven 20 October dissenters would have had to have been joined by four senators. This course might have included the following. First, ensure that John Quincy Adams arrives in time for the vote and convince him that even though the purchase might be good for the country, it is beyond the power of the government and requires a constitutional amendment. Second, persuade the other Federalist, Jonathan Dayton (NJ), that the treaty should be modified, as Article Three's incorporation of the inhabitants of Louisiana might adversely affect his vast land interests in the West, particularly in Ohio – or, if it would benefit his interest in Ohio, that his voting on it at all would give the appearance of impropriety.[56] Third, use the argument for strict construction to convince Pierce Butler (R-SC), who leaned toward states' rights, that the treaty required an amendment and that incorporation of the inhabitants of Louisiana, some of them free blacks and mulattos, might complicate matters for slaveholders.[57] Fourth, persuade Anderson (R-TN), who had defected twice on

---

55 Dewitt Clinton (NY) left after the first vote.
56 For a summary of Dayton's interests, see Charles A. Beard, *An Economic Interpretation of the Constitution of the United States* (New York: Free Press, 1913), 86.
57 In 1787, Butler owned thirty-one slaves and was instrumental in securing the fugitive slave clause. Beard, *Economic Interpretation*, 81; Clinton Rossiter, *1787: The Grand Convention*

4 November, that Article Three unfairly granted foreigners in New Orleans the same rights as the citizens of Tennessee. To ensure the defeat of the treaty, add to the required eleven by making overtures to the remaining seven (John Smith [R-OH], Bradley, Baldwin, Potter, Jackson, George Logan, or Maclay) who had abandoned the Republican leadership in at least one of those six votes. Given the inability of the Federalists to court Republicans, the prospects for those who favored ratification were certainly brighter than for those who hoped to block it, but one can presume that Nicholas had counted the votes before he advised the president to keep quiet.

Tucker and Hendrickson's argument that Jefferson was silent because of a "risk" to the treaty is correct, but the Senate record suggests that the domestic political risk was greater than they perceive. Had the president mused about his constitutional scruples, a strict constructionist like Butler might have been less willing to "risk himself" by passing the treaty than other strict constructionists such as Taylor or Breckinridge. Moreover, had Jefferson recommended a constitutional amendment, acquisition and incorporation would have been delayed by what he had already observed to be a long and tedious amendment process. By then, as the next chapter shows, Jefferson and Republicans had learned that amending the Constitution, even for correcting a flaw in presidential selection, was no easy task.

Jefferson's Silence

The application of the doctrine of strict construction to the Louisiana Purchase was most eloquently given by John Quincy Adams, not Jefferson. According to his *Memoirs*, Adams asked Madison "whether the Executive had made any arrangements with any members of any either House to bring forward the proposal for an amendment to the Constitution to carry through the Louisiana Treaty" and observed that he believed it his own duty to introduce such an amendment.[58] Adams records that Madison replied by saying that it was not "universally agreed" that the purchase required constitutional amendment. Furthermore, Madison told Adams that even if the Constitution had not "provided for such a case as this," that the treaty "must be estimated by the magnitude of its object, and that those who had agreed to it must rely on the candor of their country for justification." Adams was not persuaded by Madison's explanation of Jefferson's decision to not seek constitutional

---

(New York: Norton, 1966), 217. For the existence of free blacks and black slaveholders in Louisiana and Pierce's home state, South Carolina, see Eugene Genovese, *Roll, Jordan, Roll: The World the Slaves Made* (New York: Vintage, 1976), 408–9, 748–9n51.

[58] John Quincy Adams, *Memoirs of John Quincy Adams*, ed. Charles Francis Adams, (New York: AMS Press, 1970), 1:267.

amendment. For Adams and others in New England, the incorporation of such a large territory "was in substance a dissolution and recomposition of the whole Union."[59] With Louisiana, the Union became "totally different" in that it afforded the government "despotic powers" over the new unincorporated territories, "naturalize[d] foreign nations in a mass," brought in French and Spanish laws, and introduced "whole systems of legislation abhorrent to the spirit and character of our institutions." In 1821, he wrote of the event with words strikingly similar to those of his grandson, Henry Adams: "Jefferson and Madison did attain power by organizing and heading a system of attack upon the Washington Administration, chiefly under the banner of State rights and State sovereignty. They argued and scolded against all implied powers, and pretended that the Government of the Union had no powers but such as were expressly delegated by the Constitution. They succeeded. Mr. Jefferson was elected President of the United States, and the first thing he did was to purchase Louisiana – an assumption of implied powers greater in itself and more comprehensive in its consequences then all the assumptions of implied powers in the twelve years of the Washington and Adams Administrations put together."[60]

Like later critics, John Quincy Adams wrote that Jefferson's decision not to seek an amendment to the Constitution to purchase Louisiana indicated that the president's "opposition to implied powers" was but a "convenient weapon" to be "taken up or laid aside" at the dictates of political ambition. Furthermore, although arguments regarding the construction of constitutional powers were a political fact of a constitutional republic, such arguments would likely reflect the coming and going of political parties: "Besides, as party interprets and amends the Constitution, and as we the people care not a pin's prick for it, all arguments from that source, however solid, would avail nothing." Others, from John Calhoun to Forrest McDonald, also would point to Jefferson to say that one's construction of the Constitution depends on whether one's party is in power or opposition.[61]

In his one public explanation of the ratified treaty, Jefferson followed Breckinridge's application of the argument for the extended republic. In his Second Inaugural, Jefferson reported that the "income reserved" from cutting "unnecessary offices" and "useless establishments and expenses" had

---

[59] Ibid., 5: 401. Consider, for example, the Hartford Convention, which recommended an amendment requiring a two-thirds majority of each house of Congress to admit new states into Union.

[60] Ibid., 5:364–5.

[61] John Quincy Adams, *Memoirs*, 5: 401.

enabled the country to "extend" its "limits."[62] Here, the president conceded that "the acquisition of Louisiana" had been "disapproved by some." According to Jefferson, the source of this criticism was the "candid apprehension that the enlargement of our territory would endanger its union," so Jefferson went on to defend the Purchase against the charge that it made the country too big: "But who can limit the extent to which the federative principle may operate effectively? The larger our association, the less it will be shaken by local passions; and in any view, is it not better that the opposite bank of the Mississippi should be settled by our own brethren and children, than by strangers of another family. With which shall we be most likely to live in harmony and friendly intercourse?" By playing on American fears that European powers would settle across the Mississippi, Jefferson defended the Purchase by deploying Madison's argument for the extended republic.[63] Neither embracing the available argument for the implied power of acquisition nor elaborating on the constitutional difficulty of the acquisition, Jefferson reminded his audience that the local passions are less likely to shake large republics than small republics. "Throwing himself" on the people, Jefferson referred to Madison's argument rather than enunciating a new one.

To some extent, Jefferson's recourse to the case for the extended republic did meet the standard he had set concerning the prerogative. Not exactly a legal argument, Jefferson appealed to the extended republic as a kind of principle. Rather than following Gallatin and other Republicans in asserting the implied power of the government to acquire territory, and rather than using the oath of office or the power of commander in chief to justify the Purchase as a priority of national defense, Jefferson attached the national aspiration of expansion to the discovery that local passions and interests (arising from property, opinions, and religion) can be controlled when exposed to other passions and interests.[64] Jefferson meant for the Second Inaugural's statement of "performance" to further unite public opinion around the presidency, thus changing Madison's argument for the extended republic. That Jefferson defended the Louisiana Purchase on the grounds of this "union of opinion" rather by referring to a clause in Article Two indicates his attempt to set an example against broad construction without using words.

---

[62] Jefferson, "Second Inaugural Address," 4 March 1805, *TJW*, 519.

[63] *Federalist* Nos. 10 and 51, pp. 60, 334; and Madison to Jefferson, October 24, 1787, *PTJ*, 12: 273–9.

[64] Following Malone, Schmitt overstates his point, when he says that Jefferson "accepted Gallatin's analysis," "Jefferson and the Presidency" (see note 3), 338. See Malone, 4: 312.

But there is one more chapter to the story of the Louisiana Purchase. Instead of amending the Constitution to incorporate Louisiana, congressional Republicans successfully amended the Constitution to streamline the Electoral College. More than a partisan safeguard against an electoral surprise in 1804, the Twelfth Amendment made it theoretically possible for Jefferson to claim approval of his first term in office and therefore completed the logic of democratic energy.

8

To "complete their entire union of opinion"

The Twelfth Amendment as Amendment to End All Amendments

Congressional debates recorded in *The Annals of Congress* suggest another reason why Jefferson did not recommend a constitutional amendment for purchasing and incorporating Louisiana. When Congress convened in October 1803, Republicans already knew they had to propose another constitutional amendment fixing the Electoral College. By inserting the "discriminating principle" into the Electoral College, Republicans could be assured that the Federalists would not be left open the chance in 1804 to make another Aaron Burr president or, alternatively, a Federalist vice president. By lessening the possibility of an election in the House, Republicans could make it more likely that Jefferson's victory in 1804, unlike that in 1800, would be unambiguous. Jefferson's silence on Louisiana was thus required by a second political necessity. Had he recommended a constitutional amendment, he would have risked delaying the ratification of the Twelfth Amendment's "discriminating principle," gambling on the significance of his own reelection in 1804 and his party's chances in 1808.

When members of Congress arrived in October, 1803, for the first session of the Eighth Congress, Republicans wasted little time in proposing the amendment for designation. On 17 October, John Dawson (R-VA) introduced the amendment in the House, as did De Witt Clinton (R-NY) in the Senate on 21 October. But, again, the clear arithmetic of Republican electoral strategy and Republican power in Congress offered no guarantee of a constitutional amendment, for as Jefferson and his party would learn, the Constitution's cumbersome procedure for amendment made constitutional change difficult, even for a president whose party was in the majority. And because members of Congress considered the Twelfth Amendment at the same time they voted to allow Jefferson to purchase, incorporate, and govern the Louisiana territory, the arguments for and against the Twelfth

Amendment were cast in the context of debates on the Louisiana Purchase. Because this debate shows the potential and peril of presidential power, because shrewd politicians can elevate chance into something more than electoral strategy, understanding the Twelfth Amendment will help explain why Jefferson did not seek a constitutional amendment for Louisiana and why Jefferson may have been able to conclude that the Twelfth Amendment presented the opportunity for a larger victory for democratic energy. The relatively unknown story of the Twelfth Amendment is central to Jefferson's transformation of the presidency.[1]

The Aaron Burr Amendment?

According to the accepted wisdom, the Twelfth Amendment corrected a flaw in a Constitution whose designers did not contemplate a national two-party system. Under the original plan, members of the Electoral College would cast two votes, bound by the requirement that one vote be cast for someone from another state. Because one vote would likely be given to a "favorite son," the other vote would, the framers hoped, be cast for a person with a national reputation – some one of "those great & illustrious characters" who, in Gouverneur Morris's words, would be known by most citizens.[2] The candidate with the most votes would win as long he received a "majority of the whole number of electors." If a person did not receive a majority, then the House would choose the president from among the top five vote-getters. In this "eventual election" in the House, representatives would vote by state delegation, with each state having one vote. However, even though Alexander Hamilton once described presidential selection under the Constitution as "at least excellent," if not "perfect," the plan was seriously flawed.[3] In 1800, Republicans chose Aaron Burr to run as Jefferson's vice president because they thought he could deliver enough New York votes to give Jefferson a majority of the Electoral College. But Jefferson and Burr received the same number of Electoral College votes – because Republicans failed to cast one

---

[1] Scholars have long treated the Twelfth Amendment as the Aaron Burr Amendment without fully considering what the framers of the amendment understood of their work. See, for example, Bruce Ackerman, *The Failure of the Founding Fathers: Jefferson, Marshall, and the Rise of Presidential Democracy* (Cambridge, MA: Belknap Press of Harvard University Press, 2005); Akhil Reed Amar, *America's Constitution: A Biography* (New York: Random House, 2005); Garry Wills, *Negro President: Thomas Jefferson and the Slave Power* (Boston: Houghton Mifflin, 2003), 106–113; and David P. Currie, *The Constitution in Congress: The Jeffersonians 1801–1829* (Chicago: Chicago University Press, 2001), 39–65.

[2] James Madison, *Notes of Debates in the Federal Convention of 1787 Reported by James Madison* (New York: Norton, 1987), 308.

[3] *Federalist*, No. 68, p. 435.

Burr vote for another candidate – sending the election to the House of Representatives for resolution.[4] Because the lame-duck House was dominated by Federalists, and because Burr did not stand down, it took thirty-six ballots and, perhaps, Hamilton's intervention to make Jefferson rather than Burr president. Fixing the Electoral College, then, would serve Jefferson's interest in reelection.

Madison may have had the Electoral College in mind when he alluded to "extraneous considerations" trumping "theoretical propriety" in several provisions of the Constitution.[5] According to Madison, certain "features" in the Constitution revealed that the compromise in the convention between delegates from large and small states did not put to rest the divide between large and small states but, rather, introduced a "fresh struggle" for the greatest "share of influence." What Madison probably meant was the compromise that made the "eventual election" in the House to be decided by state equality rather than by state population. By allowing the House to choose the president in the event that no single candidate received a majority of the whole number of electors, and by requiring the vote to be counted by state delegation, the Constitution chose to count power by states rather than by individual citizens. With this nod to state sovereignty and the small states, the Constitution made it possible, even likely, that the House could select the candidate who received fewer votes than the four other persons. As opponents of the Twelfth Amendment liked to point out, the Constitution allowed the large states to have more say in the Electoral College but made the large states equal, which is to say unequal, in the eventual election in the House: the people would nominate candidates and the states would choose from among them.

That the rivalry of large and small states soon gave way to a partisan divide between Federalists and Republicans shows, of course, that Madison and other Convention delegates underestimated parties. Specifically, even though Madison and many of his colleagues surely thought that parties occurred in nature, they did not foresee the ease with which parties in Congress would be able to nominate presidential candidates as well to command the allegiance of fellow partisans in the state legislatures.[6] As is well known, there were consequences to this misplaced attention. First, as the Election of 1796 confirmed, the Constitution's allowing the second highest vote getter to be vice president made it likely that the vice president would belong to a party

---

[4] On the mistake, see Madison's later mention of "false assurances" to Jefferson. Madison to Jefferson, 14 January 1824, Smith, 1891.

[5] *Federalist*, No. 37, p. 227.

[6] Richard Hofstadter, *The Idea of a Party System: The Rise of Legitimate Opposition in the United States, 1780–1840* (Berkeley and Los Angeles: University of California Press, 1969).

other than that of the president. More than resembling the divided executive against which Hamilton warned in *The Federalist*, the system made it more likely that the vice president, after four years of presiding over the Senate, would be able to mount a more effective campaign against the president or his party's preferred successor, as Jefferson did in 1800. The second consequence flows from the first: in order to prevent the opposition from winning the vice presidency, parties selected a second candidate who, if the party was successful in winning the presidency, would also receive more votes than the intended president of the other party. But, as the election of 1800 revealed, this strategy had to be perfected by more strategy: to avoid having their intended president from being tied with the preferred vice president, parties would have to make sure that one elector cast his second vote for a third candidate. Third, parties used the vice presidential selection to improve their electoral chances by nationalizing their ticket.

But there were other consequences. Because the winner was the candidate who received a majority of the "whole number" of electors, not of electoral votes, a president could be elected by receiving only one more than one-fourth of the Electoral College votes. For instance, in 1796 John Adams received 71 of 276 votes in 1796, and, in 1800, Jefferson won 73 of 276 votes. As a result, not only were presidents denied the modern "mandate" because most presidential electors were selected by state legislatures rather than by the people, presidents could not claim that they were elected by "majority" in the same way that later presidents enjoy the exaggerated margins conferred by Electoral College landslides. More important, because the choice of president and vice president was never formally designated by a presidential elector, a victorious president could declare that he was the intended first choice only by assuming that the electors, who were meant to be independent, were following the party command. Thus, in 1800, Federalists had the Constitution, strictly understood, on their side when they said that it was impossible to discern whether electors intended for Jefferson or Burr to be president: as James Hillhouse (F-CT) argued, "You are told that, at the last election, one was intended by the people for President, and the other for Vice President; but the Constitution knows no vote for Vice President."[7] Similarly, even though a vice president lacked much authority he could say he received more votes than any person other than the president, or, in the case of Burr, just as many votes as the president.[8] If the original plan meant,

---

[7] *Annals of Congress*, 8th Cong., 1st sess., 129. Wills defends Burr by concluding that the Constitution had no way to judge intent. *Negro President*, 73–89.

[8] Adams, *History During Jefferson*, 391; Sidney M. Milkis and Michael Nelson, *The American Presidency: Origins and Development 1776–2002 Fourth Edition* (Washington, DC: CQ Press, 2003), 427.

as Hamilton wrote, to give a "sense of the people," the way it settled the results of the selection the individual president were, from the perspective of the modern elections, as unsettled as the methods by which it measured popular sentiment were indirect.

From the Elections of 1796 and 1800, partisans understood the consequences of the electoral arithmetic. Although a majority party, such as the Republicans in 1803, could rest assured that its two candidates would receive more votes combined than the two candidates of the rival party, it could not be sure that the intended office of each of the two candidates was safe. The minority party could spoil the election by voting for the majority party's vice president, making the majority vice presidential candidate the president. Or, if the majority party anticipated such a strategy and withheld its votes from its own vice president, it then risked losing the vice presidency to what should have been an otherwise weak party. Allowing the other party to win the vice presidency would afford the minority party greater access to the Senate and the chance to more competitively contest a future election, as both parties learned from 1796. In 1798, Federalists proposed – and Republicans opposed – an amendment for designation in order to guarantee majority party control of both executive offices.[9] Absent such an amendment, as the election of 1800 made clear to all, protecting the party's hold on the vice presidency risked elevating a scheming vice president to the presidency. The only way for a majority party to prevent a minority party from using the vice presidency as leverage was to nominate a vice president who was less acceptable to the opposition than the actual president. Paradoxically, the logic of the Framers' inattention to party carried the incentive for a more partisan vice president.

With Burr as vice president, the Federalists enjoyed the full benefits of the uncertainty created by the Electoral College. Republicans were understandably suspicious of Burr after the New Yorker did not withdraw his candidacy after receiving the same votes as Jefferson. Only a few months after the election of 1800 was resolved, Gallatin perceived, and explained to Jefferson, the dilemma that Republicans would face in 1804.[10] If they continued with Burr as vice president, then they would have to choose between voting for Burr and risking that he would become president with the help of a few Federalists or scattering their votes for vice president and therefore losing the vice presidency to the opposition, which also would jeopardize the party's

⁹ Tadhisa Kuroda, *The Origins of the Twelfth Amendment: The Electoral College in the Early Republic, 1787–1804* (Westport, CT: Greenwood Press, 1994), 109.

¹⁰ Albert Gallatin to Jefferson, 14 September 1801. *The Writings of Albert Gallatin*, ed. Henry Adams (Philadelphia: J.B. Lippincott & Co., 1879), 1: 51–52.

goal to make Madison Jefferson's successor. And Gallatin was right to fear collusion between Burr and some Federalists. Hamilton reported to Gouverneur Morris that Burr had attended a February 1802, dinner celebrating Washington's birthday and had proposed a toast to "the union of all honest men." And, not a friend of Burr, Hamilton warned Morris of using Burr too much: "As an *instrument* the person will be an auxiliary of *some* value, as a chief he will disgrace and destroy the party."[11]

Even though Gallatin and Hamilton surely disagreed about the source of the problem, they agreed on the means of solving it. In his 1801 letter, Gallatin explained to Jefferson that the problem of Burr would be "remedied by the amendment of distinguishing the votes for the two offices, and by that of dividing the States into districts."[12] A few months later, Hamilton endorsed, and probably had a hand in drafting, a resolution in the New York legislature that called for amending the Constitution to require each state to be divided into districts and that electors designate whom for whom they vote as president and for whom as vice president.[13] To Morris, Hamilton argued that district election was good in that it "removes thus far the intervention of the state Governments and strengthens the connection between the Foederal[14] head and the people," and that designation would allow the "people to know whom they are choosing."[15] But more than just "right in itself," the reforms would also neutralize the Republican advantage in organization: "in everything which gives opportunity for juggling arts our adversaries will Nine times out of Ten excell us."[16] Hamilton, it should be noted, favored district election before it was common knowledge that Republicans enjoyed the advantage in a winner-take-all system, for he had proposed it in 1787 at the Constitutional Convention.[17]

Hamilton's principled defense aside, the question of district election was largely a matter of Electoral College arithmetic. Because Gallatin, for instance, expected Republicans to be in the minority in the New York legislature – or at least, unable to command a majority without Burr – he believed that district election would guarantee that Republicans would win

[11] Alexander Hamilton to Gouverneur Morris, 4 March 1802, *PAH*, 25:558–9.

[12] Albert Gallatin to Jefferson, 14 September 1801, *Writings of Gallatin*, 1: 51–52.

[13] Alexander Hamilton, "Draft of a Resolution for the Legislature of New York for the Amendment of the Constitution of the United States," 29 January 1802, *PAH*: 25:512–3.

[14] In relaying the story about Burr's toast, Hamilton complains, "I often hear at the corner of the streets important federal secrets of which I am ignorant." I do not know if Hamilton used "Foederal" and "foederal" to signify the federal government as opposed to the Federalist Party, or vice versa.

[15] Alexander Hamilton to Gouverneur Morris, 4 March 1802, *PAH*, 25:558–9.

[16] But see note 4 above.

[17] Madison, *Notes*, 138. I am indebted to Robert Scigliano for pointing me to this fact.

some electoral votes in New York. But Gallatin's initial endorsement of district election was rare and was connected to the question of Burr and the New York legislature, for Republicans saw themselves as the majority party throughout the country and favored winner-take-all. Jefferson, for example, replied to Gallatin that direct election ("let the people vote directly") and winner-take-all ("the ticket which has a plurality of the votes of any State to be considered as receiving thereby the whole vote of the State") also would provide the "remedy" sought by Gallatin.[18] In 1801, a House committee chaired by Wilson Cary Nicholas recommended against district election on the grounds that the amendment would violate the Framers' of the Constitution intention to allow the individual states to use or reject district election.[19] (Nicholas did, however, recommend that Congress could and should pass a *law* requiring district election for *members of the House*). Federalists, seeing that Jefferson's victory in 1800 hinged on Republicans making Virginia a winner-take-all state, preferred district election.[20]

Amending the Constitution

Even though designation would remove the problem of Burr for Republicans, Republicans in Congress were slow in finding the two-thirds necessary to propose the amendment for consideration by the states. Late in the spring session of 1802, the House narrowly accepted the designation version of the amendment and sent it to the Senate on 3 May – the day that Congress was scheduled to adjourn.[21] The amendment failed to receive the necessary two-thirds of senators present (15:8), because David Stone (R-NC) voted with Federalists. For the next year, the amendment was considered only at the urging of Federalists who tried to force a vote on the amendment when Republicans were absent, and Republicans delayed a vote on the amendment, waiting, perhaps, for the midterm elections to provide them a greater majority in Congress or more favorable compositions in the state legislatures.[22]

Even when Republicans finally enjoyed over a two-thirds majority in each house, they did not pass the amendment as quickly as they would have liked. The principal problem was that designation opened a new question: would designation affect the significance of the number of candidates from which the House would choose in the event that no candidate received a majority

---

[18] Jefferson to Albert Gallatin, 18 September 1801, *Writings of Gallatin*, 1:54–5.
[19] *Annals of Congress*, 6th Congress, 2nd sess., 941–6.
[20] Wills, *Negro President*, 68.
[21] Kuroda, *Origins of the Twelfth Amendment*, 121.
[22] See, for example, *Annals of Congress*, 7th Cong., 2nd sess., 492.

of votes? Under the original design, the House would choose from among the top five vote-getters, but as this number included those intended by the parties to be president *and* vice president, retaining it with designation would result in the House choosing from among five potential presidents and no vice presidents. By removing the possibility that an intended vice president could be selected as president by the House, the amendment undermined the logic of the House's choosing from five – it would have been as if the original design provided that the House choose from among the ten highest vote-getters. If the spirit of five were retained with designation, then the House would have to choose from two and a half.

More than a technicality, the question posed a serous problem for the parties. If the question were in front of the current Congress, for instance, Democrats and Republicans would likely agree on two, instead of five, as the larger number would be correctly seen as an opportunity for smaller parties to compete in presidential elections. But, then, the number was connected to something more important: as the "eventual election" in the House is decided by state delegation with each state having one vote, small states saw that they would have a disproportionate advantage in presidential elections resolved by the House, at least to the extent that the more populous states would be equal with the less populous states. Accordingly, a choice from five candidates would be better than a choice from three candidates in that it would provide a greater likelihood that small states would be able to select a candidate friendly to their interests. Just as Madison had suggested that the plan for presidential selection was related to the compromise between small and large states, the designation amendment had reopened the first partisan question of the Constitution: should power be counted by state or by the people? It was this question, more than slavery and the three-fifths compromise, which might have prevented the designation principle from becoming part of the Constitution.[23] And this question introduced another in that selection from five rather than from three would increase the likelihood that a minority president could be selected by the House. At stake was the source of authority for the presidency.

House Debate

In the House, the connection between designation and number was clear when, on 19 October, John Clopton (R-VA) argued that the number should be reduced from five to two. For Clopton, to allow the House to choose from

---

[23] Garry Wills, in *Negro President*, understates the importance of the compromise between the large and small states in 1787.

a list longer than two would be to invite the House to choose a candidate who received nothing near to the majority of the Electoral College. Because presidential selections should reflect "the will of the people," precaution should be taken to ensure that the winner receive the majority, or close to the majority, of Electoral votes.[24] After some debate over number, designation, and district election, the amendment was referred to a committee with a representative from each state. Two days later, the committee recommended designation and reducing the number from five to three. The district plan was not mentioned in the committee report. Republicans must have agreed with Jefferson that designation would provide the desired object.

Debate then centered on the number, with members of the committee leading the argument. Thomas Sandford (R-KY) argued that anything in addition to preventing the vice president from becoming president was dangerous and unacceptable. Caesar Rodney (R-DE) agreed, adding that he was for five on the grounds that it would afford the small states some power. With Rodney and Sandford, James Elliot (F-VT) argued that the "federative principle" should guide. George W. Campbell (R-TN) granted that he was from a small state but said that two was closer to the original design. Debate was postponed however, when John Randolph (R-VA) argued that there was a more pressing question before the House: "Hoping that the Committee would have decided on the amendment at an early hour, he had refrained from any motion. But perceiving that a decision was not likely soon to be made, he would move that the Committee should rise, for the purpose of taking up the treaty respecting Louisiana."[25] Randolph's directing the House away from the amendment was not followed by his whole party – Dawson and others opposed it – and carried by a slim majority (60:55).[26]

On 26 October, the House resumed debate on the amendment and formed the Committee of the Whole. Even though Clopton again argued that the designation amendment, with three, would best ensure that elections represent the public will, a critical number of Republicans preferred five, rather than three, as the number of candidates to be selected in the House. Perhaps some of these were more loyal to their institutional affiliation than to their party: with each option that was made available to the House, that chamber's importance would necessarily grow. On 27 October, Elliot urged Republicans such as Clopton to compromise with the many representatives who were tenacious of five, in order to ensure that designation itself would

---

[24] *Annals*, 8th Congress, 1st sess., 376–377.
[25] Ibid., 431.
[26] Ibid., 428–31.

receive enough votes. The argument for accommodation won the day, and the House voted 59:47 to replace three with five.[27]

Consideration of the amendment must have been shaped by debate over Louisiana. In line with Republican doctrine, Jefferson submitted the treaty to the House so that it could appropriate funds to enact the treaty. Enemies to the treaty, of course, raised the question of whether the treaty unconstitutionally enlarged the union. Roger Griswold (F-CT), for instance, asserted that the Constitution provided for growth in terms of population but not in territory, and he reminded Representatives that "it was not consistent with the spirit of a republican government that its territory should be exceedingly large."[28] Similarly, Samuel Thatcher (F-MA) disputed the argument that the treaty power conferred an implied power to incorporate territory: "The Confederation under which we now live is a partnership of States, and it is not competent to it to admit a new partner but with the consent of all the partners."[29] Federalists also tried to make matters difficult for Jefferson by demanding that he submit for legislative consideration documents relevant to the purchase. House Republicans defeated the latter attempt by only one vote. Similarly, creating a government Louisiana provided more opportunities for Federalists to object to the expansion of executive power. Griswold penetrated to the heart of the matter when he declared, "The argument that the powers are necessary, though unconstitutional, is no argument with me."[30]

Emboldened by the debates over Louisiana and the number of candidates in the contingency election, Federalists aimed to dismantle the amendment altogether. On 28 October, Griswold argued that the designation principle itself was disadvantageous to the small states in that it would make the eventual election in the House less likely: "the greater the chance of bringing the States to a vote on this floor, the more advantageous it is to the smaller states." Because the designation principle would make it impossible for two candidates to receive an equal amount as well as a majority of the whole number of electors, the designation principle removed one of the two ways in which an election could be thrown into the House. Benjamin Huger (F-SC) then objected to what he believed to be Clopton's "too abstract" argument from the "will of the people," asserting that the Constitution was a "compact" among equal states: "The worn-out theory of a number of insulated beings assembled together in an extensive plain, and led by their common wants and necessities to form themselves into a body politic, cannot be applied

---

[27] Ibid., 497.
[28] Ibid., 433.
[29] Ibid., 454.
[30] Ibid., 501.

to the Federal Government, nor can inferences drawn from notions of this kind afford correct grounds upon which to build or support alterations and amendments in the national compact." Perhaps by drawing on the compact theory of the Constitution, Huger meant to offer small-state Republicans a reason for voting against their party. More important, his argument, which he conceded was "not the popular one of the present day," stood opposed to Clopton's assumption that the presidential election should represent the will of the people so precisely that it would select the single person that the people meant to elect. According to Huger – who reminded House members that he had left his party to vote for Jefferson in 1800 – neither the "salvation" nor the "political happiness" of the republic "depends so entirely on the election of any one man as President, however great or good he might be." At the heart of the designation principle, Huger discerned, was the idea that the will of the people should be expressed in terms of the election of one man instead of one party.[31]

In spite of Huger's argument against designation, the House voted 88:31 for the amendment and sent the amendment to the Senate, where debate on designation had already begun. It is important to note that House Republicans succeeded in passing the amendment proposal only by holding the number of candidates in the contingency election to five. Either loyalty to House prerogatives or fidelity to their own small states was enough to keep some Republicans from conferring a brighter majority halo on future presidents.

Senate Debate

In the Senate, De Witt Clinton (R-NY) had already proposed the New York designation amendment, which provided that the House choose from five, but Pierce Butler (R-SC) complicated the question by moving that the amendment also limit presidential eligibility to allow a president who has already served for eight years to serve no more than four years out of every next eight years. The Senate agreed, 16:15, to add the question of eligibility to the amendment, and, on 22 October, the Senate referred the amendment to a committee comprised of Clinton, Pierce Butler, Bradley (R:VT), Nicholas (R:VA), and S. Smith (R-MD). On 24 October, the committee offered its report, but debate on the amendment took another turn when Jonathan Dayton (F-NJ) pointed out that the logic of the designation amendment showed that the office of the vice president ought to be abolished.[32]

---

[31] Ibid., 517, 522, 530, 533.
[32] Ibid., 21.

Even though Dayton's argument that the amendment would weaken the vice presidency was not new, it initiated another set of events that would have important consequences for the amendment. Responding to the Senator from his bordering state, Clinton suggested that Dayton was trying to distract Senators from the present question, saying "It would more comport with the candor of the gentleman to meet the question fairly." Dayton, whose reputation had already suffered from charges that he put private pursuits over the public good, responded in kind: "The custom of the gentleman from New York has been of late to arraign motives instead of meeting arguments." Clinton called Dayton's charge "unfounded," and Dayton later replied that Senate decorum prevented him from answering Clinton accusation but added that "There would be a fitter time and a fitter place for taking that notice of it which it merited." Later that night, Dayton challenged Clinton to a duel, and Clinton left town for New York, abandoning Republicans who had relied on his vote in close counts.[33]

In addition to removing Clinton, Dayton was successful in introducing another question into the debate over the amendment, for his proposal to eliminate the vice president altogether carried the designation principle to its logical extension. Because a vice president could no longer claim to have won the second to most votes, second only to a president who may have won only one more than one-fourth of the electoral votes, the vice president could no longer substitute his lack of formal authority with informal prestige. By lessening the dignity of the vice president, the designation principle would emphasize the electoral victory of one man. Dayton was successful in buying time for Federalists. After the exchange between Clinton and Dayton, Nicholas reminded Senators that "two-thirds" or "three-fourths" of the state legislatures would be in session "in two or three months," and asserted that Dayton's proposal to abolish the vice presidency, even if correct, might 'jeopardize the main amendment of discriminating."[34] In spite of Nicholas's warning and Clinton's repeated attempts to put the amendment to a vote, some Republicans did not follow their party. James Jackson (R-GA), who thought that Dayton's proposal to abolish the vice presidency deserved more consideration, urged Republicans to take their time, "I am not for doing business on horseback."[35] Butler similarly argued for more time on the grounds

---

33 Ibid., 22–25. Plumer, however, records that Clinton left town because he had been appointed mayor of New York. Clinton's looming departure forced Republicans to act with haste. *William Plumer's Memorandum of Proceedings in the United States Senate, 1803–1807*, ed. Everett Somerville Brown (New York: Macmillan, 1923), 17.

34 *Annals*, 8th Congress, 1st sess., 22.

35 Jackson's quote is from *Plumer's Memorandum*, 20. Plumer also presents Worthington's position differently: "I have not made up my mind upon the motion respecting the Vice

that it was "unreasonable to compel gentlemen to vote on a subject who had not time to form their opinions."[36] Other Republicans must have agreed that more time was needed, for a motion for postponement of Dayton's amendment of the amendment carried by only one vote (16:15) after having lost by one vote. On Tuesday, 25 October, debate on the amendment altogether was postponed when news of Clinton's departure to New York was announced.

The postponement of the amendment lasted for nearly a month. On 26 October, debate returned to Louisiana, and the Senate voted to authorize the president to take possession of the territory. Little was accomplished from Thursday, 27 October, through Saturday, 29 October: delays caused by a structural problem with the Senate ceiling as well as activity at a nearby race track allowed members Republicans who were angry at Dayton time to cool their temper.[37] Throughout early and middle November, Republicans must have been unsure about the prospects for amendment, for they fought off attempts to consider the House version of the amendment: On 4 November, a motion to consider lost (12:19), and on 14 November, another motion to consider lost (9:22). On the 4 November vote, Butler (R-SC), Joseph Anderson (R-TN), and Samuel Maclay (R-PN) joined the Federalists. On 14 November, Maclay and, curiously, Adams and Pickering moved to the Republican side.

When the Senate finally took up the amendment on 23 November, Federalists used the Louisiana treaty to connect the small state argument to the question of executive power. John Quincy Adams attempted to introduce more questions for marginal Republicans by noting that the Louisiana Purchase would allow for more states and more foreign born citizens. After calling attention to the prospect of the dilution of the power held by the original thirteen states, John Quincy Adams put the question into its simplest form, "Was there no champion of the small States to stand up in that House and vindicate their rights." Dayton answered that he was "ready to enter his protest against being delivered over bound hand and foot to four or five of the large States." Smith responded by suggesting that the small state question was a transparent attempt to create a wedge for partisan purposes, explaining that the question of large and small states had not been raised in his ten years in Congress. One Republican, Robert Wright (MD), added that he was for the discriminating principle "in its most simple and efficacious form" but not for taking away the rights of the small states.[38]

President, but I shall vote against it – I do not wish the subject discussed. I am for the designating principle only, and therefore shall vote against a postponement."

[36] *Plumer's Memorandum*, 19.
[37] Kuroda, *Origins of the Twelfth Amendment*, 135.
[38] *Annals*, 8th Congress, 1st sess., 85–95.

But by that time, Republicans were ready to make the argument from principle. After William Cocke (R-TN) proposed the number 5 on 24 November with Dayton seconding the motion, John Taylor (R-VA) granted that the question between three or five now had put the discussion of the amendment in a "more serious air than it at first assumed." Taylor defended the amendment on the grounds that original intent required that presidential selection be kept out of the hands of the legislature: "By filling up the blank with five, you carry the election into the House of Representatives; and why do we wish to keep the election out of the House of Representatives? Because experience teaches us to avoid the danger of diets, which are always exposed to intrigue and corruption, as we avoid elections by mobs, from their liability to be misled by the sudden impulse of passion and violence. We wish to avoid both, because each by different paths leads to the same consequence." Taylor added Clopton's argument that the presidential selection could unite public opinion: "Limit the number to three and your reduce the danger, and by condensing public sentiment, you will then have the watchfulness of ambition on one side and of virtue on the other, directed without distraction to the limited number." Taylor's argument was important in that it connected the argument for independence from the legislature to popular selection. After more delay caused debate over procedural questions and by the absence of one small state Republican (Anderson), the amendment had by then come to be seen as a reform aimed at popularizing the presidency. For Federalists, "condensing" the popular vote around a designated candidate would weaken constitutional checks, including federative checks held by small states, on presidential power. For Republicans, the change would more tightly connect the results of the election to the eventual president.[39]

Taylor's confession that the discussion had become more serious confirms that the question of the relative influence of large and small states had directed debate toward the real object of the amendment. As John Quincy Adams noted, the Republican argument had changed from preventing an intended vice president from becoming president to an argument for popular selection as opposed to a selection by Congress. Accordingly, Adams showed that the argument was not about small versus large states as much as it was about whether the president would be made more popular: "The Executive, it has been said, is the man of the people; true, and he is also, as was said, though upon different grounds, the man of the Legislature – it was here a combined principle, federative and popular." Adams' appeal to the federal basis of the Electoral College was no doubt meant to persuade strict constructionists who also believed that the Constitution was a compact

39 Ibid., 99–100.

between the states. Just as such strict constructionists must have agreed with Madison's argument in *The Federalist* No. 39 that the ratification of the Constitution was federal because it was not put to a national vote, they would have agreed with Madison's, and now Adams's, point that presidential selection would be both national *and* federal. To argue that the president would be man of the people, then, was to acknowledge the lessening importance of the states.[40]

On 2 December, with the real question now out in the open, advocates and opponents finally debated the larger question regarding the connection between the president and public opinion. Samuel White (F-DE) objected to the undemocratic consequences of such an election: "upon this designating plan the public attention will be entirely engrossed in the election of the President, in making one great man."[41] Uriah Tracy (F-CT) argued that Republicans had conflated the term "public will" and the "will of the popular majority," which was also to say that the public will was the "will of the great States."[42] James Hillhouse (F-CT) stated that Taylor had been blinded by "idol worship" in that the amendment "proposes to persuade the people that there is only one man of correct politics in the United States."[43] Hillhouse went on to assert that the original design revealed intent to allow some mystery in elections in order to prevent the people from becoming too "infatuated" with one man. Accordingly, the unpredictable outcome of the original Electoral College was democratic in that protected against the possibility that a president would pose as a "friend of the people" in order to take away liberties. Pickering, although he believed that three was closer to original intent than five, also objected to the Republican argument that made so much seem to depend on "the sake of one man."[44] Tracy put the point most directly when he asked, "If gentlemen wish to shake the Constitution to pieces, if majorities must decide everything, why not go at once to a simple democracy?"[45]

Republicans defended the amendment by way of principle that elections should more closely reflect the popular will. Of Jefferson, Jackson said, "His countrymen had fixed their eyes upon him, but arts had been employed to frustrate their wishes."[46] Later, he argued that no man, with the exception of Washington, was as worthy of the affections of the people as Jefferson,

[40] Ibid., 119; *The Federalist*.
[41] Ibid., 144.
[42] Ibid., 164.
[43] Ibid., 190–92.
[44] Ibid., 123, 196.
[45] Ibid., 206.
[46] Ibid., 157.

and he went on to say that whereas Georgians believed that John Adams had violated their rights, the "author of the Declaration of Independence ... has not disappointed us."[47] Cocke went further than others and confirmed Federalist arguments when he declared that he was for a government "of the people, whether well born or by accident" and a government "not of checks and balances, but one that will not suffer a bad check upon good principles."[48] Cocke's quarrel with checks and balances reveals that Republicans believed, in John Breckinridge's words, that the Federalists had questioned the "democratic principles of the Constitution." For Breckinridge (R-KY), the question was not about large and small states as much as it was about removing the legislature from presidential selection: "If any principle is more sacred and all-important for free government it is, that elections should be direct as possible; in proportion as you remove from direct election you approach danger."[49]

After the Republicans made their last argument for democratizing presidential selection, Pierce Butler addressed the Senate. For wavering Republicans, or for those who believed in "original intent," no other Senator could have been so authoritative, as he was both a Republican and a member of the committee in the 1787 Convention that created the Electoral College. Butler argued that the Framers "were apprehensive of an elective Chief Magistrate" and wanted to "prevent the putting up of any powerful man." The original design, according to Butler, therefore required states to vote for two equally qualified candidates. With the election likely falling to one of the two – "it was totally immaterial which" – the nation would avoid the corruption associated with elections and would lessen the likelihood that one person would become too kinglike.[50]

After Butler's presentation of what he called "the intention of the Constitution," the question was called "loudly" at 9.30 PM. Over objections that the debates had lasted too late into the night and that the Republicans needed two-thirds of Senators present *and* not present, Republicans secured a bare two-third majority with a 22:10 vote. Although Republicans did not convert Butler, they did convince Bailey and Condit, who had joined Butler previously in voting for five instead of three, to join the majority.[51] The success of the amendment also depended on the Republicans holding Anderson

---

47 Ibid., 200.
48 Ibid., 153.
49 Ibid., 206.
50 Ibid., 207–9.
51 On 29 November, Butler, Condit, and Bailey joined the minority to vote for five. On that day's vote to vote for three, Bailey joined Republicans, but Condit and Butler remained with Federalists.

and Jackson, who had joined Butler in wanting to limit presidential eligibility.[52] It also required that David Stone, a Federalist-turned-Republican who had voted against the amendment in the Seventh Congress, to switch his position. For the latter victory, Wilson Cary Nicholas claimed credit in a letter to Clinton, in which he also explained that mustering the requisite two-thirds was "the most arduous work we ever engaged in, persevering and artful enemies in our front, with insincere friends in our own ranks; we deserve some credit for our success."[53] Although the Twelfth Amendment was eventually approved, as Henry Adams said "by the usual party vote," it took some time and was never a sure success.[54]

For the amendment to be proposed to the states, Republicans in the House had to move to the Senate version rather than the other way around simply because some members of the Senate had left town. Consequently, House Republicans had to cobble together enough votes to accept the Senate's requirement that the eventual election be chosen from the three, rather than five, highest vote-getters. Despite a late attempt by one Massachusetts Republican (William Eustis) to break party ranks and insist on the provisions of the original House amendment, Republicans managed to convince a two-thirds majority that the small and large state question would not be the crucial political divide in the country.[55] This time, House Republicans succeeded without a vote to spare (84:42).[56]

Jefferson

Future research needs to determine the extent Jefferson meddled in the amendment question. After his 1801 letter to Gallatin in which he seemed to favor a direct election with a winner take all scheme, Jefferson did not write about the discriminatory amendment until it had been officially passed. In fact, it is curious that one supporter of Jefferson, who in 1804 published *A Defense of the Measures of the Administration of Thomas Jefferson* under the name Curtius, noted that Jefferson never officially recommended that Congress propose the amendment.[57] But, according to John Taylor, there

---

[52] *Annals*, 8th Congress, 1st sess., 214.

[53] Kuroda, *Origins of the Twelfth Amendment*, 143.

[54] Adams, 391.

[55] Eustis had a reputation for partisan inconsistency. See John A. Garraty and Mark C. Karnes, eds., *American National Biography*, Volume 7 (New York: Oxford University Press, 1999), 590.

[56] Kuroda, *Origins of the Twelfth Amendment*, 146–151.

[57] "Curtius," *A Defense of the Measures of the Jefferson Administration* (Washington, DC: Samuel H. Smith, 1804), p. 30. I was made aware of this document by C. William Hill Jr.

was "a general meeting of the friends of the discriminating amendment (with a few exceptions) an evening or two before its passage."[58] Republicans surely met, as Taylor indicated, to discuss the new problem of whether the vice president should be allowed to serve in the case of no president being selected, but perhaps it was in also in this caucus that Stone, Condit and Theodorus Bailey were persuaded to toe the party line.[59] Whether Jefferson orchestrated this caucus is not yet fully known, partly because Jefferson himself went to enormous lengths to conceal his partisanship from posterity.

If Jefferson did not publicly appeal to the people on behalf of the amendment, he was at least a covert cheerleader for its ratification. In early 1804, he congratulated the Republican governor of Pennsylvania on his state's ratification of the amendment, adding that the Federalists would be able to oppose the amendment only on "party, not moral motives."[60] Predictably, Jefferson's interest in reelection colored his understanding of the amendment – in March, for instance, he wrote to Elbridge Gerry that the amendment would make "the election for the ensuing 4 years seem to the present nothing formidable"[61] – but he also explained his advocacy by way of principle: "That great opposition is and will be made by federalists to this amendment is certain. They know that if it prevails, neither President nor Vice President can ever be made but by the fair vote of the majority of the nation, of which they are not."[62] If Jefferson offered these opinions only in confidence to fellow Republicans, he took measures to ensure that the executive branch would be able to enforce the amendment once ratified. In early August 1804, the president urged Madison to act promptly when the required number of states had approved the amendment: "No time should be lost in publishing officially the final ratification." In his reply, Madison assured the president, "Before I left Washington a circular letter was prepared and the requisite provisional steps taken for giving effect to the proposed amendment as soon as the ratification of Tennessee should be notified."[63] Just as he had "counted

58 John Taylor to Wilson Cary Nicholas, 23 June 1804, quoted in Noble E. Cunningham Jr., *The Jeffersonian Republicans in Power: Party Operations, 1801–1809* (Chapel Hill: University of North Carolina Press, 1963), 100.
59 Taylor's letter was to Nicholas, who, as mentioned above, claimed credit for persuading Stone. Taylor's tone, which could suggest that Nicholas was not there, can be explained by the larger context in which Taylor was recalling to Nicholas whether Republicans in the Senate decided matters in "caucus" – a partisan maneuver that would have come under partisan attack. In short, this letter does not preclude the possibility that Nicholas was in attendance and that evening convinced Stone.
60 Jefferson to Thomas McKean, 17 January 1804, Ford, 8:292–3.
61 Jefferson to Elbridge Gerry, 3 March 1804, Ford, 8:297–8.
62 Jefferson to McKean, Ford, 8:292–3.
63 Jefferson to Madison, 13 August 1804 and Madison to Jefferson, 13 August 1804, Smith, 1334.

himself in" in 1800, Jefferson made sure that the executive arm would be ready to enforce the newly codified will of the people.

More than assuring Jefferson's own reelection against another Burr and more than lessening the already small likelihood of a Federalist success in 1804 and following elections, the Twelfth Amendment was part of Jefferson's larger project to transform presidential power. Jefferson's favoring the discriminating principle fit within his lifelong belief that the Constitution's method of presidential selection obscured voter preference between president and vice president. During the extended Election of 1800, Jefferson's frustration at the confused outcome led him to argue that the connection between presidential selection and public opinion should be more explicit: "The contrivance in the Constitution for marking the votes works badly, because it does not enounce precisely enough the true expression of the public will."[64] As he then put it the Republican solution of allowing "a concert between the two highest vote getters," though "bungling" and "imperfect," was preferable to the Federalist alternative, which would allow the "Legislature take the nomination of the Executive entirely from the people." Later, when precedent and party competition softened Jefferson's view, he explained to a foreign observer, "our President is chosen by ourselves, directly in *practice*" because "we vote for A as elector only on the condition he will vote for B."[65]

But he always believed the constitutional remedy for a close election was skewed improperly toward the states. In 1823, Jefferson wrote that the "constitutional mode of election ultimately by legislature voting by states as the most dangerous blot in our const[titution]," and preferred a second "appeal" to the Electoral College."[66] In the event of a second deadlock in the Electoral College, Jefferson recommended a contest between the "two highest" candidates in the House, with the states "voting per capita," not voting equally as mandated by the Twelfth Amendment. Because the latter reform would benefit the most populous states, Jefferson doubted that enough small states would ever consent.[67] With regard to presidential elections, Jefferson seemed to believe that authority derived from the people rather than the states.

The Second Inaugural and Presidential Performance
Although Jefferson may have kept his guidance of the amendment process secret, his Second Inaugural leaves little doubt as to what he meant for the

---

[64] Jefferson to Tench Coxe, 31 December 1800, Ford, 7:475.
[65] Jefferson to P.S. Dupont de Numours, 24 April 1816, Ford, 10:23.
[66] Jefferson to George Hay, 17 August 1823, Ford, 10:264.
[67] On compromise with small states, see Madison to Jefferson, 14 January 1824, Smith, 1891.

Twelfth Amendment to accomplish. With his own election guaranteed and clarified, Jefferson was able to continue attaching declarations of principle to presidential tenure. Instead of offering a new declaration of principle, he used his Second Inaugural show that the election of 1804 validated his practice of the principles announced in the first. Accordingly, Jefferson used the Second Inaugural to discuss the place of public opinion and elections in democratic government. This discussion further transformed the inaugural address.

Jefferson was criticized for simply delivering a second inaugural address. For some observers, Jefferson's speech betrayed the president's demagoguery in that it opportunistically transformed the ceremony surrounding the oath of office into a direct appeal to popular opinion. To call attention to Jefferson's parting with Washington's precedent, the Federalist *United States Gazette* titled it "Inaugural Address No. 2."[68] Similarly, Hamilton's *New York Evening Post* argued that Jefferson should not have made a second inaugural: "Mr. Jefferson has made this address without any precedent for it, and without any apparent reason but that of ingratiating himself with the people, and exhibiting a sort of defense against those severe but just animadversions which have been made upon his conduct during the greater part of his administration."[69] Such charges indicate that Federalists noticed Jefferson's parting with precedent. In the first second inaugural address, George Washington used only four sentences to acknowledge taking the oath of office a second time. After directing his salutation to "Fellow Citizens," Washington stated that he had been again called by the "voice" of his "country" to "execute the functions of its Chief Magistrate." But rather than taking the opportunity to offer a statement of the principles by which he would govern and rather than offering a second statement of thanks for being elected, Washington stated that the ceremony was an inappropriate occasion for speechmaking: "When the occasion proper for it shall arrive, I shall endeavor to express the high sense I entertain of this distinguished honor, and of the confidence which has been reposed in me by the people of United America." In place of offering a statement of principle in the inaugural, Washington marked the occasion by retaking the oath of office. "Previous to the execution of any official act of the president the Constitution requires an oath of office." Curiously, Washington added an oath he had composed to the one prescribed by the Constitution.[70]

---

[68] Noble E. Cunningham Jr., *The Inaugural Addresses of President Thomas Jefferson, 1801 and 1805* (Columbia: University of Missouri Press, 2001), 91.

[69] Ibid.

[70] Washington, "Second Inaugural Address," *George Washington: Writings*, ed. John Rhode-hamel (New York: Library of America, 1997), 835.

Nine months later, Washington reminded legislators that he had refrained from expressing gratitude in his Second Inaugural.[71] In this annual message to Congress, Washington remarked that since there had not yet arisen "a fit occasion" to reflect on being reelected president, he would do it then. As in the First Inaugural, Washington delivered his thanks by reflecting on the tension between public service and private retirement. This time, however, Washington more directly referred to the people's hand in electing him by saying that he put off his retirement in obedience to "the suffrage which commanded me to resume the Executive power." The remainder of that address, however, was devoted to the question of the enforcement of treaties with European nations and Native American tribes. In contrast to Washington, and rather than merely abiding by the constitutional requirement to take the oath of office, Jefferson found in the occasion a "duty" to once again "express the deep sense" of his thoughts concerning the "new proof confidence" evidenced by the election.[72]

Whereas the outcome of the election of 1800 was not decided until well into 1801, the election of 1804 was settled in that year. As a consequence of his easy victory, Jefferson had plenty of time to plan his Second Inaugural, and, unlike his First Inaugural, this address was edited by Jefferson's cabinet.[73] In his "Notes of a Draft for a Second Inaugural Address," the president explained the difference between the second and the first; "the former was *promise*: this is *performance*."[74] Because the First Inaugural was "an exposition of principles" by which Jefferson would "administer the government," it followed that the Second ought to be a "statement of facts, shewing that I have conformed to those principles." Reporting his performance would therefore provide the structure for the address.

That Jefferson used the occasion to report that he had remained faithful to the principles of his First Inaugural points to the larger to ambition of the address. Rather than detailing the ways that he had executed laws passed by Congress, or rather than offering a summary of his proven devotion to the Constitution or the Bill of Rights, the president used the Second Inaugural to state the ways that he had carried out the principles he himself had given: "On taking this station on a former occasion, I declared the principles on which I believed it my duty to administer the affairs of our commonwealth.

---

[71] Washington, "Fifth Annual Message to Congress," 3 December 1793, *Washington Writings*, 846–851.

[72] Jefferson, "Second Inaugural Address," 4 March 1805, *TJW*, 518.

[73] Madison received two drafts of the address, one on February 8 and again on February 21. Smith, 1556. According to Cunningham, Gallatin and Madison made "substantial" revisions but the final text was Jefferson's "own." *Inaugural Addresses*, 76.

[74] *TJW*, 1555.

My conscience tells me that I have, on every occasion, acted up to that declaration, according to its obvious import, and to the understanding of the candid mind."[75] The promise in 1800 binds performance of administration in 1804: the Constitution required the president to faithfully execute the laws, but Jefferson was also bound by his First Inaugural to administer "the affairs of our commonwealth" according to a particular set of principles. Enabled by his transformation of the inaugural address, Jefferson embraced the theory of retrospective voting before it became a theory.

Rather than treating each of the principles he had previously listed as the "essential principles of our Government" Jefferson reported on his performance in themes. In foreign affairs, he reported that he had been guided by both interest and justice, as "with nations, as with individuals, our interests soundly calculated, will ever be found inseparable from our moral duties." In matters "at home," Jefferson took credit for cutting taxes, reporting that his closing "unnecessary offices" and cutting of "useless establishments and expenses" had "enabled us to discontinue our internal taxes." Furthermore, Jefferson explained that extra revenue would be used for internal improvements during peace, and then defended the Louisiana Purchase by employing Madison's argument for the extended republic. Jefferson closed the address after detailing his activity with regard to freedom of religion and freedom of the press.[76]

The paragraphs on religion and the press deserve some attention. Concerning matters of religious freedom, Jefferson continued his project to erect a "wall of separation between church and state" by reporting that he had acted according to the principle that religion's "free exercise is placed by the constitution independent of the general government." Accordingly, he left religious exercises "as the constitution found them," and though he did not here say it, Jefferson must have had in mind his not offering any proclamations of Thanksgiving. But after saying that he had left matters of religion untouched by the general government, Jefferson used a passage on Native Americans to criticize religious leaders. Referring to the "aboriginal inhabitants," the president reported that "interested and crafty individuals among them" had stood in the way of enlightenment: "These persons inculcate a sanctimonious reverence for the customs of their ancestors; that whatsoever they did, must be done through all time; that reason is a false guide, and to advance under its counsel, in their physical, moral or political condition, is perilous innovation; that their duty is to remain as their Creator made them, ignorance being safety, and knowledge full of danger." Jefferson went on to blame these "anti-philosophers" because they "find an interest in keeping

---

[75] Jefferson, "Second Inaugural Address," *TJW*, 518.
[76] Ibid.

things in their present state" and "dread reformation." By teaching "habit" over "reason" these individuals blocked the path of improvement.[77]

By way of implication, religious leaders outside the Native American community must have felt some of the president's sting. Indeed, Jefferson planned it that way; in his notes for the address, Jefferson made clear what must have been inferred by some: "But every respector of science, every friend to political reformation must have observed with indignation the hue & cry raised against philosophy & the rights of man; and it really seems as if they would be overborne & barbarism, bigotry & despotism would recover the ground they have lost by the advance of the public understanding. I have thought the occasion justified some discountenance of these anti-social doctrines, some testimony against them, but not to commit myself in direct warfare on them, I have thought it best to say what is directly applied to the Indians only, but admits by inference a more general extension."[78] Elsewhere, Jefferson explained, "The head of the Indians was a little extended with an ironical eye to the modern declaimers against philosophy," and Henry Adams concluded that the passage illustrates how Jefferson "could not resist the temptation to strike once more" at members of the New England clergy.[79] But more than poking at a politically powerful sect of believers, the passage on Native Americans fit within the Second Inaugural's connecting presidential performance to public opinion.

Before Jefferson turned from freedom of religion to freedom of the press, he paused to assure his listeners that he did not list the details of performance in order to "arrogate to myself the merit of the measures." Rather, credit was due to "the reflecting character" of the electorate, who, "by the weight of public opinion," shape and energize the government's measures. Because the electorate used "sound discretion" in choosing its legislators, the laws would be the "foundations of public happiness." Furthermore, credit for the sound execution of those laws belonged to "able and faithful auxiliaries" who had joined Jefferson in the executive branch.[80]

After this digression praising public opinion, Jefferson went on to address the freedom of the press by alluding to the press's publication of scandal.[81] Here, Jefferson noted that though "these abuses of an institution so

---

[77] Ibid., 520–1.
[78] Jefferson, "Notes of a Draft for a Second Inaugural Address," *TJW*, 1555.
[79] Adams, 606.
[80] Jefferson, "Second Inaugural," *TJW*, 521.
[81] James Callender's publication of the allegation that Jefferson fathered children through Sally Hemings was first published in September, 1802. James Callendar, "The President, Again," reprinted in *Sally Hemings and Jefferson: History, Memory, and Civic Culture* ed. Jan Ellen Lewis and Peter S. Onuf (Charlottesville: University Press of Virginia, 1999), 259–61. See also the introduction by Lewis and Onuf in the same work (pp. 1–16).

important to freedom and science" were grounds for criminal prosecution, his attention to other matters left "punishment" to "public indignation." More than a question of Jefferson's personal reputation, the trial of the press before the court of public opinion presented the "world" with an "experiment" testing whether "freedom of discussion, unaided by power is not sufficient for the propagation and protection of truth."[82] By presenting the politics of scandal in these terms, Jefferson added to the argument for freedom of expression. Just as he placed in the minds of citizens a "wall" between church and state, the president supplied citizens with the argument that expression would not stand in the way of the progress of truth but would possibly promote it. Although the public could certainly count on the government to protect "against false and declamatory publications," it also could learn from this experiment that truth would stand its ground against false opinions.

More than a bundle of separate reports, the Second Inaugural's message of performance was a tightly woven lecture on the place of public opinion in a constitutional democracy. Indeed, the address can be divided into two addresses, the first one reporting how he had executed the promise of 1801, and the second one (six paragraphs – like his and Washington's First Inaugurals – beginning with the discussion of the Indians) an elaborate defense of public opinion. The Second Inaugural, given out of the president's "duty to express the deeps sense" of the "new proof of confidence" conferred by the electorate, aimed to continue the First Inaugural's assertion of presidential elections as the routine expression of public opinion. The election of 1804 provided the conclusion to the experiment testing truth and falsehood: "The experiment has been tried; you have witnessed the scene; our fellow citizens have looked on, cool and collected; they saw the latent source from which these outrages proceeded; they gathered around their public functionaries, and when the constitution called them to the decision by suffrage, they pronounced their verdict, honorable to those who had served them, and consolatory to the friend of man, who believes he may be intrusted with his own affairs."[83] Just as truth would stand its ground against falsehood, public opinion could be trusted to discern rumor from fact. In the summer before the election, the president reassured a partisan worried that the press would ruin Republican chances: the "discernment they [the people] have manifested between truth and falsehood, show that they may safely be trusted to hear everything true and false, and to form a correct judgment between them."[84]

[82] Jefferson, "Second Inaugural," *TJW*, 521.
[83] Ibid., 522.
[84] Jefferson to John Tyler, 28 June 1804, *TJW*, 1147.

The association of public opinion, elections, and truth points to a complication within Jefferson's political science. If the verification that truth can stand its ground against falsehood is public opinion, what is the proof that public opinion is true in its assessments? By preparing the way for the discussion of freedom of the press with the discussion of freedom of religion as the transition between the two addresses, the Second Inaugural called attention to this very problem. In the implied criticism of clergy members who had been "powerful obstacles" to enlightenment, Jefferson delineated one way in which truth sometimes loses ground to falsehood – when crafty persons can shape prejudice and habit into reverence for the ways of ancestors. Disinclined by custom to favor progress, and educated under falsehood, this public would be poorly suited for deciding contests of opinion. One object of Jefferson's presidency, as he told Tyler, was to "fortify" in the people "the habit of testing everything by reason" so as to prevent his successors from "manacling the people with their own consent."[85] But when is the public qualified?

Jefferson attempted to ease this tension in the closing of the address. Even though the election had proven that public opinion had chosen correctly and had therefore demonstrated that truth could withstand falsehood, there was a still a minority who had "not yet rallied to the same point." Jefferson reassured the majority by speaking hopefully of the minority: "facts are piercing through the veil drawn over them," and they will soon come "into the fold of their country." The "doubting brethren" would come to "see" that "the mass of their fellow citizens" agree regarding the cultivation of peace, equality of rights, civil and religious liberty, law and order, and the right to one's own industry. Because the sources of this agreement could be found in both the dictate of reason and the estimation of self-interest, the dissenters would inevitably join the majority in the "entire union of opinion." Put differently, although public opinion could be divided about the process of government, it would be united on its fundamentals.[86]

As he had famously declared that every citizen was both Republican and Federalist, Jefferson here blurred the meaning of principle. In both speeches, Jefferson suggested he meant "principle" to be something so fundamental that all Americans would agree on it – the republican form of government, Union, political equality, or the right to one's industry. To highlight this agreement, Jefferson contrasted it against the dissent of those few who wished to dissolve the Union, change its republican form, or obstruct enlightenment: because only a few believed such principles, the majority was, in principle,

---

[85] Ibid.
[86] Jefferson, "Second Inaugural," *TJW*, 522–3.

united. But, at the same time, Jefferson referred to "principle" as opinion, something that could be decided by elections: "I shall now enter on the duties to which my fellow citizens have again called me, and shall proceed in the spirit of those principles which they have approved." Just as truth's superiority to falsehood can be proven by a political experiment, a principle can be identified by recourse to a political election.[87]

Obscuring the difference between the two types of principle worked to Jefferson's advantage in his project to energize the presidency. By employing the deeper sense of the republican principle, Jefferson could rally all but a few around his principles of administration. By putting the principles of his administration into a solemn declaration surrounding a national election, he could elevate them to seem like *the* republican principle. Enabled by the Twelfth Amendment, Jefferson constructed in speech a national majority will that he himself embodied. Just as the Declaration of Independence put to words the "harmonizing sentiments of the day," the Second Inaugural positioned the master democrat as the master teacher, guiding and instructing "the union of sentiment."

Election of One Man: The Politics of Character

The Twelfth Amendment is an important, if little understood, early development in the democratization of the presidency.[88] If electors were not required to designate whom they intended to be president, partisan mischief might have resulted in a de facto congressional selection of presidents, confirming the spirit of George Mason's prediction in the Constitutional Convention that Congress would select the president nineteen out of twenty times.[89] Or, had the amendment retained the number five, the amendment might have set a precedent that a particular president need not represent a new majority of popular support, leaving future Houses freer to lean toward peer review and away from pure democracy when selecting presidents in close elections.[90] Put somewhat differently, Congress's proposing the Twelfth Amendment

---

[87] Jefferson, "Second Inaugural," *TJW*, 523. This corresponds to the problem arising from Jefferson's assertion that two political parties existed "in nature."

[88] Bruce Ackerman, most recently, missed the connection to the presidency by looking for a solution to the parties. Bruce Ackerman's conclusion that the amendment "is the very opposite of a serious attempt to think the problem through" refers to the problem of parties. Surprisingly, Ackerman missed the consequences for the mandate theory of the presidency. *Failure of the Founding Fathers*, 247.

[89] Madison, *Notes*, 577.

[90] For a discussion of movement from peer review to pure democracy, see Richard Pious, "The Presidency and the Nominating Process: Politics and Power," in *The Presidency and the Political System, 7th ed.*, ed. Michael Nelson (Washington, DC: CQ Press, 2003), 217–38.

represented a twofold defeat of legislative selection of presidents in that it made the eventual selection in the House less likely and, in the case of such an election, it ensured that the decision in the House would not veer very sharply from the results of the Electoral College.[91]

Similarly, scholars need to ask whether the failure of the Twelfth Amendment would have made less likely the later dethroning of "king caucus," the nomination of presidential candidates by the parties in Congress – could the argument against de facto legislative selection of presidents have carried if Senate Federalists had persuaded enough Republicans that the House should have as much choice as possible when choosing a president? More important, the discriminating principle required that Electors specify who their choice was for president and therefore moved control of the executive branch closer to the already developing winner-take-all system. And, by removing the mystery of the original design, the amendment made it more possible for presidents to assert that they alone represented the people. In short, the amendment gave birth to the theory of the presidential mandate.

There are serious consequences to this change. In 1990, Robert Dahl argued that the theory of presidential mandates was a "myth," at least because presidents before 1960 lacked the empirical tools – that is, the skills offered by the trade of political science – to know if voters selected them because they wanted them to carry out specific policies. More important, Dahl objected to the theoretical underpinning of mandates, asserting that the myth of the mandate was part of what he called the pseudo-democratization of the presidency. For Dahl, the democratic president parted with the Founder's design for the presidency in that the Founders intended that the president be insulated against public opinion. Further, and probably more important for Dahl, the democratic president was something of a presidential code word for the imperial president in that the claim to represent the people undermines the representative function of Congress and thus debilitates one element of democracy in the Constitution. Somewhat conversely, Dahl also worried that the democratic presidency was too democratic in that it substituted "raw will" for the "understanding" necessary in legitimate rule.[92]

Dahl's theoretical criticisms of the implications of the mandate theory were similar to the Federalist objections to the discriminating principle. Like Senate Federalists, who expressed serious concerns about making

---

[91] But see James W. Ceaser, *Presidential Selection: Origins and Development* (Princeton, NJ: Princeton University Press, 1979), 105–22.

[92] Robert A. Dahl, "The Myth of the Presidential Mandate," *Political Science Quarterly* 105 (1990): 355–72.

presidential selection about one man, Dahl objected to presidential claims that presidents uniquely represent the people on the grounds that constitutional design included intermediate forms that would mitigate the majority will. Although, like the Federalists, Dahl did not say it, the thrust of his argument was that congressional involvement in presidential selection is to be preferred over democratic reforms, perhaps because "condensing public sentiment" would make pluralistic exchange less likely.[93] Each depended on the argument that too much connection between executive power and democracy is bad for democracy.[94]

Dahl, of course, had in mind modern claims to presidential mandates, not Jefferson. Critics of Jefferson have used the Twelfth Amendment to confirm the common charge that Jefferson as president parted with his political principles: just as Federalists charged Jefferson with inconsistency on the question of states's rights, later observers, from Henry Adams to Garry Wills, have found a kind of political opportunism in Jefferson's support for the ratification of the Twelfth Amendment.[95] Because Jefferson and his party were allegedly the party of states's rights and the party of legislative supremacy, their move to make presidential selection lean more heavily on the popular will and presidents less dependent on Congress seems, according to these observers, a sacrifice of principle to politics. Just as the Louisiana Purchase was a blow to the doctrine of strict construction, the discriminating principle was a blow to the federative principle.

With a different partisan edge to the charge, John C. Calhoun saw more deeply than others the democratizing power of the reform. Confirming the predictions of Senate Federalists, he argued that the Amendment nationalized presidential selection, giving the popular majority – and the most populous states – more influence over the concurrent majority that the framers had intended, and therefore upsetting the stabilizing balance in the constitution. For Calhoun, the original design allowed for both parties to be represented in the executive, which was in his mind clear proof that the Constitution intended to restrain a president who claimed to represent the majority. So, too, with the eventual election in the House: large states and

---

[93] Federalists were more explicit in 1814, when those at the Hartford Convention recommended that the Constitution be amended to prevent presidents from serving a second term. At least one Federalist wanted the convention to urge the repeal of the Twelfth Amendment. Timothy Pickering to John Lowell, 28 November 1814, *Documents Relating to New England Federalism, 1800–1815* ed. Henry Adams (Boston: Little, Brown, 1877), 408.

[94] For an argument that mandates do matter, see Patricia Heidotting Conley, *Presidential Mandates: How Elections Shape the National Agenda* (Chicago: University of Chicago Press, 2001). Note that Conley's study begins with the election of 1828, not 1804 (pp. 52–3).

[95] Adams, 391; Wills, *Negro President*, 113.

thus the numerical majority would dominate the nominating stage in the Electoral College, and the small states and thus the concurrent majority would choose from the five nominees. Calhoun's complaint is instructive in that it shows how the real implication of the Twelfth Amendment is that it made it more likely that a national majority would choose the president. As some Senate Republicans argued in 1803, the argument from the prerogatives of the small states was simply a smokescreen for the argument against a national, numerical majority.[96]

To be sure, these charges rest on a caricature of the Constitution. If Hamilton in *The Federalist* Nos. 71 and 72 is to be believed, the basis for presidential reeligibility is that it would provide "inducements" to presidential "good behavior." A portion of his logic was negative: denying a president another term would be to tell the president to "make hay while the sun shines." But the other side of blame is credit, and Hamilton's argument for responsibility suggests that "responsibility" would make executive energy safe as well as strong. Because the prospect of reelection was blurred by partisan strategy, it is plausible that the Twelfth Amendment restored one element of the original intent.[97]

But, understood in the context of Jefferson's project to transform the presidency, there is more to the Twelfth Amendment. One consequence of the Amendment is the rise in the importance of the politics of character. When Federalists charged that Republicans were wrong to make the election of "one man" so important, they might have had in mind the new kind of politics that would inevitably revolve around such elections. In 1802, James Callendar had published charges about Jefferson's personal life – that he had had an affair with one of his slaves, that he had once made advances to the wife of a friend, and that he once had tried to pay a debt with depreciated money – in a series of newspaper articles.[98] The accuracy or inaccuracy of these charges have been the subjects of other studies and need not concern us here, but it is worth noticing that the charges, and the kinds of politics they represent, were made more relevant – more attractive as campaign strategy – by the Twelfth Amendment because the designating principle made presidential selection a contest of men as much as a contest of principle.

More important, the new relationship between the man and the principle makes possible Jefferson's understanding of executive prerogative by offering presidents a real opportunity to offer declarations of principle alongside an

---

[96] John C. Calhoun, *A Discourse on the Constitution and Government*, in *Union and Liberty: The Political Philosophy of John C. Calhoun*, ed. Ross M. Lence (Indianapolis: Liberty Fund, 1992), 159.

[97] *Federalist*, 457–68.

[98] Malone, 4:212–20.

expression of the public will. Prerogative, which requires throwing oneself on the people and therefore requires that a presidential election be "about one man," would therefore be liberated and constrained by the constitutional design. And the means by which the people may judge prerogative, the declaration of principle, would make more sense now coming from the specific man preferred by most to be president. Under the new design, the election of 1804 could test the justice of the Louisiana Purchase.

During the reelection campaign of Andrew Jackson, Alexis de Tocqueville observed that Americans "personify their theories" in their presidential candidates.[99] Although Tocqueville must have meant that the person embodies the political ideas of the masses, his phrase opens the question as to whether electing the president is as much about the character of the person as the theory. As Jefferson explained in his letter to the governor in Pennsylvania, the line between political principle and personal character can be blurred: "I am a friend to the discriminating principle; and for a reason more than others have, inasmuch as the discriminated vote of my constituents will express unequivocally the verdict they wish to cast on my conduct."[100] In truth, Jefferson himself had already blurred the distinction between the man and the office – taking on conspicuously unkingly garments, walking to his inauguration, and keeping his own birthday a secret – but the Twelfth Amendment would make the connection even more explicit. Public opinion of presidential character, and its new connection to presidential performance, was the central message of Jefferson's Second Inaugural.

[99] Alexis de Tocqueville, *Democracy in America*, trans. Harvey C. Mansfield Jr. and Delba Winthrop (Chicago: University of Chicago Press, 2000), 127.
[100] Jefferson to Thomas McKean, 17 January 1804, Ford, 8:292–3.

9

"To bring their wills to a point of union and effect"

Declarations and Presidential Speech

Jefferson's understanding of democratic energy requires a president who will use declarations to articulate the principles of his administration in order to direct national aspirations, present a standard by which administration can be judged, and, most important, bring the opinions of citizens together under a single head. Because the president's unique electoral position places the presidency closest to the national will, it is the president's job to bring public opinion to a set of declared principles; by declaring these principles, the president not only strengthens his ability to act in agency of the will of the nation but also lays down the principles by which this agency would be governed. Jefferson transformed presidential speech in order to energize the presidency, and Jefferson transformed the presidency in order to bring energy to declarations.

This is not to say that Jefferson ushered in the rhetorical presidency long before Woodrow Wilson or that Jefferson relied on popular leadership, rather than reputation among elites, as the primary resource of power.[1] Jefferson's most well-known rhetorical act as president, after all, was sending his state of the union addresses to Congress in writing rather than delivering them in person, a precedent that other premodern presidents followed until Wilson brought democracy to the presidency. Like his simple attire, this practice was part of his larger attempt to divest the office of its kingly forms. And, like other early presidents, Jefferson avoided appealing over the heads

---

[1] Jeffrey K. Tulis, *The Rhetorical Presidency* (Princeton, NJ: Princeton University Press, 1987), 56; Stephen Skowronek, *The Politics Presidents Make: Leadership from John Adams to George Bush* (Cambridge, MA: Belknap Press, Harvard University Press, 1993), 70–74; and Bruce Ackerman, *The Failure of the Founding Fathers: Jefferson, Marshall and the Rise of Presidential Democracy* (Cambridge, MA: Belknap Press, Harvard University Press, 2005), 256.

of Congress to the people in order to achieve his policy objectives. Although he expanded the inaugural address into a platform for declarations of principles, he chose against doing the same for the annual message to Congress. Instead, he found alternative pathways of influence: since the publication of *Presidential Power* over forty years ago, students of the presidency have found new appreciation for the ways in which Jefferson privately led, hosting elaborately staged dinners and confiding in lieutenants in Congress to enhance his power.[2] By placing the most important explanations of executive power in the mouths of friends and fellow partisans, he preserved the president's standing above the fray of institutional conflict yet jeopardized the teaching his own doctrine required. Jefferson famously wielded a felicitous pen, but he was no eager speaker.

But Jefferson's reputation as a prolific writer complicates the emphasis on Jefferson's silent leadership. Although studies have gone some distance in navigating Jefferson's methods of leadership through the means of political party rather than through direct appeals to the people, they fail to appreciate fully enough Jefferson's attempt to use the presidency to place declarations of principle within the practice of government. As has been argued, Jefferson parted with precedent by making the First Inaugural an explanation of his principles and again when he used the Second Inaugural to promote political harmony under his performance of the First Inaugural's promise. But there is more. When an occasion offered itself in the form of an address, Jefferson crafted his replies to further explain the principles of his First Inaugural. Or, when secrecy demanded, Jefferson used a private person to be his mouthpiece. By placing new phrases into public discourse, Jefferson used the presidency to direct the public's constitutional understanding and to unify public opinion. And, although Jefferson's annual messages to Congress were deferential, his other messages to Congress were filled with defenses of executive discretion. Significantly, by reporting executive discretion to Congress, Jefferson preserved his requirement that executives throw themselves on the people while at the same time allowing Congress to continue its constitutional function of lawmaking. But, by defending these actions and by showing how republicans could judge them, he made it clear that executive prerogative occupied a central place in his understanding of republican government.

When Jefferson became president, he continued the model of political speech he had developed throughout his life, rejecting the precedent of

[2] James Sterling Young, *The Washington Community, 1800–1828* (New York: Columbia University Press, 1966), 169; Robert J. Johnstone Jr., *Jefferson and the Presidency: Leadership in the Young Republic* (Ithaca, NY: Cornell University Press, 1978), 22, 52–7.

presidential speech set by Washington. Consider the "Farewell Address": although the Board of Visitors at the University of Virginia assigned Washington's as one of only six texts required at the university's school of law, Jefferson never offered any indication that he considered Washington's Farewell as a model for presidential declarations.[3] Rather, Jefferson first treated the Farewell with contempt for its foreign policy and then, it seems, forgot about it. That the Address was included can be credited to Madison, not Jefferson; Madison suggested Washington's Inaugural and Farewell Address to "help down what might be less readily swallowed" by some, and Jefferson agreed, confessing that Washington's speeches "had not occurred to me."[4]

Throughout his eight years as president, Jefferson inserted into presidential speech his own doctrine and practice of political declarations in order to complete his transformation of the presidency. In his annual messages, special messages, open letters, and replies to addresses, Jefferson would attempt to unify the two parts of democratic energy, public opinion and executive discretion. Guiding the will of the nation through great occasions would be the unifying theme of his presidential speech.

The Annual Message

As is well known, Washington and Adams appeared before Congress to give the annual message and to receive Congress' formal reply.[5] Jefferson, however, sent his messages to Congress and let it be known that no answer would be required. In his preamble to his first message, Jefferson explained that he had acted out of "principal regard" to the "convenience of the legislature": because legislators had such busy schedules and because they might find it difficult to answer a message without preparation, he determined it would be easier for them not to bother with an answer.[6]

In place of a statement of principles, Jefferson used his "First Annual" to report "the matters respecting the state of the nation." Specifically, the president reported peace with all nations except the Barbary States, recommended reducing the size of the national government, suggested that departments spend less money by limiting discretionary spending, offered a plan

---

[3] "Minutes of the Board of Visitors, University of Virginia, 1822–1825," *TJW*, 479–80.

[4] Jefferson to Madison, 17 December 1796, Ford, 7: 92; Madison to Jefferson, 8 February 1825, and Jefferson to Madison, 12 February 1825, Smith, 1924–6. During the next thirty years of letter-writing between Jefferson and Madison, Washington's Farewell was mentioned only twice before this discussion in 1825. See Jefferson to Madison, 13 June 1823, and Madison to Jefferson, 27 June 1823, Smith, 1861, 1868.

[5] Tulis, *Rhetorical Presidency*, 55–6.

[6] Adams, 169–170.

for reorganizing the military, presented the prospect of revising the Judiciary Act, and argued for relaxing the requirements of naturalization. Unlike the First Inaugural, which presented a strong doctrine of presidential leadership, the First Annual presented the president as the dutiful errand boy for the legislative body: "I am happy in this opportunity of committing the arduous affairs of our government to the collected wisdom of the Union. Nothing shall be wanting on my part to inform, as far as in my power, the legislative judgment into faithful execution." Not a catalogue of principles, the message deferentially laid before Congress measures for its consideration. Presidential leadership was couched in the language of recommendation: "I lay before you," "it would be prudent to," "when we consider," "I cause to be laid before you," "a statement has been formed," "it will be worthy your consideration," and "I cannot omit recommending" are the passive phrases of presidential compliance.[7]

The blandness of the First Annual caused Henry Adams to remark that Jefferson's first annual message should be studied more for what it omitted than what it contained. As Adams noticed, Jefferson remained silent as to the essential objects of the Republican Party: rather than condemning the Sedition Act, offering a criticism of implied powers, or recommending a reform of the judiciary, Jefferson chose "inaction" by passing over questions of constitutional debate. For Adams, Jefferson's silence was related to hypocrisy: rather than calling attention to the "loopholes" left over from the Federalist administrations, the president "stretched out his hands to seize the powers he had denounced."[8]

Adams was more right than he knew, for Jefferson had, in fact, included a denunciation of the Sedition Act in an early draft of the address. In this passage, Jefferson would have declared the law void and, more important, would have explained the doctrine of coordinate review, which he had elaborated in 1797 and 1798, when he claimed that the state of Kentucky could judge whether Congress had exceeded its constitutional authority.[9] In a draft of the first annual, Jefferson declared the Sedition Act a "nullity" and asserted his power as president to do so:

Our country has thought proper to distribute the powers of it's government among three equal & independent authorities, constituting each a check on one or both of the others, in all attempts to impair it's constitution. To make each an effectual check, it must have a right in cases which arise within the line of it's proper functions,

---

[7] Jefferson, "First Annual Message," 8 December 1801, *TJW*, 501–9.
[8] Adams, 170–4.
[9] David N. Mayer, *Constitutional Thought of Thomas Jefferson* (Charlottesville: University Press of Virginia, 1994), 263–276.

where, equally with the others, it acts in the last resort & without appeal, to decide on the validity of an act according to it's own judgment, & uncontrolled by the opinion of any other department. We have accordingly, in more than one instance, seen the opinions of different departments in opposition to each other, & no ill ensue. The constitution, moreover, as a further security for itself, against violation even by a concurrence of all the departments, has provided for it's own reintegration by a change of the persons exercising the functions of those departments.[10]

If the annual message was to become the time to declare new principles, this was one bold way to do it, for Jefferson even went on to invoke "the tie of his solemn oath" to declare the Sedition act contrary to the Constitution. But Jefferson chose otherwise. Historians are divided as to whether Madison or Gallatin persuaded the president in the First Annual, but it is agreed that one or more members of the cabinet convinced Jefferson that it would be imprudent to call the act a "palpable and unqualified contradiction to the constitution" and a "nullity."[11] Jefferson omitted this passage from his final message, leaving only a note in the margin to explain that the passage was "capable of being chicaned, and furnishing the opposition something to make a handle of." Instead of nullifying the Sedition Act by presidential order or even seeking its official repeal, Jefferson simply pardoned those convicted under the Sedition Act.[12]

The omission of the passage on coordinate review illustrates Jefferson's attention to the style and content of the annual address. In writing each annual address, Jefferson solicited advice from his cabinet. To Madison, he looked for special assistance: "Will you give this enclosed a serious revisal, not only as to matter, but diction? Where strictness of grammar does not weaken expression, it should be attended to in complaisance to the purists of new England. But where by small grammatical negligences the energy of an idea is condensed, or a word stands for a sentence, I hold grammatical rigor in contempt."[13] Each year, Jefferson asked Madison to revise the annual address: In 1801, 1802, and 1805, Jefferson's letters record these requests ("Will you give the inclosed a serious perusal, and make such corrections, in matter and manner as it needs, and that without reserve?";[14] "Will you be so good as to give this a severe correction both as to state and matter,

---

[10] Jefferson, "First Annual Message," 8 December 1801, Library of Congress, Thomas Jefferson Papers Series 1, General Correspondence, 1651–1827.

[11] See Smith's note on 1203.

[12] As he privately explained to Abigail Adams in 1804, such pardons were his by rights under the proper understanding of separation of powers, that is, under coordinate review. Jefferson to Abigail Adams, 11 September 1804, Cappon, 279.

[13] Jefferson to Madison, 12 November 1801, Smith, 1203.

[14] Jefferson to Madison, 18 November 1802, Smith, 1251.

and as early a one as you can?"[15]), and Madison's revisions in 1803, 1804, 1806, and 1808 confirm that the president expected Madison's assistance each year.[16] Furthermore, the notes supplied by the editor of the Jefferson-Madison correspondence indicate that Jefferson usually heeded Madison's suggestions on both substance and style. Ford's notes similarly illustrate the role Gallatin played in composing the annual messages. Later, when composing the Seventh Annual, Jefferson was particularly moderated by his Secretary of the Treasury, who counseled the president to make the annual messages more like "proclamations" than "manifestos."[17]

Proclamations

Another form of presidential speech was the proclamation. According to Jeffrey K. Tulis, the first presidential proclamation was given by Washington and recommended a day of thanksgiving and prayer.[18] As Tulis notes, in issuing his proclamations, Washington had followed British practice, borrowing the former authority of the king to give power to his words; rather than building a case or argument, the proclamation's command stems from the authority of the president.

Jefferson adopted the form even though he found much to criticize in the contents of Washington's proclamations. Of his ten proclamations, three called one or both houses of Congress into session early,[19] one designated the "district of Mobile,"[20] and one – his first – specified the building materials for houses in Washington, thus clarifying rules issued in prior proclamations given by Washington and Adams.[21] More important, just as Washington's two most controversial proclamations treated neutrality and insurrection, several of Jefferson's proclamations dealt with either an insurrection or with maintaining neutrality by the Embargo, and, in issuing these proclamations, Jefferson employed Washington's language.

---

[15] Jefferson to Madison, 22 November 1805, Smith, 1396.

[16] Smith, 1297, 1349, 1458, and 1554.

[17] Adams, 1029–30.

[18] Tulis, *Rhetorical Presidency*, 52. According to Tulis, the form of the proclamation virtually ensures that the central rhetorical appeal of any proclamation will be the authority of the president (or of the government as a whole) rather than factors peculiar to the president's persuasive abilities. Put another way, the proclamation's persuasive power derives more from the fact that the president proclaims, or commands, than it does from a case he builds.

[19] James Richardson, ed., *A Compilation of the Messages and Papers of the Presidents, 1789–1904*, Vol. 1 (1904), 357, 424, and 461.

[20] Ibid., 369.

[21] Ibid., 324–5.

In the case of the Burr Conspiracy, Jefferson employed a proclamation to inform officials and citizens that a conspiracy was underway.[22] As Jefferson put it, he had received information that "sundry persons" were "deceiving and seducing honest and well-meaning citizens, under various pretenses," to "engage" in "criminal enterprises." After speaking to citizens that might have been aiding the conspiracy "without due knowledge or consideration," Jefferson ordered "all officers, civil and military" to be "vigilant" and to prevent "such expedition or enterprise by all means within their power." After giving this order to executive officials, Jefferson next addressed citizens: "I require all good and faithful citizens and others within the United States to be aiding and assisting herein, and especially in the discovery, apprehension, and bringing to justice of all such offenders, in preventing the execution of all their unlawful designs, and in giving information against them to the proper authorities." Just as he had used a proclamation to explain to Virginians that they could not lawfully sign a British "parole," Jefferson here used the proclamation to explain to citizens that Burr's designs were unlawful. Just as Washington asked officers and citizens to assist in quieting the rebellion, Jefferson ordered citizens to join executive officials in preventing the conspiracy.[23] Later, in his proclamations forbidding intercourse with British ships anchoring near American harbors, Jefferson ordered all "citizens or inhabitants," "with vigilance & promptitude to exert their respective authorities, & to be aiding & assisting to the carrying this proclamation & every part thereof into full effect."[24] Likewise, to enforce the laws against insurrectionists around Lake Champlain, Jefferson issued a proclamation ordering citizens to "use all the means in their power by force of arms or otherwise" to deliver the conspirators to "the civil authority."[25]

Although Jefferson did not himself lead the militia to execute the laws, and though he did not appeal to his constitutional oath of office or his authority as commander in chief, Jefferson did borrow the form and vocabulary of Washington's proclamations to enforce the laws and quell insurrections. At the same time, he went beyond Washington: by speaking directly to "faithful citizens" and asking them to assist in foiling the conspiracy, Jefferson

[22] Ibid., 404–5. Madison wrote this proclamation. Smith ed., 1460.
[23] Washington, "Proclamation Concerning the 'Whiskey Rebellion'," *Washington Writings*, 884.
[24] Jefferson, "Proclamation and Draft on Armed Vessels," 2 July 1807. See also, "Draft of a Proclamation Concerning Leander" and "Proclamation Concerning Cambrian" (1806) Ford, 8:445–7, 499–501.
[25] Jefferson, "Proclamation on Embargo Laws," 19 April 1808, *The Thomas Jefferson Papers, Series 1, General Correspondence, 1651–1827*, Library of Congress.

encouraged a certain kind of citizen to act with the discretion he so often reported in his special messages.

Special Messages to Congress

The practical application of Jefferson's use of declarations of principle can be found in his "special" messages Congress. Jefferson sent at least forty of these messages, most often to communicate to Congress information he had received as head of the executive branch. Sixteen of these messages can be categorized as *Messages to Lay Before*, eighteen as *Messages to Report Executive Action*, and five as some combination of the two.

The Messages to Lay Before were messages in which Jefferson sent information for Congress to consider. Cover letters of a sort, these messages accompanied the delivery of treaties to be ratified or acted upon after ratification,[26] letters from governors reporting on affairs in the states,[27] letters from diplomats reporting events abroad,[28] documents requested by Congress,[29] communications from foreign governments,[30] or technical reports written by an executive department.[31] These messages were usually short and to the point: the president passes along news so that Congress can more ably perform its constitutional duty. Keeping in line with Washington's precedent, Jefferson kept Congress informed with events by employing these short, "special" messages.

Unlike Washington, Jefferson went out of his way to keep Congress informed with the Messages to Report Executive Action. Usually much longer than the Messages to Lay Before, these special messages informed Congress of measures already taken by the president or by another executive officer. These reports included his sending ships to Gibraltar,[32] his dispatch of troops during the transfer of power in Louisiana,[33] the shipwreck and capture of a captain in Tripoli,[34] a naval commander's installation of a new ruler in Tripoli,[35] the capture of Tunisian ship,[36] his organization of the Lewis and

---

[26] Jefferson, "Special Message," 30 January 1808, L&B, 3:460–3.
[27] Jefferson, "Special Message," 3 February 1806, L&B, 3:409.
[28] Jefferson, "Special Message," 7 December 1807, L&B, 3:454–5.
[29] Jefferson, "Special Message," 23 November 1807, L&B, 3:454.
[30] Jefferson, "Special Message," 2 February 1808, and, 17 March 1808, L&B, 3:463, 470–1.
[31] Jefferson, "Special Message," 15 February 1808, 25 February 1808, 18 March 1808, and 6 January 1809, L & B, 3:465–72, 487–8.
[32] Jefferson, "Special Message," 4 November 1803, L&B, 3:362.
[33] Jefferson, "Special Message," 16 January 1804, L&B, 3:364–5.
[34] Jefferson, "Special Message," 20 March 1804, L&B, 3:366.
[35] Jefferson, "Special Message," 13 January 1806, L&B, 3:402–7.
[36] Jefferson, "Special Message," 14 April 1806, L&B, 3:413.

Clark expedition,[37] his measures taken to stifle the Burr conspiracy,[38] military actions to detain Burr,[39] his refusal to give Congress executive papers,[40] his order to secure river deposits in New Orleans "to keep the grounds clear of intruders,"[41] and his negotiations with Great Britain following the attack on the *Chesapeake*.[42] Like the Messages to Lay Before, these messages were meant to provide Congress with information so that Congress could more easily perform its legislative duty.

In addition to illustrating the extraordinary effort on Jefferson's part to defer to Congress, these messages depict a president who spent a large amount of time defending executive actions that had already taken place. Indeed, these messages were alike in that each reported in positive language a prior exercise of executive discretion. Filled with phrases such as "gallant enterprise," "temperate and correct course," "proper decision," "promptitude and energy," "fit for the enterprise and willing to take it," "to be prepared for anything unexpected," "a zealous citizen will act," "disinterested valuable services in the prosecution of these enterprises," and "the commanding officer thought it his duty," these messages go so far as to praise executives who had followed the lights of their own discretion, some of them even temporarily moving beyond the authority of the law. Just as he had said in the First Inaugural that he would lead the country through "great occasions," and just as his understanding of the prerogative power required the president to seek approval from Congress after the fact, Jefferson used the special message as the procedure by which he could "throw himself" on the authority of Congress. Put another way, in their cataloguing instances in which explorers, diplomats, governors, military officers, ship captains, and the president himself resorted to extra-legal measures during times of great necessity or opportunity, Jefferson's special "Messages to Report Executive Action" read like the list of examples he later gave to John Colvin.[43] Although Jefferson publicly defended the Louisiana Purchase only in a few short sentences in his Second Inaugural, he did publicly and privately defend other executive officials who stepped outside their constitutional authority to achieve what they believed to be the good of the country. In these defenses, Jefferson used the same language he had used while governor of Virginia.

---

37 Jefferson, "Special Message," 18 January 1803, L&B, 3:489–94.
38 Jefferson, "Special Message," 22 January 1807, L&B, 3:427–37.
39 Jefferson, "Special Message," 28 January 1807, L&B, 3: 437–8.
40 Jefferson, "Special Message," 20 January 1808, L&B, 3: 456–60.
41 Jefferson, "Special Message," 7 March 1808, L&B, 3:468–70.
42 Jefferson, "Special Message," 22 March 1808, L&B, 3: 472–4.
43 To be discussed in this chapter.

One such official was the war hero William Eaton. Eaton, a naval agent who believed that Jefferson and his administration had been too "reserved" in their policy toward Tripoli, assembled a small army and marched five hundred miles from Egypt to the Tripolitan city of Derne. After capturing Derne, Eaton attempted to install a new ruler of Tripoli. Eaton's discretion presented the president with a political problem: his courage and success were celebrated at home, but the United States could not recognize the installation of a new Pasha. Although Jefferson's government did not officially approve of the result of Eaton's actions, Jefferson did try to protect Eaton from blame by reflecting on the nature of Eaton's task: "In operations of such a distance, it becomes necessary to leave much to the discretion of the agents employed, but events may still turn up beyond the limits of that discretion." Because distance denied Eaton the chance to consult his superiors, Eaton had to put action to judgment: "Unable in such a case to consult his government, a zealous citizen will act as he believes that would direct him were it apprised of the circumstances, and will take on himself the responsibility. In all these cases, the purity and the patriotism of the motives should shield the agent from blame, and even secure the sanction where the error is not too injurious." Eaton's daring land assault on Tripoli, and his placing Hamet Caramelli on its throne, "could not be sanctioned" by Jefferson as it had exceeded the limits of Eaton's discretionary powers. Nevertheless, Jefferson recommended that others consider Eaton's motives before criticizing his actions.[44]

The question of intent suggests that prerogative can be difficult to judge. A few years before Eaton's great military success, Jefferson told Madison that he was impressed by Eaton's "understanding" and "honesty."[45] But, later, when Eaton's military reputation prompted Burr to lure him into conspiracy, Eaton reported Burr's plot to Jefferson, but Jefferson, for whatever reason, did not act on Eaton's warning. And when Jefferson came to believe that Burr was aiming to either lead an insurrection in the Western territories aimed at separation from the Union or a military expedition against Mexico (or both), Jefferson had to rely on the governor of the Louisiana Territory, General James Wilkinson. Like Eaton, Wilkinson had been approached by Burr, but, unlike Eaton, Wilkinson's patriotism was thought be to for sale: Presidents Washington and Adams had each suspected Wilkinson of being a paid agent of Spain, and before Jefferson knew of the details of the conspiracy, he had heard new rumors of Wilkinson's joining Burr. According to Malone, Jefferson initially ignored these reports because the reports also named other

---

44 Special Message to Senate and House, 13 January 1806, Washington, 8:56l; Adams, 594–8; Malone, 5:41–2.
45 Jefferson to Madison, 28 August 1801, Smith, 1193; and Adams, 770–1.

conspirators in the West, some of whom were obviously innocent victims of partisan character assassinations. But when Wilkinson lingered in upper Louisiana rather than following Jefferson's explicit orders to go to New Orleans in order to defend against a Spanish invasion, Jefferson aired his suspicions concerning the general's "infidelity."[46] Unlike Eaton, who had warned Jefferson of Burr's plans, which would have included Wilkinson, Wilkinson left it for others to decide whether he had spurned Burr.[47]

But Wilkinson eventually sided with Jefferson over Burr. In November, Wilkinson went to New Orleans, where, after leaving his intentions in doubt for several weeks, he signaled that he would salvage his reputation by securing the city. Acting with what Henry Adams called "noise and display," he established martial law, instituted an embargo on shipping, spread rumors exaggerating the strength of Burr's forces, and fed local fears of a slave insurrection.[48] More important, he arrested, detained, and relocated suspected accomplices of Burr. His relocation of detainees was illegal, for, according to Dumas Malone, suspects were "entitled to trial in the Territory of Orleans."[49] It was also unauthorized, for Jefferson had issued a proclamation ordering civil and military personnel to arrest anyone conspiring to attack Spanish forces – the place of a trial was not mentioned.[50]

In a special message to Congress, Jefferson refrained from saying that Wilkinson's actions were ill-conceived and suggested that the suspects were relocated "probably on the consideration that an impartial trial could not be expected during the present agitations of New Orleans" and that New Orleans was "not as yet a safe place of confinement."[51] Jefferson went on to assure congressmen that the accused conspirators would receive the regular course of justice in Washington, but he also mentioned that Washington was preferable to New Orleans, as in Washington, there would be "the aid of the executive means, should the judges have occasion to use them."

Jefferson sent his tacit defense of Wilkinson to the general himself.[52] In this letter, Jefferson used the same language as his defense of Eaton to assure Wilkinson that he would be judged according to how he saw events rather than as those in Washington might after the fact. Having placed itself in Wilkinson's view of the danger, the public supported Wilkinson so far. But

---

[46] Malone, 5:223–5, 230, 244–6.
[47] The details of Wilkinson's treachery, like Burr's, are murky and disputed. The facts, then and now, seem to be colored by one's partisanship.
[48] Adams, 825.
[49] Malone, 5:266.
[50] See Proclamation of November 27.
[51] Jefferson, "Special Message on the Burr Conspiracy," 22 January 1807, *TJW*, 537–8.
[52] Jefferson to James Wilkinson, 3 February 1807, Washington, 5:38–40.

Jefferson also wrote Wilkinson to warn him against using his discretion too widely: "I hope, however, you will not extend this deportation to persons against whom there is only suspicion, or shades of offense not strongly marked. In that case, I fear the public sentiment would desert you; because, seeing no danger here, violations of law are felt with strength. I have thought it just to give you these views of the sentiments and sensations here, as they may enlighten your path." Wilkinson's discretion, then, ought to take its bearings from the state of public opinion. More precisely, Jefferson would support Wilkinson's parting from the law only insofar as his actions would be defensible after the fact, and part of such a statement of defense would make use of Jefferson's principle that discretion must be judged according to the facts available to the officer in question. As long as Wilkinson used his extraordinary power to arrest and relocate conspirators for whom there was good evidence of treasonous intent, Wilkinson could expect to be applauded by the public. Even though some had tried to arouse what Jefferson called "suspicion and mistrust" in the papers, Jefferson would protect him: "We, who knew it, have not failed to strengthen the public confidence in you; and I can assure you that your conduct, as now known, has placed you on ground extremely favorable with the public." Like Eaton, Wilkinson deserved some praise for his enterprise.[53]

Jefferson also sent his special message to Claiborne, the governor of the Orleans Territory.[54] In the accompanying letter, Jefferson again appealed to the language of his address concerning the Eaton affair. As with Wilkinson, Jefferson assured Claiborne that those officers who act outside the law will be protected insofar as their motives were just: "Your situations have been difficult, and we judge of the merits of our agents here by the magnitude of the danger as it appeared to them, not as it was known to us. On great occasions every good officer must be ready to risk himself in going beyond the strict line of law, when the public preservation requires it; his motives will be a justification as far as there is any discretion in his extralegal proceedings, and no indulgence of private feelings." To Claiborne, Jefferson repeated his formula for executive discretion: more than merely defensible, some actions outside the law are required, which is to say that one condition for being a patriotic and good officer is the willingness to depart from the law when

[53] According to Henry Adams, Jefferson's interest was hitched to Wilkinson during the trial of Burr (916–17). And there is evidence that Jefferson and Wilkinson had dined with William Blount while Jefferson was vice president and before Blount embarked on filibuster in what would become the Louisiana Territory, Buckner F. Melton Jr., *The First Impeachment: The Constitution's Framers and the Case of the Senator William Blount* (Macon, GA: Mercer University Press, 1998), 96.

[54] Jefferson to Governor W. C. C. Claiborne, 3 Feb 1807, L&B, 11: 150–1.

necessity requires it. Furthermore, that the United States possessed officers who were willing to risk themselves and put down the conspiracy proved Jefferson's claim in his First Inaugural that the republic possessed sufficient energy to meet necessity: "On the whole, this squall, by showing with what ease our government suppresses movements in which other countries requires armies, has greatly increased its strength by increasing the public confidence in it. It has been a wholesome lesson to our citizens, of the necessary obedience to their government." The public would support such discretion even though the discretion came at a cost to individual liberty. Even though the Federalists and the oppositionist Quids would try to "make something of the infringement by the military arrest and deportment of citizens" there would be "public approbation" for the arrests, so long as the arrests did not go too far.[55]

Open Letters and Replies to Addresses

If Jefferson left the formal purpose of the annual message and proclamation intact, he used open letters and replies to addresses to cultivate and educate public opinion. Throughout his presidency, Jefferson received many addresses praising his Republicanism and a few criticizing his policy. The purpose of these addresses, and Jefferson's replies, were partisan and political, for Malone notes that the addresses most often came from states in which "intra-party conflict was most intense."[56] But, for Jefferson, replies to congratulatory addresses were more than a requirement of political civility and electoral strategy, and he transformed these partisan expressions into opportunities to lead his party and educate the public. To be sure, Jefferson often sent a standard reply to bodies of citizens who congratulated his victory, but several of his replies reveal the particular care in which they were written. Typically, Jefferson devoted particular attention to replies that explained the meaning of his First Inaugural, implanted his doctrine of religious liberty, promoted his embargo policy, and shaped his decision to retire into a *de facto* term limit.

Jefferson was especially concerned with how his First Inaugural was interpreted. In his reply to the offer of congratulations by the General Assembly of Rhode Island, Jefferson referred to the list of principles given in his First Inaugural: "And I learn with pleasure their approbation of the principles declared by me on that occasion; principles which flowed sincerely from the heart and judgment, and which, with sincerity will be pursued. While

---

[55] On the Quids, see Landy and Milkis, *Presidential Greatness*, 68–70.
[56] Malone, 5:168.

acting on them, I ask only to be judged with truth and candor." Because of Rhode Island's past suspicion toward the national government, Jefferson's pointing to the Inaugural was especially important. In the first place, the most noticeable theme of the Inaugural was, as it still is, the call to political moderation and forbearance – "Our religion enjoins it; our happiness demands it; and no sacrifice is requisite but of passions hostile to both." If the call to tolerance would be welcome to the often-irascible legislators of Rhode Island, the Inaugural's promise to preserve the federal government in all its constitutional vigor would not be. Thus, after reaffirming the duty of political toleration, Jefferson reminded Rhode Island that of the "momentous truth" that "our safety rests on the preservation of the Union." Here, Jefferson offered his often repeated formula for union: "Our citizens have wisely formed themselves into one nation as to others, and several States as to themselves. To the united nation belongs our external and mutual relations; to each State severally the care of our persons, our property, our reputation, and religious freedom. This wise distribution, if carefully preserved, will prove, I trust from example, that while smaller governments are better adapted to the ordinary objects of society, larger confederations more effectually secure independence and the preservation of republican government." Jefferson described federalism first by way of making a distinction between internal and external, but he shifted the separation to one between ordinary objects of government and extraordinary objects of government. Because the extraordinary objects of government would require the effectiveness of a "larger confederation," some internal actions in Rhode Island would require the intrusion of the national government.[57]

Not all of Jefferson's replies were written in response to a friendly congratulatory address. One consequence of the First Inaugural's proclamation that Americans were both federalist and republican was that some federalists interpreted Jefferson's "declarations" promoting harmony, political tolerance, and respect for equal rights as a guarantee that Jefferson would not remove Federalists from office. Jefferson attempted to correct what he believed to be misconstruction of his Inaugural by writing an open letter to New Haven Federalists. As has been argued, the "Letter to the New Haven Merchants" connected the president's power to remove with the "public sentiment" as "declared" by the national election: the president must be allowed to control his administration in order to execute the laws as endorsed by the national presidential election.[58] As he used the letter from the New Haven

---

[57] Jefferson to the General Assembly of Rhode Island and Providence Plantations, 26 May 1801, L&B, 10:262–3.
[58] See Chapter 6.

merchants as an opportunity to explain his removal policy and correct a misunderstanding regarding his First Inaugural, Jefferson treated addresses from religious groups as occasions to teach citizens his understanding of religious liberty.

Of his many replies to religious groups asserting that Constitution removed religion from "the power of its public functionaries," his "Letter to the Danbury Baptist Association" is most famous.[59] In their offer of congratulations, the Danbury Baptists reported that religious liberties in Connecticut were enjoyed "as favors granted, and not as inalienable rights." Jefferson carefully crafted his reply, composed a draft, and sent it to Gideon Granger and Levi Lincoln, whom Malone labeled as his "chief consultants on New England." Although Granger thought Jefferson's first draft accorded with the opinion of the national majority, Lincoln convinced Jefferson to soften his language, especially with regard to Jefferson's not proclaiming a day of thanksgiving. In his final version, Jefferson famously asserted that the First Amendment amounted to a "declaration" that there should be a "wall of separation between church and state." Taking the "will of the nation" as his guide, he, as president, would "see" the "progress of those sentiments which tend to restore to man all his natural rights." By considering his audience in Connecticut, Jefferson sweetened his teaching on religious expression and furthered his constitutional project to remove matters of religion from the reach of government. In his hope that the principle would germinate into a doctrine, he showed that declarations under his watch would be more than parchment.[60]

Although Jefferson did reply to addresses often, he did not respond to every remonstrance and complaint. He was especially reluctant to reply to complaints by governmental bodies if he believed that a reply would interfere with the constitutional duties of one of the branches of government. For instance, to a Senate committee's request that Jefferson provide information regarding the qualification of a nominee, Jefferson refused on the grounds that Senators "are sensible the Constitution has made it my duty to nominate; and has not made it my duty to lay before them the evidences or reasons

---

[59] Jefferson to Messrs. Nehemiah Dodge and Others, a Committee of the Danbury Baptist Association, in the State of Connecticut, 1 January 1802, *TJW*, 510. For others, see Jefferson to the Members of the Baltimore Baptist Association, 17 October 1808; Jefferson to the Members of the Ketockton Baptist Association, 18 October 1808; Jefferson to the General Meeting of Correspondence of the Six Baptist Associations Represented at Chesterfield, Virginia, 21 November 1808; and Jefferson to the Society of the Methodist Episcopal Church at Pittsburgh, Pennsylvania, 9 December 1808, in *The Complete Jefferson: Containing His Major Writings, Published and Unpublished, Except his Letters*, ed. Saul K. Padover (New York: Duell, Sloan & Pearce, 1944), 537–41.
[60] Malone, 4:109.

whereupon my nominations are founded."[61] He also sometimes refused to reply to groups such as the Ward Committee of Philadelphia. The difference between the Ward Committee of Philadelphia and the New Haven merchants was that the latter was signed by individuals and was thus "a part of the machinery of the Constitution."[62] The Ward Committee, by contrast, was "unknown by the Constitution" yet sought "to influence the appointment to office for which the Constitution has chosen to rely on the independence and integrity of the Executive, controlled by the Senate, chosen both of them by the whole union."[63]

In addition to the source of the address, another consideration was its political affects on Congress and public opinion. To Thomas Lieper, the president explained that he could not reply to a "very friendly & flattering address" because the "question presented by these addresses cannot be touched without endangering the harmony of the present session of Congress."[64] Because any "schismatic view" might jeopardize Congress's deciding "new & great questions," the address would receive no presidential reply. If the opposition had redirected opinion away from its former unity or if the question had become dormant in the public mind, however, Jefferson would put the issue before the public's attention. A few years after his letter to the New England Merchants, Jefferson believed that the public needed a fresh statement of principles regarding the removal power. As he wrote to Gallatin, the president believed that the previous public letter had been effective: "Altho' I know that it is best generally to assign no reason for a removal from office, yet there are also times when the declaration of a principle is advantageous. Such was the moment at which the New Haven letter appeared. It explained our principles to our friends, and they rallied to them. The public sentiment has taken a considerable stride since that, and seems to require that they should know again where we stand."[65] Such was the case in 1804 when Jefferson made some recommendations to Gallatin's letter informing an officer of his removal. Jefferson's version would read that the president "determined to place your office in other hands" because the officer had used it for "active opposition to the national will." Jefferson's editing was aimed at achieving two goals: "My own opinion is, that the declaration of this principle will meet the entire approbation of all moderate republicans, and will extort indulgence from the warmer ones. Seeing that we do not mean to leave arms in the hands of active enemies, they will care

[61] Jefferson to Uriah Tracy, January, 1806, Ford, 8:412–3.
[62] Ibid.
[63] Jefferson to William Duane, 24 July 1803, Ford, 8:255–9.
[64] Jefferson to Thomas Leiper, 22 December 1806, Ford, 8:502–3.
[65] Jefferson to Albert Gallatin, 30 May 1804, Ford, 8:303–4.

the less at our tolerance of the inactive."[66] Because the president's removal power had earlier been justified by the argument that removals were central to gathering public confidence around the executive branch, removals would need to be accompanied by statements of principle that explained removals to the people. Moreover, the declarations would serve to remind friendly partisans of the administration's course.

Jefferson often resorted to the reply in order to direct public opinion regarding the Embargo. In response to approving addresses from most of the state legislatures, Jefferson reflected on the "present misunderstandings" by thanking those who sounded the drumbeat of war – "the ardor of our citizens to obey the summons of their country, and the offer which you attest, of their lives and fortunes in its support, are worthy of their patriotism, and pledges of our safety." But with his thanks he offered his defense of the policy aimed at restoring peaceful free trade: although the ocean was "the common birth-right of mankind" and the American share had been taken by a "superior force," there "could be no question" that a "policy which plants the manufacturer and the husbandman side by side" was preferable to war.[67] As enforcement of the Embargo grew more difficult, Jefferson assured Republicans in Philadelphia that the "distempered views" of some Americans would not cause war, but, in the event that they did, "we must meet it as an evil necessarily flowing from that liberty of speaking and writing which guards our liberties."[68] After receiving hundreds of addresses from organized dissent in Massachusetts, Jefferson had a reply printed and distributed.[69] In these replies, the president defended the embargo as the only honorable way to avoid war, but attributed it to Congress: "the legislature alone can prescribe the course to be pursued."[70] "A free trader in a world hostile to that notion," Jefferson used the reply to explain and defend a policy he could not enforce.[71]

---

[66] Ibid.

[67] See replies to legislature of New Jersey, the Tammany Society of New York, *Complete Jefferson*, ed. Padover, 525–30.

[68] Jefferson to the Delegates of the Democratic Republicans of the City of Philadelphia, In General Ward Committee Assembled, 25 May 1808, *Complete Jefferson*, ed. Padover, 530–1.

[69] Malone, 5:608–9.

[70] In this reply, Jefferson artfully dodged the question whether he could suspend the Embargo with regard to Spain on the grounds that a "contest" for that country's government had arisen and thus avoided a direct comparison to Washington's Neutrality Proclamation. Jefferson to the Inhabitants of the Towns of Boston, Newburyport, and Providence, 26 August 1808, *Complete Jefferson*, ed. Padover, 534–5.

[71] Marc Landy and Sidney M. Milkis, *Presidential Greatness* (Lawrence: Kansas University Press, 2000), 72–5.

Private Letters for Public Purpose

Although Jefferson believed that the president should gather and direct public opinion, and although Jefferson's democratization of the prerogative required him to "throw himself" on the people or their representatives, Jefferson sometimes left the public explanation of his policies to others. For instance, Jefferson assumed the pseudonym "Massachusetts Citizen" to argue that the president's oath of office required him to remove monarchists,[72] and Jefferson conspired with Madison and Dearborne to submit a public a response to John Randolph's "Decius": "It remains now to consider on what authority these corrections of fact can be advanced without compromitting the Executive. It would seem to be the best that the writer should assume the mask of a member of the Legislature."[73] Likewise, during his standoff with Marshall over his subpoena, Jefferson wrote George Hay public and private letters, leaving it to Hay to determine whether a private letter's argument should be voiced in court.[74] Just as he had asked Madison to answer Hamilton's writings as Pacificus, Jefferson sometimes enlisted others to make his boldest statements. Jefferson's order, "Do not let my name be connected with the business," was given in order to shape himself as nonpartisan, but it illustrates Jefferson's unwillingness to employ the authority of presidency in some of his arguments. This is particularly true of his argument for the expansion of the prerogative power.

Jefferson most clearly presented his understanding of executive prerogative in a letter written during his retirement. In reply to John B. Colvin, Jefferson reflected on the question whether "circumstances do not sometimes occur, which do not make it a duty in officers of high trust to assume authorities beyond the law."[75] Jefferson first answered by offering a general principle, one that has been quoted by many students of executive prerogative: "A strict observance of the written laws is doubtless *one* of the high duties of a good citizen, but it is not *the highest*. The laws of necessity, of self-preservation, of saving our country when in danger, are of higher obligation. To lose our country by a scrupulous adherence to written law, would be to lose the law itself, with life, liberty, property and all those who are enjoying them with us; thus absurdly sacrificing the end to the means." But because principles "are sometimes embarrassing in practice," Jefferson added examples to demonstrate the reasonableness of his position. More

---

[72] See the discussion of "Fair Play" in Chapter 6.
[73] Jefferson to W. A. Burwell, 17 September 1806, Ford, 8:472.
[74] Malone, 5: 324.
[75] Jefferson to John Colvin, 20 September 1810, *TJW*, 1231–4.

than illustrations of the general principle in practice, the examples modify and, surprisingly, expand the general principle.[76]

The first four examples concerned executives who had seized or destroyed private property in order to meet necessity. Each of the first three involved military officers: in the Battle of Germantown during the War for Independence, Washington fired a cannon upon a citizen's house after being "annoyed" from it; at Yorktown, Washington "leveled suburbs, feeling that the laws of property must be postponed to the safety of the nation;" and when the British invaded Virginia the Governor of Virginia "took horses, carriages, provisions, and even men by force, to enable that army to stay together till it could master the public enemy." The fourth example, however, was not limited to the military: "A ship at sea in distress for provisions, meets another having abundance, yet refusing a supply; the law of self-preservation authorizes the distressed to take a supply by force." In each case, the executive's decision to part with the laws was justifiable by appeal to the principle of self-preservation. Like Locke's "innocent Man's House," these examples made it clear that self-preservation trumped the right of property when the latter threatened the former: "The unwritten laws of necessity, of self-preservation, and of the public safety, control the written laws of *meum* and *tuum*."[77]

But Jefferson complicated his seemingly simple principle by offering an additional "hypothetical," posing a scenario involving something less than self-preservation. According to this hypothetical, the question was whether a president should purchase the Florida territories when Congress was out of session: "Suppose it had been made known to the Executive in the autumn of 1805, that we may have the Floridas for a reasonable sum," ought the president, "for so great an advantage to his country, to have risked himself by transcending the law and making the purchase"? In this case, Jefferson advised that the president should leave the matter to Congress to decide because "reverence for law" (lack of appropriations) would override the "public advantage" (especially if it was likely that Congress would eventually have appropriated the funds for the purchase anyway). But, as Jefferson shifted the hypothetical, the distinction between self-preservation and advantageous policy could be blurred by politics. Put differently, this hypothetical also took into consideration political necessity. What if, for instance, it were known that a powerful member of Congress, "a John Randolph,"

---

[76] Ibid. For an account of the influence of this letter on the scholarship, see Jeremy D. Bailey, "Executive Prerogative and the 'good officer' in Jefferson's letter to John B. Colvin," *Presidential Studies Quarterly* 34 (2004): 732–54.

[77] Jefferson to John Colvin, 20 September 1810, *TJW*, 1231–4. John Locke, *Second Treatise*, section 159, in *John Locke: Two Treatises of Government*, student edition, ed. Peter Laslett (Cambridge: Cambridge University Press, 1988), 375.

would stall debate on the treaty until the opportunity passed. Put differently, what if the Executive believed that the great advantage gained would be lost because a committee chair meant to pursue another agenda? "Ought the Executive, in that case, and with that foreknowledge, to have secured the good to his country, and to have trusted to their justice for the transgression of the law? I think he ought, and that the act would have been approved." In other words, the Executive could be justified for acting against the law only so long as he trusted Congress, and perhaps the public, to eventually approve his actions.[78]

To illustrate the method by which the executive could appeal to Congress after having exceeded its constitutional authority, Jefferson pointed to the *Chesapeake* Affair. After the British *Leopard* had fired upon the American ship, Jefferson had to decide whether he would wait until Congress could make the requisite appropriations before he readied the country for defending itself: "Our magazines were illy provided with some necessary articles, nor had any appropriations been made for their purchase." Rather than waiting for the more deliberative body to act, Jefferson acted first and then asked for permission after the fact: "We ventured, however, to provide them, and to place our country in safety; and stating the case to Congress, they sanctioned the act." As in the hypothetical, the condition for the president's exercising a power reserved by the Constitution to Congress is that the president asks for congressional approval when the necessity passes.[79]

But the parallel in method obscures at least one importance difference between the example of the *Chesapeake* and the hypothetical about Florida. The hypothetical presents wider latitude for executive prerogative than the military examples suggest: in overstepping the authority of Congress to acquire Florida, the president protects the public advantage not by saving the country from a foreign aggressor or internal rebellion but by making an advantageous bargain. Although acquiring Florida would perhaps have served self-preservation, as control of the Gulf of Mexico would have made the port of New Orleans more defensible, Jefferson did not then connect national defense to the argument for acquiring Florida. As with the Louisiana Purchase, Jefferson used the hypothetical to appeal to the opportunity to acquire territory rather than to an argument from national defense. Under circumstances deemed appropriate by the president himself, the military leader's obedience to the law of self-preservation became the president's preference for good policy. Although events postponed the Florida opportunity, Jefferson's letter to Colvin defended what he might have done to acquire

---

[78] Jefferson to John Colvin, *TJW*, 1231–4.
[79] Ibid., 1232.

Florida, and by extension, what he did do in the case of Louisiana. By calling attention to Randolph's opposition, which was founded on "Old Republican" principles, Jefferson meant to show that he had not been weighed down by what Malone later called the "upper and nether millstones of republican dogma."[80]

After the example of Florida and the *Chesapeake*, Jefferson addressed Colvin's specific question regarding Wilkinson at New Orleans. The general had been criticized for arresting suspected conspirators and transferring them without a trial. As Jefferson had written to Claiborne after delivering his special message to the House and Senate, Jefferson argued that Wilkinson's case should be considered through Wilkinson's perspective and information: although Jefferson in Washington knew that "there was never a danger of British fleet from below," Wilkinson "expected Burr and his band from above, a British fleet from below" as well as a "formidable conspiracy" within New Orleans. Although Wilkinson's arrests were predicated on preventing a conspiracy involving a British threat that never materialized, the arrests would have to be judged in consideration of "the state of information, correct and incorrect, which he [Wilkinson] then possessed."[81]

According to Jefferson, the question of arrests was straightforward: "all honest men" would affirm that "seizing the notorious conspirators" was just. But the question of transferring the prisoners to Washington, "when the written law gave them a right to trial in the territory," was more difficult. The answer to the more difficult question regarding due process was connected to the immediate circumstances, some of which were political: "The danger of their rescue, of their continuing their machinations, the tardiness and weakness of the law, apathy of the judges, active patronage of the whole tribe of lawyers, unknown disposition of the juries, an hourly expectation of the enemy, salvation of the city, and of the Union itself, which would have been convulsed to its center, had that conspiracy succeeded." Taken together, these circumstances "constituted a law of necessity and self-preservation, and rendered the *salus populi* supreme over the written law." As the officer given the task of preventing the conspiracy, Wilkinson was the one who had to transgress against the written law, the conspirators' right to trial in the Louisiana territory, in order to save the city from being overcome by the British or Burr. But rather than being legally conferred by the law, Wilkinson's discretion carried with it the possibility that Wilkinson would be held criminally responsible for breaking the law: "The officer who is called to act on this supreme ground, does indeed risk himself on the justice of the

---

[80] Malone, 5:73.
[81] Jefferson to John Colvin, *TJW*, 1233.

controlling powers of the constitution, and his station makes it his duty to incur that risk."

In the *Second Treatise*, Locke assured readers that the people could decide whether the executive had exercised the prerogative for the public good, but Jefferson's letter suggested that there was at least one difficulty.[82] Sometimes the people judge executives according to facts that were not available to the executive at the time of the action. Hence the "embarrassing" aspect of prerogative: with the benefit of hindsight, the people may know the circumstances better than the executive did at the time. In the case of Wilkinson, some in Washington had known that the British fleet was not on its way and that Burr had been detained before he reached the Mississippi, but Wilkinson did not. As Jefferson put it, it would be unfair to judge Wilkinson according to the facts known in Washington, for "those controlling powers and his fellow citizens generally, are bound to judge according to the circumstances under which he acted. They are not to transfer the information of this place or moment to time and place of his action; but to put themselves into his situation."[83] In order to properly judge prerogative, the people ought to consider it from the perspective of the executive. Rather than judging prerogative by determining whether its use benefits the public good in the present, the people have to consider the motives resting behind the discretion. Or, as he put it in a message to Congress, "In all these cases, the purity and the patriotism of the motives should shield the agent from blame, [and] even secure the sanction where the error is not too injurious."[84] Educated under this principle, the people can more accurately decide whether prerogative has been exercised for good or hurt.

Like his defense of the Louisiana Purchase, Jefferson's public letter to Colvin was silent regarding the constitutional source of presidential prerogative. Absent in Jefferson's expansive defense of the prerogative were questions concerning the constitutionality of the acts or whether such actions are executive by nature. Rather, Jefferson seemed to recommend that action according to the law of self-preservation extended to those who take it: not a principle to be followed by "persons charged with petty duties," it would be "incumbent on those only who accept of great charges, to risk themselves on great occasions."[85] But, as the example of acquiring Florida suggests, these great occasions were not limited to "when the safety of the nation" was "at stake" but also would include the nation's "very high interests" – similar,

[82] Ibid.; Locke, *Second Treatise*, section 161, in *Two Treatises*, p. 375.
[83] Jefferson to John Colvin, *TJW*, 1233.
[84] Jefferson, "Special Message," January 13, 1806, L&B, 3: 402–7.
[85] Jefferson to John Colvin, *TJW*, 1233.

perhaps, to the "transcendent objects" and national "hopes" Jefferson mentioned in his First Inaugural. Indeed, it was because both self-preservation and the nation's very high interests "involved the most important consequences," an executive who obeyed orders so strictly that he violated the purpose for the order was issued would be a "very bad one." Although finding the "line of discrimination" between laws to be obeyed and laws to be transgressed "may be difficult," just as determining whether the national interest or safety was at stake might be a question of perspective, "the good officer is bound to draw it at his own peril, and throw himself on the justice of his country and the rectitude of his motives." By replacing constitutional interpretation with executive discretion responsible to popular judgment, Jefferson set out to democratize prerogative while simultaneously expanding it.

To "give form and body to the floating ardor of our countrymen"

But on what basis is an officer to judge whether discretion allows him the latitude to push aside some of the law? Jefferson addressed this question in a letter to the governor of Virginia, William H. Cabell. In this letter, written only weeks after his letter to Hay detailing the "constant agency" required of the president (exempting presidents from answering a subpoena), and composed during the military preparations Jefferson had made in response to the attack on the *Chesapeake*, Jefferson answered the governor's request for advice on law, regarding an "act for accepting thirty thousand volunteers."[86] After qualifying his answer with the assurance that Cabell's own opinion would be better and noting that he then lacked his own advisors, Jefferson explained that he himself would engage in a politically risky enterprise by offering an answer to question with public implications: "I shall frankly venture my individual thoughts on the subject, and participate with you in any risk of disapprobation to which an honest desire of furthering the public good may expose us." The use of "us" suggests that Jefferson's participation was premised on the anticipation of public approval.[87]

As Jefferson answered it, Cabell's question was essentially about reconciling construction and action. By what standard is an executive to read a law, especially a law in which one section seems to undermine another in practice, when trying to effect the public good? According to Jefferson, one

---

[86] That summer, Jefferson had written the governors with the request to make military preparations. Malone does not discuss Jefferson's August letter. Malone, 5:432.

[87] Jefferson to William H. Cabell, 11 August 1807, *Jefferson Papers*, Library of Congress (see note 56).

advantage for executives is that the executive official possesses more latitude than a judge: "In the construction of a law, even in judiciary cases of
meum et tuum, where the opposite parties have a right & counterright in
the very words of the law, the judge considers the intention of the law-giver
as his true guide, and gives to all the parts & expressions of the law, that
meaning which will effect, instead of defeating, it's intention." Pushing aside
the question as to how judges might determine legislative intent, Jefferson's
point here was to make a distinction between judicial interpretation and
executive interpretation: "but in laws merely executive, where no private
right stands in the way, and the public object is the interest of all, a much
freer scope of construction, in favor of the intention of the law, ought to be
taken, & ingenuity even should be exercised in devising constructions, which
may save to the public the benefit of the law. It's intention is the important
thing; the means of attaining it quite subordinate." To the executive falls the
responsibility to carry out the laws, but more than clerically effecting the
will of another, the executive is most expert in the sphere of action and
therefore must determine the means by which the intent of the law can best
be executed. Rather than upholding the letter of the law, the executive can
and must use ingenuity to discern the means by which the public interest
will best be served. Executives who rigorously apply the law as they find
it often incorporate into the law its legislative flaws. "It often happens,"
when lawmakers prescribe the "details of execution," some "unforeseen"
circumstance arises, which if "scrupulously adhered to" in execution, would
"frustrate" the "intention" of the law. The doctrine of strict construction
should not result in the practice of narrow construction: "but constructions
must not be favored which go to defeat instead of furthering the principal
object of their law, and to sacrifice the end to the means. It being as evidently
their intention that the end shall be attained as that it should be effected by
any given means, if both cannot be observed, we are equally free to deviate
from the one as the other, and more rational in postponing the means to the
end." The executive must judge whether following scrupulously the means
prescribed by the legislature would sacrifice the end. If the executive were
to sacrifice the end to the means, then he would fail to exercise the "general
power to carry the laws into execution" and would verify the "objection"
that the United States government was an "impracticable one."[88]

After offering this "general view" of the "duty" of an "executive officer,"
Jefferson went on to answer the governor's specific questions as to whether
he possessed the power to issue commissions to officers before the companies
were organized. As Jefferson understood the first three questions, there was

[88] Ibid.

no specific authority to issue commissions before companies were created and organized according to the terms of the law. But such a reading would lead to a detrimental result in practice: "Were we to stop right here the law might stop also." To properly bring the law to action, Jefferson alluded to "other executive powers." But, rather than pointing to a particular constitutional clause, Jefferson offered a justification like the one he had given to Monroe when asking him to accept the commission as special minister to France: "because I verily believe that it will be the zeal & activity alone of those destined for commands, which will give form and body to the floating ardor of our countrymen to enter into this service, and bring their wills to a point of union & effect." Action, then, requires a person selected by nature and willing to expose himself to some risk in order to find the public good. This is as true in politics as it is in private life, for experience shows that even people who share common desires "are rarely brought into an association of them, unless urged by some one assuming an agency." In the case of a militia, this principle is even clearer in that an officer first must gather and organize the militia before he can command it. Like the person who initiates a friendship by creating the association of those with common desires, Cabell must give action to the law by getting around the rules concerning means.[89]

But Jefferson did not go so far as to recommend that Cabell himself appoint officers even though the law required that the militia be organized first. Rather, Jefferson instructed Cabell to find a way to execute the law without explicitly transgressing it. Because the law was meant to provide the means by which the militia could be called out but required that the militia be organized before officers were commissioned, a prudent executive would authorize deputies to perform the functions of officers before they could be formally commissioned. "[w]hether our constitutional powers, to carry the law into execution, would not authorize the issuing a previous commission (as they would had nothing been said about commissions in the law), is a question not necessarily now to be decided: because they certainly allow us to what will be equally effectual. We may issue instructions, or warrants, to the persons destined to be Captains, etc., authorizing them to superintend the association of the companies, & to perform the functions of a Captain, etc., until commissions may be regularly issued." Just as he had himself as governor persuaded officials to execute an expired law, and just as he ordered that possible insurrectionists be kept "out of a course of law," Jefferson recommended that the governor look to the principle of the law to temporarily set aside its details.[90]

[89] Ibid.
[90] Ibid.

Under Jefferson's formulation, ensuring the execution of the object of the law allows executive officials to modify the law with regard to the means of execution. Just as the object of the law guides the executive's interpretation, consideration of the public's judgment marks the limits of interpretation. Accordingly, Jefferson closed his letter to Cabell with the reminder that public opinion would eventually judge him according to his motives – "it is our consolation & encouragement that we are serving a just public, who will be indulgent to any error committed honestly, & relating merely to the means of carrying into effect what they have manifestly willed to be a law." But the relationship between public opinion and executive action also moves in the other direction. By putting action to the law, the president completes the unification of opinion: by gathering public sentiments under a set of principles, the president embodies the will of the nation; by carrying out the will of the nation; the president acts as its agent; by using judgment to discern the principles underlying the national will, the president gives effect to what would have been otherwise floating ardor.[91]

Jefferson's Failure

Closer examination of Jefferson's famous letter to Colvin reveals a difficulty in Jefferson's method. As is evident from the commonly quoted portion of the letter, Jefferson's prerogative includes the power to act outside the law as well as against it on behalf of self-preservation.[92] But self-preservation is not the only occasion in which the executive may use the prerogative, for other passages of the letter suggest that Jefferson also would allow its use when the public good may require it.

The second, larger, case for prerogative cannot be fully grasped until one considers the rhetorical purpose of the letter. Taken on its word, Jefferson's letter was meant to be private, and Jefferson closed this letter with a request similar to those he included in other ticklish matters: "I have indulged freer views on this question, on your assurances that they are for your own eye only, and that they will not get into the hands of newswriters."[93] But Jefferson likely understood that his words would be used for public argument, without Jefferson's name attached to them, because Colvin was a pamphleteer for the Republican cause. During the Jefferson and Madison administrations, Colvin was a State Department clerk (a patronage job), and an editor of at least two Republican newspapers, *The Monitor* (Washington, DC)

---

[91] Ibid.
[92] Jefferson to John B Colvin, September 20, 1810, *TJW*, 1231.
[93] Ibid., 1233.

and *The Republican Advocate* (Fredericktown, Maryland).[94] And during the debate over Louisiana treaty, he wrote a defense of the treaty that answered three practical objections voiced by Federalists and concluded that the treaty "compel[led] every genuine American to hail Jefferson as the Benefator of his Country."[95] In 1804, he wrote a critique of the Adams administration that concluded voters had "transferred" too quickly their confidence from Washington to his less worthy successor.[96] Even though Jefferson said he meant his letter to be read by only Colvin, Jefferson likely understood that his words would be used for public argument, without his name attached to them because Colvin told Jefferson that Wilkinson had asked Colvin for help in writing his *Memoirs*.[97]

To write the section of Wilkinson's *Memoirs* dealing with the Burr conspiracy, Colvin wrote Jefferson for his opinion.[98] But more than seeking information, the partisan writer reminded Jefferson that the *Memoirs* would include a history of events under Jefferson's administration and that the Burr conspiracy would "hereafter form a prominent feature in the history of your political life." After telling the retired president that the Burr affair would be a chapter of his place in history, Colvin submitted the following question: "Are there not periods where, in [illegible] [illegible], it is necessary for officers in [illegible] stations to exercise an authority beyond the law – and, was not the trial of Burr's treason such a period?" Colvin offered this question with a pledge of secrecy, but it is likely that Jefferson knew that his words would find their way to the pages of Wilkinson's *Memoirs*. In February 1811, Colvin wrote Jefferson to confirm that he had, in fact, used the former president's argument: "I presume that you have, by this time, read in your own words, the argument in favor of the proceedings at New Orleans against the conspirators. In truth, I copied those arguments, and gave them to Gen. Wilkinson, without the least intimation that they were from your pen: And thus, sir, you have contributed to do good without being seen in it – a thing which you, no doubt, have often done – and which, more than anything else, assimilates a man to his duty."[99] From Colvin's matter

[94] J. C. A. Stagg, "James Madison and the Coercion of Great Britain: Canada, the West Indies, and the War of 1812," *William and Mary Quarterly.* 3rd Ser., 38 (1981): 19; Adrienne Koch and William, eds. *The Life and Selected Writings of Thomas Jefferson* (New York: Modern Library, 1944), 606.

[95] John B. Colvin, *Republican Policy; or, The Superiority of the Principles of the Present Administration over those of its Enemies* (Frederick-Town, MD: Office of the Republican Advocates, 1802).

[96] John B. Colvin, *A Candid View of the Facts in a Letter from John B. Colvin to a Federal Friend* (Frederick-Town, MD: Office of the Republican Advocates, 1804).

[97] Colvin to Jefferson, 14 September 1810, *Jefferson Papers*, Library of Congress (see note 56).

[98] John B. Colvin to Jefferson, 14 September 1810, *Jefferson Papers*, Library of Congress.

[99] John B. Colvin to Jefferson, 4 February 1811, *Jefferson Papers*, Library of Congress.

of fact reply, it is plausible that Jefferson wrote his famous letter knowing the end to which his words would be used. As Colvin noted, putting words in other people's mouths was a method often used by the author of the Declaration.

Rather than being confined to Colvin's eyes only, Jefferson's words went right to the press. Later that year, Wilkinson published the second volume of his *Memoirs* in Washington, and within that volume, Colvin included an extensive defense of "General Wilkinson's Conduct in Relation to Burr's Conspiracy." Taking its bearings from Jefferson's letter, this defense included the argument that "those in executive trust," rather than those associated with the "tardy progress" of the legislative body, have to sometimes "exert extraordinary powers for the safety of the commonwealth." To support this general principle, Colvin pointed to a distinction between revolutionary Virginia and Rome: "The Romans, in great exigencies, elected dictators with absolute powers. This, in the sequel, became an evil, for every dictator did not turn out a Cincinnatus. It seems much the safest course to leave the point open, and to commit the destinies of the nation, in an imminent crisis, to the virtuous resolution of those, who may be intrepid enough to volunteer, in behalf of their government and country; to rally the good sense of the people, to an absolution of a partial violation of the laws, and to uphold the active supporter of the public interests against the vehement attacks of the miscreants and their partizans whom he had defeated." Unlike the Roman practice of providing by law a person with emergency powers, the Virginians had relied on the efforts of wartime governors who had both followed the Virginia Constitution as well as parting from it when required by military necessity. To offer this defense of Wilkinson, Colvin enlisted the example of the Virginian practice of executive discretion in the face of necessity. Under this formulation, Wilkinson's reputation would be cleared: "There is, in fact, something ridiculous in condemning a man for the infraction of a law relative to the liberty and safety of half a dozen individuals, of more than suspicious character, when by the very infraction the liberty and safety of the whole society is preserved."[100]

According to Colvin, if Wilkinson were prosecuted, then the example would discourage "future commanders" from choosing duty over ambition, as ambition would be served by trusting the "cold blooded calculations of party politicians." To prevent such a precedent, the author recommended

---

[100] James Wilkinson, *Memoirs of General Wilkinson*, Vol. II. (Washington, DC: 1810). Although Wilkinson was the author of the work, I assume that the section dealing with the Burr Conspiracy was written by, or with the assistance of, Colvin. The crucial point is that the author of Wilkinson's memoirs employed Jefferson's argument and that Jefferson would have had reason to believe that this was going to happen.

that the government pass a "general act of indemnity and protection," just as the British Parliament had passed regarding "ministers" who had acted "contrary to municipal law, in order to subserve the great and fundamental interests of the empire." The problem for Wilkinson was the distance of the "scene of the treason" from the "whole of the American people": because most did not perceive the danger of a conspiracy they never materialized, they disapproved of the "violation of personal liberty" of the accused. Even though the president had argued that Wilkinson be judged according to the events as he then perceived them, rather than what they seemed to be after the fact and from a distance, Wilkinson's transgression against rights was regarded by many to be unforgivable. To rise above objections arising from disputed details bound in geography and time, then, Colvin would have to offer a stronger defense from reason.[101]

To defend Wilkinson by way of a broader argument, Colvin asked his readers to pause and "calmly reflect" on the question with which he had earlier proposed to Jefferson: "*Whether circumstances do not sometimes occur, which make it a duty in officers of high trust to assume authorities beyond the law?*" To answer this question, the author repeated Jefferson's reply almost word for word: "It is easy enough of solution in principle, but must be sometimes embarrassing in practice. A strict observance of the written laws is doubtless *one* of the first duties of a good citizen, but it is not the *highest*. The laws of necessity, of self-preservation, of saving our country when in danger, are of higher obligation. To lose our country by a scrupulous adherence to written law would be to lose the law itself, with life, liberty, property, and all those, who are enjoying them with us, thus absurdly sacrificing the end to the means." After offering this slightly edited version of Jefferson's general principle, Colvin went on to present the same examples to which Jefferson had appealed: Washington's firing on a house, Washington's leveling the suburbs at Yorktown, the governor of Virginia's impressing horses and supplies, and a ship's taking by force supplies from another in order to prevent its crew from starving. Following Jefferson, Colvin used these examples to verify the general principle: "In all these cases the unwritten laws of necessity, of self-preservation, and of the public safety, control the written laws of meum and tuum."[102]

But Colvin changed Jefferson's answer. Between the example of the governor of Virginia's impressing supplies and the ship at sea, Colvin noted that "in retreats, we destroy roads, and boats, and bridges, and houses, force the inhabitants from their homes, and despoil the country of its stock."

---

[101] Ibid., 53–56.
[102] Wilkinson, *Memoirs*, 56–7.

Similarly, after the example of the ship, Colvin added that buildings next to burning buildings are often torn down in order to stop the spread of a fire. After adding two examples, the author then omitted Jefferson's additional hypothetical drawn from the question of acquiring Florida. By omitting this example, Colvin dropped Jefferson's expanded argument for departing from the law to effect the public good in cases where self-preservation was not necessarily at stake. Perhaps Colvin thought that Jefferson's argument was too wide or that the Florida hypothetical would have jeopardized existing treaties regarding Florida or other territories, or, more simply, perhaps the example would have too directly implicated Jefferson. Whatever the case, Colvin seemed to have preferred Jefferson's narrow rendering of the general principle over Jefferson's expansive use of the hypothetical. By omitting the reference to Florida, executive discretion would be defended on the grounds of self-preservation alone.[103]

After omitting reference to the Florida question, Colvin presented the remaining portions of Jefferson's argument, with some emendations. Again, the small corrections had wider implications. In the example of the president's making ready for war after the *Chesapeake* incident, Colvin added to Jefferson's original, which explained that the executive explained itself to Congress which in turn "sanctioned the act," by putting the example in the form of argument: "The executive was reduced to the alternative of anticipating the law, or exposing the country. He acted, and the necessary provisions were made. This might be called an usurpation, but the pressure of the occasion justified it to the government, and the measure was sanctioned by law." Unlike Jefferson's, which says that the executive "ventured" to "provide" "some necessary articles" in case of war, Colvin's use of the incident emphasizes that the president was faced with acting before Congress could meet or with being overcome by necessity. By citing a case in which the executive exercised legislative functions in the face of necessity and the legislative eventually approved of the action, Colvin also could defend the discretion by General Wilkinson. After using the example of the *Chesapeake*, Colvin added to Jefferson's argument by quoting "an authority," namely, John Randolph. During the debate on the Georgia claims, Randolph argued that "extraordinary cases" call for "extraordinary remedies" and that it was to "great first principles" that people should look "for aid" during "extremities." To carry out these remedies during extraordinary times, the nation would require action rather than legal argument: "*Attorneys and judges do not decide the fate of empires.*" Wilkinson's actions, then, were defendable

---

[103] Ibid.

according to the grounds set by Randolph, the source of Wilkinson's legal tribulations.[104]

After modifying the *Chesapeake* example and inserting the quotation from Randolph, Colvin returned to presenting Jefferson's argument. With three exceptions, one small and two big, the defense of Wilkinson and the concluding summary follow almost word for word from Jefferson's letter. As discussed previously, Jefferson's argument defended Wilkinson on the grounds that the general justly acted against the law in order to put down the conspiracy according to the information he then had. To make this argument more explicit, the author added, "Wilkinson was reduced to the necessity of putting down the conspirators, or of being himself put down."[105] The next change was in the summary paragraph. Where Jefferson made the distinction between "persons charged with petty duties" and "those who accept great charges," Colvin dropped the reference to petty officers in favor of a more general disclaimer: "In offering these principles and illustrations to our readers, we pretend not to invade the general rule, but to contend for the exception only; our doctrines apply to extreme cases and not to ordinary occasions, in the written law may take its undisturbed course with safety to the community. In such instances, the example of overleaping the law is of greater evil than a strict adherence to its imperfect provisions." In admitting that determining "the line of discrimination may be difficult," Colvin shifted the condition Jefferson had placed on those officers who accept great charges: rather than saying that such an officer must "throw himself on the justice of his country," this argument concluded by shifting the obligation away from the officer – "the good officer" must "depend for justification on the soundness of his judgment, the rectitude of his motives, and the justice of his country."[106] Rather than requiring the officer to throw himself on the public for approval, the *Memoirs* seemed to require the public to go out of its way to approve of the officer.

The changes made by Colvin point to a failure in Jefferson's indirect method. Each change, however slight, modified Jefferson's expansion of the prerogative power. Without the hypothetical of Florida, which perhaps corresponded to the larger Louisiana Purchase, the justification of executive discretion in the face of necessity lost the positive implication of the Inaugural's call to hope in achieving the transcendent objects of government. Like Locke's illustration of prerogative, Colvin's added examples of an army

---

[104] Ibid., 57.
[105] Ibid., 58. See the introduction to the 1816 edition of the second volume, published in Philadelphia by Abraham Small in 1816.
[106] Wilkinson, *Memoirs*, 58–9.

destroying property in retreat and of pulling down a house in order to confine a fire reinforced the idea that some actions are plainly defensible on grounds of self-preservation. Rather than providing the president with a power to part with the law in order to secure the country's advantage, the modified argument presented the more straightforward defense according to self-preservation. Lacking the expansive justification of prerogative on the grounds of great objects, the revised argument presented Jefferson's understanding of presidential power in a less democratic form.

At least as important as narrowing the basis for discretion, Colvin deleted Jefferson's condition that officers who acted outside the law "throw themselves" on their country. In the example of the *Chesapeake*, Jefferson noted that the president had stated "the case" to Congress, which in turn had "sanctioned the act."[107] Wilkinson's *Memoirs* omitted the account of the president seeking the approval Congress, emphasizing the degree of danger instead: "the pressure of the occasion justified it to the government, and the measure was sanctioned by law."[108] In place of the requirement that the executive appeal to Congress or the people to determine whether the parting with the law was done for the public good, the modified argument presumed that the very degree of danger, taken alongside the officer's expertise and motives, would justify the discretion to those who were not in his position. Colvin probably omitted the declaratory component of the argument for the reason that Wilkinson himself would have spurned such a requirement. In a later edition of his *Memoirs*, Wilkinson wrote that his treatment by Randolph and Madison verified what he believed to Montesquieu's "anathema against republics." In Wilkinson's view, republics depended too much upon their statesmen, and statesmen were necessarily adverse to the patriotism possessed by military commanders. Like Nathanael Greene, who had matter-of-factly argued to Governor Jefferson that the civil power must give way to the military during times of emergency, Wilkinson had little patience for politicians who could not appreciate his bold actions preventing the Burr uprising.

An Unfinished Transformation

Jefferson is often remembered for his several pronouncements that revolutions were healthy phenomena in the political atmosphere, yet his calling his own election the "Revolution of 1800" suggests that Jefferson was a new breed of revolutionary. Indeed, his enforcement of the Embargo, like his

---

[107] Jefferson to Colvin, *TJW*, 1230.
[108] Wilkinson, *Memoirs*, 57.

defense of Wilkinson as a necessary "dictator," shows the extent to which self-preservation trumps the rule of law.[109] But his letter to Colvin expanded prerogative even as it set limits on it. As Jefferson presented it, Wilkinson's decision to detain and then transport Burr and his accomplices was defensible not on constitutional or legal grounds. Nor was it justifiable on the basis of self-preservation alone but, rather, in part, because the political, or partisan, disposition of the city (the apathy of judges and the complicity of lawyers, combined with the unpredictability of citizens as jurors) lessened the likelihood that Burr would receive a fair trial. Jefferson thus answered Colvin's original question, the basis of which was necessarily political, by explaining prerogative with the simple examples drawn from self-preservation and the more complicated political hypothetical arising from opposition in Congress. Wilkinson's acting on behalf of self-preservation can be understood only after being prepared by the example of Jefferson political act on behalf of the national interest. Necessity is political as well as physical.

In place of blood-washed trees, Jefferson believed that elections and public opinion would be the symbols of revolutions won and lost. Accordingly, Jefferson found that writing a memorable phrase could energize the government by gathering public opinion around it while at the same time more clearly marking its limits. His famous description of the object of the Declaration – "to place before mankind the common sense of the subject, in terms so plain and firm as to command their assent" – reveals his method of shaping public opinion while seeming to merely summarize it. Even though his messages to Congress were delivered in writing rather than in speech, and although his annual messages were more deferential than his two Inaugurals, Jefferson used "special messages" to Congress to report those occasions that had required that he, or other executives, step outside their legal authority. By "throwing himself" on Congress by way of the "special message," Jefferson offered Congress the opportunity to approve or censure measures that he had already taken.

Because of his mild disposition, perhaps, Jefferson did not finish his project to attach declarations to the presidency. Although he cast the Embargo as part of an "epoch" in which events "embarrass deliberation," his deference to the deliberative branch obscured the fact that it was his policy. Similarly, because his advisors told him that the doctrine of coordinate review might have given Federalists an opportunity to shift public opinion, Jefferson shrunk back from offering a public explanation of it. Most important, when

---

[109] Jefferson to James Brown, 28 October 1808, Ford 10: 211. See Leonard W. Levy, *Jefferson and Civil Liberties: The Darker Side* (Cambridge, MA: Belknap Press, Harvard University Press, 1963),

the Louisiana Purchase presented him with the institutional conflict that his understanding of presidential power required, Jefferson chose silence over enlightenment. Indeed, the Second Inaugural would have been the appropriate place to teach the people his understanding – and his use – of executive power. Instead, acquiescing to the counsels of his friends, he relied on them to publicly offer the arguments that he had supplied in private. And, although he encouraged faithful and zealous citizens to undertake great objects for their country, he was too subtle in his praise.

10

Development and Difficulties

Throughout his history of Jefferson's presidency, Henry Adams traced two seemingly contradictory themes. On the one hand, Jefferson made no attempt to lessen the influence or limit the power of the executive branch and was therefore at least as Federalist as his two predecessors, but, on the other, Jefferson's presidency quickened the country's march toward democracy. But Adams failed to make the connection between Jefferson's expansion of presidential power and the democratic reasoning behind it. Like Jefferson's contemporaries who, by way of a partisan twist on an error in translation, believed that Jefferson's criticism of the "forms" in Washington's government (levees, birthdays, and apparel) was meant to recommend a revolution in the "form" of government, Adams did not appreciate that Jefferson meant to empower the presidency by democratizing it.[1] What Adams and generations of his followers have missed is that Jefferson attempted to resolve the tension between executive power and democracy by implementing a particular understanding of executive power.

To be sure, Jefferson was too good a politician, and too enthralled with experimentation, to be rigid in his views. His tenure as governor persuaded him to revise his earlier prohibition of giving the former prerogatives of the king to the governor, to reconsider the merits of an executive council and to find new ways to reign in the legislative power. Experience under the Articles of Confederation confirmed for him that a separate executive was necessary for foreign and domestic affairs. And the two-thirds requirement in the Senate for amendments and treaties, combined with the two-party

---

[1] For the translation difficulties of the letter to Mazzei, see Jefferson to Martin Van Buren, 29 June 1824, L&B, 16:54.

system he helped create, caused him to keep silent what his theory demanded he make public.

But there is a remarkable unity to his thought over his entire career. Term limits, unity of office, public opinion, strict construction, discretion by the faithful officer, and declarations of principle were brought together by the executive power. Properly understood, Jefferson's transformation of the inaugural address from oath-taking to principle-declaring, his setting of an informal precedent for a two-term limit, and his refinement of the Electoral College all suggest a deliberate and coherent project to attach presidential power to a majority will. More than the struggle of an elected official seeking to maintain power, these reforms reveal his effort to further bind executive power with republican responsibility. It is significant that he told a foreign observer that the execution of laws was more important than the making of them.

Democratizing the Prerogative

The most conspicuous feature of Jefferson's doctrine of democratic energy is its simultaneous expansion and demarcation of the prerogative power. According to this understanding, the president embodies the will of the nation by unifying and directing it, so the president must be willing to temporarily set aside the law in order to effect the public good. More than the last resource of commander in chief, the prerogative power can be used during other great occasions in which necessity would otherwise obstruct the public good. But presidents must report their use of the prerogative and defend it without recourse to constitutional argument so that the people may be able to judge it.

Jefferson used the prerogative power throughout his career. As a governor, Jefferson ordered officials to carry out expired laws, exercised a virtual pardon by instructing prosecutors to keep possible witnesses "out of the course of law," and advised military leaders to take extraordinary and secret measures to prevent insurrections. As Secretary of State, Jefferson went beyond the expectations, if not the instructions, of Congress when he proposed his plan to systemize (and therefore nationalize) the nation's currency, weights and measures. Similarly, during the 1790s, Jefferson (and Madison) organized a national opposition party, moving outside the imagination of the constitutional design, to undo the Federalist assertion of implied power. As president, Jefferson reshaped the constitutional framework when he used the inaugural ceremonies as an occasion to mark transitions of power and principle, doubled the size of the country by incorporating Louisiana, resisted

John Marshall's subpoena, and used his "special messages" to defend the discretion of other executives.

More important, Jefferson did not appeal to the understanding of the prerogative power then available. When Hamilton defended Washington's Neutrality Proclamation, he used the opportunity to assert that the absence of a "herein granted" limitation in the vesting clause of Article Two implied that exceptions to the grant of power to the president were to be considered strictly. Moreover, George Washington initiated the precedent of using the oath of office to justify extraordinary presidential powers.[2] Although the first president did not there connect the oath to the commander in chief provision, as presidents do as a matter of course today, Washington's mounting a horse to lead the militia must have achieved that affect – John Marshall, after all, included the title Commander in Chief in the extended title of his *Life of Washington*. Jefferson met similar opportunities: during the summer of 1803, Republicans urged Jefferson to assert that, as every government possessed an implied power to expand, the Constitution granted the power to acquire and incorporate Louisiana. Although Jefferson might have followed Hamilton's rationale, Washington's example, or Republican advice to defend the Louisiana Purchase, he set a precedent against broad construction by initially remaining silent, then employing the argument for the extended republic as a defense, and finally by enunciating his doctrine through special messages to Congress and private letters for public purpose.

Accordingly, his constitutional silence fit within his larger educative plan for democratic energy. Rather than claiming authority for the purchase from disputed clauses in the Constitution, as Washington did and Lincoln would, Jefferson praised the purchase only on the grounds that it would expand the empire of liberty. His example against broad construction, required by political necessity to be a silent one, was necessarily connected to his effort to place the president as the "constant agent" of the will of the nation. Building on Hamilton's assurance that executive unity was compatible with republicanism because it fostered accountability, Jefferson perceived that a loose construction would undermine this possible connection between the executive and the people. Just as his extraconstitutional organization of party and media suggest that enlightenment was central to this project in democratization, they parallel his attempt to empower these declarations through presidential speech, using the presidency to help accomplish his larger project in democratic education by teaching citizens to pursue great democratic objects.

---

[2] Washington, "Sixth Annual Message to Congress," *George Washington: Writings*, ed. John Rhodehamel (New York: Library of America, 1997), 893.

Arousing popular sentiment condenses it and makes it ascertainable, which, in turn, emboldens the people and their presidents.

Redevelopment

But Jefferson's example was altered by later presidents, beginning with Andrew Jackson. Jackson completed Jefferson's logic of reelection being about the performance of the promise when he forced his handling of the bank to become the central question of the election 1832, arguing that the people would decide this question directly. Expanding on Jefferson's doctrine of coordinate review, he declared that he may veto the bank as unconstitutional (because unnecessary) even though the Supreme Court had declared that Congress did have the authority to incorporate a bank. On cue, when the Senate responded to his veto by passing a resolution of censure, he declared that the president "is the direct representative of the American people," setting up the conflict seemingly required by Jefferson's understanding of executive power. But, at the same time, Jackson resurrected the presidential oath when he argued that Senate had gone outside the Constitution by using censure instead of impeachment: "by expressing" the president's "duty" to defend the "integrity of the Constitution" "in the official oath or affirmation, the founders have attested their sense of its importance and have given to it a peculiar solemnity and force." Indeed, Jackson had already prepared the way for such use of the oath by referring to the oath in his veto message of the bank bill (taken by "each public officer" to "support" the Constitution "as he understands it") and in his second inaugural address. Jackson left the oath, as Justice Robert Jackson said in another context, as a loaded weapon to be picked up by future presidents who wished to blur the difference between constitutional and extraconstitutional executive power.[3]

That more significant departure was brought about by Abraham Lincoln, who appealed to the Louisiana Purchase to reassert a constitutional basis for the prerogative power. In his First Annual Message to Congress, Lincoln appealed to Jefferson's example in order to propose acquiring new territory for colonizing freed slaves: "Having practiced the acquisition of territory nearly sixty years, the question of constitutional power to do so is no longer an open one to us. The power was questioned at first by Mr. Jefferson, who, however, in the purchase of Louisiana, yielded his scruples

---

[3] Andrew Jackson, "Second Inaugural" and "Protest" in James D. Richardson, *A Compilation of the Messages and Papers of the Presidents*, Vol. 3 (New York: Bureau of National Literature, 1897), 1309, 1289, and 1224; and *Korematsu v. United States* 323 U.S. 214, 246 (Jackson, J., dis. op.).

on the plea of great expediency." Lincoln's point was clear: because Jefferson set aside scruples regarding the constitutional question of acquiring territory, those in Lincoln's day need not engage in too much hand-wringing over a similar question. By reminding his audience that the great strict construc-tionist put aside constitutional questions in the face of necessity, Lincoln could himself clear constitutional obstacles on the grounds that expedi-ency required exceptional measures: "On this whole proposition, – including the appropriation of money with the acquisition of territory, does not the expediency amount to absolute necessity – that, without which the gov-ernment itself cannot be perpetuated. The war continues." In this extraor-dinary passage, which immediately followed the passage about Jefferson, Lincoln collapsed the question of acquiring territory into the question of the war, on which the fate of the Union hung. In short, the very act of enter-taining scruples was dangerous because the continuing war turned ques-tions of expediency into questions about the existence of the Union. Lincoln pointed to Jefferson to tell listeners he was prosecuting a war to preserve the Union and therefore would be impatient with some of the scruples held by others.[4]

But Lincoln appealed to Jefferson after he had already parted from Jef-ferson's understanding of the Constitution and prerogative. Five months earlier, in a "Special Message" delivered on 4 July, Lincoln asked whether a republic could be both free and strong and then answered by reporting his own solution, using force against the rebel military. Lincoln famously went on to defend one of these measures, the suspension of habeas corpus, as either a justifiable breach of the Constitution, or an act authorized by the Constitution. The first defense was offered to persuade those uncon-vinced of the second argument's blanket assertion that the Constitution's provision for the suspension of habeas corpus during rebellion or invasion was not limited to the legislative branch. This first, larger, argument thus weighed preserving the government against the harm of breaking a "single law": "Are all the laws, but one, to go unexecuted, and the government itself go to pieces, lest that one be violated?" Like Jefferson's frequent argument that the unwritten law of self-preservation trumps all written laws, Lincoln's argument reminded republicans that officers in high trust must sometimes violate the law in order to save lawfulness. But Lincoln dramatically consti-tutionalized executive prerogative when he used a reworded version of the constitutional oath of office to present the president as the constitutionally

---

[4] Abraham Lincoln, "First Message to Congress," 3 December 1861, in *Collected Works of Abraham Lincoln*. ed. Roy P. Basler (New Brunswick, NJ: Rutgers University Press, 1953), 5: 35–52.

intended agent for deciding when the Constitution's instruments must give way to its purpose. Under the logic of Lincoln's first argument, one provision of the Constitution, the oath of office, enables the president to violate other, lesser provisions.[5]

Lincoln's use of the presidential oath was deliberate, for he had already paved the way for its use in his First Inaugural. There, Lincoln spoke of an "oath" five times – three times in reference to the presidential oath and twice in reference to the oaths taken by congressmen. The first mention of the oath established the theme of the address: "In compliance with a custom as old as the government itself, I appear before you to address you briefly, and to take, in your presence, the oath prescribed by the Constitution of the United States." Lincoln next twice invoked the oaths of congressmen to support the Constitution with particular regard to the fugitive slave law. That members of Congress should obey their oaths to support the Constitution by enforcing the fugitive slave law foreshadowed Lincoln's fourth invocation of an oath: "I take the official oath to-day, with no mental reservations, and with no purpose to construe the Constitution or laws, by any hypercritical rules." So far, this use of the oath of office, alongside the pledge to resist hypercritical constructions of the Constitution, depicted the president as the errand boy for all existing law. Rather than execution implying interpretation as Pacificus had argued, Lincoln left the impression that execution was but a prudent observance of the law. Nevertheless – and here lies the departure – Lincoln's final invocation of his presidential oath implied the opposite; after he stated that the "Chief Magistrate derives all his authority from the people" and asserted that the president's "duty is to administer the present government, as it came to his hands, and to transmit it, unimpaired to him, to his successor," Lincoln used the oath to draw a line in the sand to confederates. "You can have no conflict without being yourselves the aggressors. *You* have no oath registered in Heaven to destroy the government, while I shall have the most solemn one to "preserve, protect and defend" it." Rather than serving as a contract with which a president may be bound or even entrapped, the oath became in Lincoln's hands the means by which a president may violate the law in order to save it.[6]

To be sure, Lincoln's inaugural, like Jackson's recourse to his reelection to make war on the Bank, was a direct result of Jefferson's institutionalization

---

[5] Lincoln, "Message to Congress in Special Session," *Works of Lincoln*, 4: 421–41. Early in the address, Lincoln stated that the "attention of the country had been "called to the proposition that one sworn to 'take care that the laws be faithfully executed' should not himself violate them." He did not add that this inaccurate rendering of the oath blends Sections 1 and 3 of Article Two.

[6] Lincoln, "First Inaugural Address," 4 March 1861, *Works of Lincoln*, 4: 262–71.

of the declaration of principle. Following Jefferson, Lincoln justified his dealing with the extraordinary occasion with the argument that as president he was allowed to interpret the Constitution, at least regarding *Dred Scott* and the suspension of habeas corpus. Like Jefferson, Lincoln argued that the presidential election, more than any other election, offered the most accurate measurement of a constitutional majority and that "the people" conferred authority on the president. And, in accordance with Jefferson's model of presidential power, Lincoln acted and then used the special message to report his action to Congress: a "choice was made of means" to the end of preserving the Union and "was declared in the inaugural address." Although Lincoln's declaration was tied to a particular party platform, whereas Jefferson's was not, there is a resemblance because Lincoln's military response as commander in chief derived not from a plank in the Republican platform but rather was worked out and announced in his inaugural address, as Lincoln noted. Following Jefferson, Lincoln used his First Inaugural to boldly assert a particular understanding of executive power to meet the demands facing the country and to bring unity to Unionist opinion.

But the important point is that Lincoln's invocation of the constitutional oath constituted a direct departure from Jefferson's extraconstitutional model. Rather than stating that his actions were constitutionally questionable, Lincoln offered multiple arguments for his actions, and his larger argument, which argued that the oath required him to protect the Constitution even at the cost of acting unconstitutionally opened the space necessary for his defense the suspension of habeas corpus. With his smaller second argument, that his suspending habeas corpus was not a breach of the Constitution, he had proven that the Constitution must allow for the government to suspend habeas corpus when Congress is out of session, not that the president is best suited to exercise this power. So Lincoln's larger first argument from the oath of office was necessary to make the smaller second argument seem harmless: because the president is required by his oath to break one law in order to preserve the whole of the laws, the president also must be allowed to act in the silence of the law in order to preserve the whole of the laws. Taken together, both of Lincoln's arguments point to Hamilton's conception of presidential power because each rests on the argument that a government must necessarily have any power necessary to preserve and maintain itself.[7]

---

[7] As Harry Jaffa has noted, Lincoln's first argument supplied the broad interpretation needed for the second argument to be acceptable. Harry Jaffa, *A New Birth of Freedom: Abraham Lincoln and the Coming of the Civil War* (Lanham, MD: Rowman and Littlefield, 2000), 364.

In a strange twist, it is possible that Lincoln was following the distorted version of Jefferson's argument. Jefferson, after all, appealed to the oath under pseudonym, and he preserved the draft of the First Annual that made a connection between the oath and coordinate review. More troubling, it is conceivable that Lincoln encountered Jefferson's defense of James Wilkinson as Colvin presented it in Wilkinson's memoirs. According to one biographer, Lincoln spent time as a congressman reading in the Library of Congress, and catalogs of that library show that it held Wilkinson's memoirs when Lincoln was in Congress and again, after the fire of 1851, when he was president.[8] Whether or not Lincoln was more or less in line with Jefferson than he knew, he paved the way for later presidents. Just as scholars have treated the Louisiana Purchase as a typical example of executive prerogative, presidents have used Jefferson to justify their own extraordinary actions. As Arthur M. Schlesinger noticed, FDR's Attorney General, the future Justice Robert Jackson, called the destroyer deal the most important act of national defense since the Louisiana Purchase, and Truman appealed to it when asserting that the president had "very great inherent powers," some of which authorizing him to make war in Korea.[9] Presidents have modeled themselves on Jefferson only by changing him.

Jefferson's understanding of the prerogative power offers an alternative to this assertion of a constitutional authority to transcend the Constitution. As Jefferson put it in a letter in 1804, the difference between he and his predecessors was that he believed the people could, if given the proper political education, understand and judge executive power: "As little is it necessary to impose on their senses, or dazzle their minds by pomp, splendor, or forms. Instead of this artificial, how much surer is that real respect, which results from the use of their reason, and the habit of bringing everything to the test of common sense."[10] Although Jefferson surely referred here to the symbolic remnants of the king, the references to tests by reason and common sense suggests that he also had in mind constitutional claims to prerogative that would confuse the people whenever presidents take action to meet necessity. As he saw it, the danger is that citizens will conclude that if it is constitutional, it must be in public good. Paradoxically, Jefferson's position

---

[8] Though this is plausible, it is not certain. Consider Douglas L. Wilson, *Lincoln Before Washington: New Perspectives on the Illinois Years* (Urbana and Chicago: University of Illinois Press, 1997), 3 and 14; *Catalogue of the Library of Congress* (Washington, DC: Duff Green, 1830); and *Alphabetical Catalog of the Library of Congress* (Washington, DC: Library of Congress, 1864).

[9] Arthur M. Schlesinger Jr. *The Imperial Presidency* (Boston: Houghton Mifflin, 1973), 142, 108.

[10] Jefferson to Judge John Tyler, 28 June 1804, *TJW*, 1147.

suggests that the dazzle of the president's prerogative, which exposes execution to popular judgment rather than muting it with constitutional rhetoric, becomes the very guarantee that the power will be used for the public good.

As the 1804 letter shows, the Twelfth Amendment cleared the way for Jefferson's plan to democratize prerogative. With its discriminating principle, the Twelfth Amendment emphasized the electoral connection between the president and the people, rendering the judgment of prerogative as a political rather than a constitutional or legal decision. That is, it more clearly put presidents in "great charge" of the public good and thus made the duty to prerogative more explicit, perhaps even a positive good. More fundamentally, it removed some of the arbitrariness in nature, exaggerated by the machinations of party elites, by offering proof that the people themselves had asked the executive to risk himself on their behalf. A democratic science of politics could fix what the law could not.

The President as Good Officer

If this is correct, then Jefferson's project was to not only awaken the people to their rights but also to prick presidents into action on behalf of the public good. Thus, Jefferson's constitutional theory included within it a doctrine of coordinate review. The Constitution was to be construed strictly, but it was also to be construed by the several departments. By way of this doctrine, Jefferson left room for rival interpretations between presidents and judges, creating space for executive activity. In his letter to William H. Cabell, discussed in the previous chapter, Jefferson argued that the distinction between the judicial and executive branches was operational. Judges must interpret the Constitution strictly, as the judiciary's executive function does not involve the immediacy of necessity. Presidents, however, must interpret the Constitution from the standpoint of energy because they must look to intention of the law, that is, to the assumption that the law they execute was meant to be executed. In other words, no constitution could organize itself such that it held its own destruction; therefore, verbal scruples must give way before self-preservation and other great objects, which means, most of all, that constitutions are practical things.

To be practical and constitutional, then, a law should be understood differently by members of the judicial and executive branch. Judges rightly look to legislative intent; whereas the executive, keeping action in mind, must look to other circumstances – the principles of the law, public opinion, and experience as to practice. Under Jefferson's presentation, the practical implication of strict construction, paradoxically, is that the three branches construe the Constitution differently. Members of each department would

construe the Constitution informed by their respective constitutional place –
just as the congressmen would read the Constitution with a view toward
deliberation and judges would take the time to investigate what the Constitution's framers meant, the president would interpret it with a view toward
action and energy. As he put it in his letter to Hay, there are "particular
duties" imposed on the president, which is to say that it matters that the
president must be the constant agent on behalf of the people.

Jefferson's constitutionalism moved beyond a strict interpretation of the
Constitution, for his coordinate review pointed toward an interpretation
of action and conflict. But because Jefferson's coordinate review rewarded
action, it tended toward executive supremacy and thus came to resemble the
broad interpretation Jefferson wanted to reject.[11] Recall Pacificus's argument
that the president has the power to declare neutrality because, like the other
branches, the executive has a "similar right of judgment, in the execution of
its own functions."[12] There, Pacificus meant to meet the objection that the
legislature's having the power to declare war indicated that the legislature
was the appropriate branch to decide whether the nation should be at war
or peace. According to Pacificus, by having the duty to preserve peace until
a declaration of war is made by Congress, the executive necessarily has a
"right of judging what is the nature of the obligations which the treaties of the
country impose on the government" and a duty to "enforce the laws incident
to the state of the nation." For Pacificus, the president could act until either
Congress either declared war, or the Senate ratified a new treaty. Jefferson's
coordinate review similarly allowed the president the benefits of initiative.
As the Virginia and Kentucky Resolutions and the Memorandum on the
Constitution indicate, Jefferson believed the amendment process afforded
the states a collective right to interpret the Constitution (at least when three
fourths of the states could agree to amend the Constitution), but, like the
letters to Hay and Cabell, which showed the functional requirements of
presidents, it also left the president the room to act.

Scholars have criticized Jefferson's coordinate review on the grounds that
it defies line-drawing, but that is precisely the lesson of Jefferson's resolution of the prerogative and the law.[13] Just as it is impossible to anticipate in
the law every possible contingency, it is unlikely that the powers, or functions, of government can be defined in precise enough terms that the three

---

[11] Robert Scigliano, *The Supreme Court and the Presidency* (New York: Free Press, 1971), 16.
[12] See Chapter 3.
[13] Christopher Wolfe, *The Rise of Modern Judicial Review: From Constitutional Interpretation
to Judge-Made Law* (New York: Basic Books, 1986), 97–9; and David N. Mayer, Constitutional Thought of Thomas Jefferson (Charlottesville: University Press of Virginia, 1994),
271–3.

departments of government can agree on their meaning. In other words, coordinate review grows out prerogative in that it is resistant to lawmaking and judicial finality. Thus, as the letters to Colvin and Cabell frame it, the executive, called to be the good officer, must use ingenuity and bravery when determining his relationship to the law, when "the line of discrimination between cases may be difficult."[14] The point, then, is that Jefferson sought to make these questions political rather than constitutional, which is to say that the president must respect the law by becoming lawless. Because the president looks to action, and because the president unifies and directs public opinion, he must abandon constitutional argument to the other branches. The president can transgress the details of the law in order to fulfill its purpose, and, because the president acts in constant agency for the people, he must.

Jefferson never declared this principle in public. Instead of explaining it, for instance in his First Inaugural, Jefferson chose silence over enlightenment and thus invited future executives to alter his principle even as they professed to abide by it. Again, Jefferson faced a choice. Like the problem posed by Genet for the Republican response the Neutrality Proclamation, and like the later Louisiana Purchase, declaring the principle of coordinate review risked separating executive power from public opinion. This was all the more so because of the high stakes of the First Inaugural: by so dramatically connecting coordinate review to what many would see as partisan issue, Jefferson would undermine his own cause and, just as important, render the First Inaugural a merely partisan declaration. But, as the First Inaugural reveals, Jefferson did, in a more significant way, establish his principle. By attaching the declaration of principle to the electoral clock Jefferson both encouraged presidents to claim that they alone see the whole ground and required that they frame their tenure into the performance of promise. In their lawless declarations that their principles are the people's principles, all presidents are Jeffersonians.

Difficulties

As the charge of lawlessness no doubt suggests, Jefferson's understanding of executive power presents its own difficulties. Consider the institutional, or practical, problem of enforcement. What happens when a president uses the prerogative against the public good? Presumably, Congress's power to impeach and remove would be the first recourse against the president; otherwise, the people might choose to deny him a second term – what Madison

---

[14] Jefferson to John B. Colvin, 20 September 1810, *TJW*, 1233.

called "an impeachment before the community."[15] Aside from waiting for
an election year, implementing Jefferson's understanding of presidential prerogative, then, would seem to require defining impeachment in more political, less legalistic, terms. Enabling Congress to more easily impeach a president would, perhaps, the incapacitate presidents by destroying their will,
but Jefferson seemed to anticipate this difficulty by combining his recommendations for a more muscular impeachment power with the requirement
that the executive branch be an equal player in the impeachment process.[16]
It would seem then that a political understanding of impeachment requires
coordinate review, but this is a question for another day.

A related difficulty is that the requirement to throw oneself on the people
would undermine constitutionalism. A more frequent amendment process
could render the Constitution a mere list of special exceptions to itself, unified
only by the fact that three fourths of the states at one time or another agreed
with items on the list. Such appeals, moreover, would be an incentive for
demagogy. If appeals to the people are the standard by which executives are
to be judged, the requirement itself seems to encourage executives to appeal
to the worst in democratic citizens. They may, as Jefferson did, encourage
citizens to fool themselves into believing that temporary solutions are as good
as or better than their permanent alternatives, that a mounted infantry, a
trained militia, or a gunboat can replace an actual cavalry, a standing army,
or a ship of war. Similarly, Jefferson's strange tales of natural wonders in
the Louisiana territory shows the dangers of false promises and wishful
thinking – the people believe that the president can indeed see the whole
ground, so they are willing to also believe that such a paradise must exist –
while showing that presidents might find ways to distract public attention
from more legitimate questions, such as the consequences of the Purchase
on for Indians and slaves, the importance of the existing states, or foreign
policy.[17] Tethered to public opinion, executives might seek to manufacture
it. Is it a coincidence that Jefferson's First Inaugural, with a portrait, was
immediately published on fine paper for the purpose of being framed?[18]

A third question is whether Jefferson's trust in the good officer to carry
out the great objects of democracy risks embarrassing executive power.

[15] James Madison, "Speech on Presidential Removal Power," *James Madison: Writings*, ed.
Jack N. Rakove (New York: Library of America, 1999), 461.
[16] Jefferson, Proposed Revision of the Virginia Constitution, *PTJ*, 6:301; and Thomas Jefferson
to Thomas Ritchie, 25 December 1820, Ford, 10:170–1.
[17] Malone, 4: 341–2. On Native Americans, see Merril D. Peterson, *Thomas Jefferson and the
New Nation* (New York: Oxford University Press, 1970), 773.
[18] Noble E. Cunningham Jr., *The Inaugural Addresses of President Thomas Jefferson, 1801
and 1805* (Columbia: University of Missouri Press, 2001), 27–9.

Jefferson's supplications of the good officer and the faithful citizen suggests that the few are called to use prerogative on behalf of the public good. Are these few the same he had in mind when he wrote of a "natural aristocracy among men"?[19] To James Monroe, for instance, Jefferson appealed to nature, not constitutional authority, for instructions regarding Louisiana, and to Cabell, he wrote that some are "destined" for such responsibility. If so, how can presidents distinguish those who are called from those who are not? On the one hand, a James Monroe might negotiate the Louisiana Purchase (or at least have the sense to let Napoleon sell it), a Meriwether Lewis – whom once praised as once praised as "remarkable, even in infancy, for enterprise, boldness and discretion" – might be sent to explore the Northwest, and a William Eaton might be entrusted to make an impress "as light and equal" as possible by paying "attention" to "the particular circumstances which may distinguish special cases."[20] On the other, a James Wilkinson might be asked to prevent the Burr Conspiracy, and, by most criteria, Wilkinson would have been regarded as neither faithful nor citizenly though he too believed that he was called to a task higher than citizenship.[21] Similarly, an ambitious officer, a William Eaton, might use a successful instance of overstepping the law (meddling in succession disputes in North Africa) to exert political leverage on the president.[22] If the legacy of the constitutional understanding of executive prerogative leads to a Richard Nixon, Jefferson's might point to an Oliver North.[23]

Some of these dangers revealed themselves in Jefferson's failed Embargo. The Embargo was bad policy, at least because the military had been emasculated on Jefferson's watch.[24] But there is more to this story, as Jefferson's attempt to build the military was complicated by his own words. In his First Inaugural, Jefferson defended a military composed of the militia (as opposed

---

[19] Jefferson to Adams, 28 October 1813, Cappon, 387–9.

[20] Jefferson to Paul Allen, 18 August 1813, Library of Congress, Thomas Jefferson Papers, Series One; and Jefferson to William Eaton, 7 September 1780, *PTJ*, 3:612.

[21] Wilkinson believed that his military ambition was ill served by a republic, and, had circumstances been otherwise, might have joined Burr rather than Jefferson. The second volume of Wilkinson's *Memoirs* quoted Savage on the title page – "For Patriots still must fall for statesman's safety / And perish by the country they preserve." James Wilkinson, *Memoirs of my Own Times*, Vol. 2 (Philadelphia: Abraham Small, 1816).

[22] Adams, 593–8.

[23] On Nixon as a consequence of Lincoln, see Larry Arnhart, "'The God-Like Prince': John Locke, Executive Prerogative, and the American Presidency," *Presidential Studies Quarterly* 9 (1979): 122, 130.

[24] Leonard W. Levy, *Jefferson and Civil Liberties: The Darker Side* (Cambridge, MA: Belknap Press, 1963) 93–141; Forrest McDonald, *The Presidency of Thomas Jefferson* (Lawrence: University Press of Kansas, 1976), 152–3. Marc Landy and Sidney M. Milkis, *Presidential Greatness* (Lawrence: University Press of Kansas, 2000), 74–5.

to a standing army) as a principle of free government, but the success of Napoleon later persuaded Jefferson that "a well disciplined militia" was not the "best reliance in peace."[25] Even though his party enjoyed a large majority in Congress, and even though he instructed Madison that "the classification of our militia is now the most essential thing the US have to do," his measure to classify the militia according to Napoleon's "secret" (to create a *national* militia of "young men" to fight distant battles) was soundly defeated in Congress, once in 1806 and again in 1808, by Republicans who preferred the traditional (local) militia.[26] So, too, for his request for appropriations for ships of war.[27] To be sure, Jefferson did convince Congress to triple the size of the army in February 1808, but the point here is that the principle of reliance on a militia blocked Jefferson's own attempts, throughout his second term, to more adequately provide for the national defense.[28] There is, then, a kind of justice to Jefferson's reputation for military incompetence: since Jefferson's promise of presidential performance cultivated the Revolutionary dogma of the superiority and safety of militias compared to armies, Jefferson complicated his own later attempt to enlighten citizens as to the harmful consequences of that dogma. His principled defense of militias left an obstacle that even he could not overcome.

But the real irony of the Embargo is that Jefferson, who was said to have never pursued an unpopular measure, did not explain the policy to the national electorate and therefore lost the battle of public opinion. Rather than explaining the Embargo to the people, Jefferson found what Federalists called a "secret side-way manner" to find congressional authorization of its enforcement.[29] Confusing personal popularity with public approval, Jefferson issued paper proclamations asking citizens to aid executive officials by detaining the Embargo's violators. Enforcement, especially on those who meant to make a profit by breaking the law, required more than felicitous speech. When Jefferson did explain his "liberal experiment" in the "rights of neutrals," he did so only by stating that he was executing the policy set by Congress, thereby blurring the connection between executive unity and

[25] Jefferson, "First Inaugural Address," 4 March 1801, *TJW*, 495.
[26] Malone, 4: 69, 513–4; Jefferson to Madison," May 1807, Smith, 1475; and Jefferson, "Fifth Annual Message," 3 December 1805, *The Complete Jefferson: Containing His Major Writings, Published and Unpublished, Except his Letters*, ed. Saul K. Padover (New York: Duell, Sloan & Pearce, 1944), 417–8.
[27] Malone, 5: 496.
[28] For an account that shows that Jefferson meant to make the army loyal to the Republican government rather than to decimate it, see Theodore J. Crackel, *Mr. Jefferson's Army: Political and Social Reform of the Military Establishment, 1801–1809* (New York: New York University Press, 1987), 170.
[29] Quoted in Ibid., 164.

accountability to the people. Asking private citizens to sacrifice their interest in commerce and at the same time to divert their passion for military honor to monitoring the boats of other Americans required more than the constitutional advisement that the president was carrying out a law passed by Congress. His reliance on citizens to prove the energy of democratic government by flying to its standard would have benefited from an exposition of the principles behind the Embargo.

As a result, the Embargo was rendered impossible by his own theory. Although he encouraged the faithful citizen to enforce the law, his praise for executives who violated the law on behalf of higher principle must have struck a chord with merchants who could argue that their own livelihood – a kind of self preservation – required them to find ways to get around the Embargo. Similarly, though his theory of coordinate review required the president to enforce the law over and against the objections of the states, it encouraged the states to go public with their objections to the policy. All the while, his looming retirement, which was the fruit of his campaign to regularize political change, encouraged opponents to connect the unpopular policy to the outgoing president. Having unified public opinion for seven years, he leaned too heavily on its support when dissent made the Embargo unenforceable.

But the dangers of Jefferson's theory were perceived by James Madison long before the Embargo, before Jefferson became president. As Madison argued in *Federalist* No. 49, a government that relies on appeals to the people risks losing the veneration that time confers and laws require. The principle can be applied to the questions of prerogative, which like the questions raised constitutional conventions, are often too "ticklish" to be "unnecessarily multiplied." One shudders, for instance, to think of the consequences had Jefferson resorted to an extraconstitutional appeal to the people in order to resolve the election of 1800. Indeed, Jefferson's entire public career – from the Declaration to the Bill of Rights, from forming an opposition party to running for president – might be read as a coherent project to close the constitutional pathways for stability. To this end, Jefferson opened up, or attempted to open, the pathways of democratic change to counteract the stabilizing forces in the Constitution. Put differently, Jefferson's democratization of the presidency pulled the president away from the Senate and, recast in the terms of *Federalist* Nos. 37 and 51, disconnected energy from stability and attached it instead to republican liberty. Jefferson's politics is the politics of amendments, removals, and elections.[30]

30 *The Federalist* No. 49, 323.

Madison suggested the final dilemma for the democratic executive when he tempered his friend's democratic faith by noting that it is one thing to have a nation of philosophers and quite another to have a nation of citizens. Jefferson believed that the president could both energize and democratize executive administration by bringing the wills of citizens to a single point. By bringing together the wills of each citizen, the president can argue that he holds a higher claim to democracy than any one citizen who elected him. By democratizing the presidency, Jefferson made the president the nation's largest democrat; by making the president the person whose claim to power rested on his being the majority holder and therefore the possessor of the nation's chief virtue – democracy – Jefferson pointed the presidency toward a virtue of monarchy, inequality. Thus liberated from equality, the democratic executive is free to become lawless on behalf of the people, which is to say that the democratic executive sees the people and the law as fundamentally incompatible.

We would do well to ask whether the democratic presidency is worth preserving, that is, whether its dangers demonstrate that the republican form is incompatible with energy in the executive. But finding the answers to such questions involves choosing, and choosing is a matter of alternatives. In Jefferson, we find a more accurate depiction of the origins of the democratic presidency, yet we also encounter a clear alternative to the modern practice of presidential power. Now that we have articulated the best case for one understanding, we can reconsider the other.

Index